CITIZEN OF ROME

CITIZEN OF ROME

REFLECTIONS FROM THE LIFE OF
A ROMAN CATHOLIC

FREDERICK D. WILHELMSEN

Sherwood Sugden & Company
PUBLISHERS
1117 Eighth Street, La Salle, Illinois 61301

Acknowledgments

Permission to reprint certain of these essays which first appeared in *Commonweal, Intercollegiate Review, Modern Age, Occasional Review, National Review, Saturday Evening Post, The Wanderer, Triumph,* and as a publication of the Society for the Christian Commonwealth, is gratefully acknowledged. "Why I Am a Catholic" first appeared in *Born Catholics,* edited by Frank Sheed and published by Sheed and Ward. "Captain Guilliermo Wriedt" is drawn from *Omega: Last of the Barques,* published by the Newman Press. "Schism, Heresy, and a New Guard" was included in *American Catholic Exodus,* published by Geoffrey Chapman, London.

ISBN 0-89385-005-5

First Edition

Sherwood Sugden & Company, Publishers
1117 Eighth Street
La Salle, Illinois 61301

(For ordering information, please see back of book.)

To my mother.

CONTENTS

Foreword   ix

REACTING

Hungary Speaks   3
Is There a Theology of Survival?   7
Technics and Totalitarianism   14
Babylonian Meditation   21
Catholicism Is Right—
　　So Why Change It?   30
In Defense of Sin   36
Schism, Heresy, and a New Guard   44
Empty Altar, Empty Womb   65
Introibo ad Altare Dei   74

REFLECTING

History, Toynbee, and the Modern Mind:
　　Betrayal of the West   81
Art and Religion: Felicitous
　　Tension or Conflict?   103
The Conservative Vision   117
Death of the Age of Analysis   126
Hallowed Be Thy World   135
The Good Earth   145
Pope as Icon   156
The Typology of Heresy   165
The Hour Is Late: The Hour Is Now   174
Incarnational Politics   184

REMEMBERING

Captain Guilliermo Wriedt 197

Spanish Baroque 206

The Man Who Went to
His Own Funeral 209

As You Were 212

Three Days with Mindszenty 216

Adios: Francisco Franco 222

Portrait of an Outlaw Hero 234

A Parting of Friends 237

REPORTING

The Vision of Christopher Dawson 243

Charlie and Legitimacy 251

St. Thomas Aquinas 261

A E I O U 264

REJECTING

Harvey Cox's Secular City:
City of Night 275

Leslie Dewart:
Hellene or Heretic? 290

REDEEMING

Why I Am a Catholic 305

The Sovereignty of
Christ or Chaos 314

Christmas in Christendom 326

REJOICING

The Miracle of Wine 335

FOREWORD

The papers gathered in this book span a career in letters that fill twenty-seven years of conflict, reflection, and—I trust—affirmation. Gratitude is expressed in the appropriate acknowledgements to the editors of the journals and books in which these essays first appeared. Except for a sentence here and there everything remains as originally published. Some of these pieces bear the mark of the time that called them forth. Their worth, if any, is that of witness and response to crisis. More of these essays are reflections on the age. A few are personal vignettes traced along the perimeters of a life lived on four continents in circumstances which were often foreign to the author's academic profession.

I have been guided by one principle in selecting the writing that has gone into this book: my Catholic Faith. The collection is not religious, I hasten to add, in any specifically theological or devotional sense of the term but it is religious in that I have selected work that could never have been composed by a man of another persuasion or of none at all. Two decades ago the word "Catholic", used as noun or adjective, would have required no further explanation. Today—and this is a sign of the confusion to which much of what follows is addressed—a Catholic must define or at least describe how he intends the term. I am an ultramontanist and therefore the final authority in matters religious to whom I respond is the Pope in Rome. I am a political and cultural traditionalist, at home in the civilization whose main lineaments have been shaped by two thousand years of Catholic Christianity. Whatever is personally my own in these pages is questionable, even by myself. There is an old medieval saw that runs as follows: *In necessariis unitas: in dubiis libertas: in omnibus caritas.* In Things Necessary, Unity: In Things Doubtful, Liberty: In All Things, Charity. Let it be said by some kind reader that I have preserved the Unity, gloried in the Liberty, and not sinned too gravely against the Charity. *Civus Romanus sum.*

—Frederick D. Wilhelmsen
August, 1979

REACTING

HUNGARY SPEAKS

Students: We are gathered here this morning to protest Soviet aggression in Hungary. We meet, I trust, not in the spirit of hate. The enormity of the crime committed by the Russian Army in Hungary cannot be measured in human terms. This crime staggers the reason and leaves it limp with incomprehension. It is as though men had surrendered their humanity, had created a vacuum in their souls—a vacuum which was filled by forces from another world and from an order of things so monstrous that it simply is not commensurate to the hate of man. This crime in truth cries out, in the words of Pope Pius XII, "to God for vengeance."

Not ten days ago the Hungarian people had done what no one had conceived possible: they had risen in the streets—students, workers, peasants, old men, children, Catholics, Protestants, Jews—and had wrested control from the Russian Army in the teeth of mechanized opposition in the heart of Budapest. The rebels controlled at least ten of the twenty-five departments composing their nation; they had opened the frontier to Austria; they had forced upon the Nationalist Communist regime of Premier Nagy amazing concessions; they had freed the Prince Primate, Joseph Cardinal Mindszenty, and had returned him to Budapest in captured Russian tanks; they had guarded his residence with machine guns and there were those who even dared hope that he would form the next government. The Hungarian rebels seemed to be sweeping everything before them. The Hungarian Army, darling of the Soviet satellite armies—heavily indoctrinated, privileged, babied—had come over almost to a man to the half armed rebels. The ancient Hungarian colours were broken out in the wind over the old House of Parliament. And people went wild with their new bought freedom: an old man put up

3

a cross on a wayside chapel, a cross pulled down years ago by Soviet troopers, a cross he had hidden all that time under his peasant's tunic. The effigy of Stalin and the icons of the whole Soviet hagiography were toppled into the streets and in their place men raised the venerable banner of St. Stephen.

It had been a hard fought battle and it was won by fourteen-year-old girls with tommy guns—by that child who died in the streets, her blood in her mouth, begging her mother's forgiveness, pleading that she too was a Hungarian and could have done nothing but fight.

It was the resurrection of a nation. Everyone said that it was fantastic. Our political scientists, almost to a man, declared rebellion against the industrialized might of a modern state impossible. There is hardly a political analyst in America who has not been saying for years that revolution behind the Iron Curtain not only could not succeed, but that it could not even get under way. What they forgot was the heroism of a Christian people. What they forgot was that the Faith is not of this world. There are no graves for those of us who are of the Christian West; or—better yet—graves exist solely that we might climb out of them. And Hungary, alone and unaided, rolled back the tombstone of history.

It was perhaps this taunt thrown in the face of dialectical materialism, or was it panic in the Kremlin which saw suddenly that its soft policy of the past year failed to melt like butter the will of decent men but produced only iron and the determination for freedom—was it this that brought back the Russian troops; that caused them to arrest the Hungarian armistice commission; was it the British-French action in the Suez?

Probably it was all of these, but it was something more. This act of Russian Soviet treason was brilliant, magnificent: it was inspired—by hell itself.

Today there is a band of corpses, a Soviet rosary, spanning the bridge between Buda and Pest. The frantic calls for help from clandestine radios have ceased. The voice of Hungary is silenced. Its youth, fighting tanks with pistols and rifles, is either dead or in hiding throughout most of the land. Yet they carry on; just yesterday a new pocket of resistance broke out in the south. There are still men who bring their wives and children over the border and then turn their backs on the West and return to the cemetary of their nation. They no longer hope for help. They know they were betrayed by Radio Free Europe which promised help when none was forthcoming. English is no longer a popular language on the Austrian border and the sentiment is sweeping Vienna and Munich that Central Europe is no more. Today Hungary; tomorrow Austria. Yet they still fight on, the Hungarians.

They have been fighting since before they were Christians, since the days when they came riding into the Danubian valley through the Carpathian mountains from Central Asia in the dusk of the ninth century. And as with all the great migrations, the first Hungarians—members of the Old Turkish race—followed the sinking sun toward the West, sensing in some dumb manner that their future lay in the Lands of the Evening. That they were hurried on by the Finger of Providence can be doubted by no one who sees history in the light of the Incarnation. Their first King, Stephen, received the Crown from Pope Sylvester II who cried out in wonder before the splendid and barbaric Hungarian envoys—"I am but apostolic, but thy master who sent thee here is, in truth, the apostle of Christ Himself." A light of Faith in the centre of paganism, Hungary poured out its blood through the long Middle Ages and even beyond. That land of Hungary—or, more accurately, the Lands of the Holy Crown of St. Stephen—stood as a shield against the threat from the East, in those days the Mohammedan hordes who came riding in on the same small mounts that brought the Hungarians to the West centuries before. At the battle of Semendria, during the clang of steel on steel and the shouts of battle, an unknown knight rode out of nowhere bearing a shield painted over with a black raven, holding a gold ring in its beak. He was the fabled Jan Hunyadi, one of the great captains in history, and he saved Europe and all of us by turning back the Turks at Belgrade in 1456.

The Hungarian mission to our common Chistian civilization has been for 1000 years something unique. The Magyars were a people raised to the dignity of a kingdom by Rome itself. Their kings were the Apostolic Kings. Their rights and liberties—and they knew the meaning of liberty 700 years and more before we in America wrote our Declaration of Independence—their rights and liberties, I say, stood in a unique relation to God Himself. They were not conferred by the king who was himself but the instrument of the nation; they were vested rather in the Holy Crown that had been bestowed on the whole people by the Vicar of Christ. In the halls of Parliament they spoke the common language of Christendom, Latin, until less than a 100 years ago.

No one understands, really understands, the role of this 1000 year kingdom, this nation who vested its rulers as late as 1916 in a garment woven by the wife of St. Stephen 900 years before, no one really knows this people who does not understand the meaning of the Sacred Crown of St. Stephen. When the American businessman Mr. Robert Voegeler was released by the Communists, the Russians tried to exchange him for the Crown. They failed. It rests somewhere in safe keeping, perhaps in Fort Knox. The Hungarians believe that no government can last long that does not possess the Crown, not simply symbolically but physically as has the nation always possessed corporeally the Right Arm of its sainted founder. Here is no ordinary crown. Given the land by Pope Sylvester in the year 1000, it was later built up by a headband encrusted with sapphires and enamel plaques on which are carved the saints. On its top is a globe capped by a cross and beneath is the figure of the Savior reposing: He is surrounded by the sun, the moon, and two trees. Below are the apostles. Until 1945 all Hungarian courts issued their verdicts "In the name of the Sacred Hungarian Crown." The Crown signified Hungary's Christian destiny; it guaranteed the 1000 year constitution under which the Magyars governed themselves.

Not ten days ago the image of that ancient Crown, symbol of Hungarian independence, appeared everywhere in the streets of Budapest. Children carried tommy guns and crosses in their hands, the Crown of St. Stephen in their hearts. Let us think long on this Crown, we who protest this morning and who appeal to the President for action in the United Nations. This Crown is capped by a Cross—what else would one expect from such a civilized people, a people which has always considered its national existence one with the mission of Christ? But this Cross is bent over at a crazy angle: it appears about to fall. Legend would have it that the Cross was bent in battle. Others say it was bent by a thief intent on stealing it away in the night. It doesn't matter: what matters is that the bent Cross symbolizes Hungary today, its back bent under the Soviet boot. But although bent, not broken. We must, as the apostle John writes, "harden ourselves in hope." Remember that the Cross always bends; as Chesterton wrote of the early Church, "the heavenly chariot flies thundering through the ages . . . the wild truth reeling but erect."

The Cross reels today in Hungary. But reeling it stands. And like all crosses it stands arms outstretched—crying for your help and mine. Holy God, grant us the courage to embrace that Cross.

15.xi.56

IS THERE A THEOLOGY OF SURVIVAL?

Our aging civilization, hurried on by the angel of death, seems bent upon holocaust and oblivion. The full meaning of November 3, 1964, may never be known to us on this side of history but one ominous truth, a fixed and awful face, is glaring down upon the West and we would be fools were we to fail to look and see what is written there for us to read. The West, sickened in comfort and diseased in doubt, has unleashed its sword and is about to hand it over to the enemy, blade in palm and hilt outstretched. We have lost faith in the power of justice to conquer evil and we are thus disposed to make our peace with barbarism. I can see no other meaning to the politics of co-existence and to the banner of cowardice upon which are written the words, "peace and prosperity."

I gravely doubt that many of the apostles of co-existence are convinced of any supposed superiority of Marxist civilization over our own. But despite their adherence to some of the broad principles which have made our world to be what it is, these men have despaired of victory because they think the price is too high to pay. This heresy which has today become the new orthodoxy within the free world is akin to pacifism but cannot be reduced to the simplicity of its tenets. Principled pacifism opposes armed resistance to the enemy under all forms and therefore refuses to fight even when victory is assured. The philosophers of co-existence will fight, but only provided that there is an overwhelming chance of winning and of winning without appreciable damage to oneself. These men pronounce, effectively, in favor of any kind of battle except that waged with risk. Today they are convinced that the West has passed the point where it would possibly have won its war with Communism without paying a price which would cancel out the fruits of victory. They believe that any war would involve the destruction of both parties. Thinking, as

7

they do, that this consideration might not deter the enemy under certain circumstances which might emerge at any moment, they appeal to the West to surrender whenever its sovereignty is seriously challanged. The Communist enemy is insane, according to this doctrine, and we must simply accept this fact as a dictate of history. We enter into a pact with insanity. We retreat whenever and wherever the enemy forces us to do so. We run down the flags that hitherto governed the political behavior of civilized men.

I suggest that underlying the politics of co-existence is a kind of despair: we cannot win our war, hot or cold, with the Marxist world and therefore we must cease trying to win! Buttressing this despair is a philosophical prejudice which I believe to be false: *i.e.*, success is the ultimate end of politics and if the supposed superiority and virtue incarnated in Western civilization are not sufficient to conquer *in and of themselves,* then we must realistically accept the consequences. This is the meaning of the slogan: "peaceful competition with the Communist bloc." But if the enemy still advances despite all of our "peaceful competition" (and the enemy *is* advancing!) then the enemy must be permitted the fruits of *his* victory in the war we refused to wage. Duty ceases to be a mandate of the conscience at the moment when its exercise no longer carries with it a high probability of success at a minimum of risk. Let me hasten to add that I am by no means as pessimistic as the disciples of co-existence. But even assuming that victory would be bought only at a great price or that victory would be impossible, would we thereby be absolved of our duty to defend our civilization?

It is this question which divides a purely classical or pagan conception of politics from a Christian vision of existence. To the Greeks and Romans, political victory belonged to the power of human virtue or to the irrational goddesses of Fate and Fortune. To Saint Augustine, political victory belonged to the Will of God. The classical concept of virtue, along with the civilization which virtue was supposed to incarnate, was handled roughly by Augustine in *The City of God.* Virtue, simply one among all the other gifts that God's mercy has given to men, does not guarantee political success any more than vice guaranteed failure.

Once one accepts the Christian conception of a Providence that cuts through the conventional opposition between a natural intelligibility (*i.e.,* the victory of virtue) and the unintelligibility of evil (*i.e.,* the victory of political barbarism), then a philosophy of history becomes possible. *Ex post facto*, we can see the Hand of God moving through the action of the virtuous but we can also see His hand moving through the powers of darkness because they too work, in their own way, towards God's ultimate plan for history. They also are under the Divine Government. The God of St. Augustine is truly the Lord of history.

In an orthodox context, God is neither the same nor is He totally other than the world in its coming and going. God falls outside of—better yet, He cuts through the entire dialectic between "The Same" and "The Other" which are themselves finite terms. God does not destroy the mystery of political decency frustrated nor does He dissolve its tragedy and bitterness. What was meaningless for the pagan remains so for the Christian who knows, however, that there is here a sign wrapped within a Providence he cannot see or know perfectly in this life. The Greek and Roman complaint against evil rampant in the world, against the success that is often attendant upon the forces of barbarism that forever encircle civilization, was a complaint against what is truly a surd in reality. This surd, when seen in the framework of a created universe utterly penetrated by its Creator, becomes part of the inscrutability of Divine Providence. And God Himself subjected His Son to this terrible meaninglessness when Christ was crucified upon the Cross.

The political consequences are inevitable. Should some polity come to ruin because swamped under a barbarian sea despite the good found within the polity in question, this failure will have been decreed by the Will of God for purposes known fully only to Himself. Such a polity is under the curse of sin and the scandal of the Cross. The final resolution of this awful mystery belongs to God. The Augustinian theology gives comfort to the good man with his back to the wall, to the Quixotes of our tradition. Let them take comfort in the face of the scandal of their enemies enjoying the fruits of this world, even amidst all the contradictions of life itself.

This theology of Saint Augustine is also a theology of history. Whereas the commonweal of a society annealed in virtue might very well be frustrated by the forces of darkness and irrationality, this frustration acctually would serve an end which is infinitely higher, according to Christianity. The civilization, therefore, that does its duty by the heritage of justice that it enshrines must harden itself in hope, in the words of St. John. The civilized polity must do all that it can to secure success and the perpetuation of its legacy in the future. But should civility go down, it must not despair in the hour of its defeat. Such a failure would have been written into creation for ends known only to the God of history, a failure made bearable because the Cross teaches men that even God Himself took upon His back the contradictions of human existence. Does not Chesterton teach us that only Christianity has seen fit to invest God with the attribute of courage?

It follows that the ultimate ends of politics must not be measured by a success supposedly guaranteed by the power of a virtuous life exercised corporately by the many. A virtuous life and a good polity are demanded as imperatives that issue forth from human nature itself. This has nothing to do with failure or success in any worldly sense of the term. There was a valid excuse for our pagan forefathers of Rome to balk at the scandal of barbarism on the march, of civilization at bay. This absurdity troubled their spirit because they knew nothing higher than human virtue and they had supposed, in all the arrogance that a purely human virtue breeds, that their own excellence ought to have been sufficient unto itself in the battle against evil. But our world has behind it the experience of two thousand years of Christianity. We ought to know that the victory of our arms belongs to the God of Battles.

This principle must be understood with all that delicacy involved in political speculation and action. The principle does not urge us to abandon astuteness when we treat with the enemies of civilization, be they the Turks before Vienna in the sixteenth century or the Russians in Berlin in the twentieth. The principle does not insist that we hurl all our troops and all of our resources into the breach in a desperate cavalry charge against barbarism, although the principle does not discount this possiblity. The principle does not goad us into a politics of international suicide. The principle does not countermand the subtlety and even the deviousness demanded in the actual practice of the arts of diplomacy. It rather commends all of these things and presses them upon us in the name of political prudence. But the principle does insist that these arts be seen for what they are, techniques in ther service of something deeper than themselves: the preservation and the enhancement of civilization *and therefore the ultimate destruction of civilization's enemy.* Should the arts of diplomacy convert themselves into a general foreign policy whose very end is the perpetuation of the enemy in existence, then politics would have renounced its own proper finality, a *common* good shared by all of us and not simply by those who have thus far escaped falling under the heel of slavery. Foreign policy in the West today has settled upon co-existence as an end to be achieved, as a good to be gained. This is certainly the meaning of November 3, 1964. Co-existence has thus ceased to be a temporary stratagem to be tolerated and exploited (assuming that it even could have been exploited by the West). The entire Western world with some honorable exceptions, rejoiced when President Johnson returned to the White House. The world rejoiced because the powers of irrationality have proven too strong for us. Foreign policy is thus entering into a pact with the enemy just as many Roman emperors in the centuries of decline, despairing of ultimate victory over barbarism, threw themselves into the arms of oriental superstitions in the hope of saving some shadow of civility from the surrounding doom.

Political irrationality is always symbolized in terms which appeal to the imagination and thus soothe the outrages suffered by reason itself. In late Roman times, the irrational was often symbolized by the stars. Let the stars save us because we cannot save ourselves! In our times the symbolization of the irrational takes form under the cloak of gnostic dreaming about a total elimination of poverty from the face of the earth. It seduced by its myths of historical determinism and inevitability. It confused means with ends and thus proposed "anti-colonialism" and "anti-imperialism" and "democracy" and similar nostrums as though these political instruments were in truth *ends* worthy of rational consideration. The West has seized upon this rosary beaded by the hands of secular humanism because the West today has lost the courage to face up to the only political end which can really interest any decent man in the second half of the twentieth century: the business of beating Communism or getting beaten at the try.

We began this brief meditation because the heresy of co-existence is becoming a new orthodoxy. These heretics believe that unless we keep on surrendering whenever we are challenged, an atomic conflict is inevitable. This conflict, they say, will bring with it a destruction of our whole civilization as well as that of our enemies. Since such a condition would render human life intolerable, since it would reduce a debased remnant of the race to the status of cavemen grubbing for a living on the crust of a ravaged planet, we men of the West must give up our hopes of reconquest, not only in Poland and Hungary but even in Cuba. We give up reconquest as a goal although we know that Communism will never give up conquest as *its* goal. This doctrine is preached openly by Lord Russell and his hysterical followers in a decayed England and elsewhere; but Russell's call to an open and candid surrender only masks a more profound and subtle despair circling throughout the entire occidental world today, working carefully and quietly, always moderately, towards the same end. Conscious in the minds of some men who do not as yet tip their hand openly, the doctrine is the preconscious conviction of millions who have despaired of victory.

This teaching urges itself upon us in a dozen ways: it insists that we always retire, whether it be in Hungary yesterday or in Vietnam today; it demands that we concede to them, whether it be in Korea yesterday or in Cuba today. It always advances speciously convincing arguments for every concession and it can always demonstrate, to the satisfaction of its own followers and even of others as well, that such and such a retreat is demanded by world opinion and counseled by moderation. It points to the reluctance of the Kremlin to engage us in a world conflict as instance of an easing of old tensions and of the birth of a new world in which the concepts of cold as well as hot war will have no place. It brushes aside China's brand-new bomb with the pious hope that "political responsibility" can be urged upon the Dragon of the East. In Europe, the heresy of co-existence dominates the mind and the nerve of England and of the whole Continent as well, excepting only some pockets of resistance. Today its apostle in the United States is Senator Fulbright.

Against every stiffening of opposition, the heresy raises the specter of atomic war. Against every spontaneous reaction to Communist brutality and tyranny, it raises the cry of chauvinism. Co-existentialism would never dream of surrendering the West all at once to the enemy: it does so little by little, hoping thereby to soften the harshness of the new world being prepared for us and for our children. The doctrine is thus spared the embarrassment of preaching surrender openly and crudely to a world still penetrated heavily by Christian morality. The heresy dominates the press wherein it finds some of its loftiest oracles. It occupies government. It is the new orthodoxy of an intellectuality purged of hope and altogether without chivalry. It is the yellow banner of the academy and the arts.

Were we to unfold the presuppositions lying behind this flag of defeat, we would find the same fears that worked towards the weakening of the Roman Empire. *They*—the Communist enemies—will never lay down their arms nor give up their dreams of world conquest because they are crazy with conviction—a very unhealthy state of mind. *We* live in a better world and enjoy a more humane society than they do, but we know that there is no ultimate meaning to life, that our centuries of blood spent in the name of religion and liberty have yielded nothing dearer to us than the comfort and ease that we enjoy today. We like this comfort and ask only that it be expanded and shared by the rest of the world. If we yield constantly to the enemy and even surrender to him completely when he demands that we do so, we may well be permitted the continuous exercise of our pleasures and our complacency. At the very least we will not die—right away, that is—and thus cease to be. Possibly we might even teach our barbarian conquerors the manners of civilization if not the morals in which we do not believe anyhow. In any event, we survive.

Saint Augustine and the Christian Tradition say something else. This Tradition, formed as it is of swords which flash down the ages touching one another in comradeship, tells us that ultimate survival of this our beloved civilization is hidden in the Wisdom and the Will of God. He has not entrusted us with the destiny of history, but only with the duty of making it. Our fathers wrought the City of Man out of the catalyst of time. They fenced this City all around and they set up sentinels and to each they gave a sword. They ordered us to defend the City, and it were better for the whole cosmos to go up in flames, unto the very last star and the most remote moon, burnt out—the whole of existence scorched and reduced to a cinder blown away into the awful wastes of the void—than that dishonor should unfold the banner of Hell within our walls.

12.i.65

13

TECHNICS AND TOTALITARIANISM

A new conception of politics is entering the Western world, and is succeeding in replacing every traditional political category. Today it is impossible to understand the nature of modern civilization by appealing to the classical categories of political science: democracy, aristocracy, monarchy, the mixed polity, mob-rule, oligarchy, tyranny—these ancient forms function within modern society, but underlying them are deeper currents of the human spirit, and they define the structure of twentieth-century political and social existence.

Motivating the West in our time is the fever of imanentist eschatology; man is coming more and more to place his corporate good in a secular paradise, a worldly salvation to be achieved within history through instruments conceived in his own mind, and executed by his own hands. Ths conclusions of Löwith and Voegelin on this issue seem decisive: the divinization of society constitutes "the inner logic of the Western political development from medieval immanentism through humanism, enlightenment, progressivism, liberalism, positivism, into Marxism" (Eric Voegelin, *The New Science of Politics*); the state has come to be the representative, not of the common good, but of the secular Idea.

The instrument of the New Jerusalem, fashioned patiently through centuries of Western genius and application, is modern science organized for the purpose of techincal mastery over the physical universe. Marx predicted that scientific mastery over nature would soon extend to society itself, and the widespread conviction today that society must be organized according to the dictates of mass production and scientific technology, bears out the Marxist prediction. Power is passing from the hands of statesmen and politicians, and is being concentrated in the hands of the custodians and propagandists of technical efficiency: politics is ceasing to

14

be an exercise in prudence, in morals, and is becoming more and more an exercise in technical efficiency and "know-how." This is the very meaning of the so-called "managerial revolution."

The symbolic figures of the age are the physicist, the chemist, the mathematician, the engineer; supporting them are the apostles of the new social science—sociologists, social engineers, psychologists, city planners, educationalists, statisticians, social workers; taking up the rear, following the "mechanized caravans" to use the words of T.S. Eliot, are the propagandists of the new mind: contributing little to science itself, largely ignorant of its inner nature, they nonetheless have offered their services to the wave of the future: secularist philosophers, large masses of half-educated urbanites, rootless cave dwellers of the industrialized city—fashionable, humanitarian, likable, contemptuous of the past, cynical of the present, lyrical of the future. They hold the power, and they exercise it in the name of a mechanized tomorrow.

An understanding of the eschatological drive in modern society, be it Communist or secularist, is absolutely indispensable for any theoretical penetration of the Western crisis. Nonetheless, immanentist eschatology cannot be studied in isolation from the scientific instrument it has seized upon and made its own through the past century. To view technical rationalization as simply one among many neutral forces that have been pressed into the service of political movements aiming at eventual totalitarian domination, would be to miss the point. As innocent as technologized science may appear from an abstract point of view, its full potential is charged with the power to transform society completely, to make civilization over, to alter the fabric of human personality, and even to absorb the physical cosmos within a new world created by the genius of mathematicized science. Because of this, the technologizing of society is the uniquely indispensable instrument for the representatives of any new world order, to be erected beyond the bastions of western liberty.

Totalitarian ideologies aim at the transformation of nature itself, both human and physical. A transfigured universe, a cosmos glorified not on the last day by the Author of Creation, but wrought within history by the new man: this is the ideal.

The power of science to transform physical nature, to reverse all traditional relationships between man and the world, is so well known it need not be labored here. But the power of science to achieve the atomization of society has thus far been insufficiently penetrated by political

15

theory. Atomization precedes collectivism, and both of them are preliminary phases of every totalitarian movement: the new world can only be built when the old one is destroyed, and when all forces within society are mobilized by the state for the realization of the secular goal of history.

The destruction of vertical hierarchy within society; the transfer of economic power from smaller to larger units; the drying up of folk culture and its replacement by mass propagandized commercial entertainment working for social uniformity; the stripping away of economic freedom, rendering the soul naked and abjectly dependent on the state—all of these preliminary phases of the totalitarian dialectic are the work of technologized science, and it is difficult, if not impossible, to see how they could be achieved by any other instrument.

Modern science is so well adapted for this work of de-humanization that it is sometimes hard to shake off the haunting conviction that totalitarian collectivism is a function of the scientific mind, rather than its master. As mathematicized science attempts to subsume more and more phenomena under increasingly simpler theories, hoping thus to explain the universe through a handful of axioms, so too does the technology created by this science aim at an ever-increasing simplicity of function; multiple units of production are replaced, whenever possible, by single units; multiplicity of trades and occupations decrease as time moves on; embattled workers unite in unions that resist the predatory cupidity of capitalist greed, but they dissolve with hardly a whimper when modern technology eventually gets around to absorbing them within its mammoth organization.

The peasant and homesteader are rendered superfluous; the special skill of the craftsman withers; the small businessman closes up shop because he can compete no longer; hundreds of occupations, traditional ways of life defining dozens of classes for centuries, simply cease to exist, and millions of people, finding their places in society destroyed, their very history annihilated, are absorbed into the masses where their loneliness and resentment of existence make them easy prey for totalitarian mass movements.

Technologized science has proved capable of a destruction hitherto undreamed of by the most ambitious and unscrupulous of tyrants: first Nature, then History, and finally Man—all of them become victims of the mechanized tool of the new order. The picture of the "Lion of Hungary," defying the Marxist state, refusing to bow down to the totalitarian demands of the masters of Central Europe, stands as symbol and as type of this tragedy: he entered upon his Calvary a man unbroken, intransigent, magnificent in his proud refusal; he came out and was led into court, less a broken man than a new one: technical science—chemical, biochemical, neurological—transformed him into the image of man dreamed of in all totalitarian movements: pliable, docile, frightened; he has ceased to be himself, and had become the subsisting image of the new mind. A Cardinal of the Church had become his own martyrdom: a human being was destroyed, and a new man was created to take his place. Disintegrate: destroy: create anew! This is the essence of totalitarian modernity.

Technology is thus *the* instrument, not only for social atomization and collectivization, but also for the destruction of human personality demanded by all totalitarian programs. But above and beyond all this, there is something still more uniquely proper to the technologized mind that makes it the apt means for the work of destruction and re-creation.

Sir Arthur Eddington stated the goal of modern science when he wrote that "science aims at constructing a world which shall be symbolic of the world of commonplace experience." This symbolic world is constructed, of course, so that the "commonplace" world can be manipulated. But in order to manipulate the world, science needs instruments—machines, and in order to get the machines, science must absorb a good deal of that very world within the new world of industry—technics—where things no longer are what they were, but become technical means to technical ends. It is small wonder that a philosopher of science concluded that, behind the world of scientific theory and technical organization, there rested nothing "but a skeleton structure of symbols."

Initially the world is symbolized by science, but through a dialectic of degradation the sign becomes the thing signified, and what was signified is now only sign. Thus sophomores think the solidity of a massive oak table is a symbol, constructed by sensation, for a system of electrons and neutrons standing behind the table and constituting its true reality. It does little good to tell these people they don't know good oak when they see it. The springs of realism have been so corrupted, they can be restored only by an analysis of the inner nature of science itself.

Natural creation enters the field of mathematicized science only so far as it can be stripped of its non-mathematical characteristics, or, more accurately, only so far as these can be symbolized mathematically. By denaturing the world, it can be systemazied, rationalized, transformed, mastered. The secret of total power is the refusal to look things in the face and see them as they are; when man averts his gaze from things, he can reach out and possess them for himself.

Paradox though it may be, it remains a brutal truth: scientific power over a thing is had in proportion to the failure to know the thing as it is. Conversely, a thing is known as it is, when power is relinquished, and the thing is contemplated in its very existence. The dream of total technological control over reality removes mankind from things as they are, empties the soul of the hidden reserves of loyalty to the given, and respect for the other. Thus emptied of decency and realism, the soul is open to the corrupting voice of the totalitarian dream.

When sociologists hunt for the causes of the social boredom and communal apathy threatening to engulf the West today, forming the indispensable condition for the spread of totalitarianism, they would do well to look carefully at the nature of technics and the mind upon which that nature reposes. Technical mastery follows on a dialectic of estrangement from existence, and this dialectic exacts its own price: alienation from things as they are, the suppression of nature, the removal of man from the springs of piety, the destruction of reverence.

Living a corporate existence pushed ever farther from things as they are, modern man has surrounded himself with an ersatz universe of artifacts. Nature is fenced off in parks and preserved against the ravages of a technology that everywhere else threatens the countryside, levelling it with bulldozers, spreading it over with concrete, pulling down fruit orchards, setting up antennae, destroying settled communities and bringing in the restlessness of the factory, the drab uniformity of the housing "project," the cheapness and arrogance of a way of life that leaves in its wake nothing but junk yards full of last year's machinery, now twisted, rusting under the empty sky, discarded in favor of this year's special model for raping existence.

Mankind, cut away (as Christopher Dawson noted recently) from the natural rhythm of the seasons, the benediction of the harvest, and the peace that comes of working with the springs of reality, the peace born of handling life as it ripens under the sun, man—deprived thus of the world created for his labor and play—longs for a new world, and is meantime fed a second-hand life through the mass media of commercial entertainment: the motion picture, the television, the radio, these bring with them the metallic laugh of the comedian, the tension of perpetual political crisis; the sneer of the cynic, the cheapness of manufactured glamor; so mechanized becomes life, so mathematicized the psyche that feminine beauty itself is "transformed" into a new reality measured according to a statistical calculus that reaches its most amusing absurdity only in beauty contests wherein a girl's charms are judged in advance simply by holding them up to a quantified formula: the contestants might just as well drop out of existence; their *being* is irrelevant to the issue: technologized man is so full of mathematics that he has been taught to fall in love with a set of measurements.

Clearly enough, this mentality is well on the road to a simple inability to make any judgments at all about things as they really are. The senses cannot be trusted anymore; no longer do they fill slowly with the sap of being; shocked periodically by mechanically induced stimuli, they tend to react less and less to reality as it is.

Thus a dream world settles over the West, a world full of the magic of machinery, limited only by the frontiers of a nature that has become the zero of the human consciousness. What academic idealism never succeeded in really doing, has been done for it by technology: modern man, where he is most fully technologized, has ceased to believe in the existence of Nature. That he cannot believe in the existence of God is merely a corollary.

If the unleashing of the full potential of technics has worked for the decay of reverence, the loss of piety, and the atomization of society so essential to the spread of totalitarianism, it has also furthered that curious and frightening resentement for existence that is inscribed in the heart of totalitarianism. Here is a grim proportion: power and knowledge are equated, and together they spell the dream of the absolute suppression of things as they exist independently of the scientific mind and its dependent creature—the world of technics.

Power comes finally to mean the power to destroy the world of actual existence. Mathematics abstracts from existence, as indicated, and when mathematicized science returns to the world in order to master it, mathematics necessarily gropes like a nearsighted giant through a dark and solid universe: a giant who can fashion and mold the world anew, but who cannot comprehend the hard givenness of the universe he straddles. As scientists close in on existence, their prey becomes more elusive than ever before. They possess it; they can make it do their will, but something seems to escape the rational pattern; something remains forever just beyond their grasp. As though an impressario could make an actor do everything but act, so too technical genius can make a being do everything but *be*. The world of total technical mastery can come more into, I will not say *being*, but into *use*, only when this world will have ceased to exist. The power and knowledge will be fused into the absolute unity dreamed of by both the scientific and the totalitarian minds; man will have become the secular god he desires to be, but he will be a god of destruction and slavery, not a God of creation who plays in the world, delighting in "the children of men."

This resentment for existence, for things, men, and institutions as they are, this fever to destroy the world that is, in order to make a new one, runs wildly like a diseased religion through the veins of the West today. The goal can be fulfilled, as Mr. Gilson indicated a number of years ago, only if the last traces of this world are wiped away, perhaps in some cataclysmic Hiroshima. Already men are talking of the exhaustion of the resources of the earth, and of man's impending invasion of outer space. Already the advance guard of cosmic adventurers speak as though our world existed for the sole purpose of a New City, built I know not where, perhaps on the farther shores of history, in a universe that is not, that certainly could only be, provided this our world ceased to exist.

There is only one patriotism today; there is only one civic loyalty: to the world as God gave it. There is only one enemy, and whether he disguises himself as Communist or secularist, his political label is actually irrelevant to the final issue: the enemy is the man who is so full of the spirit of totalitarianism that he refuses to look on this world and see it as it is, as Christian men have always seen it, good in its very being; the enemy is the man who would arrogate to himself the power to destroy, so that he might create.

23.iv.54

BABYLONIAN MEDITATION

The other day I was in Babylon. The approach to the ruins is through a fine arch made of the same dun-colored brick from which was built the old city of sin. Stacked up against the walls of the little museum set back behind the arch were tiers upon tiers of the same bricks stamped with the famous lion. The government of Iraq is rebuilding the city and when finished Babylon will be as she was. An unobservant visitor could not tell the difference between brick taken from the original site and that from the new arch. They build now as they did then, fours thousand years ago.

Emotionally Bablyon was a failure, or, to put the matter more justly, I failed in my efforts to find the spirit, the genie, the soul of the place. I walked down the stretch of street that leads to the Temple of Ishtar, goddess of fertility, and I experienced nothing at all. And it was only after I had left and was on the road back to Babylon that I remembered Daniel and the Lions' Den.

The Lion of Babylon is an impressive beast, reposing on a little mound set back from the pits where the workers are clearing away the earth as they bring the city to light. The lion stands over a fallen victim and looks out upon what remains of the Tower of Babel. But he doesn't remember the captivity because this lion is a fake: the real one is in the Berlin Museum. If I were asked what I came to know in Babylon I could only answer that I came to know absence. Abraham must have passed by here, and God made His Convenant with His people Israel only down the road a piece at Ur of Chaldee. But all this meant nothing to me.

I ate my lunch on the rubble of Nebuchadnezzar's banquet hall and I drank an indifferent red wine that comes from Mosul in the north where there are Christians. I surrendered every effort at comprehension. After I had eaten, I gave oranges to two beautiful little girls who played hide-and-go-seek with me in the ruins. Then I went back to my own place, the West, and resolved to read Genesis; but so far I have not gotten around to it. I have been too busy thinking out these thoughts which I set down altogether without any confidence in their ultimate truth. ´

The East is a state of mind within the geography of the Western psyche. The East is a myth invented by the West in order that the West might find a measure by which to judge itself and find itself wanting. The effort at criticism is an altogether Western thing and it has often betrayed our enemies into a false judgment of weakness. Carthage paid for this mistake with her life and even the very memory of her name. Yet it remains true nonetheless that this luxury of self-criticism that only the West can afford because of its very superiority has in our time approached a danger zone, a line which once crossed would mark the grave of our inheritance because it would mean that we had lost our soul. The Eastern myth is the most enduring and not the least of these signposts pointing to the zone of danger.

As far as the turn of the century Hilaire Belloc could exult in what he thought was the permanent reconquest of the Maghreb and the assured presence of France and the Latin Order up and down the southern shore of the Meidterranean: he was confident that the enemy would fade into the desert and that all things would be as they were, the boundaries of the Empire restored to their ancient integrity, the three sisters—Spain, France, Italy—spading and planting the African north, thus converting it once again into a garden worthy of the husbandry of free men. Belloc could not predict Algerian independence and the betrayal of France by France. These things would have had no meaning for him because he was a man altogether too knit together by the sinews of the West to ever doubt her ultimate victory. Today we are not so sure. Even when Belloc wrote his *Esto Perpetua* upon Algerian France, Gilbert Keith Chesterton wrote a fantasy about an England bereft of her liberties, given over to Moslem simplicity and the absence of wine. *The Flying Inn* was an apocalypse masked as a penny dreadful. It probed the sinews of the Western spirit until it found our permanent disease, our perpetual temptation to embrace the East.

The temptation has a long history. It is at least as old as the Crusades and the Kingdom of Jerusalem, where Frankish knights married the daughters of Levantine merchants and softened under the sun while the hopes of Europe were pinned on the already suspect Templars, men sworn to keep open the roads to the Sepulchre for pilgrims coming from the

West, but who had succumbed in their hearts to the Eastern passion for secret power built upon great wealth.

Is there some symbol or warning to us in the memory of the last king of Jerusalem, Baldwin? He was a blind man. I cannot answer my own question but I do know that it is in the cities of the Western world, far from the presence of the East, that the Myth of the East found its home. The Myth exists as a literary pretension and as an academic prejudice. It oppressed Christians (and, to a lesser extent, Jews) for centuries in little ways but today it is a formidable part of the furniture of the secularized mind, the mind that has been emptied of faith in the destiny of its own culture and of its religion. The Myth would have remained little more than a nuisance indulged by bohemians and enthusiasts had it not been for the coming of the United Nations and the enormous power that that body exercises for the dissemination of planetary propaganda and for the crossbreeding of hitherto pure cultural strains.

The many agencies for the exchange of scholars and students clustering about United Nations headquarters in New York, whose impact is felt in distant Kurdistan and Black Africa, find their activities fleshed out and perfected by dozens of private foundations. All of them together work toward a common understanding between peoples, a laudable goal whose intrinsic desirability is often obscured by some of its prophets who serve it badly because their philosophies of history and of education are vitiated at their centers by one of two fallacies. The first fallacy assumes that world is one; it preaches the doctrine of a one world within whose limits cultural differences must wither under the demands of the new mass society whose style of life is created by the anonymity that neither respects nor ought to respect any way of life foreign to its own essence. These people cannot respect the East for whatever genuine values it incarnates because these technocrats can respect nothing that is incompatible with their dream of total mechanization.

The second fallacy is apparently the opposite of the first, but it works to a similar effect in the minds of men unsettled in their ultimate convictions upon the meaning of life. This second fallacy is the Eastern Myth. It admits the existence of cultural distinctions, but it confines the meaning of the West to its scientific and technical superiority and, possibly, to a handful of Liberal and radical political traditions whose roots are more in the French than in the American Revolution. The *spiritual* dimension of life—according to the Myth—belongs to the East, which is thought to be somehow superior to the West because of its indifference to matter and its supposed dedication to the unseen things of the soul. The West, under the suppositions of the Myth, is urged to give to the East its scientific genius and accept in return the gift of wisdom and the inner peace that is the blessing of those who have known the secret chambers of the oriental mind.

The business is urged in a dozen quarters and is the implicit presumption underlying scores of books and articles that address themselves to the meeting of the East and West. The Myth has helped create Western pacificism, and even "Christian" adherents of the doctrine of nonviolent resistance find in Gandhi the doctrine they seek for in vain in Christ. The Myth invades the political order and helps keep alive the distinction between national and Russian Communism. It points with complacency to the survival of Marshal Tito's Yugoslavia as a model for the peaceful evolution of future coexistence. The Myth is altogether unmindful of the fact that otherwise decent human beings come to condone the continued suppression of a Western people who used Latin in their courts and the Dieta until the closing years of the last century; who still today publish medical journals in the same common tongue of Christendom; who were always separated from the tribes to their immediate south and east by a chivalry of manner and a high courtesy in letters and in life that are one with Europe: I refer, of course, to the Croats. But the Eastern Myth sees nothing specifically Western as being worthy of salvation.

The Myth would give French Africa to Islam and would view with indifference the insulting spectacle of nomad tribes riding in triumph through the streets of Algiers prepared to enjoy and then neglect and let fall into decay all that France has done within a century of reconquest and creation. The North would be given back again to the desert as it was when Islam first despoiled it twelve hundred years ago, although it is likely that the conquerors would subsist for a time within an empty mockery of the order that it had supplanted, because Islam would hire Europeans and possibly Americans to do the work that is foreign to the simplicity of its creed. The Eastern Myth would not have created this disaster but it would have been an ally to the barbarian within our own walls, whose only political faith is surrender to the enemy. The Myth is the main strength of Lumumbism in the West. The Myth gave Goa and Portuguese India to Nehru, this altogether despite the fact that the native population in these enclaves boasts a civilization that was launched by Prince Henry the Navigator, a civilization whose face is stamped with the high baroque of the seventeenth century, whose glory is the tongue of *The Luciads* and the citizenship of Lisbon. The Myth is the enemy of Europe wherever and whenever Europe must face a menace hostile to its presence.

The Myth has its philosophical and religious side as well. It would have us seek spiritual solace in Brahma and the Upanishads, and in I know not how many other fantastic doctrines. The Eastern Myth is a disease. In its extreme form it poisons a man like Aldous Huxley, who urges us to hashish in the name of a prefabricated mysticism. In a more innocent form it insinuates itself into fads such as the one that preaches yoga as the name of the higher life. In all cases it reveals what I consider to be the peculiar and unique danger of the East to the West: the subtle materialization of the spiritual in the name of its reverse, the spiritualization of the material.

Lacking any doctrine of the *sanctification* of the world through transformation and ultimate transfiguration as preached by St. Paul in the name of the Incarnate God, the east has had to invent every kind of cunning strategy in order to link mind and body, heaven and earth. These mysterious waves and currents, "energies," influences, and "magnetic" powers substitute for the grace of God. Highly amusing and often comical when preached by Western dowagers and school marms who have suddenly taken to what they call "metaphysics," the very atmosphere engendered by this kind of thing indicates the perpetual hurt that Manichaeanism always works in the West.

The denial or the denigration of matter removes any effective criterion by which what is *not* material can be recognized by man. I cannot distinguish two things that are identical with each other! It follows that the denial of the reality of matter works paradoxically to its own contradiction: spirit becomes matter and both of them lose that interplay the recognition of which can almost be said to define the essence of our civilization. That these aberrations belong to the Far East and not to Islam as such is a mark of the superiority of Islam to what lies to its own spiritual East. Islam preserves the values of barbarism, and, as Ortega y Gasset once wrote, barbaric values are not to be despised: beyond them the only values that exist are civilized values and these last belong to us and to those who have been penetrated by our spirit.

I have called this aberration the Myth of the East and I confess that its very indefiniteness makes it difficult to describe with precision. To a certain extent it even forms part of our own legend: who does not remember Saladin slitting the lace with his scimitar and thus shaming Richard the Lion Heart, who could do nothing better than crudely split a rock with his great two-handed sword? There is truth in every myth and I would suggest (although I confess that I advance the thesis with some hesitation) that the truth found within the Eastern Myth is the misplacement of a truth about the West itself.

The Occident, the Land of the Evening, has its *own* west and east. The issue is defined for us by the names of Rome and Greece, the one practical and the other speculative. From the one we inherit almost all our political institutions, our frontiers until we sailed west toward America, our law to the degree to which it is not the common law of the Anglo-Saxon tradition or the Basque law of the French-Spanish frontier, our roads and our engineering genius, our agriculture and our wine. From the other we inherit our critical spirit, our science, our philosophical tradition which was the form in which the Faith expressed itself rationally. The common Christian religion of the West we have from Israel but our earliest documents in which the memorials of Our Savior were written down are given us in Greek, a language heavily penetrated by the Hellenic spirit and still living its life very close to the springs of being. Our east *is* speculative, *is* indifferent to practical mastery; our west *is* practical, nervous, bent on arms and the plow, hungry for justice and the law. An east-west dialectic exists *within* the common tradition which is our own, a dialectic open to the world beyond, as was evidenced by Europe's absorption of the Germanic tribes that quickened the whole with their vigor and passion for freedom, but open to the world beyond principally because its Heart and Center was a Man from beyond its own borders.

There is a tension between the practical and the speculative within our own culture that has been stretched almost to the point of contradiction because of our own internal schisms and dissensions. (One can only dream of what the West would have been had the Byzantine Empire held out another fifty years against the Turks.) Not only are there internal contradictions which strengthen the illusion that the *real* East stands for the spirit, but there is also the paradox of medieval values traveling to our own east after they had weakened within our own west. I recall a letter sent me some years ago by Dr. Erik von Kuehnelt-Leddihn, before I had taken to my travels, lamenting the fact that I did not know the chivalry of eastern Europe, those Magyars and Poles and Croats and men from the great wheat plains and the steppes beyond, who had preserved better than the rest of us the deeds and the name of Rome. In many ways they are the aristocracy and the chivalry of the West. There was one glorious moment but a few years ago, as wrote an inspired wag in *National Review*, when it looked as though Hungary was about to liberate the entire West! For their fidelity to our own tradition these eastern Europeans have been punished at every diplomatic treaty and congress within the past forty odd years.

The West has nothing to do with race or with Western *blood*. Lebanon is an Arabic, and in many ways a Christian, country: Beirut breathes a largeness and a liberty that makes of it the Paris of the East. I have heard the Mass sung in Chaldean, in Arabic, and in Syrian and I was not surprised to learn not long ago that the revival in Arabic letters and language that now knits into one the whole Near and Middle East owes its origin to the work of Maronite Christians in Lebanon in the last century. Before then Arabic had decayed into a dust of dialects, and Algerian could not talk to Iraqi. Today a common press covers the whole Arabic world and papers published in Cairo are commented upon the day after in Baghdad. It is a Christian gift, possibly of doubtful value, given the Eastern world.

It is, I think, the awful simplicity of the desert and of the fighting faith that rode out of its wastes in the seventh century that creates in the minds of Westerners the illusion of Eastern profundity. When linked with the confusions sketched above the illusion is often impossible to exorcise. The Western mind has always been bent upon defining, structuring, understanding. Our great theological definitions of the first centuries of the Christian epoch attest this passion on a level that surpasses the merely human. Our entire university tradition is marked by the division and the autonomy and limits of each academic descipline. Our laws are complex and we have ever insisted that justice is not one thing, but many things. We have always written "liberty" in the plural when we hve been faithful to our own essence. Even the land penetrated by our genius is marked by fences and hedges and signposts proclaiming ownership; and thus they illustrate the poetry of limits.

But when the human mind denies limits, it denies itself. This can create the illusion of profundity because the absence of limitation and definition remove the conditions for human understanding, and when man does not understand he often assumes that there is some treasure beyond his capacity when there is only chaos and the void. It is here that we fall into an optical illusion. We confront the East and do not find there *our own* limits: we are tricked into imagining that we face something deeper than ourselves. We are as overawed as is a schoolboy first looking into a Greek text or as most of us when first seeing a Chinese newspaper. We don't understand it because it does not fall within the scope and defined structure of our own understanding. Therefore—and here is the fallacy!—it must contain some deep secret whose possession promises wisdom and joy. The very prohibition against portraiture in Islam suggests an untouched mystery. The intricate lacing that can be seen to such good effect in the Alhambra, so convoluted as it moves in upon itself and thus approaches an interior infinity, when contrasted with the vastness of the desert that stretches away endlessly toward the sun, seeming to swallow the night and make it its own, dizzies the mind bent on fixing itself upon an object worthy of a meaning. There *is* a secret here altogether too sinister to be named, but it is a secret that lies on the other side of Being.

Christian man surrenders sanity and reality when the limits that structure his understanding are under attack. Because he cannot find his own humble face when he looks into the mirror of the East, the Westerner is tricked into thinking that he stumbled upon the very Light of Wisdom itself. But the East has its own rationality, its own limits, and if we would understand them and do them justice we must see them from within. I reserve my observations to Islam because Islam grew up on our own borders and has preserved and even tried to magnify our great affirmation: the One God who disappears in the Far East and who vanishes within the formlessness of Buddhism, whose final teaching is its own atheism.

Islam enshrines an elaborate code of manners that knows friendship but not equality. Moslem generosity is splendid and any man who knows it will ever remain humbled. Islam preserves the family and knows all the virtues of the tribe. Islam suspects the state. Islam can expel what is not its own or, failing that, Islam can ignore it. Islam has shown itself better able to resist Communism than have the Christian minorities in its midst. Islam remembers injustice and does not permit the mere passage of time to throw a patina of respectability upon an outrage done itself. Islam is tough. Islam fixes an awful and lonely God in a heaven that is sometimes too carnal for the spirit and at other times too distant for the flesh. Islam preserves the divine transcendence by never calling God "the greatest," which would place Him within some human category. God is always "Greater" than the Greatest. There is a deep truth here.

But the limits of Islam often run to mere negation when its faithful turn their minds to the complexity of reality. A beggar will always thank Allah when you give him alms: he will never thank you, bacause to do so would be to break that solemn Fate that governs all things from before the beginnings of time. Thus the will and with it freedom are negated. The monogamous marriage which involves the mystery of trinity is denied along with the Trinity of the Christian Creed. Islam cannot change and remain itself: all alteration is violent as is the cry from *Sura fifty-four* of the Koran which proclaims that "The moon has been split." Without any theory or sense of development and therefore of tradition as we understand the term, the Islamic mind runs to a simplicity in which all subtlety of meaning and largeness of spirit dissolve before a hard and sterile refusal to face the fact of diversity within existence. Subtlety they reserve for business and for war.

Last year a book was printed in Cairo, written by the Cultural Attaché of the United Arab Republic to Jakarta, and called *Christianity*. In this book there is proven to the satisfaction of all thinking men that the so-called Gospel according to Barnabas is the only document contemporary with the life of Jesus; that this gospel was deliberately hidden somewhere in Rome until the seventeenth century; that this gospel proclaims the true message of Christ. What was this true message? Jesus proclaimed his own non-divinity and announced the coming of the Prophet *by name* six hundred years before his birth! The author also tells his Moslem readers that no intelligent or educated man—*not one, mind you!*—believes in Christianity today. Christianity, incidentally, was invented by St. Paul because he could thereby hide the true message of Jesus which was hateful to him. There are other good things in this book as well: *e.g.,* Paul invented the word "Christianity"; Christians believe in a carnal generation within the Godhead; the Council of Nicea was the work of a handful of bishops, etc. The book was praised for its scholarly virtues in Cairo. The author apparently expected it to be: his manner has all the hauteur of a camel; he is stunningly superb. Such magnificence of certitude can only be admired. Here is a confidence that utterly despises scholarship and truth as we know them. This confidence may yet be our ally against a common enemy. Yet there is about it all an absence absolute and unconditional of what I understand by meaning and truth. I did not feel these things when I was in Babylon. I felt nothing at all. This is my reaction to the East.

10. iv. 62

CATHOLICISM IS RIGHT—
SO WHY CHANGE IT?

Thou art Peter and upon this Rock I will build my Church, and the gates of hell shall not prevail against it" (Matthew, XVI, 18). These words are the promise of Christ and the boast of the Fisherman, the faith of Catholic Christians through the ages. The words proclaim to the eye as do papal trumpets to the ear the astounding claim made by the Roman Catholic Church: Only the Prince of the Apostles and his descendants, the Popes, possess the keys to the kingdom of heaven.

The Catholic claims to infallible truth have been rejected by Protestants and others as preposterous. All differences between Catholics and other Christians are rooted ultimately in the response given to that claim. Does spiritual authority reside in the person of the Roman pontiff or someplace else—let us say, for instance, in the Bible or in history or in something called "Christianity"? Is the Roman Church the indispensable instrument for salvation or is it not?

Until a few years ago the Church looked immense, impressive, aloof, and often menacing to those outside her discipline. But from *within* the Church itself, it seemed to many of us that she was slowly winning her battle. Her authority, so we thought, was advancing as the only certain torch lighting up the darkness of a world given over to increasing doubt about religion and marked by the materialist and totalitarian savagery that has ravaged our century. We noted with satisfaction that the Church was recognized as *the* focal point of resistance within and against the Communist bloc of nations. We were comforted by the fact that even Protestants and Jews saw in Rome the only fully organized and militant response to atheism and barbarism. We gloried in the conviction (and perhaps we deceived ourselves in so glorying) that the Catholic Church was on the march, a phalanx. Her yearly harvest in births, themselves a sign of the generosity of Catholic parents to what Pope Paul VI called "the banquet of life," was buttressed by a steady stream of converts.

And then the whole business collapsed. Just when traditionalist Catholics like myself thought that the enemy was about to surrender, our own defenders opened the gates and invited the forces of secularism to occupy the City of God. The council called Vatican II revealed and released a secret Catholic desire to "join the world."

The results today are everywhere in evidence. The Catholic Church is a tower of Babel. If there is one voice that stands out it is the voice of an enormous inferiority complex before the pretensions of the secular world. This voice pleads its desire to please "the outsider." The world is no longer a hostile field to be conquered by soldier saints such as Ignatius of Loyola, founder of the Jesuit order. The world has become rather an alluring mistress wooed by infatuated Catholics of "The New Breed," who address secular culture with the same prayer that St. Augustine wrote to God: *Late have I loved Thee, O Beauty!* Conversions have fallen significantly since the death of Pius XII, and conversion itself has given way to dialogue.

Catholics lecture one another on our many depravities: that is—on lack of charity toward Protestants and on latent anti-Semitism; on our intransigent authoritariansim; on our doctrinal rigidity; on our moral narrowness; on dependence upon a Roman culture; on the antiquated structure of our canon law. I, for one, grant freely that our sins have been scarlet, but I also note that previously we spoke in whispers of the blemishes upon the face of our Beloved, the Church. Today we wash our dirty linen in public—and get paid for it handsomely.

The new accent is alarmingly narrow and sectarian, despite the pretensions of "New Church" Catholics to tolerance and charity. For instance, they deplore the "Constantinian Church" and the Council of Trent, but they prohibit any suggestion that Vatican II, whatever its spiritual results may prove to be in the distant future, was a political disaster for the Church at this moment in history. The worshippers of the "New Church" invite those not of the Faith to speak to us solemnly on our many sins. Luther is rehabilitated by priests who announce on television that the Church has finally come around to his point of view. If the play and movie *A Man For All Seasons* had been produced by Catholics, Thomas More would not have been the hero and Henry VIII would have emerged as a misunderstood but essentially right-minded king.

An American Catholic who has lived abroad for many years is possibly in a better position to understand the degradation into which we Catholics have fallen. I returned to the United States in 1965 after having spent a decade abroad. I had lived in the lyrical and passionate Catholicism of Spain and then the harsh but honest negations of all things Christian in the Moslem East. I came came home to find the interminable tea and crumpets over ecumenical banalities that disguise differences and thus cheapen convictions. The shock is first felt upon encountering the new vernacular liturgy which has sabotaged Latin. The returned traveler reels with disbelief before Masses which resemble, in all things but the dignity found in Anglican services, bad imitations of Protestant worship. He senses that everything conspires to flatten our awareness that the Mass is a sacrifice of Christ upon an altar. He resents, deeply, the presence of laymen on the altar ("Mickey Mouses" as they are called by the Catholic underground).

But the problem is not principally liturgical. Many Catholic conservatives mistake the symptom for the disease. The true disease is a spiritual loss of nerve, a religious exhaustion, which reaches into the souls of men who accept with enthusiasm every criticism leveled against their faith by its ancient enemies. Let two instances suffice here to illustrate what I mean.

The dominant secular idol in higher education today is the demand for absolute academic freedom. A moment's reflection demonstrates that this claim cannot be squared with the Church's insistence that she alone possesses the authority to teach in matters of faith and morals. The claim cannot even be reconciled with the Church's insistence that the corruption of doctrine in the young (or in the old, for that matter) is a grave sin against charity. Nonetheless, when charges of heresy against members of the philosophy department at the University of Dayton were substantiated by a committee appointed by the Archbishop of Cincinnati, the president of that university, Father Raymond Roesch, publicly defied the archbishop. The heretics were vindicated, and the four professors making the charges have left the university. Time after time, at school after school, the secular dogma of "academic freedom" has taken precedence over the authority possessed by the Catholic Church. Our bishops are isolated, bewildered, and most probably demoralized by this successful show of resistance to their teaching authority.

Next, there is the demand that the Church admit a married clergy. Personally I would release from his vows, had I the power, any priest whose celibacy threatens his psychological balance. We do not want walking wrecks administering to our people. But it is one thing to rectify a mistake made by a man who is incapable of living up to his vow, and it is another thing to lower our standards for the priesthood. Where men sacrifice nothing, they can expect little respect from the faithful. Celibacy, in a normal man, is a cross he takes willingly upon his back in imitation of his Saviour on Calvary. If he would be another Christ, in the words of St. Paul, let him make this sacrifice in the name of a higher virility and a deeper manhood. If he cannot make it, let him seek another walk of life. But when the demand is made today that priests not make a holocaust of themselves as did their Lord, they must look upon their priesthood as merely another profession.

The new liberal power in the Church today—expressed through its near monopoly of the Catholic press—is bent not only on secularizing our educational institutions and our clergy. It is also bent upon leading us down the road that broadens at its base into the morass of surrender in Vietnam, coexistence with Communism, and full-fledged dialogue with Marxists. An instance of this is the howl of rage that went up when Cardinal Spellman of New York called anything less than a victory in Vietnam unthinkable. Spellman was treated roughly—but not Roger Garaudy, Central Committee member of the French Communist Party and favorite of the new Catholic Left.

The Garaudy case is instructive. The Catholic liberal-left published a book by Garaudy on the desire for dialogue between Marxists and Christians. Not only did the New Breed praise the book, but it invited Garaudy to speak at the Jesuit University of St. Louis, where he was cheered by an audience of two thousand, packed with the clerical black of priests and nuns. We seem to enjoy entertaining our own executioners, who would kill God "in the name of Christianity," the thesis being that the Christian desire for human dignity can only be realized within Marxism.

In my view the new Catholic Liberal-Left is a sociological phenomenon made up largely of educated prigs who have rejected their own lower-middle-class origins. They are ashamed of their parents and of the somewhat scrubby priests who ministered to their needs as children.

33

But there is more to it than that. These lords of the New Church are a species of latter-day Anglo-Saxon, anti-Italian populists. They hate "wops." You can see it in their attacks on the Pope and the "Roman curial system," in their rejection of the splendid liturgical trappings we have inherited from the past, in their insistence upon barrenness in liturgy and church art. The ethnic prejudice is only thinly disguised. These new breeders are little puritans at heart. They cannot bear the old-fashioned "triumphalism" because it carries with it an Italian flourish. They cannot overcome a kind of grumbling resentment more proper to sophomores trying to climb out of what they consider the "ghetto".

Such is the sociology of the New Breed. In scope it is provincial; in origin, middle class; in vision, narrow; in soul, crippled by complexes whose elucidation I leave to psychology. Spiritually, however, the whole business is best described in terms of a weakening of faith. Many Catholics today attack an ecclesiastical authority that they no longer accept in the depths of their souls. This explains the steady sniping away at the authority of the hierarchy and of the Pope. And this brings us back full circle to where we began, the heart of the affair, the authority and office of the Pope. This is, as suggested already, what makes Catholics to be what they are and what separates us from Orthodox and Protestants. Upon this issue the whole future of the Church will be decided.

It is true that the new liberalism swaggers today through the ruins of the City of God. Its troops occupy the ruins, but they do not quite yet govern them. Barbarians never know how to rule. But they are aware that a wind is blowing out of Rome—a papistical wind, and it presages a counterattack, a counterrevolution, launched by the Vatican itself. The Holy Father, himself a political liberal, has insisted recently that the ecumenical endeavors need more than love, and that they must be informed by a lively awareness of the Church's unique claims to possess the truth. His new encyclical on marriage will not comfort the hedonists. His brusque condemnation of liturgical excesses as "unthinkable" marks our return to the forum that the New Breed has littered with the broken statuary of the Catholic inheritance.

A band of men today begins to gather around the person of Pope Paul VI, a lonely figure who grows in grandeur. There are signs, I submit, that there is taking place, at long last, a gathering of the clans loyal to Peter. We can see it in France where the traditionalists today possess a powerful network of newspapers and magazines. We can see it in Spain where the appearance of the review, *Nueva Fuerza*, marks a determination not to permit the Catholic inheritance to be liquidated in the name of modernity. We can see it in South America where traditionalists make up the enormous bulk of the lower clergy, and where the New Breed to day is being challenged with renewed vigor. Possibly we are men whistling in a graveyard, but then again—what else can men do when they walk among graves at night? Let us take our title from that taunt thrown at our persecuted brothers by the reformers in the England of the 16th and 17th centuries, when allegiance to Rome was punishable by death. They were called Papists. So are we.

We see in Rome not only the Voice of God on earth but the very center of creation. Beyond this voice and outside this center there is for us—we speak for ourselves only and not for our Protestant and Jewish friends—nothing other than darkness. The desolation of our hearts in a century of anguish in which men's souls have been "shaken to the foundation" (in the words of Paul Tillich) is warmed neither by appeals to the individual conscience, nor to the written Scriptures, nor to history. For us Rome and the Keys of the Kingdom are one. Our only alternative would be the silence of a civilized skepticism before the ultimate riddle of human existence.

15. vii.67

IN DEFENSE OF SIN

The devil enjoyed his supreme triumph sometime in the nineteenth century, when mankind ceased to believe in his existence. Baudelaire, among others, proved this and eulogized his passing.

For a long time before his official demise the Devil had been relegated to the role of a mere hobgoblin so far as the peasantry was concerned. A romantic bourgeosie conceived him as a cloven-hooved satyr. Neither role befit him, for Scripture had proclaimed Satan as Morning Star! Lucifer!—a being whose beauty excelled the total perfection of the cosmos itself. Farmyard spook or sybaritic boulevardier—both suggested human qualities more proper to the Christian than to the Fullness of Pride. The pleasures promised by this Devil smacked of senility's lecherous leer more than the threat of Hell. Therefore to deny him his existence could be construed only as a great boon, the greatest conferred upon him since the God he hated had loved him into existence. Man was about to relieve Satan of his last debt to God.

No longer forced to personalize himself in human imagery, Satan happily delegated his work to gnostic lords whose messianic fanaticism promised to exceed by far his own achievements. Everyone must admit that progress was made in the shift from Halloween to Dachau, from the Cask of Amontillado to the Forest of Katyn. A paradox is posed in Scripture: to gain his soul, man must first lose it. The Devil lost his in Hitler's hate and Stalin's brutal cruelty. But his cause was advanced.

Still, this advance did not match the more recent progress of men dedicated entirely to the first of the old trilogy of the World, the Flesh, the Devil. The World requires the hand of man to fashion its fulfilment. And in the new world—desacralized, deconsecrated, laicized, purged of the holy, and served by the Human Church—men have outstripped Satan himself in their devotion to his cause.

The trouble with Hitler and Stalin is that they were, to all appearances, sinners. Even these gnostic chieftans were too human, too idiosyncratic. As Satan's stand-ins, they reproduced, in a manner incompatible with the anonymity demanded by the Secular City, the *personal* character of their master.

Hell could only meet the challenge of the age by denying the existence not just of the Devil, but of his cause, sin itself. Infernal *aggiornamento* was in order!

The opposition of the right-wing *integristes* within Hell can be imagined, but the forward-looking moderns won the day: Sin had to go. Sin had proven itself too tenacious an enemy of secular humanism, Hell's ally. So its citadels were stormed, one by one.

The first target was the sense of sin within the human person. It was rooted out of his intelligence and will, diffused through his emotions, and relegated to his subconscious. Later, sin was separated not merely from the personal center of the individual, but from individuals as such. Sin and guilt were denied the human person; they were transferred to the community of nations, to humanity. Collective sin became the mode of the day. *Vide*, in post-war Germany, the flood of articles, books, and congresses given over to the theology of collective responsibility and corporate sin. The same spirit was instilled into areas of the American civil rights struggle. As a final blow the outriders and advance scouts of the Secular City were persuaded to deny the *existence* of sin.

A careful analysis of Hell's campaign against sin would probe all of the dimensions of twentieth-century secularism. Here it is sufficient to note the core: that secularism has set itself the task of altering human nature. And it is to underrate the metaphysical daring of the secular humanist enterprise to view this goal merely as an intention to "improve" upon human nature. Although the rhetoric of progressivism is still employed by the secularists of today, most of them do not take it seriously. The old slogans are invoked because they are familiar, and because familiarity disguises the secularist revolution in the habiliments of respectability.

The alteration of human nature envisioned by the secularists belongs to what Aristotelians call the order of "substantial change." The apostles of the revolution call for radical surgery; they aim at the *total* transformation of man, which requires, first and foremost, the elimination of sin.

Are they too ambitious?

Romano Guardini contends that we have no guarantee that the psychic nature of man cannot be so radically transformed that it will cease to be what it has been formerly and is now—that it cannot become an altogether new thing. Moreover, the capacity of contemporary science to produce substantial changes under contrived conditions is demonstrable, and the ability to alter the psychic structure of human nature in highly significant ways, an actuality. Both Hegel and Marx dreamed of a future in which nature would cease to be independent of man. And encumbered now by an array of technological devices that are rapidly rendering the biological obsolete, modern man scarcely notes that nature has all but vanished from the center of his spirit. Pitiful remnants of nature, shriveled to cosmic cripples, pass before the judgment seat of the human will, cap in hand. (Prophetically, Kant predicted this very thing in the Preface to the second edition of his *Critique of Pure Reason*.)

Intense emotional experiences, even experiences that perversely simulate the highest flights of mysticism, are now induced by drugs. If physical immortality becomes possible in the next century, eliminating in all men the fear of death with its attendant moral consequences—if science in fact abrogates the independent existence of nature—then man will be cut adrift of mystery, without ever experiencing an ancounter with contingency and risk. He will have transcended good and evil by transforming both into "values" measured in terms of what secularism calls "relevance." In a word, if man does become such a Promethean Lord, then human nature will have ceased to exist.

But this gnostic end of history will not come to pass. We know this, not through reason—for such a judgment cannot be demonstrated—but only through faith. It can be affirmed only as a consequence of the Christian insistence that history began with men and will close with men. It follows strictly upon the Christian conviction that personhood can never be wrenched from even the most twisted and stunted of human beings.

The secularist dream of a life beyond good and evil, be it noted, contradicts not only Christian revelation, but any defensible phenomenology of man. Every sensitive inquiry into the structure of human existence in recent times has concluded that the Secular City's superman would be no mere anti-man or "non-human." He would be a monster, created by the assassination of man as we know him, your murder and mine. And I repeat: notwithstanding the specter of a totally technologized science at the disposal of the Secular City, this crime will not be committed. Not because of some mystique about the immutability of human nature; but because of a theological proposition involving Faith and Hope and above all Love, as understood by Christian orthodoxy.

The nature of this proposition can best be appreciated by taking a closer look at the premises and strategy of the secular revolution.

The elimination of sin is integral to the revolution because sin is an indispensable link between human nature and the supernatural order. A consciousness of God presupposes a consciousness of sin. The man without sin does not need God because the drama of his existence is hidden from him. But the man who retains some sense of sin as a mysterious laceration of the body of being, causing all creation to groan in chains, aging and falling into death—that man will affirm God and desire the Redemption and make short shrift of the pretentions of the Secular City. Who can believe that his first duty is to the world as long as he holds, in his own hand, a ticket to hell?

Accordingly, the chief strategists of the revolution eschewed a direct attack on God, or even on Christ. Both could be domesticated and pressed into the service of the Secular City under false guises. The death of God could be postponed, but not the death of sin.

For the secularists do not want souls for hell but for the world. They propose to sweep around the flanks of the awesome alternatives that are the real destiny of man. The City they would build is nothing less than a cosmic act of forgetfulness, a denial of the laws promulgated by God to govern His creation. They would create a new being, half-devil, half-angel, utterly beyond responsibility because beyong good and evil—a metaphysical monster incapable of either salvation or damnation.

This vision is new to the world. The Cross is not rejected but abolished in a breathtaking blasphemy in which the purpose of God's intervention in history is exhausted by history itself.

Naturally the revolution has sought allies in the old order, in the Christian community. In our generation two have proved particularly valuable: "sin mysticism," and the new psychology which teaches that men are moral infants.

Sin mysticism—born in nineteenth-century France and now enjoying a new lease on life in twentieth-century America—turns sin into a romantic act that demands a Luciferian intelligence and will. This school of thought has not so much shaped the American consciousness as penetrated it, and in the process has abetted the truly stunning success of that second school—the psychology that diminishes the scope of sin, without denying its reality. The latter view claims to have updated our understanding of the moral law, and thus to have found a license for many acts hitherto condemned by moralists. It also proposes a new tenderness toward human weakness.

Sin mysticism imbues evil with a quasi-divine property, thus exalting it beyond the capacities of most men. But the new ethics plays the stockmarket of the human spirit and sells it short.

And it can no longer be denied that these influences—really a combination of them—have now penetrated the bastions of the Catholic faith. Take, for instance, the teaching currently urged on certain Catholic campuses, that a man cannot commit a mortal sin until he has reached something like middle age. The idea is typically advanced by philosophy professors, as likely as not priests, who have tired of the burdens and duties demanded by the traditional understanding of human dignity. Father advises that man is an existential cripple, so gravely wounded by original sin, and as a youth so deeply victimized by emotional immaturity, that the capacity for commiting personal sin is probably beyond him—will probably be granted only as he achieves the sophistication of decrepitude.

The healthiest reaction to this counsel is, of course, to go out into the world and sin with a splendid vengeance and drink long and deeply of the sap of the Tree of Good and Evil. And disgorge it all in Father's very own confessional box.

The trouble, however, is that some students will take Father seriously and go out and do the same deeds under the impression they are *not* drinking long and deeply. Then Father will have succeeded: he will have eliminated sin from the best years of their lives.

And he will also have annihilated guilt, which is experientially one with human nature. What should have been personal guilt will dissolve into what the analytic psychologists call "existential guilt"—the guilt in simply being a man. This non-personal guilt is more devastating, more profound than personal guilt because it lacks a concrete object; so it will produce psychic trauma, and the trauma will further the deterioration of the human fiber. Like Adam and Eve, the students will go forth, "the world all before them . . . a paradise within, happier far" than if they labored through life under the severe and sometimes savage demands of Catholic morality.

But unlike Milton's Adamic couple, who left behind them an earthly paradise of innocence that knew no sin, these young persons will have abandoned a world far richer than Paradise Lost (does not the Church sing *"felix culpa"*?)—the world of Revelation which knows sin and responsibility, risk and adventure, dignity and manliness: the shattering mystery of the Cross. Secularism's Paradise Regained is a hideous parody of the Sacrament of the Altar because it proposes to effect a transubstantiation of man into a pitiful simulacrum of himself.

St. Thomas Aquinas had a higher regard for man's natural moral vigor. At first blush, his teaching strikes us as curious, even callous. Thomas maintained that an unbaptized person—that is, one living without supernatural grace—cannot be in a state of venial sin without having committed a prior mortal sin. At some point in his life, after he has reached the "age of discretion," the unbaptized youth is confronted by a choice dealing with a matter that is trivial in itself, "venial" according to the traditional vocabulary. God chooses to invest this trifling situation with all the drama of good and evil, Heaven and Hell. The youth discovers in this first temptation the whole meaning of the moral order and thereby takes account of his own end and of the direction of his being. In the words of St. Thomas, "he deliberates about himself." If he deliberates well and ordains an action in conformity with his nature, "original sin is wiped away through this grace." The youth has now received the Baptism of Desire. But should he not order his act in harmony with his end, he sins mortally.

The last end of man, God, is thus recognizable as the first cause in the order of action. On this side of beatitude God never appears to man as He is in Himself; rather He humbles His Majesty and appears in the guise of a finite thing, and in this guise permits Himself to be compared with a second, but forbidden thing. Both of these "things," which are now presented to the will as objects of choice, are little more than symbols in the real order. Nonetheless, they both satisfy a human appetite, and are both therefore, in metaphysical terms, good. But one is licit and the other is not.

One beckons to the youth and says: Choose me and I will give the happiness proper to men who love the good of the moral order! The other beckons and says: choose me and I will give the happiness proper to men who reject the moral order! Thus human freedom is born in an act sealing a youth—now made a man—in the adopted Sonship of God, or in the eternal solitude of Hell. Should the young adventurer in the Absolute be called into eternity immediately following his decision, he faces the consequences of the deliberation that produced his action. Human freedom thus *depends* on the capacity to sin.

Moreover, this primal liberty always gives more than it receives. For however a man chooses he will never obtain in this life what he wants—happiness—but simply that symbolic instrument through which he sought happiness. True, the dynamism of the human will reaches out to the Infinite, but it necessarily produces a range of possibilities that are only finite. The will is always disappointed. This is why, when man loves in liberty through his will—when he chooses—he manifests the generosity of Being Itself. Even the sinner is generous because he confers upon the person or object of his choice the whole weight of a love that can in reality be answered only by the Triune *Agape*, the Christian God.

This is the real point to be made about the secularist: unlike the sinner, he is not generous. He does not, he cannot, love. Bereft of any external norms capable of guiding his decisions, he inhabits a solipsistic universe of endless mirrors that flash back at him "values" determined by his own conception of existential "relevance." A gigantic hoax is born within himself. Because of their origin, these "values" lose whatever hold they might have had on reality; they dissolve and metamorphose into grotesque phantoms that rush down the long corridor of the soul until it opens out into the Nothingness that is man in himself.

Leibniz wrote that the only tragedy is not to be God. But St. Thomas Aquinas taught that men are nothing in themselves—zeroes made to be in the image of "the strolling carpenter's Apprentice" who is before Abraham was.

The brighter secularists have an intuitive grasp of all this. They realize that they must deal with the anguish that invades a spirit confronted by the ultimate darkness. They know they must overcome the despair that grips a world from which God has retreated, with only the sound now of a beaten army's muffled drums as it falls back beyond the last crest of the hills of being. The existentialist anguish of the past two decades was, indeed, the dumb suffering of bleeding legionnaires leaving life behind on the field of their final cavalry charge. Forsaken and forgotten by God—so it seems to the prophets of secularism—they wrote the last poem to Death as a blackness settled over the West, closing two thousand years of experience. But the existentialists' thankless heroism before the Nothingness of a world without God is now a thing of the past: existentialism, we are told, belongs not to the Secular City but to a nihilism defined in terms of the Christianity it lost.

The secularists intend, not to deny or destroy, but to forget. They propose to escape despair by forcing man to flee the spirit without, like Lot's wife, being permitted to look back over his shoulder. Thus they have elaborated an endless series of worldly tasks, urged upon man in the name of a supposed duty to perfect the world. Men who are "in the action" are too busy to look back and glimpse the vacancy of their being. They cannot despair any more than soldiers under fire can yield to cowardice when they are pistol-whipped out of the trenches. Despair is conquered in the Secular City by never resting.

Christians approach men in despair with tenderness, nay more: reverence. Such men have not feared to play the game of being and they are to be saluted in their failure. But we must approach the secularist caricature of man with the profoundest contempt. All things can be done by such "men" save one: Love. Men incapable of committing any but the most trivial of sins cannot love. We do not pity them. Pity we reserve for men.

Sin and man are one; the long procession of mumbled confessions Saturday afternoon, of "Bless me Father, for I have sinned," of guilt purged and taken on again and then purged still again; of guilty men shuffling up before the box and jostling each other for position as they rehearse their private lists of failure through centuries of sins that have long since become boring in their repetition. None of this has abstract or rational meaning at all. But it is eminently human. This is man as he is and this is man as he will be, a sinner until the end of time.

Man, suffering, makes up what is lacking in the sufferings of the Cross, teaches St. Paul. By his sins he made possible the Cross. And when the Church exults over the happy fall that made possible so glorious a Redemption, she *tells* us never to forget that sin and love are together in a mystery that is indistinguishable from human history itself. Christ took upon Himself the sins of the world. And the secularists are as far from Calvary as is Christ from their City.

ix.66

SCHISM, HERESY, AND A NEW GUARD

A writer contributing to a symposium of this nature must define his position at the very beginning of his essay. It is of the very nature of the crisis that Catholics today are deeply divided on the meaning and destiny of their Church. This American Catholic defines himself as a radical traditionalist, as a Catholic faithful to the historic creeds and as a rebel within contemporary secular society.

In a word, I am a papist, proud of the Catholic inheritance in history and grateful to God for the faith I received at baptism. This Catholic does not believe that the Church ought to adjust itself to that euphemism known as 'the world' nor does this Catholic feel the slightest repugnance towards the history of his Church, be it from Constantine to Trent or from Trent to today. I am a triumphalist, convinced that Christ's Church is the only guaranteed road to salvation and the only hope for civilization.

That a crisis grips the Roman Catholic Church at this time in history I take as evident, a fact not needing demonstration here. The modernism of the turn of the century was, Jacques Maritain insists in his *The Peasant of the Garonne*, 'a mild case of the measles' in comparison with the doctrinal deviations sweeping the Church today. I would like to explore this crisis but first it is necessary that it be defined.

In the bluntest of theological terms the Church of the post-Vatican II era is racked by internal schism; in terms more comfortable to current schools of psychology, the Church is suffering a grave inferiority complex in the effort of many of its leaders, clerical and lay alike, to adjust the Bride of Christ to contemporary secularist society. The causes of this malaise lie deeply embedded within the nature of modern Western society. Therefore, I address myself, in this study, first to establishing my

44

theological and psychological propositions; secondly, to exploring what I consider to be their causes.

Schism can be understood abstractly in two senses. Formally, schism comes into being and disturbs a Church when a body of men leave that Church in order to found another because they differ on matters of faith, morals, or discipline with the mother organization. Formal schism can also be ratified publically when the mother Church itself expels dissidents from its body because of doctrinal, disciplinary, or moral deviations. When the differences between the two ecclesiastical bodies are more doctrinal than disciplinary, schism hardens into heresy, each body excommunicating the other. But before schism is formalized juridically, it must exist really in the hearts of men. Men formulate and express heretical doctrines long before they act on them and separate themselves from a mother Church they consider to be in error on the meaning of Christ's teaching. It matters not at all that the term 'heresy' is in disrepute today. Those who chastize others for using the term consider *them* to be heretics, even though they eschew the word. Hard thinking, unburdened by sentimentality, demands that the philosopher, meditating on religious doctrine, use the term. This is offensive to the pious sensibility of the times, but only Oscar Wilde could have taken seriously the proposition that a man who calls a spade a spade ought to be forced to dig with one.

I suggest to the reader that the Roman Catholic Church today is already in schism in my second sense of the word. This schism is concentrated within the Western world, rampant in Holland, widespread in Germany and the United States, but present everywhere in diverse degrees of virulence. The disease tends to abate its fury as one moves away from the centers of the Church and out towards its periphery, in mission countries and in diaspora. Only the Church itself, through its hierarchy, can act authoritatively in dealing with schism. Thus far the Church has not so acted.

Nonetheless there is a kind of authority which belongs to the human reason itself and which ought to permit any educated Catholic to determine for himself whether or not the People of God is wounded by heresy. Let us distinguish, therefore, between an authoritative and an epistemological criterion for discerning the presence of schism in our midst. The juridical pertains only to the *Magisterium* but the epistemological pertains to good sense. If two or more Catholics do not believe in the historic creeds in the precise same way, then schism exists between them and brother is in arms against brother. This civil war actually exists today in the Church.

Can any intelligent man, be he Catholic or not, seriously believe that Cardinal Ottaviani believes in the same body of substantive doctrine entertained by Cardinal Alfrink of Holland? Can such a man—I assume here that he is a fellow marked by intellectual integrity and not prone to weasle when called upon to judge—upon reading *Commonweal's* celebrated editorial attack on Pope Paul VI's encyclical, *Mysterium Fidei*, an editorial in which the progressivist editors of that journal accused the Pope of being a bad theologian, seriously entertain the proposition that the Roman Pontiff and the editors in question hold the same substantive position on the sacrament of the altar? Can my intelligent observer assent honestly to the proposition that many contemporary theologians, talking a variety of tongues but talking all of them with a Dutch accent, believe what I believe when I recite the words of the Creed: *'Et exspecto resurrectionem mortuorum. Et vitam venturi saeculi. Amen'?* Can these theologians who begin now to question the immortality of the soul be said to maintain what the vast bulk of us Catholic faithful have believed since the dawn of the Christian era?

Can the Bishop of Cuernavaca in Mexico, who recently declared at the National University in the capital of that nation that Marxism is the only possible road to actualize the Christian message, be said to hold the same series of judgments concerning Marxism and Catholicism that are entertained by the Cardinal Prince Primate of Hungary in his self-imposed exile in the American Legation at Budapest? Does His Excellency, of Cuernavaca *react* to Communism emotionally as does the Cardinal when he peers out of his window at the booted and unifromed killers who maintain a constant watch lest Mindszenty fly the coop and embrace a martyrdom for which, we have reason to believe, he yearns?

Or, to select a humbler and more academic instance involving myself, can Leslie Dewart who recently denied the existence of God, his Being, and the Blessed Trinity in *The Future of Belief* and who was rewarded for his rosary of heresies by his fellow Canadian Catholics by having his book declared the Catholic Book of the Year, believe what I believe about God's existence, Being, and trinitarian life? Now the difference between Professor Dewart and myself is measured precisely by the fact that I believe in the above doctrines and he does not. This puts him in schism so far as I am concerned and, if he be consequent with his position, I must be in schism to him, or, to comfort his own rhetoric, I must be out of tune with the contemporary consciousness which is the only heresy he seems to recognize. One cannot walk both sides of this street. If Dewart is a Catholic, then I am not. And if I am a Catholic—the weight of an ancient tradition would seem to assure me that I am—then Dewart most certainly is not.

The most elementary textbook in the philosophy of religion has always marked out Catholicism as the archetype of an *exoteric* faith in opposition to an *esoteric* one. Whereas esoteric religions permit contradictory formulations of their doctrine to be entertained within the total sweep of the gnosis, exoteric Catholicism has always insisted that the humble Irish washer woman (remember Newman's example!) believes exactly what the pope in Rome believes. Differences look to a profundity of insight and not a shift in content. The fact that this is no longer true marks out, tragically and as would a wound, that the Church of God is internally disturbed by the gravest of schisms in all of its history.

The evidence is legion. I have made my own list but my readers can make their own. Together they would spell out the tragedy within which the Church lives in our time. And this tragedy is not confined to conceptual and propositional differences concerning Christian doctrine as though the latter were some kind of celestial geometry. Doctrinal propositions are not the faith, of course. We do not concede this to the progressivists because we learned it long ago from a Doctor of the Church who is not, as the Spaniards say, a saint of their devotion': Thomas Aquinas. But although not formally identified with the living faith of the People of God, defined doctrines are the articulation, the flowering into speech and reasoned coherency, of that secret and inner treasure conferred upon a Christian at baptism. The slightest alteration in the expression of true doctrine works to the wounding of the prayer life of the least of all the faithful. Impoverishment of doctrine is both produced by, and in turn produces, spiritual impoverishment in the deepest recesses of the heart where God talks to man in the wordless mystery of grace.

Our crisis in the post-conciliar Church is fundamentally doctrinal and to say so much is to say everything that can be said. If the heretics in our midst succeed in altering the substance of the faith; if they reduce infallibility to some vague response of the entire Catholic people, a response today engineered incidentally be the mass media that make do for the inspiration of the Holy Ghost; if they continue to rub out the sacrificial aspect of the Mass until it drains away into a familial *agape*: if they succeed in so blurring doctrinal differences with dissidents that the unique character of the Rock which is Peter is lost behind a cloudburst of false ecumenical expediency; if they implement their liturgical reforms in the direction of ever more noisy Masses that simultaneously hide God in a corner and then offer him to be handled sacrilegeously by laymen, as in Holland: if they continue to permit the 'marriage' of homosexuals while they piously write theologies condoning sodomy, if they bully Rome into silence or partial silence—and this is their tactic today: they are buttressed by the world press in their efforts—the Roman Catholic Church as we have known it will disappear.

Continuing to exist as a despised and often persecuted sect (we have Christ's promise that the Church will last until the end of time), the Church will no longer occupy the center of that civilization which she created and which has been, in the immortal words of Hilaire Belloc, 'the standing grace of this world'. The mass exodus today of priests like Davis and Kavanaugh hell bent on heresy and the marriage bed, will be followed by a truly frightening phenomenon, a quiet and unheralded exodus of millions of traditionalists, who will not deny the faith but who will have found it impossible to worship any longer, led by a new breed of priests that simply does not believe in the things or in the priorities that we have inherited from our fathers and from civilization itself.

Possibly the most hideous crime of all will be the confusion of the old, of men and women on the verge of death when faith is often tried to the point of despair in that supreme act of facing a destiny whose name is either God or Nothing at All. An uncle of mine died last Christmas. He kept repeating in the last few days of his agony, as the life was rushing out of his heaving and over-worked heart, 'There is nothing over there for me. I shall never see my father and mother again. Now they tell us there is no afterlife.'

Do not try to comfort such men—you and I, dear reader, one day or another!—with talk about building the secular city; with fantasies about omega points; with illusions about a human Church; with lies about a heaven that is this world. In that ultimate moment in which the soul traverses the Calvary of despair and is tested therein, all the modernist theologies are so much straw. It is the tradition that sees a man through, neither more nor less. 'If Christ be not risen, our faith is in vain,' says St

Paul and today it is insinuated in seminaries everywhere that he be not risen, that the resurrection was an 'event' that 'happened' inside the apostles. If this is so, then why any Church at all? Why not the despair of the pagan who at least ate, drank, and was merry before he tumbled down the abyss into nothingness? It is the dying who suffer the cruelty of the new Church. Their faith is stolen from them and this robbery of the only gift that ultimately means anything to man is something we shall never forgive the heresiarchs in our midst. For this crime against charity they merit every punishment ever dreamed up in ages past by the Holy Inquisition for they have done the last outrage to the human spirit: they have taken away hope at the moment of death. In so doing they crucify again the God in whom they no longer believe and who also was forsaken by his Father when he hung there on that cross.

A purely human Church at the service of secular liberalism, its liturgy swept clean of grandeur, its prayer life imposed upon the faithful by a vernacular liturgy whose proletarian flatness is only equalled by its artistic banality, for a time might linger on in history. It would look pretty much the way the Church looks today in Oklahoma, like that Church there that displays the photograph of a woman modeling a foundation garment (a peculiarly ugly woman, to my taste) taking the place of the Station of the Cross that remembers the women of Jerusalem who wept upon meeting Christ with his cross. A purely human Church would buy completely Roger Garaudy's Marxist-Catholic dialogue and would sink, more rapidly than slowly, into the morass of that network of international organizations dedicated to soften up the West for a final occupation by the Soviet Union. In that same church in Oklahoma a photograph of Karl Marx represents our Lord Jesus Christ. Such a human Church might command the allegiance of the peaceniks among us, of the hippies, of the New Left. It is doubtful whether Marines returning from Vietnam would care to worship in it.

At best such a Church, the dream of the Left, would not last more than a generation or so. Totally the chameleon of every last twist of the secular mind, real men would soon sicken of its lack of personality. After all—once again—what do we need a Church for, if its principal destiny consists in serving the city of man? We can do that altogether without a corps of priests who would serve the city better by becoming social workers. In a word, unless Rome can clean up this mess, unless Rome can find in the Catholic world a power structure willing to back up its every command (I shall return to the issue), I predict three consequences for the Church:

1. A continued exodus of the Left and especially of progressivist priests impatient with the 'institutional Church's' reluctance to move fast enough in the total de-catholicizing of Catholicism.
2. A subsequent drift away from religious practice by millions of traditionalists in disgust at the failure of the Church to check its own enemies from within and due to their inability to worship at the new liturgy.
3. The subsequent rapid humanizing of the Church, now purged of its conservative and traditionalist elements, until it ceases to be either a force in the world or a danger to the mythology of secular liberalism.

And, although not given to apocalyptic visions, I conclude that should the above occur we would have reached the razor edge of the precipice dividing us from total barbarism and the end of civilization. Let us repeat the proposition; it can never be repeated too often: the Roman Catholic Church created civilization and should that Church abandon its civilizing role in the world out of a desire to placate the forces of secularism, there would be left not one moral voice in all the West, not one authority capable of keeping the standard of human dignity aloft.

Saint John the Evangelist urges us 'to harden ourselves in hope' and therefore no Catholic worth the name can simply acquiesce in the above prognosis. He must look upon it as a kind of Dickensian Christmas Future which will come about only if we fail to reform from within. This reformation of our very sick Church ought to come from the following sources: our elementary and secondary Catholic schools; our universities; our seminaries; the religious orders. I suggest that these avenues are closed to us for reasons which I shall advance. The only other possibilities are reactions from the national episcopacies and from Rome. I hope to demonstrate that we can hope for little from either quarter unless there is a massive reaction from the laity itself which will take the form of what I am going to call 'Catholic Power'.

1. Our primary and secondary schools, especially in the United States, are still largely staffed by nuns, by women. They have inherited, within the English speaking world, the tradition of Irish clericalism and this

prohibits their reacting in favor of orthodoxy today. A word first about Irish clericalism. As a result of the bloody Protestant persecution of Ireland by English Protestantism, first under Cromwell and later under the Whig Establishment that dominated England in the late seventeenth and throughout the eighteenth centuries, Ireland suffered the 'Flight of the Wild Geese', the loss of its natural aristocracy that sought an outlest for its energies in the service of the French and Spanish kings. The cultural dominance of the Irish clergy was guaranteed by the priest's assurance, as he mounted the pulpit, that nobody out there in the congregation knew as much as he did about anything under the sun with the exception of farming. A kind of reverential awe surrounded the person of the priest, not only in his spiritual but in his political and social roles. Not unlovely in itself—did it not bespeak Ireland's love for the priests of God?—this awe left Ireland and went east into England and west into America. The tradition has lingered on.

Our nuns believe anything anybody wearing a Roman collar tells them. In so doing, they reiterate, in a heightened fashion, the reaction of the Catholic laity in both England and the United States. Outside of a handful of old families, descendants of the recusants in England and of the colony founded by Lord Baltimore in the United States, the mass of English speaking Catholics take the word of the priest on everything as being the voice of God. This situation possessed its advantages as long as the clergy was orthodox. Today the New Breed, despite its vaunted rebellion against the dead hand of the past, is cashing in on the clericalism that it publicly deplores. The congregations of nuns, once the strongholds of orthodoxy, are today fields of heretical mischief. Their hysterical mobbing of doubtful and dubious younger theologians such as Hans Küng is symbolic of their total dependence on the Roman collar (on the gray tie in the future, perhaps) and the male psyche. This spills over in their enthusiastic adoption of religion textbooks that systematically demythologize' scripture, emphasize the social aspect of Catholicism to the detriment of doctrine, compare—in one case at least—Christ with Martin Luther King and Buddha, and spread a sentimental humanism well suited to the feminine temper.

The results are already upon us; a new generation of little religious monsters whose religion bears small resemblance to that of their parents and whose grasp of the fundamentals of the Faith is buried in a sea of ecumenical marshmallows. Cases are multiplying of parents protesting to no avail, and of then withdrawing their children from Catholic schools in order to better preserve their faith. At this particular juncture in history, we can expect nothing from the elementary and secondary system of schools staffed by nuns. They would do an aboutface tomorrow, by the numbers, if ordered to by their male superiors in religion: such is the nature of their servility. But they will institute no reform on their own initiative in favor of orthodoxy. We can look for no hope *there*.

2. Our universities (I refer to the American Catholic universities) were formerly a bulwark of orthodoxy. Built by the pennies and quarters of a proletarian people bent upon assuring a Catholic education for their children, the typical Catholic Liberal Arts College of the past gave its students a mediocre education in the sciences; a vision of our literary tradition that emphasized the Catholic revival in England from Newman to the Chester-Belloc; a splendid discipline in Latin and often in Greek; a somewhat dry but basically sound training in scholastic philosophy; apologetics; and religion courses that did not pedantically pretend to the dignity of theology. Little science; much Latin and some Greek; Church history; scholastic philosophy; dogma; a healthy fear of hell and sex; a weakness for the bottle—this made for a sound education, vastly superior to anything found at Yale or Harvard. The system produced gentlemen, somewhat rough around the collar because these men were largely the sons of working stiffs and immigrants. But they could follow the Mass in Latin and in so doing they were firmly within the large inheritance of the best English written of the last hundred and fifty years. If they read anything at all after graduation besides the morning newspaper, it was likely to be an essay by Belloc or a poem by Hopkins. Our graduates were rapidly integrated into the commercial and financial life of America where they have been astonishingly successful despite the dominant Calvinism surrounding them. Spiritually and culturally, however, they were distinct from their fellow citizens because they were Catholics with a specifically Catholic education.

We owe to them the vast machinery of higher American Catholic education today. They paid for it, the old grads. They were far better educated men than are their sons today who can talk about Bultmann, but cannot read a page of Augustine in the common tongue of Christendom; who often know Harvey Cox but not Aquinas; who tend to be corrupted spiritually to the degree of their exposure to theological training. Their teachers today are the sons of poor men, eager to scramble out of the Irish and Italian ghettoes. Truculantly nationalist, even in their liberalism, they despise their own origins. They do not glory in being Catholics but in belonging to the National Association of University Professors. Academic freedom has become a god for them. Their excessive professionalism bears little resemblance to the dedication of an older and shabbier generation of Catholic college professors. I would dissemble were I to suggest that I liked them at all, even though I live among them.

The massive desire to secularize our universities and make them typically American at the expense of their Catholicity has already been juridically successful at Webster. Notre Dame has publicly announced that it is no longer a Catholic University. Saint Louis's invitation of the French Communist theoretician Roger Garaudy to lecture before a crowd estimated at some two thousand, laced with clerical black, plus Santa Clara's invitation to Apteker to participate in a Marxist-Catholic 'dialogue' indicates that not only are our universities secularizing themselves, but that they lack the common decency that prohibits men to sit down with the murderers of their brothers in the faith. Garaudy, after all, publicly defended Russia's re-entry into Budapest in 1956. He has blood on his hands, Catholic blood. We can hope for very little from universities with such a massive lack of common shame. Catholic University of America's show of defiance to the very episcopacy upon which it depends in the Curran case (the Reverend Father was caught guilty of teaching artificial birth control out of his own textbook) demonstrated that the press and television will back any insubordination by university professors against the teaching authority of the Magisterium. They have ceased to be Catholic. I gravely doubt whether there are enough dedicated scholars available with a thoroughly Catholic vision of life to staff more than two or three modest colleges in all the United States. There *is* no hope for us *there*.

3. The religious orders are in deep trouble all over the world. Vocations have fallen off and most orders tend to be split down the middle between traditionalists and progressivists. One older Jesuit in California reported to me tearfully that, as he sits down for meals in common with his fellow Jesuits, an abyss separates him from them, that the soldierly unity in the common cause of the defense of the Faith that has always knit into one the Companions of Jesus has simply ceased to exist. A similar spirit wounds the erstwhile soldiers of Ignatius in the Latin world where, for instance, a number of them went to the American Embassy recently and protested

the giving of a loan to the Autonomous University of Guadalajara on the grounds that it is run by 'Fascists'. These 'Fascists' in fact are the survivors and sons of the men who raised the banner of Christ the King some thirty-five years ago in the *cristero* rebellion against the religious persecution of Calles in Mexico. Yet Jesuits are offended by their lyrical and militant Catholicism. An American Dominican predicted to me that the Order of Saint Dominic would disappear within twenty years. It was a bleak and probably overly pessimistic prediction but it fingers a universal disease. Precisely those very orders that owe their existence to the perpetual war against heresy are today most willing to sit down with the enemy. Obviously they are ceasing to attract militant young men to their banners. Who wants to join sinking ships whose skippers lack the courage to blaze away at the enemy? No hope *there*.

4. The seminaries that train the diocesan clergy are in comparable trouble. Although there are many laudable exceptions here and abroad, the seminaries of the Latin rite are turning out young priests who lack sufficient linguistic training to say a decent Mass in Latin even if they wanted to. Despite the repeated exhortations in favor of the language of the West in seminary teaching by Pope John XXIII and by Pope Paul VI, but most especially by the former, our seminaries are producing young men cut away from the majesty of the Catholic intellectual tradition. Badly trained in apologetics and often not trained at all, seminarians frequently abandon their vocations in disgust because of the foreign and dangerous doctrines to which they are exposed. I know one ex-seminarian, a Mexican, who had to take turns with a friend at standing guard over a painting of the Virgin of Guadalupe in order that the iconoclasts of his seminary, professors and students alike, would not rip it off the wall on the ground that Marian devotions are today *passe*.

These young men enter seminaries because they believe they have a vocation to serve God. This not very original but certainly quite noble intention is often subtly corrupted by professors, the substance of whose teaching consists in attacking the history of the Church and the Magisterium. Too many young men who persist tend to become little prigs who despise the popular devotions of their flocks, who are contemptuous of their traditions, who whore after every liturgical fancy in the name of a specious 'relevance' that finds, however, little or no resonance out in the pews. It is instructive to talk to such priests. Almost totally ignorant of Catholic letters, they try to be painfully in touch with the last shift of wind within the contemporary consciousness. Many of these young men confuse their priesthood with social service. They would have been better off as playground directors.

Yet it is indeed a miracle that so many turn out decently despite the overwhelming influences working against their very priesthood. I salute these young priests because they have rarely been helped in coming to know the meaning of their destiny as priests. As one of these men hurries from early Mass to religion classes, from confessional to the death bed where the Sacrament he administers stiffens and sends the Christian soul to God: to rosaries said before coffins by mourners who glimpse—if but for a moment—the truth that priests are given us in order to usher us into the Promised Land of the Lord, that they have no other destiny within the economy of salvation; as he baptizes infants and seals in matrimony the young; as he mounts his pulpit Sunday after Sunday and faces the faithful who expect from him neither politics nor the social Gospel but Christ and Him crucified, the priest comes to learn that he is not like other men, that he is marked by God himself, that his vocation is fingered mysteriously by eternity. Unbuttressed by the triumphalist education of the past, forbidden crusades and warned against making converts, often ignorant of the giants of our own inheritance who could shore him up humanly in his daily going down into the world; altogether without that pride in the past that marked the older priest; incapable of decent rhetoric because good prose is always triumphalist; not even knowing that civilization is simply a byproduct of Catholicism, these young priests of whom I speak are heroes.

Crippled spiritually and intellectually in their education, bombarded towards mediocrity by the vast bulk of the Catholic press that comes their way, these men—in the very exercise of their sacred office—are undoing the pusillanimous character of their formation. They do not escape into the crowd as does that Jesuit philosophy professor at Fordham who dresses in mufti because he enjoys anonymity—and then advertises the fact in the *New York Times*. These young secular priests—the best of them—out there on the firing line of birth and death often come to know that a cross is too big an affair to carry around without being conspicuous. They look like what they are: priests—men burnt by God and no jesuitical nonsense about sport coats and coloured ties. But it is Christ that makes them good priests. Their seminaries, taken in the large and by the handful, lack both the will and the intellectual brilliance needed to pull off a successful reform.

5. Can the rank and file of the Catholic laity hope for reform from our bishops? My answer to that question, as suggested in my early remarks, will be a cautious yes . . . if. Our bishops are not simply shepherds of souls. Within the highly industrialized Western world, they are successful business men whose vast diocesan machinery not only cuts across but also weaves itself within a financial and commercial world having little in common with the transcendental claims of the Roman Church. Our bishops are civil leaders as well as religious pastors and this dual role, forming not altogether the most felicitous of marriages, constrains the hierarchy to seek respectability and to live at peace with the dominant secular society surrounding them. The bishops notoriously do not want 'trouble' and they are reluctant to criticize one another. They would have it that everything is well in Peter's Barque.

This passion for respectability within the community, wedded as it must be with the image-making power of the overwhelming liberal mass media, renders bishops reluctant to take stands which must be condemned by the world as harsh and reactionary and obscurantist. Few bishops want the public crucifixion of Cardinals McIntyre and Ottaviani. Burdened by an inferiority complex, even conservative bishops yearn for a good press. (They will never get it, for the enemy of the Church knows *his* enemies!) We have not entered into the decline of late eighteenth-century France when the King, upon being presented with a candidate for the See of Paris, exclaimed: 'But the Archibishop of Paris ought at least to believe in God.' Our bishops today in the world are largely orthodox (an exception: the Bishop of Cuernavaca, Mendez Arceo) but they suffer, most especially in the Anglo-American world, from an excess of caution which disguises itself as prudence. Perhaps it would be fairer to say that the bishops suffer from the disease of professionalism, the arch-type of which is found in the medical profession. Just as it takes a cosmic explosion involving outer space to get one medical man to even hint in public that another might have been remiss in his duties, so too does it take an even vaster cosmic explosion, invoking worlds upon worlds, to get one bishop to criticize another publicly or even to comment on liturgical or doctrinal scandals taking place outside his own narrow jurisdication. These bishops often comment bitterly in private but their remarks are always, once again, 'off the record'.

But the hierarchy in the United States at least does seem to be stirring, at last. In a 25,000 word collective pastoral, written in a prose that recalls Newman, the Bishops here have broken their silence and have issued an epistle described by them as a 'major doctrinal statement'. More than two hundred bishops have set their signatures to a document which proclaims what we members of the party of tradition have been proclaiming for a long time now: the Church is in danger. Reaffirming the infallability of the Pope and the uniqueness of the Roman Church within the economy of salvation, calling upon priests to shoulder the burden of their vocation and calling those who fail to do so 'defectors', this last episcopal statement gives heart to the defenders of the Catholic tradition. But this document must be followed by deeds.

6. The first deed looks to the restoration of our liturgy from the chaos into which it has fallen. There are those Catholics, fewer in number than we are led to believe, who do seriously prefer the new vernacular liturgy, who do find more spiritual sustenance in it than in the older Latin Mass. With such men we traditionalists cannot quarrel because the question is one of testimony. Each side can only give his own testimony and let the chips fall where they may. Nonetheless, the fact that Catholics today—after a scant three or four years—are rent into two factions, one at home in the new liturgy and the other loathing it bitterly, reveals that the innovators have succeeded in doing in half a decade what the Church's professed enemies never accomplished in four centuries of opposition. They have split the faithful and they are succeeding in creating a new sensibility at war with the old. They have broken us into a high Church and a low Church whose respective members scarcely speak to one another any more. They have artificially reproduced Anglicanism within the Body of the Church.

Traditionalist objections to the new liturgy are sufficiently well known, so that it suffices here merely to list them. The vernacular unveils that awe and mystery which is bound up with the very essence of religion, stripping it thus of the dimension of the holy and of the sacred. This leads to the fashioning of a religious sensibility from which both fear and awe have departed and this reminds us that a common pagan master, Aristotle, condemned men with no sense of awe before the sacred as being something less than human. The vernacular at best can never match the splendor and majesty of the Latin, the common tongue of the Patriarchate of the West, the visible sign of Catholic unity according to Pope John XXIII. But the vernacular offered us, especially in the new English Canon, connives to produce banality and flatness, as well as working towards an egalitarian religiosity which is hostile to the essence of

Catholicism. This liturgy destroys those moments of silence when men can enter into communion with their God. It substitutes a fake communal 'togetherness' for true worship and works altogether against any lived awareness that what is taking place on the altar is the sacrifice of Christ to his Father. The busy coming and going of lay readers—those new Mickey Mouses—with their rude instructions to the faithful to get up and sit down, with their nasal intonations of badly translated scriptural passages, violate Pope Pius XII's warning that men worshipping their God should be left at liberty to follow their own dispositions in the matter, that what is abstractly preferable—such as following the Mass with the priest—is often existentially deplorable, that the Mass is as many-mansioned as is heaven itself.

Our bishops could settle the *liturgical* differences between traditionalists and progressivists, for a time at least, by offering us a choice. In so doing, they would fulfill Vatican II's insistence that, whereas the vernacular is only permitted, the Latin must be preserved as the language of the Church, and, we might add, preserved as the last sign of the unity of the West. An effective reaction in favor of orthodoxy can hardly be mounted if the most orthodox of Catholics, those who prefer the Latin liturgy (can there be any serious doubt about *that*?), are left without any effective instrument for their life of prayer. There are tens of thousands of Catholics, possibly millions, who agree with William F. Buckley Jr, that the non-Latin Mass 'is the triumph of Philistinism', who have simply ceased to pray in Church, who fulfill an obligation placed on them by the Church, but who grit their teeth as they suffer—Sunday after Sunday—through services which to them are merely the ape of Prostestantism. They watch the Mickey Mouse flitter back and forth as he flutters pages. They suffer the indignity of interfaith services in which heresiarchs lord it over Catholics in our own temples. They sicken at the silly hymns and they rebel down in their very guts at God being called 'you' instead 'thou'. This new hate hour for us often produces the scandal of Catholics turning away from what was once the communion rail because they refuse to receive their God standing. Such situations are intolerable and the blame must be laid squarely where it belongs; on that knot of doctrinal revolutionaries that pass for liturgical experts and who sold the hierarchies a mess of pottage along with the Mickey Mouse. A sound reaction within the Church can hardly set in unless our liturgy is restored to us by our bishops.

7. Ultimately, of course, the reaction must come from Rome and it can come from Rome only if the Holy See is obeyed. There are signs that Pope Paul VI might just as well drop his encyclicals in the Tiber as address them to the Catholic world. As I have insisted elsewhere, Rome today faces a deep *political* problem which it has thus far not solved. The Magisterium of the Holy Father is purely moral as is all authority. And authority is only as good as the response that it encounters in centers of power willing to listen to authority itself. The philosophical and political distinction between power and authority, blurred in modern times, is evident to anyone who attends to the modes through which authority exercises itself in all walks of life. A physician has the authority to tell me to take a long vacation or suffer the consequences, but I have the power to accept or reject his commands. An automobile mechanic has the authority to advise me that my car needs a major overhaul, but I possess the power over my own purse. Now on this earth there is one supreme authority competent in the things of God, the Pope in Rome. His authority is so vast that what he binds on earth, God binds in heaven and what he loosens here below, God loosens above. But his authority, cascading down from dogma through morals to ecclesiastical jurisdication, is existentially only as good or as effective as the response it encounters in men and institutions who possess power. When Pope Pius IX needed a power to back up his authority he created his own army which, however, did not prove powerful enough, but in normal times, Rome has no power but seeks it in the faithful just as all authority seeks an answer in power in order that it might work its message of truth in the world.

The political helplessness of the Vatican was sealed in 1918 with the disappearance of Austria-Hungary, last Catholic power in the world. From then on, the words of Rome—be they words spoken on the social order or on matters more purely spiritual—have only been acknowledged ceremoniously by the political powers of this world. Nonetheless, Rome did command the allegiance of power *within* the Church itself. Pius XI and Pius XII were obeyed by the whole Church. Today the brutal truth is the reverse: the Pope is not obeyed, not even within his own Church. There can be no doubt but that Holland is in schism and that the Dutch, taken in the large and by the handful, are not going to heed the Vatican on matters liturgical, doctrinal, and moral. An interdict would look silly today only because no one would pay it heed. Paul's insistence, to take another example, that the prohibition against artificial birth control stands, that the entire body of teaching on the subject through to and including the teaching of Pius XII, binds all Catholics in conscience, has been defied. Priests everywhere grant couples permission to use 'the pill' and some theologians teach its licitness openly in books and classes. The Jesuit magazine *America* has proclaimed the traditional teaching impossible for our time: so much for that journal's obedience to the voice of Rome. Paul's subsequent command that the subject be discussed no longer until his long-awaited encyclical has been published has been arrogantly dismissed by Catholic journals that continue to print tons of words on the subject, thus disturbing the conscience of millions of married Catholics who literally do not know whom to believe.

Now the question does not look to who is right on these doctrinal and moral issues facing the Church. Obviously the Pope is right, to any orthodox Catholic. Although that proposition can be aired intellectually and questioned, such airing must take place *outside* the context of a common adherence to the Catholic faith. It pertains to apologetics between Catholics and non-Catholics. It has nothing to do with discussions between Catholics in communion with Rome. That 'Catholics' do in fact question the Holy Father simply buttresses my contention that they are literally in schism, that the heretics among us have substituted the Protestant principle of private interpretation for the Catholic authority of the Magisterium. Given that Rome is more often than not, *not* heeded; given that the religious orders are in plain decay where they are not actually shirking their duty; given that the seminaries are infiltrated by heterodoxy; given that the bishops tend towards timidity, the only possible power-response to the Pope's Magisterium can come from the laity.

I suggest, therefore, that the time has come for the Catholic laity in the West to take matters into its own hands when these matters are one with a positive response to papal authority exercised independently of the bishops in allocutions to the faithful and in encyclical letters, when exercised through the bishops, or by the bishops in communion with the Holy See. What I am calling for, in a word, is the creation of a Catholic *Power* in the West, of a guard of the Church that will move against the Church's internal enemies on all fronts, intellectually by throwing all the weight of its scholarly authority in the breech in the service of the Faith, placing this task at the head of its list of priorities; financially, by squeezing off funds from universities and other institutions that do not toe the papist line; physically, by preventing 'Underground Masses' and other sacrilegious profanations done the sacramental Lord.

Such a power structure, fortified from within by a deep spirituality and annealed from without by a militant and lyrical loyalty to the Holy See in time could supply Rome with the troops it badly needs if it is going to pull the Church out of the morass within which it finds itself. My suggestion is truly radical for this age because what I propose is a kind of Catholic Power, analogous to other kinds of 'power' that have recently sprung up in our midst. But although radical for our time, my proposal has many precedents in history. It was only the formation of the Holy League in the France of the sixteenth century, when the Duke de Guise organized the Paris rabble—Catholics to a man—against the money power of the Huguenots, that saved France's defection from the Faith. It was a mob plus Athanasius that saved orthodoxy in the fourth century from an Arianism that was buttressed by all the worldly power of the imperial court. Catholic Power, manned by laymen who do not yearn after worldly respectability and who glory in fighting odds, is the only effective way, to my mind, to clean the Church of heresy today and to restore to Rome, on its knees, effective control of its own house.

Not only would such a movement produce the above but its very need fingers the deeper psychological causes for the collapse of the Faith in our time. These causes must move any thinking man towards meditating upon the nature of the Church within the modern world. That world is hostile to the Church because that world is secularist and the Church must sacramentalize the whole of existence. A sacral world is one with the Faith's perpetual rejection of Manicheanism and of any dualism that sharply divorces the sacred from the profane. Just as man is a unity in being and not a duality, *pace* the rationalists among us; just as creation includes the social and political institutions men have fashioned in order that they might live decently and decorously in harmony with one another, so too are these institutions destined to be transfigured by the charism of grace. And they were so transmuted when Christendom came into its own in the Carolingian flowering of the eigth century that looked forwards to the High Middle Ages.

The point is grasped when we see that Catholics, but especially Catholic laymen, had an enormous field upon which to expand their energy in that long thousand years that hammered a civilization out of the forests of Europe. The counterpart to sacralization, secularization, dates from Marsiglio of Padua's *Defensor Pacis* in the fourteenth century, but secularization really began to gain momentum only in the eighteenth century, due to the exhaustion produced by the religious wars of the previous two hundred years. The rapid secularization of society, aided in our day by theologians such as John Courtney Murray, has progressively removed the Church from the marketplace, first isolating her from the civilization she created and then attempting to absorb her very energies into the same civilization, now drained of its Catholic blood. The apostles of a human Church or of an open Church would make of her a fifth wheel in the axis of secularism. Thus they preach a world totally stripped of the sacral and they preach a humanity totally dedicated to building this world. For these reasons they gut the Faith of its supernatural center. Their Jesus is not the Christ of the Creeds but a pale precursor of secular humanism. Their Church is not the dispenser of the sacraments, of grace, and of salvation but a progressively egalitarianized instrument in the service of a purely human society.

Thus it came to pass that Catholics, from the eighteenth century on, were progressively robbed of what T.S. Eliot would have called an 'objective correlative' for their energies, for their masculinity, for their civilizing drive. Many of them escaped into a crippling religious individualism that effectively divorced their spiritual from their secular lives. Whereas a crusading Calvinism filled a new capitalism pumped with the Protestant ethic that flooded northwest Europe and the North of America with its nervous genuis, Catholics were left defending an ever shrinking sacral order. Tens of thousands of Catholic lads marched to their deaths in that defense, but we lost the war.

In part, the crisis of our time in the Church consists in the tragic truth that we Catholics have nothing to do in history as Catholics. We have been stripped of our civilizing role. We cannot sacramentalize the real any more. It is against the law! Although a handful of redblooded Europeans took their rosaries and rifles off to Angola in order to defend the Catholic presence of Portugal in Africa, they were the last embers of a once great fire that exploded in the past into cathedrals and crusades, colonies and new provinces quickened by missionaries, an entire world of Catholic men on the march.

Given that our youth today has been denied by history an 'objective correlative', it has sought to fashion one of its own in social service, racial justice, international garbage collection, anti-war-in-Vietnam demonstrations, and other decent, dubious, and damnable causes. Religion is forbidden to go crusading. That is what is wrong with the

Church today. This explains, in part, the divorce of militancy and masculinity from our youth *precisely in its role as Catholics*. The root of the cry for 'relevancy' and 'meaning' is this failure to have a dominant and leading role in history. Due to the spiritual exhaustion into which we have fallen for having fought on the defensive for so long, our progressivists would have us join a world we could not conquer. They would find 'the relevant' by linking hands with all of our traditional enemies, by trimming our doctrine to the modern consciousness and our liturgy to the contemporary sensibility, by enlisting our forces in every secularist enthusiasm. This effort, if successful, will signal the defeat of Catholicism as a world religion.

Any salvation for the Church as a force in time rather than as a pitiful remnant waiting on Apocalypse ultimately depends on the Church's encountering a network of power—both institutionalized and private—that is willing to risk all in forging a new sword at the service of the authority of Rome. Not only could such a Power clean house at home, but it could prepare for the final collapse of western, secularist, humanist society. Although it is a well-kept secret among our brethren of the Left, their exciting big World—heavily industrialized, technocratic, slick, materialist—is on the verge of dying within the West. The presence of Black Power in our midst, the drop-out of a generation of youth drunk on drugs, bespeaks a massive abdication from a secularist society whose panaceas do not warm hearts hungering after the justice of the ultimate things. By a curious irony of history, larded with the parochialism they deplore, the progressivists in the Church would adjust the Bride of Christ to a world in full decay, to a world that has played out its three-score and seven and that has no place left to go.

When the President of the United States recently noted a 'restlessness' in the nation on the occasion of his State of the Union address, he suggested more economics as the answer. His Republican critics, given time on television immediately after his speech, simply challenged the President's economics and offered more of their own. But the Black Brother—our society's conscience—will not be satisfied with economics. The spiritual bankruptcy of our world could not be more obvious. Secularism has nothing left to offer the world but a handful of extra years after a boringly comfortable life, a new Buick, and a relaxed sexual code. It offers Sweden, in a word. But Sweden—that hellish society that has made a reality out of the dream of secular gnosticism—cannot grip the eternal adventure of youth, not for long. Youth demands risk, unequal odds, a glimpsing of the eternal hills, a cause bigger than itself.

Crusading Communism is not satisfied with Mr. Johnson's and Mr. Laird's economics, nor can it be bought off with Harvey Cox's Secular City. This Communism goes down into the sweaty jungles of Bolivia and Venezuela. It holds up the most splendidly equipped army in the world in Vietnam with sheer courage and cunning and, we must add, with the conniving of men who sense that the West has nothing more to give the world. This Communism asks nothing for itself but the sheer delight of serving a cause whose horizons seem to its followers, as they face physical indignity and perpetual danger, to be bigger than the world. Secular humanism, dying of hardening of the arteries, cannot answer this challenge. But a militant reborn Catholic Power can.

I mean a Catholic movement quickened from within by the love that Catholic men have always known for the Mother of God, Christ the King its banner, a movement dead certain of the justice of its cause and annealed in loyalty to the See of Rome, capable of any adventure, any sacrifice in the name of the Lord of Battles. Such an elite might just make possible a new flowering of Christendom. This flowering will come, this or its contradiction.

An old world once called 'modernity' is now dying. The world ages, as St Augustine insists, and the times hurry us on. We have no time, literally, to adjust to forms and to a mind already in their agony. They will be gone as are dunes in the Sahara after a great wind. As ephemeral as are men themselves, their absence—guaranteed by every sign of the times—would leave the Church with its eyes riveted on a recently dead past, as remote as the Renaissance from which modernity sprang.

But Christ is our Future, insists St John the Evangelist in a remarkable passage in which the Evangelist states that we do not now know who we are because we are what we shall be and what we shall be is Christ. Let us, therefore, prepare for a new civilization to come. Let us not penetrate it from without but rather let us let it grow up within ourselves. It will then be Catholic. Anything less is not worth the dignity of the Catholic name that we have inherited from our fathers.

1968

EMPTY ALTAR, EMPTY WOMB

It is a special pleasure to find myself here with CREDO this evening to discuss the problems and the alternatives facing Catholics in this anguished moment of the Church's history. Your banding together in Houston in a company dedicated to the defense of the Faith against its enemies, both internal and external, could well serve as a banner of hope, a beacon light to our troubled Christian community.

That the Church is in trouble, deep trouble, is a proposition that few would deny: our seminaries are empty; our convents are dmoralized; our religious orders are in plain decay: our clergy, when orthodox, is timid; when heterodox, bold, and when neither fish nor fowl, it carries the image of men who doubt the high sanctity of their own priesthood. The orthodox are confused because they, the natural defenders of the most venerable institutions of the Church, find these very institutions more often than not in the hands of men whose dedication to the full Catholic Thing is at best tepid and at worst dubious. Our liturgy is in ruins and the cult of the commonplace has reduced the Mass to the most banal of meals and the most tawdry of spectacles. Small wonder that tens of thousands of Catholics prefer to dine at home and watch far better shows on television.

Nonetheless, I suggest that the exhaustion we sense around us is not unique to the Catholic Church; I suggest that it is sensed today throughout Western industrialized civilization. A very old world is dying around us, and it is dying in the hearts and minds of men and women everywhere. We cannot understand the crisis in the Church without locating it within the crisis being suffered in this winter of the twentieth century by our entire culture. Even more: I hope to demonstrate that the defining characteristic of our very old world is, precisely, exhaustion—physical, emotional, moral, intellectual, and finally, religious.

When a physical body can no longer throw off the invisible enemies invading it; when the powers of resistance have been worn down or dissipated into sporadic and hence ineffective action, that body is ready to be conquered. Before death and *rigor mortis* set in a kind of lassitude invades the organism. And while the end may be preceded by brief moments of intense and even fevered action, these last simply heighten the general sickness of the body and finger the inevitability of death.

Translate this analogy into the spiritual life.

Spiritual vigor in societies as well as men is always produced and accompanied by—and in turn strengthens—conviction: an affirmation, a judgment about the ultimate destiny of the soul and of the meaning of man's journey through time. Every historical society that has been a force in existence has been confident in its own gods, cocky in its proper convictions, annealed in its own brush with the Absolute. Vigor is one with faith. For these purposes it matters not whether the faith in question be the true Faith or a partial version of the true Faith; whether the faith be sublime or ridiculous. The point is grasped—and all students of history will bear me out—when we have seen that a society *is* what it believes because its very belief is its most profound act of being. The crusading zeal of chivalric Christendom in the Middle Ages bent upon liberating the Holy Places in Jerusalem; the fanatic reaction at the same time of the Moslems whose zeal had overrun the entire north of Africa scant centuries earlier; the unquestioned faith in Communism that quickened the Spanish Reds during the Civil War in 1936-39; the superb Faith of Catholic Spain in reaction—these instances point to the truth of my thesis: a culture's health is in proportion to the strength or timber of its faith. This faith is very often masked as a science, as in Marxism. But ultimately faith remains just what it is: faith, the testimony of things unseen. Buttressed well or ill by reason, faith is neither rational nor irrational—because it is trans-rational.

Now there is a paradox about faith, all faith. Man desperately needs faith because he cannot live without it; he cannot act without it. Sensing his own internal nothingness, man cannot fool himself for long. He is not an anchor for the barque of his humanity, any more than a ship's mooring lines are the ship. But while faith is indispensable, it is also difficult to maintain because, as St. Paul insists, it is the witness of the unseen; and man hungers after vision. The intellect's need for vision, clarity, understanding, thus wars with man's need for faith.

So faith may decline in the individual person; and when it does, a vacuum is created—which marks the moment of spiritual sickness, of lassitude. In the case of the typical man who has changed his ultimate convictions about God and Reality the vacuum is short-lived, for nature abhors a vacuum; the crisis of doubt, the anguish of unbelief, is surmounted; and he climbs back onto the rock of security that only commitment can give him. He achieves this new security as the only alternative to breaking up. This is true even in men who abandon the true Faith for a false one, because we deal here with something within the psychic structure of human existence.

Similarly, when an entire society commences to lose its grip on its old convictions without having as yet turned to any new set of convictions, the whole social body anguishes in a kind of doubt and skepticism that shakes it to its foundations, that sickens psychologically and physically, that saps the community of its old vigor. The vacuum in this case, however, is not so easy to fill. Let me cite a striking historical instance. The late Roman Empire had already lost faith in the old gods of the Republic. Its sporadic and fevered flight after mysterious religions and eastern superstitions; its sick preoccupation with astrology and the reading of the future in crystal balls and cards; its flirtations with magic; its vain attempt to return to Nature in the Mithraic rites in which the blood of bulls flowed freely from secretly constructed stone alters—all of this frenzied activity marked, as does a fever in a body, a profound loss of faith and of confidence by the Romans in their own gods and in their own destiny. Refusing to bear children because child-bearing is beyond the capacity of an exhausted human nature; recruiting its legions from the vigorous Germanic barbarian tribes to the north, Rome soon succumbed to them and could not even be saved, in her old form at any rate, by the new Christianity which came too late to quicken the Empire from within.

History never repeats itself, of course, but historic patterns do constantly occur and reoccur in time. America of the late twentieth century resembles the Rome of the third and fourth centuries after Christ. We have lost our old gods.

What were these gods? We were convinced that the generally benevolent direction of history would gradually alleviate all the ills to which flesh is heir; we were then visited by the two most savage wars in all history. We were convinced that universal education would reduce crime and brutality; yet with more people reading and writing today than every before crime and disorder and violence stalk our streets by day and night. We were certain that democratic pluralism would produce an ever broadening level of tolerance within an enlightened community; yet we see in the Woodstock Tribe, the Black Panther Tribe and others the emergence of the most intolerant and intransigent fanaticisms that modern times have known. We were told, and we believed the telling, that the industrialized application of science would produce a paradise on earth; yet the nation today is panicked by an ecology crisis, by having to confront a burned-out planet whose natural resources are on the point of exhaustion due to poor husbrandry. We were led to believe that the atomic age would open up vast worlds upon worlds to conquer in the most remote and unimaginable distances of outer space. We now know with a resounding and even shuddering awareness that out there there is nothing but the coldness of burned-out planets devoid of life and air, resembling the earth itself in the first awful moments of the creation of the world. Our astronauts' flight into the future landed them in a past too incalculable to be put into countable years. We are left all alone in a vast galaxy and we now know that this earth is our only world here below. Science fiction has been the first casualty of the atomic age.

In a word: for a very long time progress, education, tolerance, science had been the articles of our public corporate faith. Now all of these gods have toppled. I think it a huge waste of time for orthodox Catholics to attack these idols of the market place. They are no longer believed in by anybody—not even by politicians who do continue, however, to evoke them from time to time as did atheist emperors who burned incense to the statues of the gods. I venture that there is scarcely a responsible thinker in America today—regardless of his political or religious past—who *really* keeps the faith with progress, education, tolerance and science. And this disillusion in the highest intelligences of our nation is matched by the growing disillusion with the public secular religion shown by our youth.

Now a vacuum in the spiritual realm, until it is filled by some new and more vigorous faith, not only signals sickness; it invites a celebration of sickness. When the body is ill, it is passively ill. But when the soul is ill, it attempts to justify its illness. Thus our secular-liberal order, having lost all spiritual vigor, is now attempting to institutionalize its own sterility. *This is the deepest significance of the attack against life mounted in the past few months all around the nation.*

The attack against life commences with an insistence that the federal government (and the states as well) finance clinics and so-called information centers given over to disseminating birth-control propaganda. It proceeds under the cloak of a supposed population explosion—in this, the most abandoned of nations. (Let the skeptic make a 200-mile check of almost any stretch of land in the country in a low flying plane: this is an empty place indeed!) The attack continues with a threat—veiled in high places for now, strident in others—that families be taxed for the privilege of having more than two children. HEW Secretary Finch calls for "disincentives"; the insidious totalitarian hand in the velvet glove could not be more evident. Simultaneously Senator Packwood of Oregon and Representative Bush here in Texas, the latter seeking the job of Senator today, make artificial contraception central to their political philosophies. The well coordinated campaign picks up support from conservative news commentator Paul Harvey and Senator Tower who both call for the restricted family. The targets, of course, are Catholics and Negroes and Mexicans. The "over-population" ogre, I repeated, is but a cloak hiding the panic of WASP America in the face of more vigorous peoples who breed and breed—and just go on breeding—as healthy folks have done since Adam and Eve.

And while the campaign is steadily pressed on this front, a new attack suddenly explodes on another. For several years pro-abortion forces have been gathering strength; now bills legalizing abortion bombard legislatures all over the nation, and are endorsed at high levels of government and law as a sacred "right" of Americans.

The case of Baby Roe in Washington is symptomatic and symbolic. Baby Roe's mother was refused an abortion in a public hospital in the District of Columbia. Egged on by the fatly financed American Civil Liberties Union, she appealed to the federal courts, and the U.S. Circuit Court of Appeals forced the hospital to abort Baby Roe. Also in our nation's capital a certain Dr. Vuitch performs about 400 "legal" abortions a month in a private clinic that makes fat profits by catering to fatly financed pregnant women. Four hundred a month—that means about 20 murders each working day! And the executioner of these innocent children boasts of his feat in *Life* magazine.

Now the point here is not the savage and cowardly attack on children, still in the womb, a most unchivalrous attack because these innocents are even more helpless than the Holy Innocents massacred by Herod. It is rather the profound psychic malaise, the deep ontological sickness of an entire established order getting "up-tight" about babies, specifically unborn babies. Incapable of reproducing itself or unwilling to do so, our established order wants all Americans to be as sick as it is. National genocide is the policy of this order—a collapsing order, more disorder than order—which is in the process of committing political suicide.

America—the land of the empty womb. We are about to abort our future in history because we are about to sanctify abortion itself. The very cleanliness of our sterilized murder factories gives off the stench of Death: not only the death of babies robbed of their chance at life, but the death of a society that has nothing left to do in history.

This apotheosis of murder as a national policy will pass with the advent of some new order of things, possibly savage and barbarian, but also healthy and earthy and sexy and concerned with nursing and cradling babies. This new order of things will come, either from within or without. In the meantime we face sterility, the operating room, the white garb, the liturgy of murder as the masked executioner peers over the swollen womb and pauses to study the best tactic for carrying out the death sentence.

What is the duty of a Catholic? The answer may startle you. St. Thomas Aquinas insisted—and this is engraved on the entire Catholic tradition of law—*that any law mortally violating God's Law is mortally sinful; and that an obligation, itself binding in conscience before the awesomeness of God's Eternity, rests upon those subjected to this tyranny to resist it with every weapon at their command, whether or not the weapon is condoned by the civil law.* And some, thank God, will discharge that duty. How? The occasion will properly determine the means. But let this be understood: the proper means may require the execution of the executioner.

I do not speak in my own name: I would not presume to do so in such a grave matter. I speak in the name of the entire weight of the Roman Catholic tradition of morality. That tradition does not tolerate the murder of children, and if faithfulness to the tradition requires martyrdom by the State, then let the State do its worst!

I have not discovered why the institutional authorities of the Church have not, in this matter, excommunicated the faithless, and sought to mobilize the faithful. My personal practice is to avoid the clergy on all occasions and—following my master, old Hilaire Belloc—sail off on my boat, far from ecclesiastical cowardice. But very often as I sail that little boat of mine—in the liberty of Catholic solitude and silence, forbidden me in my own church—my mind runs back to an every recurring question. What is the link between the almost total collapse of the established order in Western civilization and the apparent internal collapse of the Church herself? What has happened to us? I have spent some time this evening attempting to demonstrate the thesis that a society that has lost its faith, its convictions—no matter how false or banal they might be—creates a vacuum within itself. I have further argued that this vacuum is identical to a lack of vigor within a community that not only fails to defend itself but actively projects its own sterility. Earlier I suggested that there is a relation between the troubles which disturb us in the secular order and those which torture us in the religious. But what is the connection? Very often out on Lake Dallas, in that sailboat of mine, I have asked myself the same question. And very recently the answer came to me like a thunderbolt. The empty womb stripped of its child by the abortionist is analagous to the empty altar stripped of its God by the theological abortionist—the man who either denies, or, what is more frequent, ignores or plays down the Real Presence of Our Lord Jesus Christ in the Sacrifice of the Mass and in the Blessed Sacrament of the Altar. Both abortionists attack Life—one the life of a child, the other the life of the living Eucharistic Lord.

The heart of the Council of Trent was the solemn confirmation of the doctrine of Transubstantiation, so solemn that the Council Fathers even warned against tampering with the philosophical and linguistic formulas traditionally used to express the Mystery. Against the Reformers who insisted that the Mass is a mere meal, that the Bread and Wine *mean* Christ but *are not* Christ, Trent thundered the astounding claim that the Lord God Himself, the Infinite Wisdom of the Father, the Second Person of the Blessed Trinity, the God of God and the Light of Light, He in Whom all things were created even to the last world and the most distant star, the He—Christ: God: King: Lord: made Man, broken and murdered on the Cross—is really there upon the Altar as victim in all the awful majesty of His Divinity and the fullness of His Glorious Humanity. Trent thus affirmed the primacy of Being, of Existence, of Life—over meaning. Yes, it is true that the Eucharist means Christ, but it means Christ because It *is* Christ, the living Jesus before whose Name all are called to bow. Now this doctrine, Transubstantiation, is the very center of Roman Catholicism. Over this Europe split into two. Over this millions of Catholics have gone to their death; over this the missionary blood of apostles to the whole world has been shed in a participation of that shedding of blood on Calvary which is repeated in an unbloody manner at every valid Mass performed in every Catholic Church everywhere on the face of the globe.

We Catholics can never *know* this truth: we can only believe it. But in our belief there is itself born a knowledge because, as St. Augustine insisted, faith engenders understanding. And this knowledge is the following: that wherever this doctrine is believed, men are men; and women are women; and humanity, broken under sin and care and grief, finds its hearth. But more: this mystery of Transubstantiation presses the mind further down a corridor without end (for this is the nature of mystery) wherein it encounters a paradox. The God on the Altar is as helpless as is the child in the womb. If this observation shocks you, then its point has been made. There was a good deal of piety in the last century, and even until quite recently, about the lonely Jesus in the Tabernacle on the Altar. I remember, as a very small boy, how we were urged on Holy Thursday to spend an hour with Him so that he would not be alone. We did this, surpliced and cassocked, kneeling on white benches, a sea of candles glowing before the mystery of the Tabernacle. And we kept Him company through the night, remembering that He complained that His own apostles could not watch even one hour with Him. The only thing wrong with this conception is that it was sometimes reduced to sentiment. Today men talk sentimentally about "the human Jesus"; yet such men know nothing about men. Our God was a Man. He wanted company. Today He is more often than not hidden away in a closet, an embarrassment to a dying clerical establishment that dies along with its secular counterpart because it cannot understand, sense, intuit, divine, sing—the mystery of grandeur in poverty; power in weakness; glory in ignominy: of God in Man.

There is no point for point relation between the white-masked abortionist in his sterile clinic and the modernist theologian or liturgist discomfited by the presence of the Living God. The relation is analogical. Therefore it is all the more real. The empty womb mirrors or reports the empty altar. Both bespeak an exhausted world. That world, remember, has long since forgotten the miracle of Easter and the Resurrection. In this light, everything falls into place: the empty womb and the empty altar follow on the denial of the empty tomb.

But I leave you not with pessimism but with optimism. The negation of life, whether of Our Eucharistic Lord on the Altar or of the child in the womb, is transitory. All of this will pass, and pass more rapidly than we might think. A new world is upon us, an older order is going out. The future is ours, who know that a helpless God is the only hope of helpless man. Orthodoxy, in truth, is the only possible rebellion of tomorrow. And the rebellion will begin when an aroused Catholic laity beholds in the very helplessness of the Cross the shape of a sword.

vi.70

INTROIBO AD ALTARE DEI

I am among those Catholics who once fought for the restoration of the Old Mass. I am *not* among those Catholics who today believe that this battle is antiquated and that, therefore, we ought to resign ourselves to the present liturgical situation and set about the task of doing other things. I hold, rather, that other things cannot be done except out of a liturgical ground. Man is a liturgical being. The Latin liturgy made the West; Eastern liturgies made the East. Let the invidious draw the comparison.

Speaking only for myself, then; and *Thomistice loquendo;* I offer a number of propositions, personal and otherwise, about liturgy, our Catholic liturgy in 1974.

I begin by being pedantic. Doctrines are lived long before they are articulated. They are gestured and danced and woven into the nerves of men before they are spelled out in specific propositions. And this gesturing of doctrine, in all cultures, finds its culmination and its heart in liturgy. Liturgy binds men into a common creed. Cult makes creed: creed does not make cult. Were it otherwise, the Last Supper would have followed upon the First Council of Jerusalem rather than the other way around. Lest any rationalist who might read my words be shocked, let me ask him this question: do you kneel before the Tabernacle of the Altar because you are reverent or do you kneel in order that you might be made reverent? Do you act decently because you are good or do you act decently in order that you might be made good? Action always precedes its own articulation precisely in the way in which being or existence is prior to its own internal configuration, essence, or meaning. Does a child do what he ought to do because he knows he ought to act in this or that manner or does the child's being taught to act in this or that manner engender in him his knowing that he ought so to act? Activity always precedes intellection even as does the object of intellection itself depend upon the act of intellection. (In God this Business is Otherwise, of course.)

Now, to set the record straight: I abominate the new vernacular liturgy; I abominate it when it is done badly and I abominate it even when it is done reasonably well. I do not rejoice in the *Novus Ordo* in Latin. But I also recognize that fifteen years of liturgical innovation have worked their yeast into the sensiblities of millions of my fellow American Catholics. These people—it remains a perpetual surprise to me!—are at home in the new vernacular liturgy. They sing the new songs obediently and without any suspicion of internal rebellion. These millions have come to like what, for lack of a better term, has been called "the New Church." In my own parish I watch young nuns lead long haired children with guitars in choir—they also wander about my end of the church—and I would be a fool or a pharisee were I to deny that they *are* being hallowed in the Lord in their own way of approaching the Mass. Only a totally blinded traditionalist (I am a one-eyed traditionalist, a veritable Cyclops) could deny that the new order of things in the American Church not only appeals to, but, more profoundly, seems to satisfy the religious sensibilities of millions of our fellow Catholics.

There seems little point in instructing these people on how they were conned by a gang of ecclesiastical gangsters, a Mafia in orders, whose game consisted in demolishing our ancient liturgy. It would be untoward—I use a Ciceronian *praeteritio*—to point out how the clerical radicals worked their will upon the Body of Christ and then abandoned her for a marriage bed elsewhere. These mute millions, today affluent and influential, know nothing about their own Faith but they believe in It: this will get them where they are going.

Nor is there any point in insisting that a new iconoclasm has swept our churches of beauty, has bent itself toward protestantizing and rendering flat and ugly the Bride of Christ. Many "new" Catholics know this vaguely: they see that the statues are gone and sense that the altar is now a table but "Father told us it was o.k.," and they think no more about it. I know about this conspiracy: dear reader, you know all about it as well; but millions of American Catholics do not know these things, would not care about them, would not believe them if you told them so. They are perfectly content to worship in churches that are Puritan barns.

"Let us break bread together on our knees . . . When I fall on my knees with my face (raise voice, please!) to the rising sun, Oh Lord (raise voice! again) have mer-c-y on me." Yes—Lord, have mercy on *me*: every time I hear that song sung to guitars, and others like it, I suffer a small death. I die way down inside myself and I remember that Boswell said that every moving out of one house into another is a small death. I was not moved out of my house: I was kicked out and my new house is no longer my home. I am not given solace by the knowledge that those who kicked me out of my house have now gone to live elsewhere. I am reminded of the common experience of a momentary blackout which lasts but a second and the subsequent reaction: what am I doing here? But I look around in the church and nobody else seems to share my reactions.

But I am wrong. This is a visual trick. Nobody says anything, not there, in church pews—but get them talking over a drink or two. They will never tell the truth to "Father" or "Sister" because the clergy in this country exercises an enormous psychological dictatorship that is equaled nowhere else in the world, not even in Ireland from whence it came (Ireland, of course, having got it from Jansenist France). Millions of American Catholics are not happy at all with the new order of things but they keep their mouths shut: American Catholicism has always excelled in obedience if not in intelligence. These millions obey: with tongues slung sideways, hanging out, and eyeballs rolling, they repeat by the numbers: yes, we like these new changes! We are the emerging laity—because Father told us so! After the passing of a decade or so they do truly come to like these changes. Articulation, as suggested earlier, follows upon practice, upon its being done. If you do the new Mass long enough, you will like it too. (Typical genesis of a traditionalist American Catholic: 1967-1970—he answers in loud Latin; 1970-71—he says his Latin to himself; 1972—he says nothing at all, either to God or to himself; 1973—he begins to join timidly in the English.)

But there does exist a massive testimony that millions do not find themselves at home in the new Mass, even if they have begun to join in the English responses. They take no spiritual sustenance therefrom. They know that Christ is offered on the altar but they find His Presence obscured and they are uncomfortable because they are not encouraged to kneel and therefore they are not encouraged to adore. They miss adoration. For millions this new Mass is castor oil administered by Mother. And Mother is always right. A country still ridden by Momism makes of these millions obedient children who take the castor oil but wonder why they should.

Here I will not enter into the thorny issues concerning the legality of the continued use of the Tridentine Mass, except to say that most of us garden variety Catholic traditionalists (*Católicos secos*—dry Catholics, as the Castillians put it: this, incidentally, is a compliment over there) do not spin off into the insanity of denying the validity of the *Novus Ordo*. We are Papists. But it is worth recalling that in matters liturgical the Church has usually *followed* the people. Legalities emerged as the recognition of realities. Certain doctrines are *done* in the old Mass that are simply not done in the new Mass. Possibly the new Mass does a number of other doctrines. I have suggested that people finding sustenance in this new liturgy are not to be contradicted: testimony cannot be contradicted and they testify to their satisfaction with what they have.

But we testify to our *lack* of satisfaction in what we have. Millions, here and elsewhere, yearn for the Old Mass of St. Pius V and for the entire liturgical ambient within which it was celebrated for centuries. (I will not raise here the interesting but expected resurgence of interest by the young in the Old Mass: this phenomenon would require another article.) The Mass of St. Pius V (nobody knew it by that name years ago: it was just "the Mass") knits them back to the trumpets of their youth, to the time when the Faith was clean and simple and direct. The Old Mass haunts the backwaters of memory and imagination and its splendor recalls a Church Militant and bent on triumph. Give to those who like it the new liturgy; it fulfills them; from this worship something good may come. But give to us the Mass that has always been our own. A largeness of spirit of the part of the hierarchy would be a balm of charity badly needed today to make us one again in the Latin Rite. *In necessariis unitas, in dubiis libertas, in omnibus caritas.* If the entire Church embraces a variety of rites—following, thus, the genius of its catholicity—why can there not be a variety within the Latin Rite, one variant of which would be Latin! This ought to appeal to the irony of the Latin temper.

Recently I watched on television a uniate Coptic Mass done in Ethiopia. I was astounded and profoundly stirred by its barbaric splendor. To be a Catholic is not necessarily to be a Westerner. Rome did not "permit" that Coptic Mass: Rome encouraged it because Christ comes to Ethiopia in an Ethiopian way. In the West, presumably, Christ comes to us as to Westerners. For centuries now He has come to us in that Mass in which, at the foot of the altar, a small boy answered the priest: "Introibo ad Altare Dei" with "Ad Deum qui laetificat juventutem meam." I go unto the Altar of God, to God who gives joy to my Youth. God has, in truth, given joy to the youth of many of us and that joy was our joy in bowing deep down before altar lit up in candle time at darkness, in churches waiting dawn, on early mornings long years spent, and finding there—only there—He Who can be found and Who can be found best—there.

iv.74

REFLECTING

HISTORY, TOYNBEE, AND THE
MODERN MIND: BETRAYAL OF THE WEST

Open controversy in the field of ideas is an intellectual exercise rarely indulged nowadays. Because of this, Mr. Douglas Jerrold's brilliant critique of Professor Toynbee's *The World and the West* was a double triumph: but the destruction was executed in the best traditions of English polemical writing. (*The Lie about the West*, Sheed and Ward, 1954.)

Mr. Jerrold put his finger on what is perhaps the deepest danger to the western mind today, when he accused Toynbee specifically, and liberal humanism at large, of preparing the way for the assault on the citadel of the West by inviting all of us to view history from a universal point of view. From this bird's-eye view we can see, it is supposed, that the West is feeding upon the world as a parasitic organism feeds upon a parent body. As organisms grow, decline, and die, so too did the West grow and decline, and so must she now die; but this destruction of our civilization will be no real catastrophe (from the universal point of view) because the decline follows the law of challenge and response: "a dialectical view of history which sees each civilization offering a challenge to those outside its orbit, and by this challenge engendering a response." Jerrold went on to locate this doctrine within the general context of the progressivism of the liberal tradition. Since the dialectical movement of the historical process is upward, since the response is spiritually superior to the challenge, we are asked to give our allegiance, not to an historical heritage, but to the historical process itself. Putting the matter more concretely, we are told to commit ourselves to a process inevitably moving away from the religious and cultural traditions of Christian civilization.

The position is by no means peculiar to Professor Toynbee, nor does it customarily achieve the high level of conceptualization achieved in his own work. The doctrine is held everywhere, if not as a philosophy, then as a prejudice; its tenets are insinuated into the most typical art of the moment; its pretensions are paraded by the most representative members of the contemporary intelligentsia; an adherence to its platform guarantees a hearing in more than half the halls of learning of the day, but disagreement, even the most tempered, brings the weapon of ridicule or the sanction of neglect. The leading characteristics of the doctrine at hand are well known: the investing of the present direction of history with an aura of necessity; the suggestion that an attempt to struggle against the powerful forces moving toward collectivism is futile; the abandonment of traditional ways of life beloved to our historic West; the sanctification of naked power in the name of "history."

This conception of history is, of course, fundamentally dialectical; it supposes that there is an intrinsic "meaning of history," that this "meaning" is identified with the flow of time, and that it is capable of being known by the human mind, if not in all its details, at least in the broad sweep of its direction. It is this philosophy of history that I should like to explore and challenge in the present essay. The doctrine in question reaches back to old style British Liberalism, and beyond, to that mingling of the Enlightenment and the English temper that gave birth to the Whig conception of history. Paralleled and challenged on the continent by Hegelianism and eventually by Marxism, Liberalism had in common with its totalitarian enemies a theory of history necessitating the wearing-away of traditional political and religious institutions by the dynamism inherent to the historical process. At first "the meaning of history" was some Utopian future toward which the law of progress inevitably tended. In time, this "meaning" was sophisticated to the point where progress to a fixed goal was dropped, and history was reduced to sheer change. From this point of view, Professor Toynbee would appear slightly out of date: he still hopes for better things to come. Most of his contemporaries, moved by the frightening events of the last fifty years, have dropped the earlier "meliorism," and have simply surrendered to the sheer mobility of the historical process.

In any event, the attempt to place the essence of history in time, *taken as sheer change*, tends toward a double rejection of the western heritage: one political and cultural, and the other philosophical. First, to identify "the meaning of history" with the flow of time results inexorably in the rejection of any intelligibility that is traditional, because a tradition, although it grows in time, itself endures, and therefore blocks any dialectic thought to be immanent to time as such. As the past gives way to the present, and the present to the future, if there be an inner teleology to change as such, it must be at odds with any heritage transcending or resisting this death of the past in the fleeting life of the present. For example, the western heritage of law and justice was not built, it is presumed, in order to wash away in the stream of becoming; but if "the meaning of history" is contained within the changing process as such, then this tradition is doomed. The rooting of human intelligibility and historical rationality within the law of change is a betrayal of the whole culture we have inherited from the past: a betrayal extending to the highest ideals of liberalism itself, because if everything obeys the dialectic of time and is overcome by the future, why should not liberty suffer the fate of all history?

There are really only two paths out of this dilemma, and both of them are dead ends: to equate freedom with an alienation from the restrictions of historical tradition, is to fall into an absurdity; for where is this liberty cherished by all liberals, if not within the fabric of the classical Christian inheritance? If, on the contrary, liberty is equated with mere action or an automatic response to a challenge, then what is left but the word? Secondly, the philosophy of the primacy of the historical process must entail the rejection of the Christian claim that man's deepest finality is transhistorical: beatitude with a God who is not only immanent to time, but transcendent as well. Man owes a duty to God that is by no means fulfilled simply by entering into the stream of historical becoming. It is not the God of the future who commands my allegiance: it is the God of the present who elicits from me a decision in the now, even though that decision demand that I stand against the world. *Athanasius contra mundum.* This is the Christian vision of man with his back against the wall; and to ask him to surrender to the "forces of history" under the guise of meeting "the challenge of the times" is to ask him, frequently enough, to abandon courage and to betray that sense of honor that was born on the Cross two thousand years ago.

To ground the meaning of history within some law thought to be consubstantial with the flow of time is certainly a denial of the ethical and religious drama of the moment, but it is even more a denial of the unique dignity of human personality. This follows quite naturally from the rationalization of time inherent in the dialectical conception of history. As time has a past, present, and future, so too has "the meaning of history"; since existence is always in the present tense, so do we always stand in the center of history's meaning, looking back on the first stage now completed, and looking forward to the third stage still to come. From this follows, not only a sense of condescension and superiority to the past, but also a hatred of present existence, a resentment of the given. If we stand at the present moment of time, itself destined to give way to the future, and if the meaning of history is the very process of the destruction of the present in the victory on the future, then "the meaning of history" can never be found in present existence; it must always be projected into the future, whether that future be thought of as fixed and knowable, or as undetermined and unknowable. Therefore an act placed in time by a man must be viewed exclusively as an instrument, a means, to the future fulfillment of the dynamism inherent in reality itself. Here is a curiously vicious conception of ethics: not only is man commanded to live in the future, not only is he cautioned against preserving those traditional values he has inherited as a legacy from the past, but the very morality of his actions is measured, not by human nature, not by the needs of living men and women, but by the supposed future direction of the historical process. Not only can Marxism enslave and murder millions with a perfectly good conscience, but the heirs to liberal humanism, the latter-day secularists, can lecture the rest of us on our duties to an historical dynamism which would sweep away the civilization that has alone made life bearable for man because it has shown him his soul. No wonder Gabriel Marcel has cried out against "this crowned ghost, the meaning of history."

Although the advocates of historical determinism and "futurism" disagree widely with one another on the actual direction of the historical process, they are all united in holding that this direction is away from our western origins, nor merely as a fact, but as a law: cultural alienation is of the very essence of history. Even where the theory of an inner dialectic to history is rejected as a law of nature, it is reintroduced as an ethical imperative. For example, Mr. Karl R. Popper in his *The Open Society and Its Enemies* rejects any scientific penetration into the meaning of history; he rejects the historicism of Professor Toynbee; he has no patience with Hegelianism of any kind; he declares that "history has no meaning," but he really doesn't mean it! He takes it all back when he tells us that "we can give history meaning," and the meaning we give it is the "democratic process." Upon closer inspection, Mr. Popper's "democratic process" (equated with the march of history) turns out to be an ethical abandonment of all trans-temporal absolutes: non-commitment, cultural alienation, dedication to the future conceived as the death of our religious and cultural heritage—this is Mr. Popper's "open society." The Platonic-Aristotelian achievement in ethics and politics is rejected because it struggled against the "open democracy" of Pericles, Socrates, and Democritus; but this "open democracy" reveals itself to be an irrevocable opponent of the whole classical-Christian conception of man as a person, owing allegiance both to God and to the common good. Mr. Popper's own brand of anti-historicist historicism seems to have little to distinguish it from the Blanchard theory of history as an ever-widening extension of the equalitarian principle, moving to a secularist paradise wherein everyone will be as equal, and as equally trivial, as everyone else.

The "open society" of undedicated men closely resembles the way in which Mr. David Riesman has read the meaning of history (cf. *The Lonely Crowd*). Despite his avowed pragmatism and his suspicion of conceptual frameworks, the dialectical philosophy returns in his own trinitarian symbolism: until the Renaissance, western man was "tradition-directed," motivated by religious and ethical absolutes; from the Renaissance until the close of the nineteenth century, western man was "inner-directed," "fashioned by the interiorized voices of ancestors"; in our time, we stand at the threshold of the "other-directed"—man purged of faith, ethics, and history. The historical process makes sense, it has meaning, when it is seen as a *progressive* stripping of every dimension of existence, save that of the visible. There will be no room within this new barbarism of the playground for a commitment to an absolute ethic or to a transcendent God. Nobody will suppress our heritage; it will merely wither away, because the inner logic of history would seem to dictate such a destruction.

Mr. Riesman's society admirably fits the way in which the philosophers of the "managerial revolution" have read historical intelligibility. The real revolution giving point to history, sweeping away every traditional hierarchy, uprooting ways of life beloved in the East as well as in the West, is the work of mass production, represented and forwarded by the new business elite. The coming society will be neither capitalist nor socialist, as we understand those terms today. It will be an order dominated by technicians, scientists, educationalists, intellectuals, and psychologists; the new order will reach hitherto unimagined goals of industrial production; small independent businesses will give way to a multitude of "service" industries dependent on, and subservient to, gigantic corporations whose arteries will be fed yearly by the hundreds of thousands, even millions, of young men educated at the expense of the state. Independent farming will yield to agricultural factories. What was once a capitalist system will be so closely linked with governmental control that an observer would not be able to categorize the new order. I confess freely that I am filled with dismay when I contemplate the "new order" supposedly being born from the womb of history. A society headed by men, in the words of Mr. Russell Kirk, who are "schooled beyond their proper worldly prospects or, indeed, beyond their intellectual capacities, lacking property, lacking religious faith, lacking ancestors or expectation of posterity, seeking to gratify by the acquisition of power their loneliness and their nameless hungers"—such a society of white-collared barbarians is held up before us, not only as the fulfillment of history, but as the *fiat* of Nature.

No one denies, I should imagine, that the West is drifting in the very direction indicated by these propagandists for an equalitarian future. Only a man blind could fail to see that the United States and Great Britian today, perhaps France and Canada tomorrow, are headed toward a consumers' society, dominated by engineers, technicians, advertising artists, and the like: men who, although good enough in themselves, are nonetheless cut away from the larger rhythm of Christian civilization; men so "open" to all "values" that they would lack the spiritual toughness needed to meet the challenge of Marxism. The point is not that the West may betray itself: the point is that the West is invited to betray itself in the name of an historical determinism.

The pattern that emerges from an examination of typical social and political theorizing today is grimly repetitious: allegiance is neither to our cultural, nor to our Christian, legacy; loyalty is to history, not as to an immemorial tradition summing itself up in man and giving direction to his destiny, but as to a sheer process conceptualized in a dozen different ways. Perhaps John Dewey's suggestion that we rewrite our history every time we act is the most frightening proposal yet advanced by those men who would rationalize the temporal process. This proposal, undoubtedly advanced in all innocence, looks as though it could have come from the world of Big Brother, wherein yesterday's news is rewritten to fit today's crisis. History's meaning would seem to dictate her destruction.

A most significant and sophisticated defense of the dialectical conception of history as an impersonal force, grinding to pieces all values inherited from the past, appeared in *The Partisan Review* ("The Myth and the Powerhouse," Nov.-Dec., 1953). Mr. Philip Rahv pointed up the tension between myth and time in contemporary letters. Myth, kept perpetually before the corporate consciousness through its reenactment in rite, represents the timeless, the eternal; it promises "to heal the wounds of time." Myth is thus at odds with history which is "that powerhouse of change which destroys custom and tradition in producing the future." This drive toward the traditionless future results in "the disenchantment of reality carried through by science, rationality, and the historical consciousness." Except as a literary device, Mr. Rahv would have the man of letters drop his preoccupation with myth, and accept the challenge of historical time. Perhaps in some future social order, says the author, the "paradox of progress will be resolved," but "a conquest so consummate will take place not within our civilization but beyond it, on the further shores of historical necessity." The fulfillment this dream promises "is the hope of history . . . and its redemption."

Mr. Rahv's essay is extremely significant, not only because of the high level on which he develops his thesis, but also because his conclusions illustrate, not only the meliorism of the whole school of historical alientation and determinism, but also the moral prejudice that seems to buttress the tradition of Liberal Humanitarianism. First, granting that an escape into myth is an ineffectual way of meeting the challenge of the times, does it thereby follow that the only alternative is total allegiance to the historical process, in the desperate hope that "the further shores of historical necessity" will offer us temporal and spiritual salvation? Second, why does Mr. Rahv commit himself ethically to "science, rationality, and historical consciousness," and why does he discard so cavalierly the "customs and traditions" of a people? Does he imagine that science has any more title to existence, any *more right to be*, than the customs and traditions of a civilization? Clearly enough, both have a place in any good society, but if it came to a choice between them, I have absolutely no doubt where the greater good would lie. If the customs and traditions of a people serve their needs, if they preserve the family hearth, if they shelter faith in God and shore up common human decency, then neither "science" nor "rationality," nor what the author calls "historical consciousness" has any right to touch them: they are inviolable: they are sacred. Should they be tampered with, not only will the corporate soul be torn and wounded in its very essence, but powers and passions hitherto kept in check by the good sense of a civilized people will be unleashed, and future generations will feel the impact and will suffer the bitterness and the loneliness brought about by this initial tinkering with the spirit of a nation, and with the structure of a society, in the name of "science."

Mr. Rahv speaks of the "disenchantment of reality caused by science." I presume throughout this entire discussion that he refers to the nature of post-Cartesian science, which aims not at knowing, but at controlling and making. The science in question, good in itself, is not a disinterested contemplation of things as they are, but is a mathematicized instrument capable of total power over, and transformation of, the physical cosmos; in the hands of secularists—drunk with the future—this science would not only make the weight of the world easier to bear (which is its chief ethical value), but it would substitute a new mechanized world for the organic creation God gave us. It would transform the face of the earth, uproot older ways of life everywhere, and blot out the historic memories and the hallowed pieties of those countless obscure people in fields and towns all over the West: men who desire nothing more than to live their lives as did their fathers before them, to bequeath to their sons a patrimony maintained in its fullness, to hand on a way of life bound up with poetry of possession, integrity of service, and dignity born of Christian freedom. Where these things have been destroyed by technologized science, man is undoubtedly disenchanted; anyone would be, were he given a cheap copy for the real thing. The principle of the complete rationalization or "humanization" (so goes the euphemism) of the universe has removed too many men from any but the most obvious contacts with reality as it is. Contemporary society, wherever it has been thoroughly technologized, moves through its communal life surrounded by, and formed in the likeness of, a world of images and flickers—mechanized illusions—created by the "scientific spirit." This vast and complicated world of artifacts and machines is looked upon exclusively in terms of use. The remnants of a raw nature, the frontiers of the new field of vision, exist simply as a distant quarry of stuff, to be mined, disciplined, and then absorbed within the universe of utility. Existence has value for this advance-guard of the future only in so far as it can be worked. A thing as it is—a zone of unrepeatable actuality, unique and irreplaceable—is an affront to the technologized mind, or at best, it is a challenge to be met and conquered. Thus we squander our substance while the dream of total exploitation corrupts the heart. It is no wonder man is "disenchanted," bored, altogether without mystery and reverence, stripped of that piety for things that should fill all life with the sense of poetry.

Still, Mr. Rahv maintains that this onward march of "science and rationality," which he equates with the historical process and which he maintains is the final meaning of history, has resulted in a growth of "historical consciousness." But how can he say this when the rationalizing and technologizing of society has resulted in the very destruction, not only of religious and cultural traditions, but even of family memory? Although not often noted by social scientists, the loss of family history since the mid-nineteenth century has been overwhelming. It is the most striking historical blackout in the Western World. We are rapidly producing a race of men without grandfathers. The "historical consciousness" of a small class of alienated intellectuals seems beside the point in this context; I am concerned with the history of families, the very seed plot of history itself. Where modern man is most fully himself and least western, where he is most fully the creature of the new world of demiurgical science, *i.e.,* in the giant housing units, the shabby tenements and the fashionable suburbs of the American city, in the New Towns of Great Britian, history has ceased to be a category of the human consciousness.

In all probability, Mr. Rahv would accuse me of equating history and its "meaning" with remembered tradition. On his own premises and on the premises of those who equate historical intelligibility with alienation from our past, the accusation is perfectly correct. The point is that I deny the premises. But before turning to a defense of that thesis, let me pose the question I think is decisive on the level of concrete political and cultural action. What values would emerge if we did succeed in finding an intrinsic intelligibility within the historical process? Where would this historical law take us? Where is it taking us now? Only a Marxist would answer that question with any degree of certainty, but if the question is posed negatively, it can be answered by everyone maintaining the primacy of the historical process: what western values will be overcome by the "new civilization" that is supposed to be unfolding from the womb of time? If the civilization "on the further shores" of history is *really new*, if it is not western, then it will be foreign to those characteristic marks that stamp the historic West and cause it to be the thing it is. I turn *again* to Mr. Douglas Jerrold, for a description of the essence of the civilization that time is supposed to be destroying:

"Christian civilization is not just one among many; it is, and the world today provides overwhelming evidence of the fact, the only civilization built on the rights of the human personality, rights which derive from the belief in the immortality of the soul of man. . . . The doctrine of man's fall and redemption, of the equality of all men before God, of the ability and obligation to win salvation, and consequently of the sanctity, dignity and responsibility of the individual personality, these doctrines changed the face of the world. They gave a wholly new direction to human activity. . . . The 'rights' which are deducible from these doctrines are today universally recognized by all who are heirs to the traditions of Western European civilization, even by those who deny in whole or part the doctrine from which they have derived."

To the above I can only add the following supplementary comments: man free under a law, rooted, not in the vagaries of the majority principle, but in the very fabric of human personality; the free family, the free Church, the free society headed by the legitimate state: these are the marks of the Christian heritage. Deducible from them is the conviction that political freedom is an illusion unless linked to economic freedom; that power—both economic and political—should be vested, so far as possible, in the human person; that a decent society admits of the widespread distribution of property, so that private ownership sets the tone of the whole community; that personal and social peace necessitates a living continuity of the present with the past—a continuity carried forward first of all within the family, extending naturally to the region and its traditions, and finally to the nation itself; the respect for privacy, and the perennial watch against uniformity and collectivism; above all, the supremacy of the spiritual over the temporal, of the ethical over the economic, and of the economic over the technical; the enchantment of reality.

The West honors analogy and suspects univocity; the West lies on the side of diversity against dead-levelling, quality against quantity, the valley before the world, the shrine against the cosmos.

To penetrate the heart of the world that was once Christendom, the world that is the very strength of the West today, a man must make an imaginative thrust into the very soul of that culture which is our own. Few men, if any, have captured the poetry of Christian civilization with more power and sympathy than the late Hilaire Belloc. Writing of our common patrimony, he summed up the essence of the West under two points:

"The City . . . and what we have come to call chivalry . . . these two are but aspects of one thing without a name; but that thing all Europeans possess, nor is it possible for us to conceive of a patriotism unless it be a patriotism which is chivalric. In our earliest stories, we honour men fighting odds. Our epics are of small numbers against great; humility and charity are in them, lending a kind of magic strength to the sword. The Faith did not bring in that spirit, but rather completed it. Our boundaries have always been intensely sacred to us. We are not passionate to cross them save for the sake of adventure; but we are passionate to defend them. In all that enormous story of Rome, from the dim Etruscan origins right up to the end of her thousand years, The Wall of the Town is more sacred than the limits of the Empire." ("The Men of the Desert," *Hills and the Sea.*)

These things make up the culture of the Christian West. Whether that civilization be looked at theologically, politically, or imaginatively, it adds up to one unique Thing: "the standing grace of this world." It is a culture sealed only in the sense that it has achieved the Absolute: its freedoms are relative to nothing but God their Author. It remains an open question whether this culture was largely created by Christianity (Dawson), whether it was transfigured in the fires of Christianity (Belloc), or whether it is the human face of Christianity (Eliot). Perhaps these three distinguished defenders of the traditions of Christendom are saying the same thing in different ways. In any case I shall not attempt to deal with the issue here. However the delicate realtionship between culture and faith is finally decided, the answer will never alter the massive fact: the classical-Christian tradition raised up an edifice that gave man dignity under God, and freedom within the law. If the "new conservatism" rising in the United States today is to prove effective, it must go into the marketplace to defend this very patrimony. On the practical level of political and social action, should the "logic of history" demand the suppression of this heritage, then so much the worse for logic.

If commitment to our religious and cultural traditions as opposed to an allegiance or surrender to the historical "process" is the practical issue dividing thinking men in the free world today, it must be affirmed, nonetheless, that the theoretical question goes much deeper. Is there some law or necessary principle governing the flow of time? Does this law *demand*—as an imperative of the structure of reality itself—that our civilization be swept away in the stream of becoming? To a Christian the law governing time is eternal, but this eternal law englobes time itself; history is not a check signed in advance by Divine Providence; God's Will encompasses the freedom of man. We are not playing out our parts in a scenario written in advance: we are not puppets: we are Christian men, which is to say that we are free men, and that *we alone* are blessed with the certitude of our own freedom. An appeal to the Will of God to justify the collectivist trend of the times would be a monstrous presumption and a betrayal of our own responsibility. The question of historical intelligibility must bear on a law—a finality—immanent to the temporal order, and therefore capable of being discovered by the mind of man, and rendered an object of secular science.

The attempt of Anglo-American liberalism and continental Hegelianism and Marxism to discover an inner intelligibility to the flow of time fails both extensively and intensively: extensively, because, as Professor Eric Voegelin has pointed out in his *The New Science of Politics*, "the course of history as a whole is no object of experience . . . the meaning of history, thus, is an illusion . . . created by treating a symbol of faith as if it were a proposition concerning an object of immanent experience." The only certain conclusions we can make about history concern the past: civilizations have died; that they had to die because some law dictated their death is a deduction from a dialectical framework that can never be abstracted from the facts themselves, facts that are inextricably entangled both in the mystery of human freedom and in the unknowability of existential contingency. Intensively, the hunt for "the meaning of history" is buried in the theoretical collapse of positivism, and of that positivistic "social science" that copied the methods proper to the physical sciences. The issue needs elaboration:—

The characteristics of scientific rationalism are known well enough that it suffices merely to list them: the reduction of qualities to quantities; the patterning of the universe after the dead dynamism of the machine; the mechanization of causality; the suppression of the richness of concrete existence; the ideal of a horizontal and featureless cosmos; the postulate of an impoverished universe. The modern mind has been called "sensate." On one level the judgment is true enough; but on a deeper level modern civilization has a profound distrust and contempt for sensation, because sensation presents a universe that contradicts, point for point, the world according to the gospel of scientific rationalism. The senses yield to the human intelligence a world peopled by unique concentrations of richly endowed actualities—underived, uncontrolled, unproduced: a world of things that are simply *be*-ing, and causing, through this primitive action, the assent of the mind to their existence.

By theoretically denying, and by practically ignoring, the irreducibility of existence, modern science found it was possible to unite all things under the concept of quantity. Since quantity is the measurable, and since the measurable can be controlled, the quantitative can be predicted. This method worked so efficiently in physical science that it became the ideal of the new social science. Social science set before itself a goal that was both empirical and logical: social scientists were given the duty of reducing to logical order massive blocks of political and historical phenomena, objectively controlled by principles that would permit deterministic prediction of future events. The future course of history could be understood, so these men thought, provided the facts were rationalized. In this way the goal of total political power was given a theoretical basis.

This program required a self-conscious alienation from history as a cultural tradition within which a man situates himself. Non-commitment to a national or to a religious heritage was the ascetical price exacted for the promised mastery. It is here that the positivist dream failed, and still continues to fail. The dream of scientific historical "objectivity" perverts the very reality of the historical act: an act placed in time by a man is not a bit of refuse lodged in the consciousness of a scientist. In a very profound sense the historical act is not "objective" at all. It is an act issuing from the depths and the densities of subjective personality, proceeding forth from the center of a soul wounded with the responsibilities and the dignity of freedom. It is an act of the spirit of man, and it cannot be reduced to the counting house, let alone to the dialectical slide-rule. To pretend that an "objective" scientific grasp of an historical act as it faces experience is the same as an understanding of that act is both an affront to common sense, and an insult to the sacredness of human personality.

The theoretical failure to come to terms with the over-all course of historical time and with the uniqueness of human freedom has been masked, because the apostles of historical determinism are really nothing but apologists for powerful forces operative within history, forces which are at odds with the main stream of Christian civilization.

To face the problem of history we must locate it historically. Throughout the long life of the West—classical, Christian, and post-Christian—three distinct attitudes have divided men on the nature of history: history is time invested with an inner law or intelligibility, which law dialectically overcomes the past in favor of the future: history is time, but time is unintelligible, and therefore we can know nothing at all but history; history is a cultural tradition enduring and progressing through time, and although time as such is unknowable, the enduring tradition itself carries whatever intelligibility man has succeeded in salvaging from the darkness. The first conception is post-Christian and contemporary as indicated; the second is Greek; the third is Roman, and this last has penetrated the entire Christian world, and is still operative in the minds of all men who have not surrendered to any dialectical philosophy of time.

Unless we go back to the Myth of the Cave, the classical locus for the Greek philosophical conception of history is the Aristotelian corpus. For Aristotle, the scientific necessity found within any thing was located in the order of universal essence—form—the measure of the mind and the source of rationality. Whatever lacked this essential necessity was hidden within the darkness of matter and the unknowableness of time: the realm of change itself. The universal and the necessary belonged to science; the particular and the contingent to history. Eventually history was given back to time, or to those inscrutable deities—Fate and Fortune—that brooded blindly over the world, dispensing favors and wreaking vengeance, reducing to a harsh comedy the plans and schemes of men.

There is no doubt about the sincerity of Aristotle's belief in Fortune; nonetheless his reduction of history to the mythology of Fate and Fortune masked a philosophical tragedy; the inability of reason to cope with the historical fact precisely as existing and as individual. In yielding to historical knowledge the order of existence, history tended to break down under the task, and to content itself with the modest role of the chronicler, recording facts and maintaining a prudent silence about their meaning.

When and if any Greek historian *did* attempt to find some meaning within historical time, he was faced with the intolerable tension between the free act of a human being faced over against a blind nature controlled by necessary and universal laws. The laws were understandable by science; the free historical act, as well as the full course of time, blocked rational penetration. Every time a Greek historian rationalized this dual mystery, he dissolved human freedom within the order of nature and her laws: a nature controlled, disciplined, wheeled about cyclically, spinning forever in a circle that was really a chain. It was better to let Fortune alone, and exclude her from the order of science. To admit her to the Temple of Athene, as did Herodatus, was to destroy human freedom by reducing liberty to the laws of nature: "That which is destined to come to pass as a consequence of divine activity it is impossible to avert. . . . Of all the sorrows which afflict mankind, the bitterest is this, that one should have consciousness of much, but control over nothing." (Herodatus, ix, 16)

Aristotle's theory of history escaped this bleak pessimism because he refused to consider history intelligible. His refusal saved the unpredictability of the free historical act, but man's freedom was saved only because Aristotle failed to come to grips with history on its own terms. All knowledge began in the sensation of existing things, but scientific causal certainty was achieved only when the concrete individuality of the existing thing was left aside. Even poetry was closer to science than was history, because poetry looked to the universal through a particular that mirrored essential perfections. "Poetry is something more philosophic and of graver import than history, since its statements are of the nature of universals, whereas those of history are singulars." (*Poetics*, 1451a36-1451b8.)

Despite the recognition of the philosopher's duty to society, salvation for the Greek mind was achieved only by a flight from time, contingency, the darkness of matter, and the world of opinion. Human perfection was not found within the historical order (although man had a duty to that order), nor could history give to men a meaning to be found only in those eternal essences that singular things can but shadow forth, seducing the mind into the kingdom of the abstract—a kingdom beyond existence. The Good of Plato and the One of Plotinus are the loftiest expressions of a spirit that hungered for release from the prison of history; this is the same spirit that carved forever an ideal of serenity and peace, universality and beauty, unspoiled by the vagaries of time and matter. The soul of Hellenic Greece can be seen at its best by contemplating that sculpture that remains to this day a marvel and a testimony to the classical spirit. The Greeks—at the apex of their glory—never painted men: they sculptured Man.

It is not accurate to think of Plato and Plotinus leaving the world to an Aristotle who kept his feet resolutely on the ground. The Greek philosophical spirit was all of one piece. For Aristotle, history serves political theory. Political theory ministers to ethics. Ethics teaches that the good life must be sought in the highest part of man. The highest part of man is the soul. The highest part of the soul is the intellect. The highest act of the intellect is the act of philosophical contemplation in which the

Truth is known purely and simply for itself. Among the order of contemplative acts there is one which is the end of all the others, and this act is the end of man, whose end is the end of the universe. This is the act of philosophical contemplation, Wisdom, the understanding of the First Cause of all things in the order of finality. This First Cause is the perfection of Thought thinking Itself. Contingency and time and the things that pass may never enter the temple of the eternal, a god too good for providence, a god who neither creates the order of time, nor knows the things that are. Man's highest end is the contemplation and the imitation of this Pure Intelligibility. Human life would be very good indeed were there no history to know. History is the tragedy of human existence.

I am convinced that this was the essential attitude of Greek philosophy toward history. That some of the Greek historians flirted with the temptation to reduce history to science can be attributed, perhaps, to the perennial need man feels to organize the concrete richness of historical existence into a rational pattern. Among all such experiments, that of Polybius is crucial for an understanding of the profound abyss separating the Romans from the Greek philosophers on the question of history and its meaning.

The thought of Polybius wavers between historical description and historical theorizing, and his analysis of the facts of the Roman constitution could never be made to fit his own variation of the "science of history." Borrowing heavily from the political theories of Plato and Aristotle, Polybius constructed an historical science his masters would have rejected with contempt. The traditional doctrine of the three good forms of government and their three evil opposites, worked out as logical possibilities by the early philosophers, appeared to Polybius to be something of greater than merely speculative import. The six forms were ordered in historical time in such a fashion that one kind of government necessarily followed another, until the cycle, now completed, began anew. Kingship degenerated into tyranny; tyranny was overcome by aristocracy; aristocracy corrupted into oligarchy; oligarchy gave way to democracy; democracy sank back into mob rule; mob rule was suppressed by monarchy, and thus the cycle commenced to wheel about once again. For Polybius, the cycle was neither a shrewd guess, nor was it a highly likely possibility, nor was it a logical deduction from some abstract science of ethics. It was an historical fact that could be understood rationally because it partook of the principle of necessity; the law was as necessary as the laws governing the angles of a triangle. Polybius concluded his analysis with a declaration of independence for history: "Such is the cycle of political revolution, the course appointed by nature in which constitutions change, disappear, and finally return to the point from which they started" (Book VI, 9.10). The cycle was "appointed by nature." This is the key: for the Greeks, "nature" was always the order of law and necessity. If history had been subsumed under the order of nature, history had finally become a science. Even the Roman Republic, then at the zenith of its glory and power (so thought Polybius) was destined nonetheless to undergo a "natural decline" and thus "change to its contrary" (9.14).

But the theory of cycles that made history a science could not be made to fit the history of the Roman people. No matter how hard Polybius tried, he never really succeeded in pressing Rome into his own Procrustean bed

The Roman Constitution broke the cycle. By combining the three possible good forms of government, Rome had overcome the supposed "natural" necessity of a state's decline into its logical opposite. The Roman Consititution was an instrument that was a tension created by the intersection of monarchy, aristocracy, and democracy. Since the very essence of this state was the tension itself, Rome transcended each of the three forms taken separately. Hence Rome escaped the very real dangers inherent to any single unmixed form of government—the dangers that had engendered the theory of the cycle. The Roman consuls together formed a political instrument monarchical in structure; the Senate, composed as it was of the nobility of the City, was by nature aristocratic; the *comitium* represented the people acting and voting in a body, and was thus essentially democratic. The evils germane to any one of the three governing arms were checked by the powers of the other two. "It was impossible even for a native to pronounce with certainty whether the whole system was aristocratic, democratic, monarchical" (VI, 11.11). The system of "checks and balances" keeping any one part of the constitution from dominating the others and thus resuming the cycle, forced Polybius to conclude that the Roman State was sufficiently powerful and elastic to meet all emergencies; possessed of powers adequate for the suppression of abuses, the "mixed" state provided the proper equilibrium for continued political existence. The Romans broke the cycle, not be inventing new political forms, but by synthesizing the old forms recognized and tried by the Greeks. In so doing, the Romans implicitly accepted the Greek political theory concerning the six possible forms of government, but the Romans succeeded in locating the three good forms *simultaneously* in time. Abuses inherent to any good governing arm did not necessarily lead to an opposite evil order, itself destined to give way in time to the contrary good order.

Behind the Roman mind on this issue reposed an implicit rejection of the whole Greek attitude toward time and history. Polybius understood this on the level of politics. There is no evidence that he or any other Greek understood its full profundity: a rejection implying a new conception of historical existence.

The late Professor Collingwood has noted what I choose to call the dramatic quality of Roman historical writing. The imagery of Livy, Tacitus, and Suetonius was dramatic—the imagery of the theatre. Rome was talked of as though she were a person, a Character: Rome was a she: a heroine. Roma steps, mature and fully clad, into the arena of history as though she had just come on stage from behind a backdrop. She plays the leading role, and if we push the figure a bit, we might say she soon steals the show. Rome marches through history from the burning of Troy to the burning of Carthage, but she comes through unharmed and erect. Menaced by wars, by age and decay, she emerges from out of the chaos and dust of the centuries, triumphant, and herself. Aeneas carries father Anchises out of burning Troy, and the saving of the household gods assures the perpetuation of the fatherland. From the fabled age of Romulus, and even beyond to the "glory of the Antonines," Rome is conceived by the Latins as though she were some one Thing, carried forward by a people whose very immortality is bound up inextricably with the destiny of the City. The modern man has met history when he has changed with the times; the Roman felt he had met history when he had mastered the times. History wasn't the times; history was the City of Man.

Collingwood and others have complained about what they call this "substantialist" or "static" theory of history permeating the Roman mind. Rome failed, so goes the complaint, to grasp the nature of the historical process; Rome never understood the dynamism inherent to history. When a Roman acted, Spengler once wrote, he acted as though the full brunt of all the forces of history went into his present decision; when a Roman acted, wrote Ortega y Gasset, he clothed himself, not only in the virtues, but in the garb of his ancestors. This attitude of mind has been condemned as "static," but the complaint falls to pieces when we face the overwhelming truth that this "failure" made the western world. Christian Rome succeeded, as Jerrold points out, not because of the fall of the Empire, but in spite of it. The staying power of the Roman spirit was rooted deeply in the conviction that if a man builds, he builds against the ravages of time, or he simply does not build at all. To have told a Roman that he was part of a dialectic soon to overcome his "moment" in history, would have been as absurd as it is to ask anybody to build a house *in order that it might collapse;* true enough, the house may collapse; true enough, it probably will, but if it gets built at all, it goes up because a man feels he is, in some measure, the master of time. The dialectical conception of history, no matter how good it looks on paper, is fundamentally at odds with common sense, and if the Greek heritage of science and ethics is enshrined in the West today, it is because the Romans were essentially a practical people, who refused to be seduced into an historical determinism by the vagaries of a psuedo-metaphysics.

The poetry of Rome points to something deeper than myth; it points to the conviction that human society, both familial and corporate, is a spiritual unity, linking together all generations. For this tradition of the comradeship of all men—be they dead, living, or yet to come—for this tradition to exist, it must, by definition, resist the rhythm of generation and corruption intrinsic to nature.

The dramatic imagery of the Roman poets and historians did not fade away in the dust and confusion of the centuries dividing the Empire from the high Middle Ages. The conception endured and is the heritage of the entire western world. It is by no means so antiquated or provincial as a number of academicians might imagine. When a twentieth-century American, unencumbered by the baggage of what has become a latter-day scholasticism, looks for a symbol of the history of his country, he draws a picture of Uncle Sam. So too the Englishman has his John Bull, and the citizen of the old Germanies had his *alter Michael.* If the historical symbol was taken from physical nature, as the Scots took the thistle and the Frenchmen of the old regime took the *fleur de lis,* the symbol was stylized and thus humanized. All the black and gold riot of heraldy emblazoning our western past suggests an attitude toward history fundamentally Roman. History was thought to belong, neither to nature nor to dialectical laws, but to an order essentially capable of transcending the ravages of time because it partook of the dignity of spirit. Rome brought in our common patrimony of civic loyalty, and it was not loyalty to any "powerhouse of change producing the future."

This attitude, an historical fact itself, is so imposing that it cannot be brushed aside as mere folk-lore. Society was looked upon as a circle of light incarnating traditions of living and dying inherited from the past, and destined to be projected into the future. Society was not one dimensional: it included the past, and looked toward the future. History was what added depth and being to what would otherwise have been a mosaic of mechanical and abstract principles, devoid of human associations, altogether lacking in that civic poetry without which patriotism can never flourish. Men looked back with gratitude to those from whom they had inherited, and they looked forward with dedication to those to whom they would give. Committed to a patrimony whose very being was enshrined in history, history was a gift received and an inheritance transmitted. This sense of history as a corporate Thing, an unfinished story, within which the existing person finds himself, ran through all arteries of life: the farm, the estate, the town, the city, the region, the nation, the West itself. Nor did such a conception prevent progress; if progress be conceived as a flowering from roots reaching back into history, then the condition of progress is the perpetuation of the heritage of the past. The above, of course, is a figure for a reality that is essentially spiritual, and the spiritual advances, not by destroying itself, but by becoming itself.

It is with Rome, as Hannah Arendt has pointed out, that the reality of tradition entered for the first time into the western consciousness. History was no more the order of sheer mobility and unintelligibility. What lay beyond the City and the Imperial Order was the chaos of barbarism: the barbarism of men who had not yet fully entered into history. The citizen did not identify his destiny with the cosmic order, nor did he consider himself the representative of a supposed law of nature as did the oriental masses of the Eastern Empires, as do most primitive people today, and as do all intellectuals touched by the spirit of Hegel and Marx.

To put the issue precisely, let us say that the Greek philosophical discoveries concerning the nature of man, the good life, and the rule of law, would have remained largely ineffective had they not been linked with the Roman sense of tradition. In order for that tradition to endure, the men within the community had to become committed to the tradition. This dedication extended to the fathers who gave the law, as well as to the law itself. In order to *be* at all, an absolute must become a family heirloom.

The famous Roman *pietas* was the instrument perpetuating the classical mind.

Of course this is reading history after the fact. The Roman sense of historical tradition was not a philosophical deduction; it was a psychological necessity to a nation of peasants. The family is knit together by blood and a common land turned over by hands that have received their patrimony from a line of ancestors stretching back to the youth of the race. The dusk falls on the back of each man as he retreats down the road of time; but as he has received from the past, so has he given to the future; and as they lived in him, so shall he live in them. And this is promised him by the household gods, and even when he no longer believes in his gods, he keeps them, because they are the badge of his service, and the pledge of his immortality.

This immortality was corporate and political: *fatum* perpetuated by *labor* and *pietas*. Essentially incomplete, the Roman vision subordinated the individual to the community. The ideal of the common good at the expense of personal perfection was pagan, and it was corrected and transcended by the Christian emphasis on the unique dignity of the human person. The doctrine of the Incarnation shattered the course of history once and for all, and the debt owed time was paid by Eternity. This redemption has always filled the West with a sense of awe before the human person, because he is an absolute: destined for beatitude with God, he comes into his eternity, while still a wayfarer within a world that passes.

These truths may not be believed by many today, and indeed the destruction of Pelagianism by orthodoxy attested to the Christian conviction that they cannot be believed without the grace of God. But if any man—be he Christian or not—does not see in them the source of his freedoms, he is without any sense of history. These Christian rights make up the legal traditions of the West, and they inform the rich and diverse national traditions subsisting within the lands penetrated by the cross and by the mitre. They bring me back to where I began. Not long ago a man wrote that it was "natural enough that liberals, with their faith in reason, should today accept science and its method as the highest development of mind. It is just as natural that conservatives, with their faith in tradition and precedent, should emphasise history and law" (Ralph Gilbert Ross, "The Campaign Against Liberalism, Cont." *Partisan Review*, Sept.-Oct., 1953.) I forgo comment on the remarks concerning science: I trust I have made my attitude on that score clear enough. I am concerned here with the supposed conservative emphasis on history and law. I should imagine *all* men of letters genuinely concerned about safeguarding personal rights would take a lively interest in conserving the traditions of freedom and decency that are the patrimony of the West. If they do, I suggest they drop their futile search for an inner "meaning to history" which could only result in a still further academic betrayal of our heritage. I invite them to see history, not as a "powerhouse of change which destroys . . . tradition in producing the future," but as the full inheritance of civilization to which we all owe a sacred allegiance. Still further, I invite them to stop talking about "the open society," the City without walls, prostrate before the barbarian flood. Finally, I invite them to join us in defending the citadel. Should they do, they may recover, not only the poetry of limits, but the sense of chivalry.

vii.57

ART AND RELIGION:
FELICITOUS TENSION OR CONFLICT?

Religion bends the knee but art makes man walk erect on his two legs. Precisely here we encounter basically antithetical drives in these two fundamental aspects of human existence. This essay addresses itself to the tensions and conflict attendant upon religion as worship and art as making. The reader is cautioned that I am not using the word "art" as did the Renaissance and Humanist tradition. The distinction of art into fine and useful, while itself useful, is too narrow and blocks any successful confrontation with art in the broad sweep of its meaning and power. What is art in the most universal sense of the term? Aristotle, in posing the question, noted that art is marked off, fenced away from, everything that goes under the rubric of nature.[1]

The Stagirite pointed to an evident truth of human experience, needing no validation from anything more fundamental than itself: *i.e.,* whereas nature possesses its own principles of activity immanent to itself; whereas nature gets that way not because of anything that man does, a work of art has its principles imposed upon it by man. Wood in a tree is natural; the same wood worked into a rowboat is art. Aristotle's observations remain perennially true but their application today is blurred enormously and this blurring began when man first took to himself the task of civilizing nature, bringing it to heel, and putting it to his own service. For those of us who live in a civilized order and not in the jungle, we rarely encounter what old fashioned romanticists called "raw nature." The nature civilized man knows has been domesticated and converted into art. We simply need to call to mind a well-ordered farm with its rows of wheat; its growing corn; its domesticated animals; its cross-bred fruits: the mark of man is everywhere. In this sense of the term, nature is not obliterated by art but is fulfilled by art thus completing the scriptural injunction that man take unto himself the task of fulfilling creation.[2]

We do·not fall into the pathetic fallacy when we note that there is something in nature that demands that it be perfected by art. Within this zone of reality art shocks nature, enters into tension with nature, a tension that can be either fruitful and friendly or hostile and even bitter. The ecologists today have noted a backlash in a nature genuinely abused by four hundred years of mechanical technology. The romanticists among us—and there ought to be, I imagine, at least a dose of romanticism in every sane man—bemoan the loss of forests and their conversion into houses or boats or furniture. The forest certainly has its beauty and can bring out virtues that are often lost in the city, but if these considerations were pushed to an extreme, if Rousseau were given his head completely, there would be no houses or furniture or wooden boats.

The good inherent in pure nature, nature unworked by man, is essentially a good to be contemplated. Essentially this good does not belong to the moral order (although it can have moral consequences). Man's awe before a nature untouched by his own hand is aesthetic. Following Aquinas who insisted that the beautiful is that which pleases when it is simply contemplated,[3] I judge then that the delight which man takes in nature as it comes forth from the Hand of God is principally disinterested and hence properly aesthetic. The experience of natural beauty is a *stasis*, not an *ex-stasis*; experiences of this type freeze action, and the will and emotions are halted in joy simply because something exists and exists as it does.·Man marveling before the splendor of the universe is content with merely "letting-being-be," Heidegger's *sein lassen*: it is good that this tree or brook or flying fish simply be and man thus blesses, as with a benediction, the mystery of a world which he has not brought into being.

But the drive of art in man comes from another source. At its most primitive, a primitiveness that is never surmounted even in highly developed civilizations, art answers the need in man for self-preservation and for betterment. All art, all *techne*, is an extension, as Dr. Marshall McLuhan has noted,[4] of man's sense powers as is the hammer an extension of the arm and the wheel of the leg, the telescope of the eye, the telephone of the ear, and the atomic bomb of the fist. Man thus extends himself initially in order that he might survive and prosper. If man contented himself with sitting by the side of the road contemplating the glories of the world, he would perish. And he would perish even in some mythological Tahiti. Secondly, man is simply built physically in such a way that he literally stands on the earth and takes it·in his hands. Crawling on all fours is awkward for any artist. But man takes the world in his hands by imposing formal patterns or meaning on matter. Art is, therefore, to borrow a title from a book by Karl Rahner, *Geist ins Welt,* spirit in the world.

But "spirit in the world" must be understood delicately and with philosophical precision. If by spirit we mean, again following Aristotle, "the return of the soul upon itself" in reflective activity;[5] if by spirit we mean the taking-of-man-in-hand-by-himself, consciousness, then man's spirit is unlike the Spirit of God or the spirit of God's messengers, the angels. God's Spirit certainly is *in* the world but it is not *of* the world. The Spirit of God makes the world be and outside of this creative act there simply would be no world at all. The angelic spirit, according to the scriptural tradition, can be sent *to* the world but is again not of the world. But man's spirit, his soul in intellectual and volitional activity, is spirit constituted *in* the world, spirit enfleshed. Man's spirit does not sigh through the body as though it were some transcendental ghost but exists and operates in and through the body, in the world itself. These propositions, the formal defense of which would take me away from the business at hand, I offer nonetheless as principles for an understanding of man as *homo faber,* as "making man." We all know that bees make hives and that spiders spin webs but they do not know what they are doing and hence their activity lacks that precise element of self-consciousness and of freedom that marks true art and makes man a maker. Given that this constitution is man's very nature, in man nature fuses with art: the artist is the man.

In a very true sense man can fashion himself, at least to a degree. Health is natural but when achieved through medicine health becomes what—art or nature? Is the "Six Million Dollar Man" of television fame a natural spectacle or an artistic one? The question seems bizarre but it is less so than the situation it attempts to probe. Today the entire cosmos is being converted into an art form.[6] Nature is being absorbed so thoroughly into art that often it is difficult to determine, according to Werner Heisenberg,[7] where man leaves off and nature takes over. Heisenberg's remarks pertain, of course, to contemporary physics whose mental constructs, artefacts, so mesh with the atomic and sub-atomic world they attempt to understand, that any understanding we do have of that vast sub-microscopic universe is achieved only within our own scientific and hence artistic patterning thereof. Aristotle's distinction between art and nature does not cease to be true but it ceases to be relevant. Is the effect of cosmetic surgery art or is it nature? People who have had such surgery successfully are uninterested in the problem. The new nose today is as much part of the man as was the old nose he discarded yesterday.

This mastery of nature and its transformation into art by man follows, as suggested, man's very utilitarian drive to survive and to survive well. And it is exactly here where we encounter a zone of danger capable of revealing a sharp tension between art and religion. This tension must be explored because it lies close to the heart of historic conflicts between religion and art.

If art is initially a human necessity, a utility in the deeper sense of the term, religion is not initially useful at all. Religion wells up from another source in human existence. The word "religion" is used here in its broadest sense to cover every religion in the sociological and anthropological meaning given the word. At this point of the discussion the difference between revealed and non-revealed religions is not pertinent. Religion is universally natural but too little attention has been given by philosophers and others to the very concept or intelligibility of natural religion. My exploration here follows the pioneering work done by the Spanish philosopher, Javier Zubiri.[8] In part my reflections depend upon certain conclusions achieved more recently in *Gestalt* Psychology. The synthesis, nonetheless, is purely personal.

The word "religion" semantically suggests a "binding back" of some reality to a source or ground of being: *re-ligare*. Initially the imagery that swarms into the imagination is spatial. Trees and bushes are grounded in the earth. By a refinement of meaning the purely spatial connotations can be eliminated. We need only think of the wings of birds in flight that are "bound" by the laws of aerodynamics. An "unbound" being, so far as human experience is concerned, is simply not to be found anywhere, look as hard as we might. Everything is *relegatum*, bound back to some source. In this sense everything that exists is "religion." But only man consciously and deliberately binds himself "back" (*re*) to a source of existence. All things are contingent and dependent but man takes this contingency in hand, lives it—most especially in moments of crisis and anguish and danger—and this makes of him not merely a being conditioned by relegation but constituted thereby. Man is religious by his very nature. The ground to which man refers himself is what Zubiri has called "the divine."[9] Let the term "the divine" refer to the ground in which man stands, or—to void again the spatial metaphor—the source of his existence. This is no so-called "proof" for the existence of God: such a proof comes later, if it comes at all. I am simply pointing out the evident truth of experience that man is naturally religious in that he experiences no inner anchor to his being and that he spontaneously seeks to anchor himself in "the divine" in one or another fashion. Relegation itself makes atheism a philosophical and practical alternative to theism. Atheism is essentially negative and is made possible by what it denies. The young Karl Marx once wrote that any man who attends to his contingency must admit the existence of God but "this question is forbidden to socialist man."[10] The admission is startling in its candor. If you attend to, meditate upon, your contingent or "grounded" status in being you must admit that you are dependent on The Independent, God. Personally, I do not hold that a mere attendance upon contingency of itself and without the introduction of other considerations leads *eo ipso* to the affirmation of God; here Marx goes faster than I do, but I do agree that such an affirmation will begin with just this awareness of contingency.

These considerations cross Aristotle's insistence that only a beast does not know awe. To be bound back and experience the self as contingent, as floating and unanchored in the real, to be a ship at sea with neither sails nor motors nor anchors, to be in the air without a parachute, is to palpate the truly ultimate mystery of existence, human and even non-human. The last mystery to which all religion is an answer was well summed up by Heidegger when he wrote: "why is there, in general, being rather than nothing?" To which I add: at first blush it would seem far more reasonable that there be nothing rather than something because nothing grounds its own being. Existence is a scandal to pure reason.

But although a scandal to pure reason, existence is a joy to man. From these experiences there have grown up all the festivals and feasts of pagan antiquity and of Christendom, indeed of men everywhere. The being-bound-back yields awe which then gives way to thanksgiving to "The Divine," to the gods, to God. Dr. Josef Pieper in his little gem of a book, *In Tune with the World,*[11] has pointed out that the feast, the festival, while not necessarily always religious, is bound up with sacral ritual. The ritual festival consecrates a time and a place and ordains that man cease his working in order that he might rejoice in the goodness done him by the gods and, in his affirmation of anything at all at ritual time, man implicitly affirms the totality of that which is.[12] "*Ubi caritas gaudet ibi est festivitas*—where charity rejoices, there is festivity."[13] In festivals man offers up his arts in the service of the divine.

But this very offering, in one specific and deep dimension, runs counter to what seems to constitute the inner dynamism of art itself. Have I not insisted that art primatively grows out of man's drive for self-preservation? Have I not insisted that man simply dies unless he becomes what he already is potentially—a *homo faber?* Through his arts man transforms the universe and thus makes himself its lord. All art, understood in this strict and somewhat narrow—but important—sense renders man *independent* of his surroundings, of his environment. Art is nervous, active, domineering, and in so being art tends to overcome man's contingent state, to chisel away the ontological fetters that make him dependent, to challenge fate, to release him from the bondage of a very precarious existence. Even the art of the actuary and the insurance agent tries to circumvent death and I am reminded of the mortuary that issues credit cards: "One call answers all." Art is the enemy of necessity.

Religion recognizes the necessarily contingent state of human life and eventually comes even to celebrate it through acts of thanksgiving. Religion, as mentioned earlier, is the bending of the knee. Art is man walking through the world on two legs, knees not bent at all. Art independicizes; religion dependicizes. The contrast is made as sharply as possible for the sake of illustrating a hidden tension and a possible source of conflict. To insist that there are antithetical drives in man as artist and man as religious is not to insist that these dynamisms are necessarily opposed as are enemies. Art and religion do, however, grow out of differing needs found within man. Therefore they can be in conflict with one another.

Through a kind of catalyst worked at the heart of human existence religion and art reveal themselves to be supremely human but there is a kind of impersonal humanity, if the term be permitted, that characterizes art and that never marks religion. Even in the savage cruelty of Aztec religion the offering of living sacrifices was eminently personal. Presumably any of the victims could have testified to *that* truth. But the artistic act as exercised by a man transcends that man. Art is formally and strictly *work* and an act of work is such that the full perfection of the act transcends itself in fulfilling something else, in imposing some perfection on the often intractable density of matter. Yves Simon used to say that "work is the generosity of being" because no work act is done for its own sake: work is always undertaken by man to perfect something else. The worker can grumble and can shirk and complain bitterly about his lot but his work nonetheless brings into reality some product. We encounter here two distinct drives in *techne*: (a) artistry in producing something which is not man helps man preserve himself in being; this is the human motive or finality of the artistic act; (b) but the finality of what the artist does lies within the thing he makes. A homely example ought to illustrate this truth: if the perfection of the act of operating surgically on a patient remained in the physician operating, the patient would die. But the surgeon himself can have a dozen personal reasons for doing what he does as a physician. Despite these reasons what he does is thoroughly impersonal; it terminates in someone who is not himself. The interplay between these drives is one with civilization. Art is thus supremely personal *and* impersonal.

But all artistic activity does not simply aim at executing results, producing useful artefacts. Here again Aristotle can help us. Art also imitates nature but art does so in its own mode of operation. Unlike Plato for whom artistic imitation is merely a matching or copying of a supposedly "real" form or idea subsisting independently of our own world of experience, Aristotle understood the imitative arts in a non-copybook fashion: they analogically refract activities going on in nature but they do so by being themselves. But Aristotle could not have known, because he was ignorant of Revelation, that the artist not only imitates nature in its own mode of operation but that the artist also imitates God in His Divine mode of operation. St. Thomas Aquinas brought this home in his discussion of God's knowledge.[14] God does not know something, let us say myself, because I am there to be known the way in which someone knows me because I am there before him to be known. God knows something by making it exist, by loving it into being, and before he makes it exist, "it" is simply not there to be known; "it" is not a Platonic idea hovering in God's mind; "it" is simply nothing at all! Therefore, concluded Aquinas, God's knowledge is better compared to the knowledge that an artist has of what he makes than to our speculative awareness of what exists in independence of ourselves. The artist knows the artefact in bringing it into being and unless he knows it by producing it, the artefact will never be known because it never will be. Inventions not thought through and poems unwritten are non-inventions and non-poems. Artistry emerges thus as novelty. Strictly speaking the boat is not potentially in the wood of the tree; left to itself the tree will never convert itself into a boat. The boat—as a form of human transportation—is engendered in the fertility of human reason. A poem is not in its materials—metaphors, stories, symbols, etc.,—not even potentially: these raw materials must be integrated, synthesized, and that act of integration is productive, creative. The artist thus mimics God by making things *be* but with a profound difference. God makes things exist totally out of nothing; the artist must use pre-existing materials. Human creativity depends hence on man's contingent status.

And here again we encounter a possible conflict between art and religion. Art both imitates and makes, but art would make without reference to the world could art do so. There is a magical quality to all art but when fully released from dependence on the real, magic bewitches—or would bewitch—a new order of being into existence. Magic would make something be simply by intending it; sign would produce the signified. Magic both fascinates and frightens because the magician is a mock God. Technology can be read historically in terms of one long battle by man to overcome his contingency and to master creation. Modern art, running ahead of contemporary consciousness—as art always does—has frantically battled to free itself progressively from its own materials. Thus, occultly or openly, art has attempted to deny the contingent and grounded, hence religious, state of human existence. This temptation is intrinsic to art itself because of its quasi-creative power. Possibly this drive to liberate man through art goes back to Nietzsche's Superman; possibly its roots are driven far more deeply into the soil of Western man. If Alladin's Lamp came from the East that lamp has been lit in the West. These historical considerations lie beyond the scope of this essay but certain examples do come to mind: French impressionism in the last century: the passion of the devotees of "pure art"—art purified of objective content, art that would form a world all of its own in independence of this one. But what the artist cannot quite tick off, cannot quite put over, is precisely to make the artefact be in such fashion that its very materials are independent of nature (in Aristotle's teaching) or of God's creation (in Christian teaching).

Art today—*all* art or *techne*—aspires to such a total dominance over the world that the cosmos itself, to the most distant star and to the last frontiers of our galaxy, will be cradled in the hand of man and thus dependent totally for its being on a new ground of being, a new "divine principle"—Man. Any modest acquaintance with the history of technology constrains the intelligence to affirm this truth but the dream of total dominance is gnostic; it cannot be pulled off because man cannot create out of nothing. But although mankind is doomed in advance as it lives this Promethean dream, mankind still marches forward with it. Our technology today, under electric conditions, does not "work the world over" but our technology sweeps the world into itself, converting it—in McLuhan's words—into an "art form," a new stage.[15] This has produced in many of us, individuals as well as societies, a forgetfullness of contingency, a gradual fading away of the natural religion that is consubstantial with human life, a dimming of the need to offer thanks, a damping of all the feasts and festivals of what was once Christendom. The marks of this are everywhere: the conviction that every problem has a technical solution; the petulance and impatience we sense before limitations placed on our activities by chance and contingency; the contempt we have for societies that do not run on time, that have not mastered creation as we have; the reduction of death to a social and medical problem; the refusal to see any good in pain and suffering; the withering away of the sense of awe; the loss of mystery. (The revival of the Occult in the United States is a conscious reaction against technology, but at bottom the occult manifests the same desire to bind the Powers From Beyond to the will of man.)

Promethean art promises liberation. The truth that it has enslaved and has enslaved in no more striking way than in robbing man of his sense of the divine need not be labored here. The truly grave problem facing man today is not so much the denial of God. The truly grave problem is that man in industrial technologized societies does not sense any need for God. Contemporary art, both as technology in the accepted meaning given that word and as "art" in the sense of imitation, would render the divine superfluous.

But the artist can transcend the inner finalties of his own art if he consciously puts it at the service of the Divine. Art in one dimension deviates in its finality from what religion does in its inner dynamism. We have explored this tension. But an art that self-consciously attends to its inner functionalism tends to be bad art just as a boxer who overtrains is likely to lose in the ring. The fanatical funtionalism of European art between the two World Wars is an instance in question. We are all aware of the contradiction contained in an art that parades its own practicality and utilitarianism. Such art forms end in sterility and have thus mocked their own goal of supreme usefulness. We are all also aware of art forms that were, true enough, designed specifically to be supremely practical but that nonetheless delighted the hearts of men by their beauty: we need only think of the silversmithery of colonial New England and of the sheer splendor of the hull of the American clipper ships designed by Donald McKay. But with all this said—and I do not now intend to gainsay it—the intrinsic dynamism of *techne* is towards that which is useful, to man's *esse* and to his *bene esse*.

All arts that look to man's "well being" as opposed to his mere survival tend to surpass themselves. They contain a kind of overdrive in their inner dynamism and this overdrive symbolizes and more often than not what it symbolizes is sacral. This is obviously true of the didactic arts in a conventional sense of the term but it is also true that *all* arts of this type tend to overflow their own limits and thus to be didactic in that they say something which transcends their own formal structures and finalities. This is very true in homely familial situations, in which an attractively decorated cake, a delight in itself at a birthday celebration, becomes a symbol of the celebration of life, of the bonds knitting together the family, of gratitude for still another year of life. This is even true of the world of advertising. Did not G.K. Chesterton once write that only an illiterate could appreciate the beauty of Times Square? When the specific content or import of the neon signs is suppressed, something remains—and it is poetry.

Now this "something beyond" in all works of art, even the needlework of a grandmother making a dress for her grandchild, must not be reduced to the merely psychological. The psychological is present and does deserve our serious attention. But the "beyond" spoken of here is consubstantial with art and finds its true home only when art is dedicated to the service of religion. This "more than itself" found in every artistic act (but subdued or even suppressed in arts of mere survival), even if it be but a gesture or a song whistled by a boy on a country road, is burnt into the very artistic act itself. Art thus transcends its own immediate end which is to produce something, but art does so not by offering itself to man as a contemplative object but as inviting, signalling man, to lift himself beyond the work to its ultimate Home, its *Patria*, the Land of the Lord. There is, of course, a danger in this transcendence. The danger consists in reducing the work itself to a mere symbol—to fail to see it as it is. This is bad enough but it is even worse to fool yourself into thinking you have grasped—even loved—a reality because that reality symbolizes something

112

beyond itself. Nobody can really appreciate a Rolls-Royce who sees it as nothing more than a status symbol. The Reduction of the world to a tissue of symbols is a kind of subtle Manicheanism whose advocates are incapable of understanding anything under foot or at hand on its own terms. Human experience teaches us that unless you grasp the reality "in-itself," in its own dignity and worth and function, you cannot understand it as a "more-than-itself," as a symbol. At the risk of over-simplification I suggest that Byzantium overly symbolized whereas our technocratic and secularist society undersymbolizes. Between these two dangers lies the truth and the road to sanity.

All art imitates, as pointed out, nature. All art imitates God's creative activity. This imitation, rooted as it is in artistic activity as such, is both an act making an artefact to exist and an act flashing beyond itself, through imitation, to God. The theory here grows out of historical observation. We need only return to the religious or sacral sense of the festival pointed out by Dr. Pieper.[16] The festival—I follow Pieper's reasoning on this point—cannot be reduced to pure play, to a simple suspension of the world of day to day work. Play, understood rigorously, is activity which is done purely and exclusively for itself.[17] Play involves a delight taken in any activity merely because the activity exists and is as it is. We need only contemplate children at play or watch greybeards playing chess in a public park. But even here we can easily trick ourselves: the waves lap over the sand castles made by children and we sense something awesome about the littleness of all things human: *we* experience this transcendence but the children who made the sand castles did not; they were just playing. Play needs no justification: play is play and is thus self-justifying. Hence the same Chesterton could write that God does not work: He plays. But the festival, while playful, involves a significance and is a sign pointing beyond itself. The festival offers thanks, celebrated some moment in man's life and thus celebrated the Lord of life.

In so doing art surrenders—better yet, offers—its internal dynamism which is factive to something beyond its essential structuring, art reveals itself to be a kind of "plus" or "excess" that is proper to being as such.[18] Art weds religion by surrendering its pretensions to autonomy in the service of the work of man. Every religious festival involves using up a surplus.[19] We eat more and we drink more on festival days. The fruits of labor are consumed. Now consumption belongs to the essence of sacrifice. Every feast sacrifices something by consuming the fruits of man's labor:

hence, Thanksgiving Day. Art sacrifices itself in order to be "more than itself." Pieper exemplifies this through a description of the Feast of *Cropus Christi* in Toledo:

> The streets, canopied with canvas, are transformed into a vast festive tent whose walls are formed by the tapestry-decked façades of the houses and whose floor is strewn with rosemary and lavender, which gives a stronger perfume the more they are walked on. High Mass in the Cathedral is followed by the procession: a musical performance, military parade, social display, and Exposition of the Sacrament. The bullfight in the afternoon is, of course, as secular as at other times, but it is the Corrida del Corpus.[20]

Art in occasions such as this is put deliberately to the service of what is not art—festivity; festivity in turn always looks beyond itself and thus signifies or signals something deeper than itself. Man affirms the goodness of creation and in so doing affirms a Divine howsoever he might articulate that transcendent source of his being.

Art as secularized is stripped of this movement towards self-transcendence and art thus bends back narcissistically upon itself. The early Harvey Cox, in his *The Secular City*, advanced as desirable what in truth is a frighteningly drab vision of the world, of a civilization whose artistic structure is totally stripped of the divine. In this completely secularized world the cribs at Christmas are chased from the lawn at city hall, the bells are silent, the churches swept bare of statuary. The historic marriage between art and religion is annuled on the grounds that Christian faith is *so* transcendent that it can never enter into union and enflesh itself in the public artistic structure that forms the life style of a culture.[21] Cox' secularized "Christian" is as lonely in his faith as was the anonymous Christian of tomorrow sketched by Romano Guardini in his *The End of the Modern World:* alone, some secretary in a vast clinical office with two hundred other girls pounding on typewriters or tending computers slyly signals her Christian adherence to some other lonely Christian at the far end of the office.[22] This underground Christianity is a necessity in countries enslaved by Marxism but when advanced as a desirable situation the theory flies in the face of this natural synthesis between art and religion that has been sketched above.

The symbiosis of art and religion is nothing forced or dictated; it is a natural condition found in both pagan and Christian societies and even in iconoclastic Islam is not absent. The divorce between art and religion harms the artist because it refuses to his art that superabundance, that pouring of art outwards beyond its own proper formality that in itself—I grant that the assertion is bold—is constitutive of artistic activity if not of artistic essence or nature. By this I mean that a movement towards the transcendent cannot be discovered in artistic structures studied abstractly but that this movement is rather observed in artistic achievement—and it is observed in all cultures. The divorce between art and religion also harms the believer because the believer can only encounter his religion initially in art. The proposition is so evident that it is almost embarrassing to formulate it. I receive the Message of God, the Good News, through words. We hear the Word of God. Words are fashioned into sentences and sentences are artefacts, both logically and rhetorically. There is no possible way that an adult can affirm the faith that is in him outside of some symbolic, artistic structure, the most fundamental of which is language. The proposition is epistemologically valid, but it has a peculiarly theological significance in the context of Christianity: in Trinitarian theology, the very *work* of creation is done *in* the *Word* by the Father: "work," "word"—both lie at the heart of all artistic production; no product comes into being until it has been "expressed" by the artist. Even logic, according to the classical tradition, is an *art*. The divorce of religion from art in the name of secularization is not only an undesirable ideal; it is also contradictory in itself. If the enemy of religious art and art in the service of religion is successful in his polemic, it is due to the artistry of his rhetoric. In a word: all discussion about religion, for being discussion, involves its incarnation in art.

Art is the instrument of evangelization. This is true not only of the Catholic tradition with its emphasis on visual art, but it is also true of the Protestant tradition with its emphasis on song. In all religions we discover artisanry at work in fashioning sensibilities and molding cultures that reflect convictions that transcend this world. Frightening consequences follow on the artist's conscious separation of his art from religion. (I am not suggesting, of course, that all art ought to aim at being religious; if art simply follows its own bent it will signal beyond itself to The Whole of Being.)

Art exists thus in tensison and it can flourish only within this tension. As a mastering of the materials of being, art liberates man from the tyranny of raw nature and thus diminishes his contingency. As a "more than itself" art adumbrates the Divine which recalls man again to his contingency and which brings forth his private and corporate thanksgiving for the gift of being and of life. Art, as indicated, does not have to intend its own overdrive consciously. If man will only let art have its way, art will heal the wounds of contingency even as it hallows a very precarious world. Blessings and sacraments are works of art. But then so too is God's creation.

iv.75

NOTES

1. Aristotle, *Metaphysics*, 1070a4—1070a30; 1046b-28.

2. *Genesis*, ch. 1 and 2.

3. Thomas Aquinas, "Pulchra dicuntur quae visa placent," (*Summa Theologiae*, I, Q.4, a. 4 ad. 1); "Pulchrum dicatur id cujus ipsa apprehensio placet," (*Summa Theologiae*, I-II, Q. 27, a.1, ad. 3).

4. McLuhan, Marshall, *Understanding Media: The Extensions of Man*, (New York: McGraw-Hill, Inc., 1964).

5. Aristotle, *De Anima*, 417, b. c; *Metaphysics*, B. IX, 1048 b. 18—1049 b. 34. *Cf.*, my discussion: Wilhelmsen, Frederick D., *The Metaphysics of Love*, (New York: Sheed and Ward, 1962), pp. 53—67.

6. McLuhan, Marshall, and Nevitt, Barrington, *Take Today: The Executive as Dropout*, (New York: Harcourt Brace Jovanovich, Inc., 1972), *passim*.

7. Heisenberg, Werner, address given before The Bavarian Academy of Fine Arts, Nov., 1953.

8. Zubiri, Javier, *Naturaleza, Historia, Dios*, (Madrid: Editoria Nacional, 1959), pp. 309—340.

9. *Ibid.*, pp.321—322.

10. Marx, Karl, *Writings of the Young Marx on Philosophy and Society*, (New York: Anchor Books, Doubleday and Company, Inc., 1967), pp.65—66.

11. Pieper, Josef, *In Tune with the World*, (Chicago: Franciscan Herald Press, 1965 *passim*.

12. *Ibid.*, pp.10—17.

13. Attributed to St. John Chrysostom by Josef Pieper: *op. cit.*

14. Thomas Aquinas: e.g., *In I Sent.*, d. 19, q. 5, a. 1 ad 1 et 7 et 8; d. 19, q. 19, a. 2; d. 19, q. 5, a. 3.

15. McLuhan and Nevitt, *op. cit.*, esp. p.6 and *passim*.

16. Pieper, *op. cit.*, esp. pp. 25—39.

17. Jünger, Friedrich, Georg, *Die Spiele*, (Frankfurt am Main: Vittorio Klostermann, 1953); pp. 197—198.

18. Thomas Aquinas, esp., *In De Divinis Nominibus*, ch. 5.

19. Sacrifice and holocaust came together in this insistence that the fruits of the earth be consumed; they differ in that in holocaust the victim literally consumes himself; in sacrifice which is not a holocaust the victim is consumed, of course, by those who offer up the sacrifice.

20. Pieper, *op cit.*, pp. 25—26.

21. *cf.*, my: *Cox's Secular City . . . City of Night*, republished elsewhere in this volume.

22. Guardini, Romano, *The End of the Modern World* ed. by Frederick D. Wilhelmsen, (Chicago: Henry Regnery Co., 1968), pp. 68—133.

THE CONSERVATIVE VISION

The spirit of abstraction is abroad in the world and it threatens to drown us all in violence and barbarism. This world, lurching drunkenly on the verge of self-destruction, is the backdrop for the present-day discussion in our country between liberalism and conservatism. In the light of the above, the discussion seems sometimes to be the irresponsible play of children who do not know the night is upon them. Thus it must appear to ironic skepticism, but the conservatism of despair is forbidden a Christian by the apostolic injunction that he harden himself in hope. He may expect the worst: he is bound to hope for the best.

But hope without charity is a contradiction. Unless we close ranks we are doomed. Conservatism—in simple justice if not in charity—must cease blaming latter-day liberalism for all the evils of the times; conservatism must respect the historic role of liberalism as the social conscience of the age. In turn, liberalism must cease sneering at conservatism for its failure to come to grips with the concrete issues of the day: we conservatives do not hold the power; if we did, the world would dance to a different tune. Liberalism must cease its weary preaching: it does no good to advise those of us who, in spirit, are of the party of tradition to exorcise our illusions and face the modern world. We face the modern world every day and we have lived our whole lives in it: it confirms us the more in the vision which is ours.

Since the conservative vision defines the modern temper by opposition and contrast, an exploration of that vision may go far toward suggesting a cure for the crisis of the West.

We see a world wherein science, liberated from traditional life, has been permitted to go its own way and build a new universe which is intolerable to the very psychic structure of man. We see a world wherein art, divorced from the living culture of the people, has fashioned an esoteric dream foreign to the faith and aspirations of Western man. We see a world wherein the state, freed from the religious convictions of the nation, has pushed its own nature to the limits of totalitarian slavery. We see a world compounded of abstraction and violence.

There is no doubt that this process of separating the part from the whole has resulted in enormous change and considerable advance. Science and poetry, technics and mythology, the secular and the sacred, have come into the purity of their own essences within the past centuries. They have done so, however, only by trampling upon the corpse of what was once a traditional society within which all things coalesced in the unity of historic existence. Mr. Russell Kirk has written eloquently of "the broken cake of British custom." But the cake of custom was broken all over the West and the world has grown grayer for it. Modernity has been one long attempt to rationalize and isolate, one from another, the diverse elements that go to make corporate existence. Modernity is man's disenchantment of the real. So far as I can see, conservatism makes no sense except when seen as the party of enchantment.

That conservatism represents enchantment has been missed in our day by many conservatives, as well as by their critics. The educated mind has tended to take over the identification of conservatism and classicism made by T.E. Hulme, who, incidentally, had a highly romantic and unreal notion of Original Sin. The identification has been furthered because of the marked preference of some conservatives for classical forms in verse and prose. But although classical elements enter the conservative vision, they do not constitute it.

The classical inheritance of law, for instance, belongs as much to the liberals as it does to the conservatives: both parties, when faithful to their professions, adhere commonly to our classical traditions of civil rights and liberties. In fact, Greek classicism, taken as a whole, better fits the liberal than the conservative mind. The rejection of traditional wisdom, the contempt for the inarticulate, the exaltation of formal education, the emphasis on the civic rather than the familial, the cult of rationality—these are both Greek and liberal attitudes: they are foreign to the centre of historic traditionalism. Aristotle used the same principles to justify a slave society that many contemporary liberals use to justify a mechanized world: in order that man be free he must have leisure in which to educate himself for his responsibilities to society; thus the free man is the man who is released from labor, either by a slave or by a machine. That he might find not only dignity and fulfillment but poetry and salvation by uniting himself with the things that are, is a consideration too elusive to enter either the Parthenon or the Syntopicon.

The conservative suspicion of abstractionism was summed up magnificently by Dr. Johnson when he said that "the Devil was the first Whig." But what do Whiggery and the Devil have to do with the present discussion? Nothing on the level of the abstract and rationally formulated; everything on the level of the psychic and mythic.

To the Christian, the Devil represents the quintessence of ontological perfection, shuddering before the impact of matter and the mystery of the Incarnation. To the Tory, the Liberal State represented the withdrawal of the cultivated mind from the mystery, variety, and impurity of traditional life. The analogy is fruitful for an understanding of conservatism, but it is fraught with danger because it risks making God a party to the forces of reaction. This is just as bad as making Him a party to the forces of progress. The danger is surmounted only if we are aware that the analogy simply symbolizes a profound stirring in the Western world of powers hitherto kept in check by the silent rhythm of traditional life.

The conservative reaction cannot be understood unless we go to its medieval sources. But it is important to remember that traditional life is not necessarily medieval. Western traditional societies, surviving from medieval times, have been altered deeply by the modern world. For example, the traditions of French and South German peasant economies stem, in part, from the French Revolution, and the fierce sense of proprietorship and independence of these free men—they are the bulwark of continental conservatism—is, in a very real sense, an inheritance of the Revolution. But I think it fair to say that the mythic substructure, as well as the corporate substance of these societies and others like them, are in a living continuity with the traditions of the High Middle Ages. To grasp traditional society at the peak of its development and thereby come to terms with the conservative mind, we must look to medieval Christendom.

Medieval man had a firm grip on the difference between distinction and separation: poetry and morality, economy and technology, the temporal and the spiritual were distinguished one from another and these distinctions lie at the basis of the delicate hierarchy articulated by the men of the thirteenth century. But where distinctions abounded, sometimes without reason, no one element of cultural life was separated from, or permitted to dominate, the whole.

An archaic compactness governed medieval society which saw itself as a closed world of meanings branched out in different directions abstractly, but which were fused into a cultural unity by the catalyst of existence. As Romano Guardini has pointed out in his illuminating little book—*Das Ende der Neuzeit*—existence, for medieval man, was not only that through which something "is": it was also that which "means." And since the meaning of existence is fundamentally theological, everything in any sense claiming title to existence was given a religious significance.

Medieval man sacramentalized the whole of being. This sense of the symbolic issued into a fruitful and dense mingling of things formally distinct. Thus the Holy Roman Emperor wore a blue, star-spangled robe, representing the arc of the heavens and he carried the imperial globe representing the world. He symbolized the temporal fellowship of all Christians in Christendom and his coronation in Rome at the hands of the Pope signified the very dependence of the globe of the world on the creative will of God. (I would suggest, with all respect, that a man can learn more about the history and meaning of the West by meditating carefully on the misnamed "Crown of Charlemagne" than he can by reading any number of books arbitrarily called "great.")

As with political existence, so with man's life in space and time. The Word is incarnate in a Body, and the Church is that Body Mystic. Now all bodies are extended in space; it follows that the Church must extend herself through space: thus the Episcopal seat symbolizes the headship of Christ, and as the head has a body, so is the local church building the extension, the *situ*ation, of the Incarnation. The church building, in turn, stands in the same analogical relation to cemeteries, chapels, and wayside crosses. In this manner the Church spreads through the open spaces and hallows the land.

The symbolization of space is paralleled by that of time. The earthly pilgrimage moves seasonably through time, and, since we are saved by a Man who lived out His years and died on this earth, each day and month and year of a man's life repeats the life of Christ. Hence the great liturgical feasts weave themselves into the rhythmic pauses of the seasons as they return forever upon themselves. But lest man fall back into the "eternal decadence" of the pagan cycle, he is always brought up short by the vision of the Judgment—confronting him in stone and glass all over Europe. The drama of present existence approached, at the moment of death, the mystery of the timeless freedom of the angels who accept or reject their Creator forever in any act admitting neither progress nor decline. Thus the here-and-now takes on a sacred awesomeness psychologically compelling medieval man to make himself the center of the physical cosmos. The eyes of God are upon him and the world circles around his body as its very center. Hell is at his feet and heaven just above his head. He is separated from the Absolute by the thin crust of a material world that might dissolve any moment leaving him standing before his Judge.

If the cult of the Virgin shone at its brightest in medieval Europe, it was because Christian man had penetrated the meaning of existence: "God with us." And since *to be*—for a man—is to be *in time*, and since to be in time is to be *in matter*, it is no wonder that medieval man turned to the womb of God. Modern psychology, under the influence of Jung, is rediscovering, painfully and slowly, the role of woman in the economy of psychic existence. She is the enemy of abstraction and clarity. She represents passivity and patience, obedience, the traditions of the hearth and the continuity of the race. The Greek world had an almost effeminate horror of matter and physical existence: matter, said more than one philosopher under the spell of Greece, hungers for form the way woman hungers for man. The Greeks could not conceive matter in the timeless perfections of an abstract essence; therefore they consigned it to the darkness and unintelligibility of history, a "reality" so worthless that the discipline engaged in its penetration ranked even lower on the classical scale of values than poetry. Western historic existence, begun in the peasant Rome of Cato and the fathers, cannot be said to have come into its own until the Incarnation sanctified the things that pass.

Thus the God who is Being signs all things with His Name, and His Signature underwrites the order of historic existence. The Lord gives being to the material world and He legitimizes His gift by entering history in the womb of a woman and by hammering out His living over a carpenter's bench.

I am convinced that this medieval dream of this unity of all things in existence is the mythic foundation for what I would call the conservative vision: this is what I mean by the enchantment of reality.

A modern traditional society gets its heart from the medieval dream. Although the religious vision begins to recede down the corridors of time, although the symbolic battalions of God begin to march out of history, their muted drums can still be heard sounding through the fields and forests of the fatherland. A sense of the sacred lies over all things, and man, in the words of that great and haunted figure, Martin Heidegger, is content simply to "let being be." If modern man is the demiurge who reworks creation in his own image, traditional man—even as he survives into our day—is the man who celebrates the things that are.

A traditional society does not permit dissection into the categories of contemporary academicism. Reality is fused into too tight a cultural unity for rational analysis: like existence itself, such communities defy conceptualization.

A monarchy might turn out to be highly representative of the spirit of a people and thus fulfill the dream of democracy far better than a parliamentary republic: I am thinking of the Bavaria of the Wittelsbachs, where even today the people call the old gentleman of Nymphenburg, "Our King." The extent of "formal" education might be trivial and yet the level of popular culture high: I am thinking of the Andalusia of Lorca and the ritual of the ring. The amount of literature published, the numbers of students enrolled in university and college, might be low and yet the arts might flourish, only they will be the arts of pulpit and chase, cuisine and dress, custom and manner, arts which do not separate themselves from the community in order to find their own proper "essence", but which fill all society with poetry and thus soften the tragedy of life: I am thinking of the Old South and the Cavalier tradition. Finally, the existence of sharply defined classes might ironically mask a fundamental egalitarianism, the equality of all men in the face of Death who is made a guest at every table: I am thinking of Castile and the somber dignity of the poor of Spain; I am thinking of the *santos* of the Indians of my own Southwest, of the cottonwood Christus on the way to Golgotha in a cart, surrounded and escorted by an army of marching skeletons.

It is only the rationalist mentality, enamored of books and degrees, ignorant of history and innocent of the mystery of life, that insists on judging such communities in the light of an abstract company of essences inhabiting a ghostly republic of ideals foreign to the rhythm of being and becoming.

A venerable society, born in necessity, nurtured in courage and annealed in conflict, is the creation of experience. It throws around itself a mythic cape woven of symbols—poetic, social, religious—representing its marriage with reality and its compromise with the absolute. These symbols cannot be penetrated fully by reason. They touch the springs of being and there sounds about them the drama of salvation and damnation.

Before a society toughened by the impact of nature and hallowed by the passage of time, the wise halt in contemplation and wonder. Only the rationalist presumes to judge the goodness of an ancient community by an unreal and abstract standard of what society and government ought to be. And if the rationalist does grant some share of truth and value to a traditional society, he does so out of a concession to human weakness: these people, he says, have not yet been "educated" to assume their responsibilities to the modern world, etc. To the rationalist, history and existence, human affection and the poetry of a people, are "weaknesses" which his social and political ideal tolerates out of the largeness of its spirit.

In the old days, these people were called "rationalists;" today they are called "essentialists." Call them what you will, they remain forever the same: men who ignore diversity, who are embarrassed by tradition, and who are blind to mystery.

The conservative has always known—even though he could rarely express it philosophically—that essence is for the sake of existence, not existence for the sake of essence. The essence of a thing or of an institution must be judged by whether or not it fits that thing or institution to take its place in the economy of being and in the rise and fall of the tides of history.

All of this, of course, is in utter contradiction to the spirit of disenchantment and rationalization. The genealogy of the Western mind since the break-up of the medieval unity can be read in more than one valid way. But with so much said, permit me to hazard the guess that the role played by Calvinism has yet to be written. Tawney, Weber, and Belloc began the work, but no one has followed it through to its psychological and metaphysical depths. With Calvinism, the unity of all things in the bosom of traditional life was shattered for all time. Power fell to the "godded men" who looked upon temporal society as nothing but an instrument to bring about the golden world wherein the Lord would dwell in the midst of His saints. The state ceased to incarnate symbolically the convictions of its people.

No longer was God with man in the drama of the present moment of time. God was before him in the Kingdom which was to come into history.

Thus the unique value of the present, so densely symbolized by medieval man, dissolved before the dream of the new world to come. Reality was no longer something *conserved*, cherished, and seen as the robe of God.

The double revelation of God to man, one supernatural and the other natural, was discarded as Papistical sophistry. Natural theology was legislated out of existence and with it went the songs and feasts of Christendom. The symbolic value of creation fell to pieces, and God—"the Totally Other"—retreated to the lonely splendor of His transcendent majesty.

With rejection of matter, came the rejection of Mary: principle of darkness and mediation, she offended the need Calvinism felt to approach God directly, without the aid of sacraments, ritual, or mummery. The universe became nothing but the "raw material" of Manchesterianism, good only to be exploited and hammered into use. Thus a terrible psychic tension between a loathing for matter, linked with an almost fevered engagement with it in the mass production of industrialized goods, filled the Puritan with a restlessness and a burning energy that opened up *new* worlds less grossly connected with this one. The machine, as has been suggested, becomes the bride of man.

Freed from the restrictions of traditionalism, economics worked out its own laws, unaffected by morals and prescription. Poetry, discarded by the middle-class, went its way and sought a lonely destiny. Work, divorced from the limitations placed on it by medieval law and from the sense of play with which it was infused in the old sacramental order, came into its own and remade the world in the image of the machine.

Lest it be thought that I am making this all up out of my own reactionary head, listen to the words of Dr. Werner Heisenberg, speaking with all the authroity of his genius before the Bavarian Academy of Fine Arts, in November, 1953: "Natural science stands no more as a spectator before nature, but recognizes itself as part of the game between man and nature. . . . We are constantly running up against structures built by man. Thus man is always meeting only himself." The Calvinist tension between spirit and matter is now dissolved by eliminating one pole of the dialectic.

As far as art is concerned, listen to what a critic has to say of the dream of Mallarmé who sums up faithfully art's attempt to divorce itself, not only from culture and morality, but from natural being: "To construct a poetry which would have the value of a preternatural creation and which would be able to enter into rivalry with the world of created things to the point of supplanting it totally." Thus life purges itself of poetry, and poetry purges itself of life.

Abstract perfection running riot, uniting with a subterranean passion, divorced from the constraints of tradition and fed by a resentment born of boredom: this is the modern world. Charity demands that we save *this* world: it's the only one we have. But we conservatives cannot heal the age. In Latin America, we are blocked by one hundred and fifty years of anticlerical prejudice, and in some countries our people are even barred from the polls. In England, we are cracked between two parties both committed to the mass state. On the Continent, we went from Dachau into British concentration camps because we pledged allegiance to an old order. In the United States, our very name is stolen from us by oil millionaires and seasoned character assassins.

I repeat the thesis: we conservatives cannot cure the modern world: we do not hold the power, nor is it likely to pass into our hands. But if liberals—and they are in the saddle almost all over the West—will make the descent into the maelstrom of the modern soul, they will find in conservatism a diagnosis of the disease of our time. We conservatives have lost our kings and our chivalry; our craftsmen are gone, and our peasantry is fast disappearing. Our horses have been shot from under us. We have nothing to offer the world but our vision.

vi.55

DEATH OF THE AGE OF ANALYSIS

> But still a question, *the* question: Is Being a mere word, and its meaning a haze, or is it the spiritual destiny of the West, of the Land of the Evening?—Martin Heidegger, *Einfuhrüng in die Metaphysik.*

The Heideggerian question—and it is a sorrowful question, for these are the words of a man who understands himself to be the gravedigger of a dead world—brilliantly illuminates the profound crisis in which the Western spirit anguishes today. For it locates the roots of that crisis in the metaphysical order. Heidegger insists that the Occident was born with the discovery of the "Is" by Parmenides, who subsequently veiled his own intuition because it blinded him with light that did not illuminate; and suggests that the history of our civilization simply articulates, as would a play—a tragedy—the loss of being that commenced with its very discovery. For Heidegger, that loss has become, in the post-Hegelian epoch, total exhaustion: we are left with no alternative to nihilism.

If we pass over Heidegger's paganism and the univocist understanding of existence he derived from his early studies in Scotus, we can learn a lesson he has been trying to teach the philosophical community for a long time. The lesson is that the West has indeed converted being—"our spiritual destiny"—into a "mere word" whose meaning is only a "haze"; to which I add that the historical culprit—the Age of Rationalism, the Age of Analysis—is now also dead, although its death rattle is still very much with us. Let us see why this is so.

Rationalism and the analytic method it fostered depended upon s systematic forgetfulness of being in the sense of actual existence. The Industrial Revolution and the technology issuing from it were made possible by a kind of epistemological trick, a theoretical suppression of the organic, of the qualitative, in favor of the mind's concentration upon the quantitative, those aspects of the real that can be manipulated, projected, repeated. Why was the trick played? Because whatever is measurably predictable, whatever can be foreseen or projected, can be *controlled*.

Aristotle pointed to the possibility of man's control over the real by noting man's ability to symbolize physical and hence organic aspects of reality in mathematical terms. The sciences employing these terms, formally mathematical but materially physical, he called *scientiae mediae*, "middle sciences," because they manifested neither the conceptual purity of pure mathematics nor the contemplative innocence of pure nature study (as we would call Aristotle's physics today). These "middle sciences" were the rather modestly developed optics, astronomy and music known to classical antiquity. Even though they granted a measure of power over the real to society, they were nonetheless subordinated to an ideal of science as *scientia* which was overwhelmingly contemplative—subordinated to philosophy, that is.

With the Renaissance development of mathematical physics this symbolizing power released the full demiurgical thrust of what was soon to become modern science, and the application of the mathematical to the technical order on a grand scale became possible. But this new science was not self-generating: it depended above all on the new philosophy of René Descartes. He it was who made possible European Rationalism, that movement which so radically shaped the destiny of the West for four hundred years and which has made us all, in part at least, for better or worse, what we are.

The heart of Cartesianism is not, as is often supposed, the reduction of the complex to the simple; or even his famous teaching on the reduction of the qualitative to the quantitative. Cartesian reductionism, of course, has marked the entire Western spirit, and every effort to translate what is uniquely proper to one order of the real into terms intrinsic to another is an instance of the rationalist conviction that the complexity of the many is somehow explicable in terms of the simplicity of the one. But the ultimate secret of Descartes, the psychic root of his dream of a universal science of conquest over the real, is embedded in the famous *ergo* linking the *cogito* with the *sum*. "I think; *therefore*, I am." With this supposedly unshakable first of all truths, Descartes would remake philosophy and fashion a new world.

Students of philosophy have been taught for decades that Descartes here was merely offering a new "proof" for existence—one that had somehow escaped the scholastics. This is nonsense. The *ergo* does not point out mere factuality. If I am sensing or imagining or reasoning, I obviously *must* exist; this truth is pointed out equally by psychic states other than that of thinking. The "*ergo*," on the contrary, most profoundly asserts that *meaning itself engenders being*, that essence precedes existence, that signification bewitches into existence the signified, that *esse* is ultimately simply a function of *intelligere*. The *ergo* does not make a sterile *a priori* demonstration; it is a command placed upon the real by exigencies which are one with the consciousness, with thought. The essentialism of Descartes is thus not passive but supremely active: intellectual assent to essence is for Descartes an order, a dictate. The point is emphasized by his insistence that even the Divine Being depends on its essence: God's own essence, the very inteliigibility of sheer Will, *commands* the Divine Being to be.

The domestication of being to conceptual meaning has nowhere been better expressed than in Leon Brunschvicg's preface to his truly remarkable book on Descartes: "Whatever cannot be reduced to the reason is at the most non-existent and at the least uninteresting." This victory of meaning over being had its ultimate illustration in the shift from the Eucharist as Being, the Catholic doctrine of transubstantiation—the formula of Trent—to the Protestant insistence that the Eucharist *means* Christ but is not His very Body and Blood. The historical consequences are well known: the withering away of reverence and awe before the complexities of life; the increasing desacralizing of the social and political orders wrought under the conviction that the secular and the sacred are rationally distinct essences and, therefore, ought to be separated compartments of the body-politic; the substitution of number theory in politics for dynastic loyalties, which always resist rationalist analysis; the decline of craftsmanship and its replacement by the principle of mass production, and so on.

From these and other developments it can be seen that the Cartesian flight from existence involved a double movement. Technical power over the real was the consequence of an interior centralization in which the world was explained through increasingly simpler theories. But centralization depends on atomization, because only homogenized units capable of being arranged in linear sequences can be subsumed under power structures which bend them to univocal ends. Therefore interior centralization went hand in hand with an external atomization of society, and together they achieved the humiliation of being.

There was a man in the thirteenth century who understood that the opposite of being is nothing, and therefore that being can never be tacked on to anything, never adds to anything as does one unit more in a series: being is sheer novelty. But by the time Rationalism had swept all Europe, Thomas Aquinas' wisdom had been effectively lost to the West, and thus it was no Thomist, but a recalcitrant Scot, David Hume, who finally threw the bomb of existence into Descartes' world. Hume, by an ironic because totally innocent return to Thomistic epistemology, pointed out that simply because ideas "B" and "C" flow necessarily from idea "A," it does not follow that either "A" or "B" or "C" actually *exists*. The analytic order, he was recognizing, is totally bankrupt when it enters the kingdom of actual existence. Hume's subsequent despair of science ought not to blind us to the true scope of his genius. Like Chesterton after him, Hume discovered that: "Existence was itself so very eccentric a legacy that I could not complain of not understanding the limitations of the vision when I did not understand the vision they limited."

Immanuel Kant was "aroused from his dogmatic slumbers" by Hume, and refined the Scot's insight. He pointed out that every analytic *démarche* commences from some whole whose parts are already there, synthesized into unity before the analysis itself is possible. Synthesis is thus a precondition for all analyses. Kant even sensed obscurely that synthesis is not irreducible to analysis, but is somehow a transcending novelty; but he was incapable of handling his own discovery. His ultimate reduction of synthesis to the *a priori* in the Transcendental Ego was a victory, within his own system, of the Rationalism his system was designed to conquer.

It would be presumptuous to explain the complex genius of Georg Wilhelm Hegel exclusively in terms of his relationship to Kant; but it is intrinsic to Hegel's thought, no less than to Kant's, that any transcendence of rationalism—of a sterile and tautological analysis of the already given—demands a principle capable of orchestrating this transcendence. Thus the famous dialectic.

The Hegelian dialectic was principally an intellectual construct aimed at rendering progress or novelty intelligible—in the entire gamut of the real but most especially in history. Keenly aware that analysis—be it logical, philosophical, literary, or scientific—is only an intellectual moment, as it were, in which the mind looks back upon the already done—the given, the past, the *nunc stans*—Hegel understood that this analytic moment of the human spirit was not open to progress, to the new: it was simply the mind doubling back upon what it already possessed.

The condition for the dialectic was not a mere domestication, but the murder of being. Since being was, for Hegel, an abstraction—the most abstract of abstractions, in effect—and since reality was concrete, and not abstract, if followed that being was literally *no-thing*. Being, that is, due to its vacancy and emptiness, generates its own negation, non-being—and thus commences the dailectic, the very ground rules of existence. Being is lost in the sea of becoming as history moves toward the identity of concentration and consciousness in the Absolute Spirit. Note carefully that being's emptiness is the condition for synthesis in Hegel, and hence for his dialectic of progress.

But Hegel's insight that the structure of reality is synthetic was sound; but his understanding of that structure was crucially flawed. If the unity of disparate essences is not reducible to any analysis, but constitutes rather its pre-condition, it follows that this unity *is*—that it exists.

Anything real is recognizable to me as a fugue whose disparate elements are susceptible to objective and analytic dissection; but their orchestration into a oneness, a unity, is not a deduction, as in an analysis, but is given me as radical novelty, as *be-ing*. This is what St. Thomas called the plus, the *excessus*, which is *esse* and which escapes every analysis. A synthesis *à la* Hegel is ultimately a masked analysis, like a motion picture run backwards, which puts the parts together again into a composite whose reality is merely a sum of the parts. Hegel thought he had surmounted the tautology of Carteisan rationalism. But is not his deduction of the world dialectically another instance of meaning generating being? Is not the entire dialectic already compressed within the *ergo* of Descartes' "*Cogito ergo sum*"?

Reality is positive contradiction in Hegel's dialectic, but it is non-contradiction for St. Thomas. Each being is absolutely diverse, so absolutely diverse that the very concepts of "the same" and "the other" break down when the mind confronts the act of existing. And it is only by viewing *esse* as radical novelty, as creation (as the proper effect of God—the "To Be") that it is possible to transcend the dialectic theoretically—to break out of the prison of Descartes' *ergo*, and to prepare for an age that will have surmounted the West's internal and structural Manicheanism.

This internal Manicheanism has been one of the two chief characteristics of our civilization in the past four hundred years. As articulated by Hegel, the dialectic insists that reality is fashioned out of opposites. Men, in turn, as they act out the drama of history, are forced to choose between these opposites in such a fashion that every "yes" must be countered by a "no."

This was forcefully underlines in a brilliant lecture given last year by Don Francisco Canals Vidal. Canals points out a curious phenomenon marking the last centuries of our epoch. All revolutionary movements have been absolute negations of the going order and they, in turn, have been negated by conservative movements which are defined by the very negations they negate. Extreme dialecticians of the revolution have aptly called this "yeaing" and "naying" the "perpetual revolution." In any event, it is at the center of the dialectical situation within which our very old world is now anguishing upon its deathbed. Canals traces this aberration through Hegel back to Manichean dualism and even beyond to Pythagorean number theory which saw the world in terms of odd or even. In all cases, the dialect insists that we choose, not between good and evil, but between slices of the cake of reality which have been conceptually hardened into oppositions. On a more vulgar, but not for that reason inconsequential, plane the West has been divided into the hostile camps of rich and poor; blue-collar and white-collar; hard workers and loafers; the washed and the unwashed; the beards and the beardless; the liberal and the conservative; the literate and the illiterate. Each term of the polarity in question has raised its own banner and created its own mystique.

However, there are signs everywhere today in our youth that these dialectical oppositions are breaking down. They no longer cut any ice with the generation under twenty. Working hard is no longer a virtue, and professors who sweat their students bring to mind those masters of sweatshops celebrated in infamy by Dickens. Whether we are equal or unequal means nothing to a generation which tells us that each one must "do his own thing." And this doing of one's own thing totally breaks the dualism inherent in Hegelian Manicheanism. (I pass over the obvious excrescences and overreactions of youth as themselves hangovers from the dialectic and analytic age; youth has not escaped the dialectic, but it is on its way to doing so.)

The breakdown of the "yes" and "no," of dialectical pluralism, is accompanied by the rapid obsolescence of the second characteristic mark of the West of the past four hundred years—that machine technology which grew out of the Rationalist Spirit.

Machine technology is process attempting vainly to convert itself into independent existence. This is its nature and therein consists its inner contradiction. A machine is so constructed that it is pure "being-for," a mechanism so formed that once turned from the use for which it was built, it is distorted. Imagine an automobile used for anything other than driving, or a machine-gun which did something other than spit bullets. Machines, diverted from goals which are their internal dynamic principles, are either violated (pistol-whipping violated not only the man whipped but the pistol), or they are antiqued and thus declared *fuera del combate*—Mississippi side-wheelers converted into restaurants; San Francisco cable cars decorating gardens. Machines, moreover, are so utterly functional that the world fashioned around them has tended to be purely functional. Its very art and style of life, its music and literature, as well as the rhythms of its psyche, reflect and thus symbolize the mechanical basis upon which our world has rested.

Consider: Were a machine to convert itself into an independent reality, into *being* rather than *process*, it would look like a Rube Goldberg contraption. It would go round and round, and *do* nothing at all. It would simply *be*, and this *being* would reverse its teleology, which is *not to be* but *to do*. This is the basis of Friedrich Georg Juenger's prediction that the very success of machine technology would destroy it. It is amusing to note that Juenger's famous book, published in the original German as *The Perfection of Technology*, was changed in its English edition to *The Failure of Technology*. They both amount to the same thing.

But Juenger did not take account of the newer electronic technology whose phenomenology is pioneered today by Marshall McLuhan. The Industrial Revolution based on mechanics has avoided collapsing into being (sterile nonsense for machines) thanks to the gradual introduction of this new technology which could be bent to the old, as was ignition to the combustion engine. Electronics finds its own perfection, however, not in any instrumental services it might render machines, but in media which move information. The genius of McLuhan's famous aphorism, "the medium is the message," is that it properly compounds sign and signified. The insight might also be expressed by stating that a medium is "being" rather than process or "being-for." Show a savage an automobile and he will not know what it is for, what to do with it. But put that same savage in a room lit by an electric light and he will experience light, just as does the most highly civilized of men. The savage will find himself in a new state of existence, the state of "being-illuminated." He need know nothing at all about the nature of electricity; he will experience light just as he will a voice if handed a telephone, or a moving, talking image on a screen if led into a theater. Once electronic technical media are "switched on," they produce modes of being which are indifferent to the use man makes of them. Do with them what he will, man is now involved within them.

Thus the older mechanical technology, while progressively dependent upon man-the-user, progressively attempts to escape this dependence; and electronic technology involves man more and more as it approaches its perfection. The results, obviously, are antithetical. The war between these two technologies—the older approaching fullness at the moment of its imminent obsolescence even while it mingles with the newer—has produced an intolerable tension within the psyche of modern industrialized man. He is forced to live an increasingly tribalized life due to his being bombarded, invaded, decentralized, by a host of omnipresent media. Simultaneously, the life rhythms of his day-to-day work, be it in shop, factory, or school, reflect the atomized, solitary, and solipsistic fragmentation of the Age of Analysis. Synthesized by electronic media and shattered analytically by machine technology, contemporary man is torn to pieces, and the contradiction will not be tolerated much longer.

The shape of the future is not difficult to see. The sharp oppositions between subject and object, symbol and symbolized, being and doing, meaning and the meant, will dissolve back into organic and synthetic existence; reality, once again, will be a style of being, a manner, a play, a mode—in the vigorous slang of the Common Doctor of the Catholic Church, a *modus essendi*, a manner of "izzing." We are returning, thus, after an interlude of four centuries, to the corporate, to the familial, to the dynastic, to life and death, to love and glory, to the real. We can say good-bye to the dream of Descartes.

The future may bring a new barbarism; or it may bring a transcending, because totally novel, traditionalism. That depends on the use that is made of freedom. The horizon of the future remains hidden in the shadows of wills, both divine and human. But we will certainly be bathed in a new order of being—call it *esse electronico* if you like. Meaning will once again be consubstantial with and derivative of being. The Cartesian "*cogito ergo sum*" will not be turned on its head—this would be a dialectical response: the *cogito* will be transcended. Nature itself, unto the last and the most remote of the solar systems, will simply be one more environment within which tribalized man lives his frightening life. I say frightening because the existentialist terror of non-being will remain. St. Thomas said that everything is nothing by nature, that meaning by itself is zero. A world that will seem to depend for its every existence upon the will of man, even as it is cradled perilously in his sinful bosom, will force upon humanity that last and most sundering of questions: "Why being at all?"

It is truly terrible *not* to be, but only those who *are* can understand this terror. It is even more terrible *to be*. When we strip away every analytic dimension of the real; when we cease busying ourselves with How, What, When, and Where; when we confront that ultimate beyond every essence or nature, that Is which is truly an indecent excrescence to the rationalist spirit; when we take account corporately of the final ridiculousness of any world at all and most especially of a world wrapped inside our own miserable wills, then we will come to know the *terror* of the *Lord God Who Is*—"I am Who Am"—and is nothing else. Or we will come to know the terror of nothing. In this way, very truly, the spiritual destiny of the Land of the Evening shall be revealed to us: and we shall know all these things in a shining light, the glory of a new Christendom, a glove of the hand of God; or we shall know these things in the light that does not illuminate, but that blinds and darkens the hollow sockets that once housed the eyes of being.

x.69

HALLOWED BE THY WORLD

Religion means, as the word itself suggests, a binding back of man to the source of his being and a recognition by him of his own contingency. Since this is true, and all sound scholarship on the meaning of natural religion affirms that it is, then we must admit candidly that orthodox Christianity is much *more* than a religion. The Catholic Faith cannot be fitted into the category "religion" as though it were an instance or a species of some common genus.

The Catholic Faith is unique. While paganism in all its forms manifests an acceptance of contingency and thus binds man back to a divine source identified ultimately with the order of nature, Catholic Christianity is not satisfied with this: it proclaims, through its faith in the Incarnation, a vocation to fashion creation anew and to hallow all things so that they might participate in the Redemption of Our Lord Jesus Christ. This is spelled out explicitly in Pauline theology which insists that The Fullness of Time Who is Christ calls upon men to "fill up what is lacking in the sufferings of the Cross." By redeeming the world we remove, to the degree of our intentions, the sufferings of the Cross. We thus assume a burden that otherwise would be Christ's.

In this awful mystery we see God's infinite graciousness to man in permitting him to lift from God Himself a portion of the burden of Redemption. This is the very meaning of human freedom: I am free to help Christ help me. Any other freedom condemns itself to triviality and vulgarity.

We live now in the Last Age, insists St. Augustine; and an aging world, hurtling like an arrow toward Apocalypse and Judgment, cries out for Redemption. Nature, crippled by sin, cannot come even into the fullness of its own promise unless it be quickened from within by the grace

135

of Christ that pours through the veins of the Mystical Christ, the Church. As St. Thomas Aquinas taught: in no sense shackling or inhibiting creation, grace perfects nature and thus enables nature to be not only what it would have been without the Fall but to be more than itself. This is why the Church can sing on Holy Saturday—*felix culpa*—"blessed fault that merited for us so glorious a Redemption."

Christian religion is thus marked by an internal experience which consists of two moments: an initial acceptance of our utter dependence upon the Lord of Being, and our response to His call to sancitty the whole of creation and to lead it back to the Father through the Son and in the Spirit. This means, in technical theological terms, that whereas there are only seven sacraments there are as many potential sacrament*als*—every one of which conveys actual grace—as there are beings themselves. This sacramentalizing of the real, be it the high act of anointing kings in medieval Christendom or the picturesque blessing of the Portuguese fishing fleet today, is the essence of what I would like to call the *civilizing* aspect of the Incarnation. We are called upon not only to save our souls but, in so doing, to save the world. Hilaire Belloc exaggerated when he wrote that "Europe is the Faith and the Faith is Europe"; but this famous statement would have been theologically unshakable had Belloc not inverted the terms of the proposition. Europe, in the sense of Christendom, was the historical consequence of the call to Catholic men to incarnate the Truth and the Grace of Christ in a civilization whose lineaments bore the marks of the Faith.

This public and out-going character of the Faith makes Catholicism the archetype, possibly the only real instance, of what scholars call an *exoteric* religion. In an *esoteric* religion the saved are initiated into a series of quasi-mystical rites designed to withdraw them from the impurities of existence. They are saved not by sanctifying the world but by receiving a hidden doctrine, a *gnosis*, that cuts them apart from the broad mass of humanity and that permits them, through the manipulation of the *gnosis*, to dominate a hostile nature and to create eventually a new dream world fashioned in the image of men for whom reality is a burden too intolerable to face.

Messianic or gnostic dreaming always repeats this common error: from the dawn of the Christian era, when a swarm of sects sought to prevent the essence of the Faith, down to the Marxist secular-humanist heresies of our own time, it rejects the idea of redeeming creation through sacramentalization. It proposes, rather, some new creation to be fashioned out of the womb of history by a select group or class that believes itself to be the possessor of the secret laws of Time itself. It is the essence of gnostic heresies that they deny nature on principle, and then destroy it in fact in the name of some future paradise. It is the essence of Christian civilization that it builds upon nature, upon things as they have come forth from God, and that it perfects them through a communication of that grace which only the Church can dispense.

Gnostic heresies, incidentally, always reject the Mother of God because God's humility in entering history through the womb of a woman and by her *fiat* offends the messianic view of creation. But to the Catholic the mysterious sanctification of the womb of the Virgin by the presence of the Uncreated is a type and a promise of what Christian men are called upon to do to nature within history: to sanctify the real, to sacralize it, to redeem it.

Now if the above analysis is substantially correct, it follows that the act of civilizaing is integral to the full profession of the Catholic Faith. Sacramentalizing the real includes the political and social orders, and our general vocation to redeem the world is specified in a human fashion by a call to rear up a truly Christian order of things. This conclusion, deducible from the theology of the Incarnation, is buttressed by the massive testimony of history itself. The alliance of the papacy with the Franksih kingdom, which grew out of the dust of the dark ages following the collapse of the Roman Empire, gave birth to a precarious but brilliant flowering of Christian culture in the Carolingian Age. The coronation of Charlemagne in Rome on Chritmas Day in the year 800 not only infused the best traditions of classical antiquity with the promise of a new order, of a *res publica christiana*; it also marked an advance beyond the Christian politics of St. Augustine.

The *City of God* envisaged a Roman Empire led by Christian princes and staffed by Christian magistrates and soldiers. Are not Christians both braver as soldiers and more honorable as magistrates than pagans? This was the proud boast of the Bishop of Hippo. But he did not conceive the possibility of a new cluster of institutions, themselves temporal, which would be integrally Christian. Augustine's "Mirror of the Christian Emperor" looked to the old Roman order, now to be administered and governed by Christians. But the Christendom that emerged from the papacy's throwing in its lot with the Frankish Latin West was not simply a restoration of the old Empire. It was a new civilization, unmistakably Catholic.

A pagan could have governed the Rome of Theodosius simply by removing the pro-Catholic laws that St. Ambrose of Milan had jammed down the imperial throat. But no pagan could have governed the Empire of Charlemagne or the Europe that flowered from it because he would have encountered the configurations of a social and political order that made sense only in Christian terms: the pre-eminence of the family and the hallowed place of woman; the gradual conversion of the slave into a serf and the serf into a free peasant; the free university whose authority stood so that kings consulted it on the morality of political adventures; the sacredness of customary law; the institution of chivalry and the Christianizing of the profession of arms; a society of families governed by fathers, expressed politically in the popular Christian dynasty, and unencumbered by the quasi-totalitarian character of the pagan polis; the limitations placed on political power by the Church and by Christian society itself; the subordination of temporal to spiritual authority: the public recognition that the only Sovereign in Christendom is Christ the King to whom all kings owed whatever portion of power and authority might be theirs.

No pagan could have understood a society rooted economically in an agrarian order plowed into being by Benedictine monks who civilized as they saved. No pagan could have grasped the meaning of all those hospitals and monasteries and free guilds, self-governing and going about their business and God's as they fed the poor and assumed, almost absent-mindedly, the entire burden of public charity. No pagan could have worshipped his gods in Chartres; the Mohammedans were able to worship their lonely deity in St. Sophia in Constantinople only by defacing its visage and by rubbing away every trace of what Catholic men had etched in glory in that masterpiece of the Catholic spirit.

This public and exoteric dimension of the Faith is not shared by the Protestant sects. Luther's removal of God to the awful transcendence of a "Totally Other," coupled with the Luthern rejection of Aquinas's analogy of being, reduced man's link with God (as Barth never tired of repeating) to the "extrinsic denomination" of grace which covers man like a cape, but does not penetrate his nature and transform it. The political consequences of Lutheranism were patent almost from the beginning. The sinfulness of the social order and the intrinsic corruption of the political order—themselves consequences of the depravity of human nature—demanded that the subject suffer the prince in all things, even in a tyrannical exercise of his power. The Lutheran Christian was willing to lend himself to any crusade in favor of the faith of Augsburg, but he never thought of defending a specifically Lutheran civilization. He withdrew from society and gave up any real effort at founding or maintaining a *res publica christiana*. In Anglicanism, the frank subordination of the ecclesiastical to the political worked a similar effect and jelled beautifully with the new European adherence to the principle of nationalism. In Calvinism, the rejection of the goodness of nature blocked any sacramental view of the world or of society. With Calvin, nature even ceased to have a symbolic role in pointing man toward God: the only relation binding man to God was a divine *fiat* which saved or damned altogether without any absorbing of human liberty into God's Freedom (as in Aquinas).

Protestant Christianity, in short, witnessed to the truth of Christ as it imperfectly understood Christ; but in no sense did it call man to the specifically Christian task of civilizing the world. This call can follow only from a highly sacramental view of creation, which is uniquely Roman Catholic.

The final supreme effort of the Church to create a civilization was made in the Age of the Baroque. Thrown up as a brilliant and self-conscious protest against the negations of the north, the spirit of the Baroque was articulated theologically by the Council of Trent which reaffirmed the sacramental universe both by insisting upon Transubstantiation and by advancing the Church's unique claim to dispense the grace that Christ won for mankind upon Calvary. Under the spur of the Company of Jesus, as the army of a purified papacy; served by the House of Habsburg which deliberately turned its back on the new Machiavellian politics of the Renaissance (did not the Emperor-King Charles V pledge "all my friends and all my kingdoms, my wealth and my life, to the service of the Holy Catholic Church"?); finding its sword in the infantry of Castille and its mystical lyricism in the same high plains that were blessed by the presence of St. Teresa of Avila and St. John of the Cross, the Counter-Reformation won back for the Church a third of Europe and simultaneously spread the Cross to half the world in a stunningly brilliant half century that came within an ace of reestablishing the unity of Christendom.

But the counterattack failed, and the full consequences of the failure have now worked themselves into history. The Protestant principle of the primacy of the individual conscience over the authority of the Church has become a public orthodoxy in the secularized West. This new orthodoxy has outlawed any corporate incarnation of Christian principles in the social and political order. The sacral universe has itself been outlawed.

The secular state's central meaning is to contradict the proposition that the act of civilizing is integral to the full profession of the Christian Faith. The secularist contention simply reverses the terms of the proposition: religion can be anything it cares to be to man provided it leaves to the secular state the task of civilizing. Man's relationship with God (if there be a God) is totally vertical and individualist; it has nothing to do with the horizontal task of fashioning the social and political order. This view of the state's role was articulared as an ideal as early as the fourteenth century in Marsilius of Padua's *Defensor Pacis*.

Philosophically, the secularist position was elaborated brilliantly and wittily by Thomas Hobbes who urged, however, a state religion in order to spare England from religious strife; this solution would eliminate potential martyrs, who might be moved to deny that Peace and High Standard of Living are the ultimate ends of life. Hobbes's state religion was, of course, only a precursor of state atheism.

Secularist assumptions were also insinuated into the American *Federalist Papers*. Publius urged upon our forebears the accumulation of wealth and the cultivation of private interests because these activities drain off enthusiasms that otherwise might harden into religious fanaticism which could lead the various factions to make the nation a battleground for their respective creeds. The end of politics was thus deliberately lowered from the high virtue preached by pagan antiquity and by the Christian polity which emerged in the *res publica christiana*. Let creeds multiply merrily, the American "solution" proclaimed: latitudinarianism will eventually dilute conviction; religion will retreat to the "private sphere"—to the attic of the individual conscience, and to sacristies whose doors are closed to the public forum. The American founders wrote wisely from their point of view. They brought forth the only great power in history that has not been guilty of anything so indecent as a religious war.

On the European continent the secularist view marched from victory to victory. The splendid Catholic rally in the nineteenth century, following the shock of the French Revolution, produced in Pius IX, Leo XIII and St. Pius X the condemnation of the proposition that the Roman Pontiff ought to adjust himself to the modern world, and a reaffirmation of the

Church's right to civilize. But these popes had no secular arm, and the last embers of the Baroque spirit burnt out in the Carlist wars in Spain and in the papacy's inability to recruit an army big enough to defend even its own lands against Italian secularist nationalism. The destruction of the Austro-Hungarian Monarchy in 1919 by the liberal politicians who met at Versailles left the Church for the first time since the conversion of Constantine altogether without a major secular power willing to listen to its authority.

The success of this anti-Christian politics forms a secularist rosary whose beads are simply negations of Catholic civilization: the drying up of local autonomy and the suppression of those concrete rights belonging to regions and townships that date from medieval times; the abolition of the guilds in favor of a savage liberal economics that recognized no master beyond the market; the confiscation of the free universities and their absorption into the new state; the persecution, at times petty and at times vicious, of the civilizing religious orders; finally, the supplanting of the Church's spiritual authority by the authority of the positivist religion of material progress. In a word, every typically Catholic institution in the political and social order either disappeared or was reduced to a simulacrum of its ancient status.

The liberal nineteenth and twentieth centuries can almost be defined in terms of a purposeful dismantling of the civilization that the Catholic Church had erected over fifteen hundred years. The hostility of liberal secularist governments today to any semblance of a Christian order—whether in Spain or Portugal, in Diem's Vietnam, in the Greece of the generals, or in the first flush of Catholic hope that swept Ongania into power in Argentina—is simply a logical consequence of a politics whose true meaning is the de-Christianizing of the social order.

The result of all this is so tragic that it is embarrassing to set it down baldly. But let us follow the example of the *Peasant of the Garonne* and call a spade a spade.

We Catholics have been robbed of our civilizing role in history. Living in a wholly secularist world, *we have nothing to do in history.*

We have been robbed of those Christian institutions that were once the channels through which we directed our dynamism. Looking at the world today, and excepting two or three pockets of resistance, there is not a single political or social "objective correlative" for whatever Christian drive we might have within us toward sanctifying the world. Outside of a direct revolutionary appeal to the masses, the only way men can get things done in history is through existing institutions. But those that exist today—everywhere—are hostile to the Faith. No democratic politician could conceivably get himself elected if he ran on a platform of sacramentalizing the political order. In most nations, including the United States, such an ambition would be tantamount to treason. Our youth, even when they are prepared to make sacrifices, are told either to fight the wrong wars or to fight the right ones for the wrong reasons, as in Vietnam. Whenever a brilliant opportunity emerges to strike a blow for the Christian Order, as in Hungary in 1956, our governments not only do not act themselves, but they forbid individuals to act, even on their own initiative and as private persons. At the very moment a splendid system of Catholic universities in this country was challenging the intellectually bankrupt secular Academy, it surrendered, and went hat in hand, to secular treasuries for its own share of anti-Christian money. Whenever an opportunity to civilize raises its head, it is seized by the secular authority and directed to ends which are either indifferent, or hostile, to Catholic culture. I think especially of the Peace Corps and of the Alliance for Progress in South America; this last is practically definable in terms of its fastidious refusal to take into account the massive presence of Catholicism south of the Rio Grande. I repeat: there is quite literally nothing for Catholics to do anymore—except, perhaps, to homestead in Angola and take part in the last Christian venture in the world sponsored by a specifically Catholic politics.

Now this situation in which Catholics find themselves cut away from a role in history has produced predictable consequences inside the Church. The existential failure of Catholicism to maintain its exoteric dimension has led the "new theologians" to repudiate even the *concept* of Christendom—of Christian civilization. And this withdrawal of the Church from politics, from civilization, has understandably produced a backlash in the sensibilities of the faithful. Although incapable of continuing a millenium and a half's work of evangelizing and civilizing mankind, Catholics could not simply withdraw from history as though the Faith had nothing to preach but a vertical relationship between God and the isolated human soul. The ecstatic character of orthodoxy still demanded some externalization of the Faith in things political and social. So today many Catholics have bought the assumptions of secular humanism and are attempting to graft the Church onto a tree whose roots are utterly foreign to the Faith. Robbed of their own culture, they have accepted an ape of the real thing, and have launched an elaborate campaign to accommodate the Church to secularist society. Just as the French royalists in the last century attempted, with far more justification, to identify Throne and Altar, our liberal Catholics today identify Democracy and the Meal Table. These men would drown the Church in a sea of sociology and thus make her "relevant to the modern world." But in so doing, they seem to be totally unaware that they are perverting the Church's call to sacramentalize creation—to raise up a society integrally Christian in character.

Nuns busily throwing off the habit in Los Angeles are poor mimics of nuns ministering to the wounded at Mont-Saint-Michel in World War I. Jesuits agitating for social legislation in *America* are pale imitations of Jesuits under sentence of death administering the sacraments to English Rescusants under Elizabeth I. Priests captaining Castroite *guerrilleros* in Colombia are parodies of priests going into the Mexican hills some thirty years ago to give spiritual comfort to those *cristeros* who took up arms against a persecuting Masonic government in the name of Christ the King. Christian Democrats swamping their Christianity in their democracy and their democracy in their socialism are distorted images of Catholic kings in the past proferring their swords and their manhood to the Roman Pontiff. Liturgists who busy themselves in writing creeds and canons and "bible services" in a secularized language and a style that blots out every sense of the Holy are unworthy descendents of the mendicant Franciscans who spread to all the poor of Europe a popular piety centered around Bethlehem and the Child Jesus. In short, while the campaign to adjust Catholicism to the world reveals a spirit still sufficiently Catholic to *want* the Faith to spill over into the market place, it is not Catholic enough to realize that *we are called upon to shape the market place itself in the image of the Faith*. The crippled spirit forgets that the Church of God does not stoop to conquer, but elevates to save.

I have said we have nothing to do in history; but in fact I lament only a temporary state of affairs, which will not long last. For nothing is clearer to men capable of evaluating history than that secularism—the process of desacralizing the real—is nearing the end of the road. The modern world is in its last agony; the age that began with the Renaissance is thrashing on a bed of death prepared by history itself. The orthodox need neither "adjust" to this world nor join the courtiers before the coffin; for their time is soon coming.

St. Paul teaches that history will be consummated only when we have carried all creation back to the Father, through the Son and in the Spirit. What does this mean but that Augustine's "Last Age" is really only beginning—that a world purged of the temptation to play God is again waiting to be hallowed?

vi.68

THE GOOD EARTH

William Anders: *In the beginning God created the heaven and the earth. And the earth was without form and void; and darkness was upon the face of the deep. And the Spirit of God moved upon the face of the waters. And God said, Let there be light: and there was light. And God saw the light, that it was good: and God divided the light from the darkness.*

James Lovell: *And God called the light Day, and the darkness he called Night. And the evening and the morning were the first day. And God said, Let there be a firmament in the midst of the waters, and let it divide the waters from the waters. And God made the firmament, and divided the waters which were under the firmament from the waters which were above the firmament: and it was so. And God called the firmament Heaven. And evening and morning were the second day.*

Frank Borman: *And God said, Let the waters under the heaven be gathered together unto one place, and the dry land appear: and it was so. And God called the dry land Earth; and the gathering together of the waters called the Seas; and God saw that it was good. . . Merry Christmas and God bless all of you—all of you on the Good Earth.*

Man had to journey 500,000 miles from home in order to discover that he had one. The amazing feat of Apollo 8 was comprehensible to the mathematical mind and to the technological genius that planned it. But it was totally foreign to both imagination and sensibility which simply cannot experience such an enormity of space traversed at such incredible speed. December 1968 forced man back into believing what he sees even though he cannot comprehend what he sees. This demand for mass humility has seemingly disturbed the mediators of our secular culture, but it is precisely what gives historical meaning to the adventure of the astronauts. They ushered into history a new epoch and a new order of things alien to everything the past four hundred years has made familiar—as witness our almost total inability to date to handle the event rhetorically and poetically.

For one thing, the event repudiated the modern myth in the West about space. The vastness of space, paradoxically caught within twenty-inch television screens, produces awe and reverence. It does not elicit any thrill, or pride in "conquest." That word was foreign to everything beamed to earth by our three astronauts. The cold, silent world of the Moon with its burnt-out craters and valleys whence drift weird, blue dust formations was a prehistoric world that recognizably lies within the hands of God even as it is fixed there in lunar light. It held no promise for a bright secularist future, as our cultural masters had assured us it would. Apollo 8 has not led upwards to a secular paradise—awaiting us tomorrow. The arrival at the Moon, out there in a space beyond physical comprehension, has hurtled us all backwards into time through the vortex of the imagination; it took all America and most of the world, on those fateful Christmas days, to Genesis and to beginnings—to the creation of all things from nothing.

Now the party is over and the music has stopped. Man knows silence once again. In the past he found it in deserts and monasteries as he fled a noisy world. Today he has found it beyond all possible noise—in space; he has found it altogether without desiring to, in a cosmos which has forced the only three men who have ever been there to their knees. They prayed and they prayed publicly, without fear of petty reprisals: they were half a million miles away from secular fanaticism. They could tell us what they experienced.

Silence without God is intolerable. This is why atheists talk so much. The lunar world, and beyond it all space and a potential infinity of worlds, was silently swept into the technological genius of man even as our Earth was photographed side by side with the Moon, both caught—at different moments—with the telescopic instruments of the spacecraft. The only way to break the silence, the only possible human response to this new world, so hideous in its utter lack of humanity and of the spirit, was to affirm God the Father.

But the grandeur of this affirmation was compounded by a terrible awareness that created existence now depends for its continuance, increasingly, upon the wisdom and will of its human master. Although our science can make nothing *be* out of nothing, it has the frightening power to undo what God has made. The soul is greater than the heavenly bodies,

146

insisted Aristotle, because the soul can know them whereas they know nothing. The Moon's knowing nothing—its utter vacancy and burnt-out visage—confirms the Stagirite! But the soul today is even greater because not only does it know the cosmos, but in the future the soul must participate in God's providence, even to keeping the whole universe in being.

Indeed, any attempt to probe the cluster of symbols, bigger than the world, that surrounds Apollo 8 encounters the whole galaxy of paradoxes which define human existence. Awe before the inhumanity of the Moon was mingled with, and therefore heightened, out piety toward the Earth. The final telecast of Apollo 8 was completed Thursday afternoon; the spacecraft was almost 97,000 miles above Earth; better than half the return trip from the Moon was completed. "See you back on the Good Earth soon," said Borman. One was reminded of Chesterton's fantasy of the English yachtsman who joyously discovered England under the impression that he had landed in the South Seas. The Earth (everybody capitalizes it nowadays!) had not been spoken of with such warmth and affection in decades. In becoming very small indeed, the Earth grew to the gigantic proportions of any home, anywhere in Dickens' world at Christmastime: lights and the tree and a roaring fire, good company and cheer, warmth and shelter from the snow without. This piety toward a common *patria* suggests what St. Thomas Aquinas taught about all piety: the virtue gives gratitude toward that which has sheltered us, and it promises a return in kind.

The piety of officers Borman, Anders and Lovell was shared analogically by most of us, thanks to the simultaneity of electronic media. But this awe and reverence toward creation, which welled up in millions of men, could not be expected to sit well in all quarters of our dying secularist society. Accordingly, various secular fanatics immediately informed the news commentators that this public affirmation of the Christian God originating from Outer Space had violated the sacred doctrine of the separation of Church and state! These quaint protests, moreover, were surely but a prelude to a more serious counterattack from the scientific and rationalist community. Future moon flyers will no doubt be warned against exploiting their trade on behalf of religion, and be instructed to wax less enthusiastic from now on about God's Earth. Houston will be advised of the desirability of integrating atheists (would they care to make the trip?) into the space program, and avoiding Christian feasts for the celebration of secular triumphs. Mr. Justice Fortas will be asked to write the Supreme Court's opinion deciding that Apollo 8 cannot be reconciled with the First Amendment.

We must try, however, to sympathize with these secularists. They are bleating out their banalities in this their very last moment in history. They have propagandized us for half a century about the miseries of this planet and the joys of the space-world to come. They spent $25 billion of our money without consulting us in order to spit artificial moons into space. In so doing they spat metaphorically on our shrines and valleys and hallowed places, on all of our pieties. Finally they blundered into putting three men on the key trip who proceeded to read Holy Scripture to them from the real Moon. It is as though Mankind, a gigantic Paul Bunyan, heaved himself mightily off the throne of secular-liberal democracy and relieved himself from the height of the Moon. Splashdown for the secularists did not happen on Friday when our men landed in the Pacific. It was delivered on Christmas Eve, by three Christian lads a quarter of a million miles away. God bless you all, you little Unitarian Atheists—wet—one and all!

One lesson to be drawn from Apollo 8, then, is that millions who have had a front seat to the Creation of the World and a total experience in the Metaphysics of Being will increasingly be able to recognize the strident strictures of professional secularists as the empty ukases of a dying order. But there is another good lesson, which may be less obvious to the non-philosopher. I mean that Apollo 8 has exquisitely fingered the radical difference between the new age that is beginning and the old one that is ending; and in so doing has existentially touched a dimension of God's Plan and His Creation that before our time could only be imagined by Christian theory.

Awe, reverence, piety—these are virtues totally opposed to the analytic mind which has dominated the West since the Renaissance; but they are attitudes toward the real demanded of man today if he is to master humanely his own impending exploration of space. I advisedly use the term "exploration" rather than "conquest." The first suggests knowledge; the second domination by violence. A mark of contemporary electronic technology in opposition to the older mechanical order is its propensity to move information *about* reality, rather than to conquer reality. Both computerized electronics and electronic media reveal new modes of being which analogically mimic and further elevate the material order into the spiritual consciousness proper to humans. Father Teilhard de

Chardin had a lively awareness of this dynamism inherent in the new technology, much more lively than many of his critics. Teilhard failed, however—as have his critics—to see the parallel with human knowledge; most probably the French Jesuit was imperfectly trained in the Thomistic theory of intentional existence. Theilhard thought that the "noosphere" or "skin" thrown over nature by science will progressively eliminate nature as it is absorbed more thoroughly into scientific hypotheses. Thus the apex of man's scientific achievement will so spiritualize nature that the distinction between subject and object will disappear into an Omega Point, an identity of consciousness and nature suggestive of its model, Hegel's Absolute Spirit. But if the argument is merely that nature follows the curve of ascending consciousness, then the philosopher is urged to stop shouting at Teilhard for being a heretic, and to correct him on the point of what happens in ordinary instances of higher consciousness. What we know is not altered or destroyed in our knowing it: the known is given a new or second existence, and is thus "spiritualized" without in any sense losing its original being "in nature." The proposition is an epistemological commonplace in the Thomistic tradition, but its consequences have thus far been unexplored.

Electronic technology reiterates in its own fashion the integrating activity of human knowledge, both sensorial and intellectual. Marshall McLuhan has pointed this out, but the message seems to have been lost on his swarm of critics who are divided into those who fear him as a mummer in a medieval masquerade and those who envy him as a high-paid Madison Avenue huckster. (Being sympathetic with the twelfth century while making plenty of money in the twentieth is a sin that is unforgivable in the academic establishment.) Electronic technology, nonetheless, integrates the real not by violating its structures but by elevating them to what we may call "electronic existence": *esse electronico*. Nature is not altered any more than were Earth or Moon on the shots we got from Apollo 8. *What was* now *is* in another order of being. The Thomistic tradition calls this order "intentional," and Cajetan warned his reader when he approached the mystery of knowledge: *disces elevare ingenium, aliumque rerum ordinem ingredi*. Sharpen your brains because you are entering into another order of things!

Four propositions follow from this reasoning: 1) electronic media, reflecting their human masters, reintegrate, within structures uniquely proper to themselves, worlds upon worlds of information; 2) these worlds no longer simply *are* "out there" in nature: they also *are* in consciousness, thanks to the media in question; 3) since man's psychic structure is profoundly shaped by his being symbolically "informed" by media, *he* is "within" them; and therefore (recalling that all technology involves power over the real) we must conclude 4) that nature depends upon man somewhat the way in which an aged mother depends upon her grown sons. Although she brought them into being and nourished them to maturity, she now lives in a house built by them. We have thus come round-robin back to classical piety compounded by Christian paradox: the cherishing of what cherishes; the humbling of the mighty before the weak; the Wise Men bending over the Child; the Lion lying down with the Lamb.

The analytic mind, typical of the rationalist and secularist spirit, plainly cannot cope with this new order of things. Dominant in the West for more than four centuries, modernity is now bankrupt, not only because it succeeded so well that it ran out of objective correlatives for its old dynamism, but principally because the very way in which the modern mind looks at reality precludes its coming to grips with the newer scientific breakthrough wrought by electronic technology. The issue can be sharpened by noticing the three overarching ways in which Western man has historically expressed his relationship to the world and to the Absolute.

In pagan antiquity, man conceived himself as forming part of a Nature which was coincidental with and therefore exhausted by the totality of Being. To be was to be part of Nature. Beyond was Nothing at all.

Thanks to Revelation and the Christian teaching on the created structure of the world, medieval man saw all things as holding existence on suffrage from the Lord. Nature was no longer the Mother Bosom but the fragile Sister of St. Francis of Assisi. By being divested of its old divinity ("all gods within; none without"), nature lost its absolute character but took on the shimmering beauty of a fragile chandelier. As Chesterton put it: smash a chandelier and it will shatter into a thousand pieces; let it be, and it will last forever.

With the advent of the Renaissance and the new mechanized science perfected by the rationalist mind, nature became something different. Symbolized by mathematical constructs, conceived as a clock governed by rigid laws, nature was looked upon as a network of moving bodies devoid of qualitative differences and of ontological density. Nothing new ever happened because everything was just as predictable as the movements of pistons and rods within a well-oiled machine. Thus nature could be dominated—provided nature were treated in a purely analytic fashion. So the world was given to the mind in a series of clear and distinct Cartesian ideas from which future behavior could be deduced with iron rigor.

The necessary fruits of the analytic approach are worth elaborating. All analysis assumes a whole which is subsequently reduced to its constituent elements—the "resolution," in Aristotle's terms, of a reality to its "causes." This *resolutio* is an act of taking apart in the mind what is "put together" in the real. It is the key to the rationalist mentality. Reduction to causes is not bad in itself, of course. Crime-solution, possibly rationalism's crowning achievement, would have been impossible without the method. But when reduction to causes becomes *reductionism*, the complex shrivels to the simple; the many to the one; the qualitative to the quantitative; the hierarchical to the horizontal; difference to sameness; mystery to banality; poetry to prose; prose to linguistics; linguistics to linguistic analysis. Eventually the synthetic wholeness of existence dissolves into a dust of mathematical symbols.

The analytic *mind*, fragmented within itself, produced in its image the atomized world of the last centuries. In the political order families and dynasties and local laws and ancient traditions and pacted privileges gave way to individuals because the latter could be recognized by numerical count; and number theory gave birth to egalitarian democracy. In the economic order, the analytic mind invented mass production which both "divided" labor and atomized nature. In the theological order, analysis reduced the Trinity of Persons in the Unity of Divine Nature, first to Unity of Divine Nature and then to Unity of Divinity within Nature; and more lately, to One Secular World. Of course, I have taken instances of analytic reductionism of which I do not approve; but presumably everyone either likes or dislikes the process according to the direction it takes. The point, however, is that analysis *always* moves from complexity to simplicity and from mystery to clarity. It always moves *down*, never *up*; more accurately, analysis moves "out," not "in": it fragments rather than integrates; it is hostile to the synthesis constituting actual existence within the wholeness of being.

If there is an apt symbol, bathed in irony, for all of this, it is not to be found in the poetry of the imagination, but in the far better poetry of life. He is Dr. S. I. Hayakawa, acting-president of San Francisco State College.

The poor man spent his life trying to banish connotation from speech; in a valiantly puritanical effort to tidy up language, he tried to purge from spoken and written diction any symbolic undertones that hinted at transcendent convictions. Now, pressured by the times and a new world—and moved, presumably, by a noble soul—Hayakawa disappoints his semanticist friends and becomes a hero. His act of walking into a crowd of Black Power extremists and yippie barbarians and yanking the wires out of the truck from which they had been preaching revolution on his campus moved the nation in an entirely *trans*-rational fashion. The Hayakawa tam became the symbol of resistance to street tyranny but his own language tests deplore a hat being anything "more than" a hat.

It is this "more than" the merely analytic order which medieval man vividly lived in his harsh and poetic encounter with nature. Each and every thing, from the distant castle on the hill to the shroud that covered over death, was intensely itself—but simultaneously "more than itself." In being thoroughly themselves, all things somehow fingered the Lord of Creation, but the symbolized passed into their symbols and both were compounded in a density of being and meaning which forced everything first *to be* in order that it might *mean*.

This truth, that things always mean more than they are, was, of course, the supreme lesson of Christ: who came and died and rose—fleshly, bloody, dirty birth, death and resurrection. And behind every future "demythologizer" of the Virgin Birth or the physical Resurrection there would be the Manichean disease, the latent homosexual hatred of the very good dirt of God's very splendid world. Unless I place my fingers in His wounds, said the Christian . . . unless this flesh and blood . . . unless Christ be risen—all is in vain! This religion which insisted against the Arians that He was "more than Man" and against the Patripassionists and a dozen oriental heresies that He was "more than God" has lived for two thousand years affirming the paradox of transcendence in immanence. The doctrine was first suggested to the nascent Christian West by the dogma of creation—I do not receive the gift of being as though I were before I am: *I am that gift*. The doctrine was given the flesh it needed by the specifically Catholic teaching on Incarnation and Redemption: I do not suffer the fate of nature, but nature is granted the high dignity of "suffering" my fate—union with the Father, in the Son, and through the Holy Ghost. I shall live in a final *patria*, the Land of the Father, but nature itself—my world, this Earth, today a cherished inn on pilgrimage—is destined to share in this ultimate glory. There is only one orthodox answer to the question of the ages: what will I do in Heaven? You will do, my boy, whatever gives you joy because your joy is simply Our God, Your Blessedness. And this last Mystery is Being: Trinity: God.

The Age of Rationalism, of Analysis, mortally violated this sacral fabric of the real. What had been the Glove of God for Christendom—the world—became the raw material of Manchesterianism, its threads taken apart and then fed back into spinning jennies. Calvinism, hating the world, married the rationalist spirit; and both of them, pumped by French lucidity and the greed of Dutch and English capitalism, engendered that Modern Age which today passes out of history.

The modern world was unlovely, in short, because it was never "more than" anything. Subsisting on a systematic dissection and thus violation of the real order, this world fed off nature by absorbing it into machines which in turn demanded even more raw stuff from nature in order to function. And like a man diseased on sex who wants more and more and gets less and less from every woman progressively violated, bought or seduced, mechanical technology and the world built around it would have burnt themselves out had not the principle of electronic technology appeared on the stage of history in the last century.

I have already suggested that while mechanical technology exists by destroying nature, electronic technology exists by conferring new orders of being upon nature. The heart of mechanical technics consists in taking things out of nature, while the heart of electronics consists in moving information *about* nature. Of course, borderline cases abound in which the two technologies mingle and buttress one another, but let us concentrate here upon the essential dynamisms, and the indications that the new one is now displacing the old.

Vico, a seventeenth-century pioneer against Descartes and rationalism, pointed out that changes in the human spirit are played out in life long before they are ever understood in theory. The truly pragmatic structure of human existence adjusts to new circumstances well in advance of philosophical justification. Universities today begin to introduce studies in "communications theory" not quite certain of what it is or where it will go, but knowing infallibly that the future lies in *that* direction. Hitherto analytically divorced academic disciplines frantically, often comically, seek "interdepartmental" integration and thus flee older subject areas once fenced off from one another with all the rigidity and grace of flower beds in a Franch formal garden—itself one of rationalism's more charming products. Women revolt against living up to analytically fabricated models of what constitutes beauty. Men seek defiantly picturesque clothing out of a romantic Edwardian reaction against standardized mechanical civilization. The *New Yorker*, sniffing the times, blazes advertisements adorned with young bloods sporting frock coats and brocaded waistcoats, smoking pencil thin cigars (at the very moment when the American Catholic Church, true to its reputation for being there latest with the least, sweeps its temples clear of color and drama and assumes the pose of Grant Wood's nineteenth-century *American Gothic*).

Nor are the astronauts, who discovered at the Moon the beauty of silence, really ahead of the times. The most sensational motion picture of last year, "The Graduate," though swamped by a medium altogether too perfect for its message, brought forth a little song which has become a hit with teenagers:

> Hello darkness, my old friend
> I've come to talk with you again
> because a vision softly creeping
> left its seeds while I was sleeping
> and the vision that was planted in my brain
> still remains, within the sound of silence.
> And the people bow and pray
> to a neon god they made,
> and the sign flashed without warning
> in the words that it was forming;
> and the sign said:
> the words of the prophets are
> written on the subway walls, town and halls,
> and whisper,
> The Sound of Silence.

A medieval canticle, "The Scarborough Fair," was also played in the film: the worlds of the two songs seem to blend.

This new-bought silence suggests to the meditative mind that all the principles of noisy mechanical technics are marshalled immanently in a horizontal field. Nature is over here; and The Analytic Mind (Mr. Kaufman has him on the bookjacket of his *The Age of Analysis* as a very grim young-old man, baldpated, doing figures in his head which actually are much better done today by computers) is over there—glowering at Nature, the Enemy.

But meantime a new world born along with Apollo 8 has cracked the game wide open. Nature—both Moon and Earth and everything else—are today inside man and both depend upon him for existence. If this be true, then it follows that man tomorrow will have so transcended nature, be it lunar or earthly, that both will be swept into the scope of his liberty. It follows that man transcends *all* nature. Freed of tasks which once divided his kind into technically superior and inferior, confronted by an analytic order rapidly domesticated by computerized technology so that it no longer can dominate the life rhythm of an entire culture, man in the near future will have to give himself over to the important, the sundering questions. Why an Earth peopled by men, a home warm as a cottage in winter and tiny as a hidden grove sanctified to the gods? Why a burnt-out crater reached after an incredible cost to Earth? (Could we not have licked cancer with the same money?) Did we go to the Moon for nothing or have we discovered, having been there, that God's creation is as paradoxical as His birth in Bethlehem? Why an Earth and a Moon? Why anything at all? Why not the long sleep of nothingness? Why did the astronauts, sent for information about creation, signal home information about the Creator? The secularists who conceived and launched the enterprise were convinced with Fichte that *"Im Angang war der Tat"*: *in the beginning was the Deed. But the boys who went there signalled back: "In principio erat Verbum"*: in the beginning was the Word spoken in the silence of space.

These questions cannot be answered by rationalist analysis, and these are the questions of tomorrow. Possibly tomorrow we can say in a spirit that remembers Hilaire Belloc: take no fear: the night has passed. Finally there has come a dawn which can be our very own, if we have the intelligence and the will to seize it, even as it floods with new light a very old world. It promises an order of things so ancient that it must look to the young like the Good News of the Gospel heralding release from a past long grown intolerable to the human spirit.

ii.69

POPE AS ICON

In the town of Ravenna, lying close by the Adriatic, there is to be found a marvel of the Christian Empire, the mausoleum of Theodora, the consort of the great Justinian. In it, Christ the Good Shepherd is shown tending his flock and St. Lawrence embracing martyrdom. Both compositions breathe an air of peace suggesting the fulfillment of Resurrection. In this both look back to an earlier Christian tradition and foreshadow the coming hieratic triumphalism of Byzantium. Christ is not yet Pantokrator, the Lord and King of Creation, but He is already at peace with His sheep. No shadow of the tragedy of the Cross disturbs an airy and almost insubstantial pastoral. Saint Lawrence advances at a stately pace toward the gridiron set on a carpet of flames. He holds aloft a cross but it symbolizes neither pain nor death but rather the fulfillment of a martyr's faith. And upon leaving that miracle of art a man is struck as though by thunder when he recalls the truth that the mausoleum itself honors a prostitute turned empress.

The Christian East stylized everything. In so doing the East chained the cruelty of time, softened tragedy, and suppressed the idiosyncratic. In contrast, the Latin West, full of a nervous energy that precluded repose, not only exalted the Sacred Humanity of Christ but it also created gargoyles and griffins. The West would have invented the elephant had not God already done so. This very good humor toward, and puzzlement over, the personal and the incongruous was paradoxically linked with the cult of the Passion and the Pain of the Divine, the sense of personal sin and of a temporal world groaning in every lacerated and violated tendon of its existence upon the wood of the Cross.

That human propensity emphasized in Byzantine Christianity to stylize life, to formalize existence, to universalize being, to live beyond

156

time and therefore to experience eternity as a hope even here on this side of the grave, is the *iconic* in man. Although emphasized in Eastern Christianity, the necessity to fashion icons symbolic of the timeless is rooted in all mankind. The icon is contrasted to what we shall call here the idiosyncratic: the itch to individuate, to dig deep into matter, to scratch the unique, to glory in the flux, to wax. This has been weighted in the Latin West but it too is common to all men.

My thesis is this: the post-modern world will be, is even now becoming, increasingly iconic. This new age will be quickened by the leaven of the Church, and the Pope will emerge as Icon of all icons, omnipresent in a world in which space and time have been so thoroughly altered that older concepts of both will have been rendered obsolete.

Both the iconic and the idiosyncratic are common to all men because they are rooted in two different dimensions of the same creation and two corresponding acts of man's intelligence. On the one hand, the mind concentrates on the "*is*" aspect of reality; on the other hand, the mind concentrates on the "*what* is" aspect.

Naturally, in creation the "what" and the "is" cannot be separated, but the mind is sufficiently subtle that it can consider the complex as though it were simple. The mind halts the projector of being and freezes the dynamism of the real, thereby producing a still life or a slide of the cosmic motion of the universe. In this fashion it discovers structures that are repeated in individual instances in the real. That which has being spatially and temporally now comes to exist timelessly and universally within the soul. When man works his soul back into matter, artistically and morally, he forms an order which consists, largely, of repeated structures or forms. Thus the *icon* confronts the consciousness as an "after the fact," as an already synthesized whole capable of analytic differentiation. The icon, thanks to its universality, is projected into a future of indefinitely repeated instances, of "more of the same." Icon is expectation; transcendence of the fickle; promise fulfilled; loyalty rewarded; immortality. Icon is Order.

The non-iconic, on the other hand, is grounded on the "unpredictable" aspect of reality, on the fact that since the principles of the real that make up the whatness of things are not prior to their be-ing, nothing, existing in time is already constituted: all things, rather, are now being constituted. A green field of grass is a composition for mere contemplation but in the real it is a "green-ing field." *Time* in a burst of genius once wrote that if all the features of a certain woman were taken apart one by one by a critical mind they would add up to a series of imperfections; but that un-ited in Sophia Loren they make up one gorgeous woman. Active synthesiz-ing, thus, in one with creating, with being, with novelty. Thus we en-counter the idiosyncratic, the new, the never repeated, the contingent, the free. Let this cluster of terms, taking into account their differences, make up our understanding of the non-iconic; the unexpected; the spontaneous; the paradoxical. When irrational, the non-iconic is the absurd of Sartre: when transrational, it is the gratitude of a Christian.

There is no dialectical opposition between icon and non-icon, but there is a danger of confusing the two orders; the danger of iconizing the human person in the same way that no man is a hero to his butler. Thus, thanks to its stylistic generality, the icon is more closely associated with institutions and offices, with rites and liturgies, than with the men who ex-ercise their functions. Perhaps the family is the closest analogue in the per-sonal order to the icon: generations come and go but the family, if for-tunate, remains. The traditionalist and legitimate monarchy of the Mid-dle Ages invested the crown in a dynasty and not in a man. Moreover, the office was distinguished from the person of the king: any king who violated the sacred trust placed in him by the character of the office lost the "legitimacy of exercise." He could not govern tranquilly and take his repose in the dignity of the crown simply because of any supposed per-sonal charisma.

In this way the icon is different from the "image" of any one man as an individual; image, in the modern sense of the term, is charismatic per-sonality, and there is a rough but traceable inverse relationship between the decline of the icon and the ascendancy of the image. The dis-appearance of the three European empires after World War I and the crippling crisis that tortured all institutions inherited from the immediate past was followed swiftly by the rise of the great personalities: Hitler, Mussolini, Franco, Churchill, Stalin, Rosevelt, Adenauer, de Gaulle. The Emperors they replaced—Wilhelm II, Nicholas II, Franz Josef I—were all interesting and even good men in their own ways but whatever charisma attached to them belonged to their offices and not to themselves. But the giants of the midcentury imposed themselves upon a ravaged world by the sheer weight of their genius. They were the last flowering of the in-dividualist spirit. They have given way to Jungean *personae*, artificially fabricated out of essentially mediocre men in the laboratories of the clinical masters of the new communications media. These images, masked as reality, do duty for the absence of the praetorian hero who, in the classical tradition, imposes himself upon the chaos of an order which is disorder, a disorder within which the iconic role of institutions has already disappeared.

But icon and image, if distinct, are nevertheless related. The icon in the Russian liturgy represents a saint—a person; and is carried by a priest—a person. The icon, in our extended use of the term, is fulfilled and its meaning is "done" by a living flesh-and-blood man. Only persons can have images, and the man who puts on the mask of the image in this age of total electronic exposure participates totally in the public timelessness and universality of the icon. His image—has not McLuhan told us delphically and has not McGinnis spelled it out crudely?—must invoke consistency and predictability, the most common and least idiosyncratic of human traits, here transfigured magically by the media. He must be both intimate and remote, intimate because he is in every man's living room but remote because his behavior there is far more controlled than is that of those who own the house. Mr. Lyndon Johnson had a "bad image" because he acted in public the way the rest of us behave in private. That is why he had a credibility gap. The credibility gap is only closed by iconicizing the image. Life, on the contrary, *is* a credibility gap.

Now, if these reflections are substantially valid, the icon plays its proper role in the economy of the political order when it is non-personal (which is not to say, as indicated, *im*-personal). The icon is a formal structure within which a society incarnates its way of being. Better yet: society itself is a tissue of icons. (There is, for example, an iconic way in which men greet one another in differing cultures and this style reveals differing encounters with the absolute. Whether we shake hands or bow or embrace is not indifferent to our generic intention to greet. Whether we kneel or stand to receive Communion fashions the very being of our adoration. Those highly moralistic people who brush aside considerations of form on the ground that forms are mere neutral instruments need to be instructed by St. Thomas Aquinas that forms are causes of being. They determine or structure content to be *as* it is.) The iconic is also properly static, not in the sense that the iconic cannot grow up slowly in time or even appear suddenly in history, but in the deeper sense that the iconic must be *experienced* as something permanent even if it is new, as assuring continuity, and as healing contingency. The iconic is legitimate: it can be altered or smashed only by an act of violation that threatens the public orthodoxy. The iconic is universal and is accepted as such by the members of the community in which it is enfleshed. The iconic is sacral in that it adumbrates in diverse ways man's brush with the mysterious heart of the real.

With these attributes of the iconic as background, the roles of the icon in the post-modern world begin to take shape. As national structures dissolve under the impact of electronic technology, a new proliferation of lifestyles is produced, and these new modes of culture cut across older loyalties. Tribes spring up and their members recognize one another wherever they might be: the jet set, the black tribe, youth, the Woodstock tribe, the university students, the Confessional tribe—all spontaneously group themselves in relationships which are increasingly mobile and are identified with no fixed place within geographical space. We begin therefore to see rearing its head in history a cluster of iconic structures that are not only often merely different from one another but increasingly in active conflict. The national state for these tribes is not a fixed and absolute political entity to which they give their deepest allegiance but rather an instrument at their service, when fortunate, or a hinderance to their goals.

Older icons are shaken and newer ones stare across chasms of misunderstanding in which tribe is literally unintelligible to tribe. Men still loyal to the older liberalism attempt, often with the best of intentions, to use the new media to break down hostilities and to heal the racial and doctrinal wounds separating man from man. They fail, however, to take into account that it is the media themselves which have rendered it possible for the new tribes to be and to sense themselves at one with their brothers wheresoever they might live. Only if the media were literally shut off for five or ten years could the tribal wars cease, the tribes dissolve, and mankind be recentralized around the older mythic patterns. But this last Luddite gesture will never occur unless the entire technology collapses, and that is the dream of romantics or the prayer of integrists.

Now, to be sure, the enormous psychological pressures that follow on society's emergence from the private and lonely world of the mechanical and individualist past *are* producing reactionary movements and gestures in which men attempt to escape, to flee back into solitude, into the personal, the unique, the non-iconic. In general these counter movements involve some kind of return to nature. We need only think of how many young men, and very old men as well, take to navigating the globe single-handedly nowadays. We need only think of the thousands of affluent parents who send their children out into the desert on short survival courses and pay handsomely for the privilege of offering their youngsters the primitive and personal life for a few weeks. And yet, life forces almost everyone today to be a polyglot, to move back and forth between tribal structures at war with one another. You need either real poverty or real affluence to escape. The better a man can master these hostile languages and keep his own to himself within *his* tribe, the better he makes his way in life. But the psychological price is savage. And the lines are hardening and the swords are being drawn.

I have already stated that the iconic forms a cosmion of meaning, a network of intelligibilities, that constitutes a relatively stable order in which reality reposes timelessly and universally, thus portending the peace of eternity. In the past man escaped the iconic by conquering nature or facing the density of the *personae*. Today, however, *the new technology forces man back to an iconic understanding of the cosmos as such.* Newton's universe of infinite space beckoning men to cross it and conquer it involved "being-here" and "going-there." "In here" was the supposed oppressiveness of culture with its rigid iconic structures; "out there" was liberty. The adventure of the Renaissance and the age of explorations depended structurally on a linear cosmology. This smashed the older Ptolemaic world in which the earth—a round ball of moderate dimensions—was literally the center of the entire order of material being, circled perpetually by nine concentric spheres. The Copernican world humbled this earth by subordinating it to the movements of the sun but it liberated man for his conquest of nature. But now that Copernican world is dead. Mankind returns through the new electronic technology to a new Ptolemaic galaxy. The older spheres have come back with the satellites that circle the earth. The new electronic and computerized technology covers not only earth but moon; tomorrow—Mars; then—the entire solar system. *Where* man is within this new technology is utterly irrelevant to technology itself. This extension of man iconicizes nature because it lifts nature into the intelligible, predictable, and universal order of meaning out of which the iconic is fashioned. In a word: the philosophy of nature has become a part of the political order. Thus nature has been given an iconic and hence quasi-sacral status: pollution is a sin.

And yet if nature is swept into politics for its very preservation in being, then it follows that there is literally no exit for mankind on a purely immanent basis. If everything is already constituted in being; if even our sense of the dynamism of time has given way to the staticism of electronic simultaneity; if all ages are present to us technologically so that we might entertain them as an entire global synthesis of the history of man; if everybody's information from birth to death is computerized, as data is beamed to us from distant worlds, then it follows that man once again is a "center" of everything; but a "center" without a periphery to win or toward which he can thrust his innate bent toward novelty and liberty. Moon dancers, after all, are the most publicized and charted and controlled human beings ever known to history.

Sir Francis Chichester can escape as an older individualist in his cockle shell of a boat in the rugged confidence that out there in Atlantic and Pacific, beyond a totally organized and technologized world, he will be able to find some reality not yet constituted, not yet done. But his bizarre and attractive adventure is beyond the possibility or the talents of most men. Still, all men need to know that there is even yet something "going on" in being, some unfulfilled tale to be told. They need the assurance that being itself spells out within its heart the magic name of creativity, of creation. Mankind needs to know that it still has a future, that its future is more than the mere conservation in being of world after world thrown up before its consciousness by a technology that does not specifically alter or rape the world (as did the older mechanical order) but that makes all things a burden before they were even a promise. Here we encounter the panic running through the apostles of the ecology crisis.

But everything, of course, is *not* already structured and constituted in being, waiting to be iconicized. The entire creation, as suggested at the outset of this essay, is here and now being made to be God's creative act. Even the relative domestication of reality achieved by the "simple" understanding of everything that exists materially through our enormous technological and Ptolemaic system is itself now being-made-to-be. Man senses this because he knows that the entire fabric of the galaxy itself now depends on the exercise of his own will, and that exercise, prudently and heroically, can never be something done and finished. Like the angelic acceptance or rejection of God, this will to let things be will be a perpetually perduring and continuing act until time's end and the Last Judgment. Man will need the grace of God because he will come to know that his active composing of the principles of a world he never made but only assembled is simply beyond any innate power he might possess. He will need an icon beyond all icons that lifts in prayer a *universal* petition to the God of Being to lighten this awful burden of tending the entire garden of creation.

And here I enter into matters deep and I do so with trepidation. Man possesses the power to bind here below, short of making things be, but he does not possess the *authority*. This authority is possessed only by the Vicar of Christ for whom, Scripture teaches, even Heaven is bound. The Pope in Rome teaches in Christ's Name not principally because of the intrinsic merits of what he says but—the proper theological conditions being met—by *who he is*. The office of the papacy blends into the person who exercises it. Icon and bearer are one. Increasingly in the years ahead the Pope will emerge, not as a learned theologian parrying the thrusts of a secular world with his wisdom, but as the single iconic figure in all creation who depends neither on a prefabricated image nor on any psychological or intellectual charisma. He will be released—and this will be liberation indeed!—from the need to rely on the older mechanical chain of command in order to transmit the awesomeness of his authority and power. Freed by technology from the need to transmit the Word and the Will of God through lesser figures, the Pope will bypass the possibility of being constantly misunderstood. He will be everywhere and at once in the very immediacy of his person. Even now his iconic power is sensed by Hell: the long knife, frustrated in the Philippines, hidden symbolically under a black cassock, was a corporate dagger aimed not at the heart alone of one old man but at Christ and His Church and *therefore* at this old man's heart! The whole world saw Paul VI bless those islands and bowed down in prostration before him as did those two hundred newly ordained priests. The future will see the pontiff in every room throughout, and thus transcending, a world of seething tribes at war with one another.

The magical power of the name of Rome was once sensed as a distant hope and a dim promise by monks in the Island of St. Patrick and far north in the Hebrides, and this during those dark ages following on the fall of the Empire. There was then only one City, and it was remembered by all men but present to very few of them in those centuries when the forests came back to Europe and civilization dissolved in a swirling vortex of barbarian tribes.

We enter once again a new dark age. There will soon be only one city of any significance: the *only* City: *Civitas Aeterna*: Rome. The increasing obsolescence of cities as viable economic and political centers is today patent. They came into being in modern times in order to govern stable and static populations fenced in by boundaries roughly coincidental with national tongues created by the printed word. The new technology will not be delayed much beyond the turn of the century in its task of sweeping away megalopolis. The internal decay of cities, already a plague to politicians who would keep them alive artifically, will follow upon the increasing decentralization of industry and politics. A decentralization of the Church itself will coincide with the withering away of the need to govern through chains of command. The Pope need depend on no messengers as he sends forth the Gospel of love. He will be there wherever there is any "there" calling out for salvation. As the Vatican comes to learn—slowly and painfully—that the structure of the new world permits the Pope to imitate materially the ubiquity of God and thus, in the metaphysical levity of Christ's words, "be perfect" as is the heavenly Father, the Tribe of Christ the King will have their Pastor with them in word and image as they roam a world, soon a galaxy, now wrapped within the bosom of mankind. As the number of priests decline, the presence of the Pope will impose itself as he anneals the faithful in their burden of con-stituting the cosmos in being and of returning all things to the Father through the Spirit. The Pope will teach and exhort but he will principally *be*. Giving the eternal blessing, *Urbi et Orbi*, arms stretched out in a white cross that will embrace all creation, the Pope iconically will impose Christ lovingly on the world more by simply being than by what he might say. In Christ and through His Vicar men will then enter into a peace and repose that have fled the earth, taste a promised eternity, heal the wounds of con-tingency, find an exit from pure immanence, and come to know the one high adventure to which they have been called.

i.71

THE TYPOLOGY OF HERESY

Heresy is a word that has had a long and bloody history. A term of opprobrium in the Christian tradition, heresy has become a badge of honor in our permissive and relativistic world. Defined as the contrary to orthodoxy, heresy certainly has a better press in our century than does its opposite number: To be orthodox is redolent of being smug and self-contained, of being narrow of mind and parsimonious of person. But both etymology and history give the lie to this reversal of meaning. Any student of heresy—and this essay is an attempt at getting at the generic and philosophical meaning of the term—must be struck with curiosity about the history of the word itself.

Heresy is of course of Greek derivation. But the Greeks were the most tolerant of people (to their own), and their easy going paganism even put up with Socrates for over thirty years. Yet the heretic is the man you persecute and drive out of the community or the man you burn at the stake. Nonetheless, the very meanings inherent in the Greek term suggest the opprobrium that the Western tradition was to lay on the back of the heretic. These sinister connotations must be dug out of linguistic history.

Opening my Leddel and Scott's *Lexicon* I find a bewildering number of meanings given the word, and at first blush they seem to have little in common: "to take with the hand, grasp, seize; to kill—to win, seduce." Now I "take with the hand" gently some child or old woman crossing the street, but I do not "grasp" or "seize" them. "To take away" suggests stealing off with something or, possibly, separating one thing from another; when I "steal off" I do, in effect, "separate" something from that to which it had been attached. And what I have "taken away" is now "in my power," hence "conquered," "overpowered," "won," and "seduced." And does not a man "win" by killing his enemy, and is not "seduction" a kind of rape and hence a "killing" in the broad sense of a violation, a murdering either physical or spiritual? Now this "conquering" and "overpowering" also has the sense of a "choice": I choose something, but, given that I also "conquer" and "kill," my choice implies a rejection, a casting off.

Heresy thus emerges as an act in which a part is ripped from a whole and that part is stolen away by the conqueror. Thus it is that the word heresy has come down to us as meaning the selection of a part of a doctrine, large or small—be it philosophical or political or religious—and the rejection of the whole of which the part functioned precisely as a part. The heretic is the man who runs with one dogma, enlarging it to such an extent that other doctrines are rejected. The recognized meaning of the term belies the current prejudice that the heretic is broad and the orthodox narrow. If the heretic seizes a part and rejects the whole, the heretic is narrow by definition—narrow at least when defined in terms of the orthodoxy that he abandons. If an orthodox Christian balances the two truths affirming both justice and love of God, and if the heretic takes justice to the exclusion of love or love to the exclusion of justice, then the heretic is the man who has narrowed the scope of his convictions. The heretic is a one-eyed Cyclops: He sees, but he does not see enough.

Heresies are thus defined in terms of the orthodoxies from which they have deviated. No man can be a heretic unless there is some regnant orthodoxy whose tenants or dogmas he has violated. Only the twentieth century has given us men boasting of being heretics. This abuse of language suggests an ultimate relativism. Given that orthodoxies are the context within which heresies are intelligible and given that orthodoxies define heresies as being false because deficient, and deficient because exaggerated, it follows that the heretic is the man who languishes or agonizes or snarls in his error. We may take it as evident that no man wants to be in error and that no man consciously is comfortable in preaching or holding fast to falsehood. (This statement will be slightly modified further on in the text.)

This profound reverence for the truth of things made the early Christian Fathers, culminating in St. Augustine, look upon heresy as the most vile of all sins, surpassing by a hundred fold the other evils to which the flesh is heir. Heresy is *the* enemy because heresy denies that what exists does in truth exist. Heresy is the negation of being. As such every heresy—in its typology, at least—is pregnant with the danger of nihilism, the resentment toward creation. The heretic, as Chesterton once wrote, would pull down the lamposts because they shed light—the light of being which is the truth. But when all the lamposts are stricken to the ground and when the world is given over to the darkness of error, then somebody will strike a match and that match will be the hope of orthodoxy because it will be the flickering flame of truth—man's cognitive conformity to things as they are.

No man annealed in an orthodoxy in the truth of which he is utterly convinced is ever completely comfortable in the company of heretics. If he is a belligerent or crusading type, he tries to bring back the prodigal son to the house of his father. If he is a polite fellow, his conversational gambit will avoid touching on the painful subject of the other fellow's heresy. He does this for the sake of public peace, possibly for the sake of friendship. A kind of distance and ultimate alienation is the price paid for loving profoundly an orthodoxy and for loving friends who do not share it. This pain in things human is not felt by the fanatic.

Tolerance is always an act exercised in the service of a political good. The tolerant man recognizes error and recognizes that he can do nothing about it, things being as they are. Tolerance is not indifference. Tolerance is restrained anger. Tolerance is a virtue, but indifference bespeaks a total lack of interest; there are orthodoxies and heresies by the bushel about thousands of subjects, and most of us are utterly indifferent about most of them. Indifference lies outside both heresy and orthodoxy, but if this lack of concern is pushed to the ultimate questions, indifference becomes an insult to the structure of being: "Each man's opinion is as good as the next man's" means "Each man's opinion is as bad as the next man's." "Your opinion is as good as mine" means that my opinion is not really my opinion after all; such statements are insults to the intelligence. Total difference, metaphysical ennui, is the "I don't care" about the world. To tell somebody who has questioned you with intense interest on an issue, "I don't care," is the last and most ultimate of insults that could be hurtled at him. Care belongs orthodoxy *and* heresy; care belongs to truth.

An ultimately indifferent society would know no orthodoxies or heresies. It would not care about anything at all. And that society that cares about nothing is already doomed because the society unwilling to fight must die, and we fight only about those things that elicit our care. If heresy makes no sense except in the context of some orthodoxy, if both are intelligible in the light of caring about the truth, if indifference is a lack of concern about the truth, if indifference bespeaks a refusal to fight about things thought to be true, then it follows that the indifferent society will not go out with a whimper but with a yawn.

Orthodoxy ultimately is the truth as known, and every mistaken orthodoxy is at least a compliment paid to the truth, an innocent failure. No man is saved because he is invincibly ignorant of the truth, but he might well be saved despite his being invincibly ignorant. The proposition is both theological and philosophical.

And the philosophical problem of heresy resides precisely in this paradox. Both paradox and problem are political. Political philosophy cannot determine the content of the common good. That content—the "public orthodoxy" as I have called it for some years—must be judged on non-political grounds. The convictions and affirmations by which any polity conducts its business and celebrates its rites are ultimately non-political. Their roots are religious and metaphysical, reflecting an ultimate brush with reality and a society's reaction thereto. And these ultimate convictions—even the ultimate conviction that there are none—form the spine around which every body politic stiffens itself into a society of men who thus believe and love something in common. Without this common love, as St. Augustine insisted, there simply is no community at all, only an aggregate of isolated individuals.

What the political philosopher *can* do is articulate the conditions which make possible the existence of any viable political order, taking into account the truth that every polity—simply in order to be a polity—must possess some orthodoxy, publicly entertained and privately—so far as possible given the human condition—believed and cherished. In the light of these considerations we can formulate the problem of heresy: How can any society come to terms with its heretics, with those who reject the presuppositions around which the polity has made its very being—presuppositions which, once flouted publicly and violated corporately, dagger that political order to death?

It would seem that there are only four possibilities that can elicit our attention: The society can tolerate its heretics; the society can silence them; the society can kill them or drive them out; the society can reconvert them. Let us move to a consideration of each of these alternatives with the intention of delineating their characteristics.

1. A community can tolerate heretics only when they constitute no immanent threat to the psychic existence of the community itself. This presupposes that the heretical segment of the polity is relatively small and,

if small, not possessed of those instruments of propagation that could make it dominant: the media, the schools, financial and economic preponderance. Thus it was that Louis XIV struck against the Huguenots, not because there were all that many of them, but because their economic power in the France of the seventeenth century made them an internal threat to a nation that had emerged from the wars of religion overwhelmingly Catholic in conviction and practice. Thus it is that England gives its fringe lunatics Hyde Park because they can do the polity no significant harm. Should the advocates of Thuggery or Moloch get strong, such tolerance would be simply intolerable. England could not exist as she has for centuries if there emerged a strong party advocating ritual murder or human sacrifice. Thus it is that a basically Christian society with anti-homosexuality laws can tolerate its practice in a few provided that practice be kept secret and not become a public flouting of the morals of the nation.

2. A society silences its heretics by preventing their spreading their own doctrines. Whereas Anglicanism is a heresy from the standpoint of Roman Catholic orthodoxy, Catholicism is heresy to Anglicanism. When the Elizabethan settlement, confirmed by the Revolution of 1688, assured the victory of that religion in England and its identity with the political order, the Catholic minority was simply silenced and the public expression of Catholic faith was prohibited. Fines levied on Catholics for the profession of their religion successively reduced the numbers of those who adhered to the Old Faith. Toleration only came much later when any possibility that England would return massively to the old religion had long passed.

Silence can take many forms. If the heretic is not talked about, if his books are not reviewed even when published, if he is treated as a nonperson with a non-alternative, he has been effectively reduced to impotence. The mass media use this tactic in their treatment of conservative alternatives to the regnant liberalism. The universities do the same by refusing to hire men whose intellectual positions are considered dangerous to the going orthodoxy. The refusal of many philosophy departments to hire anybody who is not a logical positivist or an historicist is an instance of this tactic of silencing opposition and not permitting students to hear enemies of the dominant intellectual creed.

Silencing can also work the other way: The heretic can silence himself by publicly observing the pieties of the polity of which he is a member. Evidence points to a secret atheism in Cicero that he never expressed publicly because it would have wounded the basis of the Roman order. Charles Maurras, personally a Comptean atheist until the last two years of his life, was the leading champion of the Catholic cause in France in the early decades of this century. Lord Bolingbroke was a High Tory and defender of the Anglican Church in eighteenth century England, but he was a notorious freethinker in his private life. Cicero and Maurras and Bolingbroke were motivated by piety toward the public orthodoxies of their times even though they could not come to accept them as literally true in themselves. In our country there are many professors teaching at church schools proclaiming religions that are not their own. These men, many of them at any rate, simply refrain from disturbing the orthodoxy of their schools; they go about their business, but they do not corrupt the faith of their students. The principle of academic freedom does not extend to destroying the basis upon which a college or university or school is founded.

3. A society can kill heretics it considers dangerous to its very existence. The Athenian Assembly against Socrates is the most dramatic instance in the history of philosophy. The Spanish Inquisition was matched by the Elizabethan slaughter of Jesuits. The public execution of religious heretics was a commonplace in the sixteenth and seventeenth centuries. Religious persecution in time was matched by, then surpassed by, political persecution. The American Civil War was a bloody duel between two factions each claiming that its interpretation of the Constitution was definitive. The advocates of secession today are few and far between, tolerated because they cannot undo Lee's surrender to Grant.

History gives us few examples of such a resounding and irrevocable victory as that of the North in our Civil War. In this business of political orthodoxy, history is more often blurred than not. The French Revolution tore France into two bitterly opposed factions for a century and a half. The two Frances lived side by side waiting for the right moment to dagger each other to death. Even today the public orthodoxy of France is blurred, representing a compromise between Old and New, with a preponderance of weight in favor of revolution and against tradition. Franco's Spain stood as a long interlude after a century-and-a-half civil war between Liberals and Carlists. When nations thus split down the middle in their allegiance to the ultimate things, political stability is the exception and not the rule. A truce is often possible, but no truce ever ended a war. Given the broad consensus that has marked the American political order since the Civil

War—a consensus thin in its substance but accepted overwhelmingly throughout the nation—the party system worked fairly well. Parties are viable only when a common orthodoxy concerning ends is shared by all of them. When parties differ on ends, as in Europe, a common *patria* has ceased to exist.

In a word: No society can tolerate its heretics should they be bent on destroying the going orthodoxy and should they threaten to gain the power needed to do so. Tolerance in such a situation is equivalent to suicide, and the tolerant stance toward a militant and dangerous heresy is always a sign that the going public order has begun to doubt the assumptions underlying its existence. The easy-going tolerance of that most open of all societies, the Germany of the Weimar Republic, was more indifference to ultimates than tolerance. This permitted the victory of Adolf Hitler by way of democratic procedures that Hitler blatantly despised and that he abolished by *fiat*. The kind of tolerance that is no longer tolerable bespeaks a loss of nerve and hence of faith. The descent into sheer relativism and indifference is the act of a society that throws away its power, thus creating a vacuum soon to be filled by a more vigorous creed. The polity that refuses to draw its revolver when the heretical enemy attacks is doomed. Kill or be killed are the only choices open to a beleaguered orthodoxy, whether political or religious or a blend of both.

4. Finally, an older orthodoxy can set for itself the task of reconverting the newer heretics. Poland and the Rhine valley and the larger part of Hungary were reconverted to Catholicism, largely by the Jesuits. But these historical examples are rare because the very nature of heresy involves an act of violence done the orthodoxy from which the heresy is derived as a deviate body. Although young people tend to rebel against the convictions of their fathers, their heretical enthusiasms often die with the decline of the sap of youth. But a heresy maintained well into maturity against an older set of convictions is abandoned with great difficulty. The return of the Anglican Establishment with the Restoration did not eliminate Puritanism from England, and even less was Puritanism eradicated in Scotland. The power of Puritanism was defused only when, by an internal dynamic, Puritanism scattered its strength by shattering into a bewildering swarm of sects.

And this last consideration leads me to attempt an exegesis of the act producing the heresiarch. How does a man fall into heresy and thus come to reject a doctrine previously entertained as the truth? Given that heresy feeds off orthodoxy and is an exaggeration of some truth or constellation of truths found in the rejected doctrine, the heretic, as suggested, narrows the scope of his vision. Why he does this remains a philosophical and historical puzzle that has simply not engaged the attention of students of the subject. Possibly heresies emerge when technological or cultural grounds of an older society shift. Jansenism with its rigid moral stance seems to reflect the spread of the new print culture in France in the seventeenth century. Pascal's rejection of the subtle and even blurred approach to moral problems that marked Jesuit casuistry was marred by a kind of impatience before moral complexities, a desire to have everything moral spread before him in sharp and well defined contours, as would a mathematician, as would any early rationalist for whom philosophy was no longer the give and take of spoken dialogue but the sharply delineated intelligibility of the printed page. Donatism would seem to imply the egalitarianism of the proletarian African Church through its rejection of any ecclesiastical authority, bishop or priest, who had once sinned by denying the Faith during the persecution of Diocletian. Arianism was initially the snobbery of Hellenizing intellectuals who simply could not swallow the formula "Mother of God," the battle cry of the orthodoxy of the streets.

Every heresy is a simplification and hence an unwillingness to maintain in tension a constellation of dogmas. Islam could not take the complexities of Christianity, and its lonely and awful God, bereft of Trinity, does conjure up the vast and empty infinity of the African deserts from which came that crusading religion that forever remains a threat, dormant or active—today again active—against the West. The well-known thesis that Calvinism could not have gotten off the ground without its cultural base in the new commercial society that burgeoned into being in the Europe of the early decades of the modern age has been defended by Sombart and Weber. In no way can heresies be reduced to their technical, economic, or cultural causes, but these causes, if ignored, lead to an exaggerated intellectualism or "spiritualism" in any attempt at understanding the genesis of heresy.

In truth every heresy in its genesis is both retroactive and anticipatory. The heresy spreads its shade backward toward the past and forward into the future. There is no cutoff point at which a man formally abandons his old faith and elects his new one. The heresiarch knows one day that he has already become a heretic, that he has been on that road for quite some time, and that only now has he become conscious of the path he has tread. The flip from orthodoxy to heresy is always retroactive, and the tension within which a man lives in orthodoxy is now known to be released, and the heretic revels in having overextended this or that doctrine and glories in having rejected the whole within which he once lived.

Heresy in its *substantive* content means error, but the determination of precisely what is error falls outside the scope of this essay. These reflections have attempted to throw some light on the *formal* structure of heresy, abstracting from what their author considers to be orthodoxy or heresy. Nonetheless, the typology of heresy is sufficiently public for anyone to study it, and that study recommends itself today, most especially to Christian philosophers, because there are grim signs in this nation of ours that Christianity itself is well on the way to becoming a heresy in the eyes of the courts which are making secularism the new religion of the land.

Western Maryland College, supported by the Methodist Church, was forced to capitulate before litigation that insisted that the school, in order to receive the federal funds it needed to survive, "neither sponsor nor conduct any religious services . . . and remain totally neutral to the spiritual development in a religious sense of its students," and even to refrain from conducting prayers or singing religious hymns in its graduation exercises. Federal courts have struck down Tennessee's law to permit creation to be taught in its schools as an alternative to evolution. This decision was reached on the ground that creation is a religious doctrine.

Are we Christians about to be persecuted on a plethora of issues because a new orthodoxy of secularism has insinuated itself into the very laws of the land? These decisions against the public manifestation of the Christian Faith point to a general collapse in the West of its ancient convictions. In the meantime, before the collapse, secularist law has four ways to do away with Christians: tolerate us if we are reduced to impotence, silence us, kill us or drive us out, convert us to godlessness.

iv.76

THE HOUR IS SHORT:
THE HOUR IS NOW

Can the new electronic technology be sacralized?

The question cannot be answered in any simple-minded fashion. Our answer must, to cite the most important complexity, take into account the difference between an historical ground and an historical figure.

The ground of a civilization is the technology according to which it runs. That technology largely shapes the civilization's psychic and social understructure. When print, for example, replaced the spoken word in Western culture during the late Renaissance, print became the new ground for all Western civilization. Protestantism exalted this technical ground into a self-conscious figure by insisting that salvation comes through the Written Word. Catholicism was not much at home in print culture and never gave it the stature of a figure; but Catholicism did *use* the new technology.

The *Spiritual Exercises* of St. Ignatius Loyola are an instance. The highly elaborate strategy of Jesuit spirituality—with its tactic of a "Composition in Place" in which the retreatant imaginatively places himself in the Garden of Olives and accompanies Our Lord to Golgotha—depends upon the peculiarly heightened visual imagination which is the product of literacy: the Ignation Exercises are in this sense a product of that enormous shift from oral to written culture, the Exercises in no sense transform the new technical ground into a self-conscious religious and aesthetic figure. The missionary who uses a power boat to visit his scattered flock in the Pacific, the lecturer who jets around the country from campus to campus—neither exalts into religious significance his mode of transportation, unless, of course, his message is one of salvation by technology. Sanity in these matters involves never confounding ground with figure. A mark of gnostic messianism is the investing of any ground of society with

174

transcendental significance. The other side of this coin is that an older ground *can* be retrieved *as a figure,* in play and art, without risk to sound philosophy or religion.

It is my contention that in the nature of electric technology, and what it is doing to our society and the men who live in it, are seeds of hope for the development of an Incarnational politics, a Catholic politics, whose lineaments can be dimly glimpsed on the horizon today.

The problem of sacralization in the post-modern age is enormously complicated because Western man, especially American Western man, lives today within *two* technical structures, the mechanical and the electric (cf. Wilhelmsen and Bret, *The War in Man: Media and Machines*, University of Georgia Press, 1970). Although the electric is rapidly replacing the mechanical, that replacement has not yet been fully achieved. Thus liturgical attempts to make the mechanical a sacral figure always collapse—because the mechanical is still very much with us. Churches that look like factories bore us because there are so many factories around.

The blurring of technologies in our historical moment demands a reaching back, *way back,* for appropriate figures for worship. The new Mass, to indicate our most striking collapse within the Church on this issue, is entirely too full of print and reading to be fit liturgy for the historical moment—a moment in which literacy is, to be sure, less and less a ground for the going order, but still very much a necessity thanks to the crossing of the new order with the still quite vigorous older mechanical order. These distinctions are utterly lost on those who have inflicted the "relevant," "contemporary" liturgy on us, thinking that worship must march in step with the going technological ground when, in fact, it ought to do just the reverse.

More than twenty years ago John Cogely, in a stroke of generosity and genuis in total contrast to the overarching direction of his teaching, wrote a splendid article called "The Gold and the Glory" in which he spoke of hurrying as a boy, daily through cold Chicago mornings, with the snow crunching under his young feet, to Mass at his parish church. There, in the darkness of those silent gestures of early worship, he found—God? Cogley confessed that he did not know and that he was too far removed from his youth even to make a judgment. He suspected, however, that what he sought and found was beauty. The Latin Mass—its majesty, its silence, its resonances—all of this contrasted with the bare mechanical ground of the Chicago of his boyhood. In that contrast, in seeking beauty as a figure, he found the God of the Tabernacle. (Cogley, of course, did not structue his analysis of his own experience in these terms, if only because the *Gestalt* technique of figure-ground analysis had not yet emerged; but the reality of his experience is all the more poignant because it was not clothed in a scientific construct.)

The old Latin Mass in a slum or in a ghetto Catholic neighborhood was counterpoint to the barren mechanical uniformity and shabbiness without. The Latin Mass came into its own, most truly, within the industrial age. That Mass had all the "archaism" that anthropologist Victor Turner finds in all successful liturgy (see the commentary on his work by my esteemed colleague W. Marshner in "Contra Gentiles," *Triumph,* Dec. '72). Those of us who, like Cogley, grew up in such neighborhoods knew in our bones exactly what worship was all about. The door to our parish church was our one opening into transcendence. Garry Wills knows these things too: therefore he hates his childhood.

Another illustration of the structure of the figure-ground relationship: Medieval chivalry depended, formally, on the earlier invention of the stirrup: no stirrup, no mounted knight. But the chivalric ideal really came into its own within the commercial and town society that developed in Burgundy, as Archduke Otto von Habsburg has pointed out in his work on *Charles V.* The commercial ground accentuated all the more the knightly ideal. When pushed to an extreme, this contrast between figure and ground produces Don Quixote and Sancho Panza.

Technologies change men and these changes simply cannot be fitted in to the Aristotelian category of "accidents" as opposed to "substance." These changes are not incidental; in many cases they strike the very springs of spirituality. Here, Aristotelian psychology is far more faithful to the facts than Aristotelian political philosophy. The latter is sound so far as it goes but radically incomplete because it does not take seriously Aristotle's own contention that man is just as much a *homo faber* as he is a rational animal; that, in fact, he discovers his rationality in his *techne* or art. Unless a man study technological structures and study them sympathetically as objects worthy of the highest kind of philosophical attention, he cannot seriously study Incarnational politics.

The issue demands elucidation. Western political philosophy has never taken account of, nor speculated seriously upon, the technological order. The Integrist antipathy for machine technology as well as for the newer electronic technology is a visceral reaction. This antipathy is not reasoned; or, if reasoned as in Marcel, it fails to distinguish between technologies and to take account of what technologies do to men, what effects they produce in society and in nature. This failure to study the ontology of technics can, I think, be corrected in large part by the development of a more delicate understanding of figure-ground relationships.

Many traditionalists hate the automobile with a passion. The passion is in some ways understandable, but the hate is superfluous. The automobile will certainly survive in the electric world—but increasingly only as play or leisure. The new electric technology will punish the automobile if it is taken too seriously; what the radar screen does to a speeding car is an early example of the emerging relationship between the two technologies.

Another illustration of the complex figure-ground relationship is the current popularity of the agrarian way of life. The agrarian ideal, be it the Distributism of Chesterton and Belloc or the platform of the American Southern Agrarians, is today a real possibility again—but only if it be taken as symbolic figure, as play. If taken seriously as a potential ground for society, the old agrarian style is simply not viable.

This fact indicates where the line is drawn between romantics and realists. Replacing a technological ground is the dream of romantics—the mistake, for example, of communes like Owens Farm. Restoration of the pastoral life as the ground of society is not merely practically difficult, it is theoretically impossible. For a symbolic figure can alter the going ground of society only insofar as and for as long as it remains a figure, a contrast. Communes live off the society they reject. Were they to become independent, they would cease to alter the non-communard society.

Technologies are not neutral instruments, like tools lying on a work bench in a garage; more than instruments, technologies are what these instruments do to men, how they alter them in the most profound and subtle ways.

A tribe makes sense if it plays. It comes apart when it takes itself seriously. Rejection of the going order has collapsed, and will continue to, to the degree to which it is done not in a spirit of play but in one of work. When you play at being a farmer or sailor, you are really replaying symbolically an earlier ground. But this is not to say that such replaying is without significance, because the replay today is *more* real than the intitial play: this is why you sense that you have not really seen the pass on the gridiron until it is played back for you. As a medium for watching football, television is far superior to a seat in the stadium. And replay is a mark of electronic technology. The replay is the conscious articulation of what is being, even has been done: it is a "saying" of being—*dicere: Verbum: Word.* Replay is not second rate—unless the Son of God is a second-rate God. He is, after all, the perfect Expression of all that the Father Is. Son is Figure to the Ground of the Father.

Our secularist society today offers enormous opportunities for symbolic replay of the sacral. Conscious sacralization against a background of secularism is all the more sacral. Did not Chesterton say that in order to see white on black you had to see black on white? Today everything in history can be replayed.

And this leads me to what I have called the Augustinian/*Opus Dei* posture: infiltrate the going order and Christianize it from inside itself, altogether without altering existing institutions or structures. Neither St. Augustine nor anyone I know of in the *Opus Dei* suggested that this attitude was anything more than a tactic, and a tactic that is open to any Christian who wishes to incarnate his faith in the world. If, however, this tactic is raised to the level of theory then it blends into Western political philosophy's general absentmindedness about technology. Technologies are, to be sure, instruments that can be used well or poorly: good content on TV presumably is better than bad content; pistols used to shoot criminals are better than pistols in the hands of criminals shooting innocent folk. This is not philosophy; it is simply common sense.

But technologies, more deeply, change men and change them all the more significantly to the degree to which they do not know that they are being changed. Integrist rejection bespeaks an at least emotional conviction that technologies do something to men; technological "neutralism" does not even see that far.

To look at the world and attempt to understand it in terms of technological grounds can illuminate history and help us prepare for tomorrow. It might render possible a truly realistic Incarnational politics—a bringing of Christ into the very marrow of society—for it would remind us that He did not disdain the technical order—He was no Greek—but made His living as a carpenter and thus did what the rest of us do: extend ourselves in space and time and transform the world technically, artistically.

Were we to turn our philosophical attention to the formal study of technologies, I believe we would see that our own electric ground makes society particularly susceptible today to being affected by Catholic symbolic figures. I think we would find, in fact, that the ground may finally be ready for what the Holy Fathers have been asking for in their social encyclicals throughout a century and a half. We would discover that the *personal* world we have long wanted and preached is already here—possibly it is altogether too personal for *us*, formed, as we have been, in an older mechanical order of things. We would find, if we have the imagination to sweep away all the moralistic and basically Puritan nonsense about the evils of television, that we have been back in the Middle Ages—*formaliter sed non materialiter*—for quite some time now. Television and electronics in general are far more compatible with the Catholic spirit than are printed books. The new technology imitates the ubiquitous playfulness of the angels. Christ, after all, had some harsh things to say about writing; it was Martin Luther who extolled the written word. Let us accept the new barbarism and Christianize it. It is far closer to the sixth and seventh centuries than we have been in a long time. Charlemagne, were he alive today, would flunk fourth-grade reading.

I am convinced that some of the nineteenth and early twentieth-century battles alluded to ealier in this essay, which helped to seal the defeat of Christendom, would end in Catholic victories if they could be refought today. The statement, of course, is not to be taken in terms of history understood as a trajectory, any linear section of which could be lifted out of the tracks and placed further down the line. No, the point is that Christendom's late battles were fought by zealous Catholics still reposing upon a popular culture, buttressed by a splendid clergy truculent against compromise and deeply committed to the Church—advantages we sorely lack today; but these battles were fought against the grain of the age. Now, however, the age is running away from the monolithically mechanical and individualistic structure of the past that militated against Catholic victory. In the past we lost everywhere, not because our people were always and everywhere bunglers (some were, of course: we Catholics are not good efficiency experts), but because the weight of the times conspired against us.

The Holy Fathers were preaching a decentralized economy and society when the existent technology was driving the West toward an ever-increasing centralization. Our thinkers extolled a rural society and the small farm, the artisan and the small businessman, when these were losing their viability. The linear and rationalist bias of the times went against that sense of the mystical and the transcendent which quickens our Catholic inheritance.

But the linear and rationalist bias today is gone as a ground of our civilization. Using the physics of the last century, we cannot even do the calculations needed to get astronauts on the moon. Democratic individualism and old-fashioned classical liberalism, surviving as hot-house figures in movements like Libertarianism, are obsolescent; Libertarianism is a figure without a ground. The classical, book-oriented society and education inherited from the Renaissance, perpetuated somewhat preciously in our time by the Great Books Foundation and certain academic institutions based upon the proposition that the gates of Heaven open with the covers of a number of well-defined and selected books—all this is simply funny when looked at from the standpoint of Catholic Doctrine, but it is dogma to dozens of Catholic educators. Our proper heritage is the historic and defined insistence on the preeminence of the *spoken* Tradition: the Canon of Holy Scripture, remember, is as it is because the speaking Church said it should be; therefore, it was and is. The Holy Father is infallible when he *speaks* from the Chair, not when he writes something down. The illiteracy of our American youth is no barrier to evangelization. What stake do we have in literacy anyhow? Is an ability to read books a prerequisite for the Kingdom of God? Old William George Ward used to say he wanted a papal bull with his *Times* at breakfast. We ought to want a papal discourse weekly by television. That would put an end to the incredible array of bureaucracies and "interpreters" now standing between the Vicar of Christ and His people. (Liberal Catholicism is an effort to escape the consequences of the invention of the telegraph. Once the telegraph was invented, according to McLuhan, papal infallibility had to be defined; technologically we did not need to go through intermediaries anymore. This is all the more true in the age of television: liberal Catholicism is a throwback to the nineteenth century.)

And this moves me to the last consideration of this very tentative essay. What Incarnational politics needs far more fundamentally than a political program is a a political philosophy. Programs come and go but philosophy, as we understand the term in the Catholic Tradition, attempts to discover something permanently true (even if the permanently true concern itself with the ephemeral: after all, *we* are all ephemeral!). The Truth will set you free. Nothing could be more refreshing in the political smog in which we live today than a genuine political philosophy. Such a political philosophy—sophisticated: deeply traditional: thoroughly post-modern—could light up action already under foot and point toward the direction in which action might move.

It happens that the potential of such a philosophy is accentuated by the fact that ideology is rapidly dying everywhere (cf. my *Telepolitics*, in collaboration with Jane Bret, Tundra Press, Montreal and New York, 1972). Marxists are in a panic about their own obsolescence. Ideology is being replaced by concrete interests which have little to do with abstract "issues" or "ideas." A neighborhood needs cleaning up? Help clean it up. A rapid-transit system needs to be established in this or that town? Help establish it. Youngsters need better food at the local school? Get them food! And hand in hand with this personal character of our world today goes an emphasis on the personal nature of politics.

Now the curious thing is that our philosophical tradition has not paid much attention to personality in politics. Nor do I know of a treatise in classical political philosophy that is devoted the the "you-scratch-my-back-and-I'll-scratch-yours" syndrome. I know no treatise that looks to the nature of charisma in leaders and to why men follow them, cost what it might cost. In classical philosophical theory, I imitate, if I am a good man, the best, the aristocrat. This works, however, only in an aristocratic society. Hilaire Belloc's *The Nature of Contemporary England* demonstrated, with a clairvoyant brilliance, that neither democrats nor royalists can found the basis of an aristocratic order because democrats and royalists simply do not admire aristocrats. And Dr. Alvaro D'Ors—Spanish Carlist and preeminent authority on Roman law—has authored a study of familial politics (*Legitimidad familiar y formas de gobierno*) that carries Belloc's demonstration further. D'Ors shows that three typical situations emerge in Western political life: (1) a society structured around the individual in which the family is denied any political role is necessarily democratic; (2) a society, such as Republican Rome or eighteenth to early twentieth-century England, that divides the populace into those with illustrious names and those without names, no matter how famous and rich these latter might be, is necessarily republican; (3) a society whose broad base is familial reposes its authority naturally in a dynasty, a traditional monarchy whose very family sums up the familial nature of the polity. In

181

the past these three forms were circumscribed territorially. With the abolition of frontiers today due to electric conditions, with the growth of the new tribalism that marks our time, all three forms mingle and interface. Television has brought back the dynastic principle. The Nixons are far more a royal couple than their crowned Scandinavian counterparts. the new American dynasties are in constellation: Kennedys, Percys, Rockefellers, Eisenhowers, etc. People tend to vote for names and not for platforms. The *nomen* has returned as political talisman. This new American style is nowhere more dramatically illustrated than in our public funerals. Nobody buries the great with more solemnity and splendor than we do!

But this new ritualism in our politics has not abolished the older American tradition of spartan, democratic individualism; it has made of this individualism a symbolic figure. Thus does the "work ethic" assume its central place in Nixonian rhetoric when it has no practical place in real American life. But even as older forms jostle with the newer, we find that personal loyalty tends to dominate the going political order. All legitimacy is again based on personal loyalty. And we Catholics, thanks to our personalist religion—we believe in a Three-Personed God, not in any abstract ethic—are uniquely at home in this kind of political order. We do not take secular issues very seriously because we are cynical about life; but we do take persons very seriously—and very little else indeed! We like to play with secular issues, but we play with them as well as we do because we do not invest them with messianic solemnity. Electronic conditions have thrown up, as ground, a new personalist order made for a people like us. You cannot ideate deep thoughts electronically today. You can only participate in a familial and personalist order. The technical ground is ripe for a Catholic figure, for an incarnational politics.

Yet I am haunted by the scars of our defeats, by my fear that Catholic traditionalists—and I am a Catholic traditionalist; indeed, I am a Carlist—will not respond to this splendid moment in time, that the Integrist temptations will paralyze our wills; that we will dissipate our energies condemning the wrong things or condemning the right things for the wrong reasons; or that we will slip conventionally into the going order and swim like fish who know everything except that they are in the water, totally absentminded about our moment in history.

The hour is very short indeed. Everything happens so fast today that tomorrow is conceived as a possibility only after it happened yesterday as a fact. We must seize this moment for the sake of Eternity. If we do not do so, we will not be worthy of our heroic traditionalist forefathers. Alfonso Carlos, in exile, dedicated his land to the Sacred Heart. General Ongania surrendered the vast plains of Argentina to the Immaculate Heart of Mary. Dollfuss died with a bullet in his back on his knees before Our God. Colonel Stauffenberg crumpled, a living cross, before Nazi machine guns. They, at least, had the honor of stitching banners to Our Exiled King in their hearts. Will we have done even that much when it is our turn to die?

iv.73

INCARNATIONAL POLITICS

Don Alfonso Carlos, exiled and legitimate King of Spain, more monk than soldier but very much the soldier indeed, dedicates his homeland to the Sacred Heart of Jesus: this, now, more than fifty years ago. General Carlos Ongania, President of the Argentinian Republic and in full power, dedicates his nation in the teeth of clerical opposition to the Immaculate Heart of Mary: this, now, a scant five years ago.

The fifty years marking off the distance between these two Catholic gestures have been full of controversy concerning the proper relationships that ought to govern Church and state in Catholic societies. Full confessionality, the *thesis* of older theologians, became the *hypothesis* of the now fading school of John Courtney Murray. What was once considered an optimum was reduced to the status of a tolerated inferiority. Alfonso Carlos came and went and if he is remembered at all, he is remembered for having commanded the pope's army of volunteers aginst the Italian Masonic State in 1870: another failure. Ongania seized power after having been moved by a profound religious experience that followed on a private retreat structured around the Exercises of St. Ignatius of Loyola: within two years he had frittered away his credit, and he too has stepped off the stage of history. Argentina today still waits on the sacramentalizing of her political and social order even as Spain seems hell bent on desacralizing her own.

The beads of failure marking Catholic politics in our time could be extended into a rosary of desolation. Those of us who are interested in Catholic politics could esaily follow the counsel of despair and conclude that God has not willed us to win a world for His Son, Our King. We might well conclude that we have somehow failed, that we have bungled our chances, or that the tide of modernity has simply been too powerful to swim against with any reasonable hope of success. This last conclusion, of course, is the mark of Integrism.

Possibly an insight into the Integrist spirit, the temptation peculiar to Catholic traditionalists, might open the door, not to immediate political success, but to the very nature of an Incarnational politics. For Integrism, I shall argue, does not understand the Incarnation in the political order; but Integrism *thinks* that it does. And this is the rub! The roots of this self-deception lie hidden in history. They lie hidden, most especially, in the history of political philosophy.

I use the term "Integrism" with great hesitation, for it means different things in different nations. Brazilian and Portuguese Integrism simply meant allegiance to the legitimate royal line of Don Miguel against liberalism: in the Portuguese and Brazilian sense of the term, I am an Integrist. In Spain the term was used to designate a schism within the Carlist movement between those who backed the allies during World War I and those who did not: the Integrists were these latter and they placed themselves against their own claimant to the throne, Don Jaime. Integrism, psychologically, bespeaks a kind of total intransigence against the going order. I am honored to have been called an Integrist in the Spanish press by liberals. But the philosophical and theological usage of the term is largely French: it does not designate a specific political commitment but rather a way of looking at the world, a tactic of survival elaborated since the French Revolution by men and women whose lives are often splendid witnesses to the truth of the Faith. An Integrist is a kind of 150 percent Catholic, at least in his own reading of himself. In this sense of the term, Integrism—presumably—is at least an aberration; when entertained consciously, it is a sin. The term is taken throughout this study to designate the aberration.

The late Willmoore Kendall, certainly America's most brilliant interpreter of its own political experience, used to complain that there was no specifically Catholic political philosophy. There was, so went his complaint, a handful of nineteenth and twentieth-century papal encyclicals that addressed themselves to specific evils of the times; there were a few brilliant pamphleteers such as Chesterton and Belloc; there was the astonishing but lonely figure of Donoso Cortes, himself a practicing diplomat and an *ad hoc* writer; there were a few French sociologists; three or four nineteenth-century Spaniards and—no more! Something of a paltry body of literature for a Faith which made Europe and whose contributions to every other dimension of life defy the specialist's itch for cataloging.

Political philosophy historically has been a rearview mirror, an "after-the fact" articulation of a passing or dying age. In this sense of the term, political philosophy is a creative figure whose historical ground has shifted. Plato and Aristotle articulate the structure of the Greek *polis* at the very moment when the *polis* has ceased to be viable politically and when Alexander the Great is fashioning his huge empire. There is not a whisper about the politics of empire in either Plato or Aristotle; this is all the more remarkable in Aristotle because he had been the tutor of the new lord of the world. The *Republic* of Cicero is a nostalgic backward glance by a reactionary republican to a world that was dying around him and whose successors finally daggered him to death. St. Augustine's *City of God* is principally a *theology* of politics, not a philosophy. Let the Christians take over institutions already fashioned by pagans, he reasoned, and run them better and more honorably than do the pagans themselves. Augustine's theology of politics resonates today in the *Opus Dei* tactic of Christians doing better what everybody else is doing—running banks, filling cabinet posts, building bridges, and so on. This tactic essentially ignores, without necessarily denying, the religious *roots* of institutions. The tactic sees all institutions as neutral and understands "incarnationalism" in terms of occupying and Christianizing whatever happens to exist socially and politically.

A return to the calssical "rear-view mirror" marked medieval political speculation. An entirely new world had been created between the death of Augustine and the birth of Aquinas. This world, the *res publica christiana*, was not run by good and saintly Christians administering institutions fashioned by pagans; it was marked, rather, by good and bad and indifferent men administering *institutions fashioned under the aegis of Christianity*. The gradual disappearance of slavery and the rise of the free peasant; the purging of the chivalric ideal of its Islamic origins and its full incorporation into Europe; the sacramentalizing of kingship; the decentralization of authority and its diffusion throughout a largely self-governing society—all of the typical medieval political institutions would have been impossible had it not been for the yeast of the Faith ever working its health into the body politic. But none of the great medieval theologians comment on the situation in which they were living. As though they were blind to the on-going politics of their own time, they comment—when they formally bend their attention to political theory—on Plato and Aristotle, on a social order already in full decay eighteen hundred and more years earlier.

The articulation of medieval Christendom does not occur until the late eighteenth and nineteenth centuries. What the Middle Ages did for Greece, the nineteenth-century traditional Catholics did for the Middle Ages. The horror of the Revolution, itself the product of a kind of philosophical mind—the rationalist—moved Catholics to meditate on what a truly Christian political order would be. But it must be remembered that this meditation took place in the nineteenth century. We cannot understand the Catholic reaction to the Revolution if we isolate it from that century's prevailing tone.

Thus the Catholics who articulated medieval Christendom in the last century were initially confused in their theorizing because many of them simply identified sane political life with the *ancien régime*, itself the effect of a rationalism and a technological revolution that had already run through two hundred and fifty years before it found its logical conclusion in the Revolution. Catholic traditionalists almost had to see the Middle Ages through the prism of glasses ground in the Age of Rationalism. Then, too, while the content of the Catholic reaction was motivated by the Faith, its *form* was universal to the age of classical liberalism.

The technological ground of the nineteenth century was mechanical: this is the age that produced the steamship, the railroad, the percussion rifle, the internal combustion engine, the enormous and inhuman factory cities of Leeds and Birmingham and Manchester. But every society expresses itself poetically and artistically, in style, by retrieving an *earlier* ground and converting it into an artistic symbol, or, to use the language of *Gestalt* psychology, a "figure." In the nineteenth century, the style that seized the mind and sensibility of the West was Romanticism—a kind of idealizing of the medieval past linked with a buying back, in poetry and philosophy and life-style, of nature, which was at the very moment being raped by mechanization. The Romantic movement was the full flowering of the Enlightenment in the eighteenth century and in its nineteenth-century consequence, classical liberalism. The last century's apostles of tomorrow, of progress, of mechanization and centralization, were themselves liberal reactionaries who longed to repose once again in the glories of ancient Greece, or, at the very least, to identify spiritually with the Noble Savages of North America. Neoclassical art is itself an instance of the romanticizing of antiquity. A man simply has to stroll through government Washington or study the French painting that followed on the collapse of Napoleon III's tin Empire to grasp this truth. The world was filling up with machines but everybody governing that world and living handsomely off the machines was thinking about ancient Greece and Rome, but especially Greece.

Catholic traditionalists, meanwhile, with a fine sense of horror before the dehumanization surrounding them, with the abandonment politically of the Catholic inheritance, reacted to the Middle Ages, not to antiquity. We can almost define the opposition: everybody was living in a machine world; the dominant half of that world thought about classical democracy; the large Catholic minority turned medieval. *Nobody* wanted to look at the nineteenth century, the century in which they were living; nobody, that is, except the popes.

The initial reaction of Catholics to the Revolution had little about it at all of the romantic. In both France and Spain as well as in Metternich's German system, the Catholic political response was couched in the name of "the natural order of things." Christendom had always been structured into social orders or "estates"; it must be so restructured against the new power of industrial money and the intellectuality of the universtities and the press. The weight of public orthodoxy had always reposed upon the land and not the cities because virtue is of the land; it must so repose again. The pact of peoples with their dynasties reflected tha pact of God with His Church; this pact must be defended against all republican ventures and against the pretensions of the new middle classes. The crowns of Europe had always defended the little man against the power of big money; that defense must be reinvigorated; the crowns must be freed from the shackles of party domination. The whole spirit of the Treaty of Vienna, backed by a natural desire to see matters return to where they had been before the Revolution and the nightmare of Napoleon, was buttressed by a new Catholic awareness of what medieval politics had been—but an awareness sifted through the prism of the Romantic age.

But the Catholics' idealization of the medieval order went hand in hand with a very hardheaded conviction that the *res publica christiana* represented "reality" whereas the Revolution represented messianic dreams. This understanding was well illustrated in Spain at the Constitution of Cadiz, which met in 1810 and broke up in 1814. The "innovators" (*los innovadores*) were the Frenchified liberals. The word *liberal* dates from that congress. The "conservatives" (*los conservadores*) simply wanted to roll the clock back to the eighteenth century. This affection for the "old regime" was rendered possible by an absolute blindness to the nadir to which Christian civilization had sunk in the eighteenth century. The fact that poor Louis XVI, with more irony than history credits him with, insisted that the See of Paris at least ought to belong to a prelate who had the decency to believe in God was lost on Catholic "conservatives" who failed to see that the Church was flowering again in their time and had been in terrible shape in the age they were romanticizing. The "renovators" (*los renovadores*), precursors in Spain of the perpetually vigorous but never quite successful Carlist movement, wanted to go *behind* the Age of Absolutism and find the true political roots of their nation in a tradition that still survived with the people and that had its origins in the High Middle Ages. These "renovators," the first Catholic traditionalists, were right. They *did* stand for the natural order of things in their own world, though it was a curious, underground world having little to do with the dominant liberal institutions that were occupying the front of the stage of the era. But before the nineteenth century was over, that "natural order" upon which the "renovators" based themselves just withered away. Mechanization in the technical order and secularization in the political order destroyed the broad rural base upon which Catholic reaction had rested. A *renovador* in Spain could say with pride in 1830: "I stand for the nation with its traditions and its way of life." He could no longer say that in 1900. The so-called immutable "naturalness" of what remained of the medieval order was dead in most places and hung on in others as rough but merely picturesque survivals.

It was this age that produced the despair of Integrism and, in so doing, wounded Incarnational politics.

The Romantic "figure" of the nineteenth and early twentieth centuries suited the Catholic temper even when it was used by non-Catholics. Catholic culture is full of color and flair. We invented pomp and circumstance. Go through any picture book of World War I and note the gorgeous plumage of the age, the emperors and kings as splendid as peacocks, their guards magnificent in scarlet and blue. But then remember that this is the war of trenches, of Big Bertha, of hundreds of thousands of men sacrificed at Verdun for a few inches of real estate. The violence of mechanical technology was covered over by a romantic façade and more novels about a return to nature were written then, when nature was being systematically destroyed, than ever before. The castle loomed large as myth in literature and politics when the factory glowed as reality. The rhetoric might suggest that the author of these lines is passing a moral judgment or expressing a preference; nothing could be further from the truth. Any sophisticated anthropology today teaches us that the articulated symbolic structure of an age is always something other than, often opposed to, its technological base. The myths with which we interpret ourselves are usually throw-backs.

The political symbolism of today is highly mechanical because the new technical ground of the age is electric. The resurrection of the work ethic by Mr. Nixon, his neat and somber clothes, his business-like image, are all new figures which retrieve the mechanical nineteenth century within the electronic twentieth. (In the meantime, of course, "the kids" react all the way back to the Middle Ages and crawl our cities dressed in motley.)

All of this is background to a consideration of the Integrist temptation in its contemporary effect on Incarnational politics. Integrism today is a political figure without a ground. Embittered by failures everywhere, Integrism tends to freeze Catholic political order, to identify it as necessarily bound up in the *forms* of some privileged moment in human history, usually the Middle Ages, occassionally the Age of the Fathers or even the baroque seventeenth century. For this reason, Integrism is marked by a despair of victory in the political order. This translates itself into a spiral movement "within," in which the Integrist seeks to incarnate the Faith in specifically symbolic ways in his own life, in that of his family, and in that of like-minded fellows. The back to the soil movement of American Catholics in the 1950s was an instance of the Integrist spirit, as was the 1960s' effort to retrieve from the remote past a supposedly "purer" liturgy than the one that we inherited from Trent. As these examples suggest, Integrism is elitist by nature. It tends to be excessively moralistic and to read damnation everywhere on the broad screen of the contemporary world: We—the chosen ones—have the key to the truth; we alone know what it means to be Catholic in a truly dense and incarnated fashion.

The new tribalization of our society, pressured into being by electronic conditions of decentralization, has given to the Integrists a golden opportunity—we might again say, a temptation—"to do their thing" just as everybody else is doing his own. A Catholic tribe wrapped around with a golden political symbolism woven out of a sacral past could very well co-

190

exist with the swarm of new (and old) tribes that have lately proliferated throughout the western world. Today *every* historical past has become a present. Why not another resurrected tribe, the Catholic one?

The solution is attractive. It is probably viable, perhaps even necessary as a holding action. But in the long run, the Catholic tribal solution is going to face danger from the Integrist temptation, and if that danger is not seen clearly, Catholic politics may turn in an elitist direction, in the direction of Port Royal—may in fact abandon any effort to evangelize and hence truly incarnate the Word of God in history.

The danger arises from the fact that, while Integrists understand the theology of Incarnational politics, they do not understand its anthropology. In order to grasp this we must indicate, if only in a sketch, the structure of Incarnational politics.

Classical political philosophy sees the political order as ultimate and self-sufficient. The classical *polis* gives opportunity, and sums up, the very best in human nature. Within the "City" there is secular salvation. Even the Roman awareness of immortality was bent to the political order. The dead, mere "shades" of what they had been in life, are sheltered by the living and the very gods themselves are *our* civil gods: hence Varro's coining of the famous term, "civil theology."

But the Incarnation of the Son of God in time, united with the dictate to "restore all things in Christ," calls for a sacramentalizing of the real, a hallowing of creation, an extension of the sacramental system by which Christ saves through His Church. This laying of hands upon the political and social order transfigures institutions, sanctifies work, and turns everything human into a sacramental. Wayside shrines: blessed fishing fleets: blessed burial grounds: guilds dedicated to the saints and to the Mother of God: oaths exchanged in court and vowed under promises made to God: coronation rituals woven into sacral liturgy: the lively promotion by magistrates of sound morals: the material aid given by government to Church in its evangelical mission—all these things and hundreds others like them tend to weave a golden web of sacrality around the world and to spread outwards into space and carry through time the Incarnaiton of Our Lord. In Danielou's terminlolgy such a politics makes it easier, even possible, for the poor to bear the tragedies and hardships of life with Christian fortitude and joy.

Incarnational politics, therefore, add a dimension to the politcal order. Politics remains politics; it is not transformed into religion. The world remains the world. But to the political ground of life there is added a new religious figure, a dimension which internally affects what would otherwise be merely secular. Once the Incarnation happened, a neutral politics became a contradiction. Every polity tends either toward sacrality or away from it, tends toward rendering efficacious the Incarnation or away from this efficacy. Anthropologically, the religious figure thrown over society tends inexorably, if slowly, to alter the social ground. Political institutions, abstractly "secular," tend to become molded by their own sacramental dimension. The faimly is not a specifically Christian institution, but the Christian family gets stronger and takes on new meaning in a Catholic order. Human dignity is not something specifically Christian, but men gain a newer and deeper dignity within the Catholic order. Responsibility and self-government are not uniquely Christian but Christian societies seem to create and then shore up institutions which permit a maximum exercise of personal responsibility and autonomy.

I suggest that Integrism, despite its laudable intentions, misunderstands the figure-ground relationship in Incarnational politics. *Because*—so runs the Integrists' implicit argument—a sacral politics existed at such and such a time in history, the very same set of institutions that marked such a polity must be restored in its integrity. Integrists are restorationists. To a thorough-going Integrist the sacral *figures* he perceives as having marked an older political order must become the political *ground* of any new Christian order. Permit me to cite a few examples: if the small farmer and artisan marked an earlier Christian polity, then we must rearrange the economy in order that we might re-establish small farming and artisanry as dominant ways of life; if small shops dotted an earlier and healthier order, then we must abolish super-markets; if the horse marked earlier orders in warfare and transportation, then let us abolish jets and automobiles. But a figure can never be restored as a ground. I can bring back the horse as sport and as play but I cannot bring back the horse as a dominant ground of transportation, anymore than I can turn the American hotel system into a network of medieval monasteries serving foot-sore travelers. The older ground can become an aesthetic and liturgical symbol, as the inn had become a symbol of Christian cheer and warmth by Chesterton's time. But nobody in old England found in the inn the density of spiritual significance that Chesterton found in it—because inns were part of society's ground. The institution had to become archaic—not necessarily dead, let it be understood (the archaic is not dead)—for it to be useful as a symbol of the good life.

Because he is so fascinated by his own tradition's historical models, the Integrist cannot react intelligently—imaginatively and creatively—to his own situation in time. He has the good sense to come to see, finally, that the restoration is not about to come. Therefore he despairs.

As already suggested, this despair could be converted into some kind of positive action, into hope, because the new electronic conditions have simply rendered the older mechanical ground of life obsolete as ground (if, however, very much alive as figure), thus making possible any kind of life-style, even a medieval or baroque life-style. Abolition of space-time limits linked with massive decentralization of industry, causative of the imminent disappearance of the big city as a viable social institution, creative itself of the new tribes—that is the new technology which dominates the world today; and *that* is the ground, the ground needing sacralization even as it makes possible any and every previous life-style as symbolic figure. Now, it has always been very difficult to sacralize *any* technology in the West. Either technics are turned into a religion as in progressivism; or technics are hated as in Integrism; or technics are ignored as in philosophy. Can the new electronic technology be sacralized?

iii.73

REMEMBERING

CAPTAIN GUILLIERMO WRIEDT

Guillermo Wriedt, *Capitán de Travesia*, has been master of the barque *Tellus* for twenty-eight years. Before that he was master of the *Claudina*—the old *Clan Ferguson*—and before that he sailed in ships that no man but he remembers. He was born some sixty-four years ago in the port town of Flensburg in North Germany, on the Danish border. As a boy, he knew my father's family, but as my people were wagonmakers and as he went to sea at the age of twelve, the acquaintance was a short one. His first vessel was a three-masted schooner in the North Sea lumber trade; she carried a complement of four, and they were at the pumps twenty-four hours a day. It was a cold and bitter baptism to a life promising only work, danger, and whatever satisfaction can be wrested from a career of combat and communion.

Those were the days before the German merchant service had brassbounders. This was still a uniquely British institution. Wealthy parents apprenticed their boys to some big shipping company, secure, independent, promising rapid advancement after four years of indentured hell. Boys from the Continent who wanted to become maritime officers worked their way up through the hawsepipe. They went to sea hardly more than children and many of them soon quit in disgust and drifted back to shore to set up shops in the big seatowns or to take again to the land. Others kept to the sea but settled back in the fo'c's'l and gave up any dreams they might have had of gaining a station abaft the mainmast. A few carried on and gathered through the years their packets of discharge papers, testifying to honourable service in ship after ship. They learned navigation; they mastered the art of loading and discharging cargo; they studied rigging and sails and the winds. They presented themselves for second mate's papers and, if they passed, they went out and looked for a ship, preferably in some line offering advancement and a vessel of their own after years of service.

Many of these last, however, weary of the routine and hardship, drifted to the Far East where they mixed in with the strange life of the Orient and became one with that swarm of western adventurers who sought in those lands fortune and relief from the rigours of the sea.

A few came to the Americas, brought down here by I know not what satisfaction that forever attracts the men of the North to the regions of the South. Wilhelm Wriedt was one of these last: a German sailor who became a Peruvian citizen about 1912.

He advanced rapidly to the *Claudina*, first as mate and then as master. The *Claudina* was an iron barque launched in 1876 from the Clyde. Christened the *Clan Ferguson*, she weighed 799 tons, was 199.2 feet in length, 31.6 in breadth, and 19.3 in depth. She was the work of the old Scottish firm of J. Reid of Glasgow: one of Dunlop's nine "Clans," she outlived them all. She was a beautiful ship, and I have seen her photograph, mounted and occupying a place of honour in the house of Captain Wriedt. I have it on his own word that she was a most admirable vessel, and if someone object that a captain's testimony concerning his own ship is prejudiced, I can only answer that prejudices are often born of deep feeling and a sense for real beauty.

The *Clan Ferguson* was sold by the Scots to a Peruvian firm that renamed her *Juan Peral*, and then finally *Claudina*. Wriedt's barque was given him by Scots who knew how to care for a ship by giving it attention, rather than money. Clipper-bowed, fleet, low, one of the first of the iron sailing ships, she was nonetheless entering her old age when the German-born skipper took command. She was tired: she was past her prime, but she was coaxed into a second youth and a new glory. Wriedt's seabag was full of tricks and he tried them all on the quarter-deck of his little clipper. He liked to run her right in under the coast, catch a favorable land breeze and an ebb tide, and then skip on south under all plain sail, full and by. She ghosted down the coast, defying the trades, and while all other windships stood off and beat back and forth, thrashing about for weeks before they made Callao, Wriedt did it in days. She was known as the "White Witch of Peru," and her master often stood aft and threw a tow rope to steamers as his charge boomed home after a season in the islands. He made her sing in her old age; once he loaded at Santa Rosa in eight days and sailed her back in seven—the record both for loading and sailing from that port to Callao. When the *Claudina* was almost fifty years old, she ran on one day from 9:00 a.m. to 3:00 p.m. at a steady twelve knots and clocked better than forty-eight miles the watch. For a guano barque, in these waters and with these easy winds, that was first-rate sailing.

The *Claudina*, like all ships, came to an end; in 1926 a tug ran her into the coast of Peru; she filled; she soon sank, and thus ceased to be a ship.

Guillermo Wriedt took over the barque *Tellus*. He has been sailing her all these years, and it was only in the December of 1952 that he sailed her into Callao and was told she would sail no more.

If the *Claudina* was the youth of this man, the *Tellus* has been his manhood and the promise of his old age. He has built himself into her very substance, and she is stamped with the full vigour, the tempered skill, and the love of this German-Peruvian seaman, one of the last of the sailing ship captains. He cannot conceive of an existence apart from his quarter-deck. He lives, with wife and family, in a small and exceedingly neat house in La Punta, only a short walk to the line of the sea. Behind the captain's house, a man can see the masts of the *Tellus* mingling with those of the *Maipo*, rising above the cluttered roof tops of La Punta and the workshops that command the bay. Every day, about ten in the morning and then again in mid-afternoon, Captain Wriedt has himself rowed out to the barque. He goes below and looks over the logbooks and papers that record the life of his ship, all written in an old-fashioned Castilian script whose letters curl as they sweep gracefully over the yellowed page. They are the work of this one man and they are the history of the care of half a lifetime. This ritual completed, the captain is likely to pace the deck and study the bay. He glances aloft at the rigging and runs his fingers over the bulwarks, now just beginning to rust from too much time spent in port. He goes forward and inspects the pump, the only thing—he swears—that still works on the vessel. Two seamen wait for him somewhere forward of the mainmast; one of them is the bosun, and he has been with Captain Wriedt for the last twelve years. When the Master is ready to leave, he blows a whistle, and his men bring the dinghy around to the port side and all go ashore, the two sailors rowing silently and rhythmically, and the captain at the tiller.

The *Tellus*—said the captain—"she is dying a little every day." Gradually gutted of equipment from end to end, her gear is being sent to the little steamers operated by the guano firm that administers the industry for the government. Wriedt simply refuses to recognize the fact that the *Tellus* has been condemned by naval engineers. He denies their competence. He knows the old barque is for sale. He knows that if a buyer cannot be found she will be broken up and sold for scrap. He knows that the weight of a modern government is behind all its experts and authorities: he defies the authorities and has nothing but contempt for all "experts." He will not leave his ship. His loyalty is an absolute: "The vessel—she is good! The skipper—he is good too!"

The *Maipo* is being stripped along with the *Tellus*. But somehow nobody feels very strongly about the *Maipo*. She is really a pitiful excuse of a sailing ship. German built in 1893 by no less a house than that of J.C. Tecklenborg, she was rigged originally as a fullrigged ship. Steel hull, 246 feet long, 39.2 breadth, 22.9 depth, she shipped out of Hamburg in her younger days. The Peruvians have worked her long past her normal life span and they have not treated her well. Her rigging, both standing and running, is in abominable condition, and the saying is than when something comes down it never goes back up again. In 1941 they cut her down and forever ruined her looks. Her sails are mere rags, and even with her reduced sailspan, I doubt if she could spread canvas on every yard. I know that half her jibs and stays'ls are gone. Still, she has sailed all these years, and, although a bit tubby in the bows, it is not her fault that she has been treated badly. Nor is it particularly the fault of her officers and men. Nobody ever stayed long enough on the *Maipo* to find out what was wrong, and as the years ran on so many things were wrong that captains, after a season or two, just quit—appalled at the old wreck. It need not have been that way: the *Maipo* was a well built vessel; Tecklenborg never turned out a bad ship in his life.

A sailing ship to serve as it should demands continuity of command. So has it always been with the things man has made that depend, not on machines and such tricks, but on art, skill, and the knowledge born of a communion with those forces with which he has endowed a soul. This has been the way with *Tellus*. After each season's run, all the rigging came down and was worked over by the captain himself or by men brought up in these skills under his own tutelage. The *Tellus*, like her companion barques, is a "poor" ship: little money has been spent on her. When something wears out it must be replaced by the ship herself, by men who are not only sailors, but who are carpenters, sailmakers, riggers, fishermen, and boatbuilders as well. The *Tellus* carries, for example, every footrope she had when Wriedt took her over in 1926. But no sailor ever went to his death because a rotten footrope gave way under him on a swaying yard. Traditionally, the captain sails and the mate works the ship. Here the skipper both sailed and worked. From the time Captain Wriedt took command of the *Tellus* to the December of 1952, he sewed two complete sets of sails, gradually replacing her original hemp with cotton.

In 1941, the *Tellus* was stripped of her royals as were the *Maipo* and *Omega*. It was an economy measure, but it was a low trick to play on a self-respecting sailing ship. Wriedt refused to let his barque look like a clipped bird. He raised the fore and main upper t'gallant yards, deepened the two sails, and, as a result, the *Tellus* has more canvas today than she possessed before the reduction. A novice looking at her would say she carried double topsails, single t'gans'ls, and royals. He would never notice that these last were missing. The *Tellus* is the only vessel I know whose looks have not been spoiled by the loss of her royals. Her master has an eye for beauty.

When I was rowed out to the barque by the captain, I could not help but admire her as she lay there in the bay, waiting for orders that could only mean the acetylene torch and death, or servitude to some American millionaire. Black above the waterline and red below, she is pencilled around with a thin yellow band. Her spars and masts are tan, and her lines begin well forward (like all Dutchmen) and promisingly sweep aft, only to be sawed off square by men who were either absent-minded or who feared feminine beauty fore and aft.

The *Tellus* is a steel barque built in 1881 for Rijkee and Company of Rotterdam by Wachsmuch and Krogmann. Her dimensions are 238.2 feet in length, 27.5 in breadth, and 24.1 in depth. Like the *Maipo* and *Omega*, she sailed out of Hamburg before the war. Her decks are not cluttered and unsightly. Only one house rises abaft the foremast and extends almost to the mainmast: it is divided into a fo'c's'le sleeping twelve, a sail-locker, and the galley. Forward under the fo'c's'lehead, the barque carries the bell of the old *Claudina* engraved with her original name: *Clan Ferguson*—1876. The bell is the oldest thing on the vessel, and remains the symbol of her antiquity.

The pumps midships are from the old clipper barque as well. Powerfully built, they are the work of the men of the Clyde. They stretch back to the days of the wooden ships when pumps had to draw true. The *Clan Ferguson*, one of the very first iron sailing ships, was outfitted with the same kind of pumps carried by the wooden ships of the time, and they have served her well.

It was ludicrous to hear the pumps turn over, after the captain ordered his two remaining seamen to prove to me that the ship was not yet stripped completely of life. At his command, the silence of the ancient barque was broken by the shudder of pistons thrashing up and down on the body of the old seabird. The captain stood there grinning with pride as the sparks coruscated about the deck like miniature pinwheels. But the spectacle filled me with a kind of subterranean horror, a horror I know whenever I am faced with things mechanical that mimic and thus mock life. I was oppressed by the thought that a machine lived on, while a ship of sails died. And then I remembered that this is always the way with things mechanical: like all those old tales about men and women who never die, but who retain through the years the faces and figures of children, they emit the frost of death. But I soon exorcized these unworthy illusions and went aft, happy to leave this sorry remnant of what was once the full life of a good ship.

In his saloon, Captain Wriedt settled himself in a chair and smoked and told me many things about the sea and the ships that sail. As he sat there, short, powerful, ruddy, he seemed part of the *Tellus* herself. Holding forth under the old bronze lamp swinging from the lowhanging ceiling, surrounded by walls of sturdy Scottish paneling—walls almost as old as the skipper himself—he seemed to mingle with all the elements that went to make up his ship and indeed to be their bond and their life.

He showed me wooden models, made by himself and used in the old days to teach navigation to the Peruvian boys sailing under him. He taught not merely the science of naviagation, but the art as well: how to sail a barque by the look of the sea, the show of clouds, the flight of birds; how to feel your way across a body of water, and how to smell the tides.

Just two years ago, the captain overhauled the rudder; to get at it, he had to tip up half the saloon. He pointed out the places where he had cut through the walls and he explained just how he repaired them afterwards. He talked of her plates: very old now, but still sound. He spoke of the men who had sailed under him, of his bosun and the man's twelve years service. He recalled his own record for safety: not one man lost in twenty-eight years. (The *Omega* lost three, and one of her skippers went mad.)

I talked to many seamen, later in the bigger *Omega*, who had sailed under Wriedt. One evening, weeks after my visit to the *Tellus*, I was given eloquent testimony of the regard Peruvian sailors hold for the little barque and her master. The *Omega* was making for Punta Pacasmayo. We were on a course steering north, and the old four-master was doing about three knots in a gentle but firm breeze that just filled the square sails, whose outlines—tall and black—could barely be made out in the night from my station on the quarter-deck. I sought the company of the helmsman, and we talked quietly before the big wheel that needed only a spoke now and again to keep the *Omega* true to her course. I spoke of the *Tellus* to my companion and said it was a shame she was to be broken up. The name of the little barque, dropped in the quiet of the night, seemed to agitate the young helmsman. Speaking rapidly in his broken English, he told me that he too had sailed with the *Tellus*. He knew what she could do when touched by the magic of *El Capitán Wriedt*. One day—three years before—outside Callao, Wriedt had put on an exhibition of sailing for the benefit of the British Navy, whose personnel looked on from their huge battleships and cruisers, astounded at this seabird of a barque, heeling over, wheeling round, tacking back and forth under full canvas, and then sailing in to a safe anchorage. This was no command performance. Wriedt saw the English ships anchored before Callao and he knew that those thousands of sailors had never seen a square-rigger in their lives; he knew that hundreds of them were lining the sides of their ships and grinding away with cameras as the *Tellus* sailed in, drinking in the beauty of the old windjammer but smiling indulgently to themselves in their lordly cruisers and battleships. The opportunity was too delicious to let pass. Wriedt *had* to strut his square-rigger before all those eyes and let them see some real sailing at least once in their lives. He sailed between cruisers; he ran around battleships, dipping the Peruvian ensign from the mizzenmast as he crossed their sterns; he sailed in toward San Lorenzo as though to run on the rocks and then, at the last moment, he brought her up short on the new tack and bowled back to sea. My friend at the wheel that night swore he would never forget that day: he had never seen such sailing in all his years at sea, nor had anyone in Callao.

If his men respected their master and his ship, it must be confessed that the captain's purest love was for the sheer art of sailing itself. Once he brought the *Tellus* into Callao waters and stood out beyond the breakwater, mainyards backed, waiting for a tug. None came. They were all busy with foreign steamers, and the tug-masters apparently felt the familiar old windbag could wait until the other ships were towed in. Wriedt, tiring of this insult, squared the mainyards and sailed the barque through the narrow breakwater, past the busy traffic of the harbour, and thus brought his ship to the quiet south anchorage that has always been her own. He was fined a hundred *soles*, but he considered the sail well worth the penalty.

He talked on in his cabin that day for many an hour; talking in German and English, which I understand, and in Spanish, which I understand not at all. In time we ran out of matches, and he got up and rummaged around looking for more. "The vessel—she's still got matches, but not one damm thing else. You should have seen her in the old days. I kept her up like a yacht. But that's all gone now."

I asked the captain if I might take his picture, standing on deck at the break of the poop. He waved aside the suggestion: "When we are going along at twelve knots under all sail—*then* pictures! *This* way—the way she is now—no! The ship, she is dying, but not the skipper. They can kill the vessel. They can't kill the captain."

We rowed back by the bosun and his fellow seaman, and while the captain sat in the stern of the dinghy, hand on tiller, he kept insisting, again and again, that the *Tellus* could still sail for another five years or more. "The vessel—she is good, and so is the skipper." His voice trailed off, and then, as an afterthought, he leaned over and asked me in a low tone, half confidentially: "You want to buy her? I get her up to the States for you."

That afternoon I dined with the captain at his own table. We ate cheese and sausage, washed down by the heavy coffee grown in these parts. The captain and I talked about the *Preussen* and the great *Potosi*, and the *Tusitala* and the *Kaiulani*, last of the American sailing ships. He gave me a copy of *Sea Breezes* which is the bible of all sailing ship men and which is unquestionably the finest periodical in England, with the possible exception of the London *Tablet*. The captain kept hinting that I could do worse in life than buy the *Tellus*. I agreed and, considering the price—$40,000—helped myself to more cheese. My hostess asked me what I thought of Lima, and I answered that I was surprised to see such a great city so worked up over a beauty contest. It was the time for the annual selection of a "Miss Peru," and the city was filled with partisans from the provinces, each group violently proclaiming the proportions of its own native flower. Sra. Wriedt commented dryly that there were better women in Peru than these. I was quite willing to believe her and have more cheese while I delivered my own convictions on the subject, but it was time for me to return to Lima. I had a dinner engagement that evening and I could not afford to be late, because my stay in the capital depended on such invitations.

The captain walked with me to the trolley line, and as we swung down the streets of Callao that late afternoon—he wearing a black beret and a checked suit, and I, old army trousers and a leather jacket—I knew that I would never see him again. It was at the precise moment when this sentiment crossed my mind that he wheeled around, and looking me full in the face, threw the sundering question:

"Sind Sie Katholisch?"

"Jawohl—und Sie, Herr Kapitän?"

"Nein," he thundered and stormed. *"Ich bin ein Freidenker."*

"Glauben Sie an Gott,"

"An jenen Gott?" he exploded, gesturing wildly at a church across the thoroughfare (a church that housed a splendid and barbaric Christus: a suffering and sorrowing Christus, a black Christus fixed with myriad knives and spears—spears and knives removed through the years, one by one, from the bleeding body of the figure, and placed by the suffering and sorrowing faithful upon a cloth of gold). *"An jenen Gott? Nein! Ich hab' zu viel gesehen und zu viel gelesen."*

Zu viel gelesen! He never read a thing in his life. I wish there were more like him.

He put me on a train, and that evening I dined like a prince and my every need was filled by twelve servants, one of whom came running with whisky and water every time I sounded a small silver bell.

1956

SPANISH BAROQUE

A man need but wander through El Prado, Madrid's magnificent museum, to *see* with his eyes the soul of that nation that forever scorned fashion and gloried in opposition. This is true because Spanish art specifically and the Baroque in general is an art form that a man *sees*: it exists to be taken in by the eye and therefore it is intensely realistic.

Baroque is not symbolic in itself. It is, rather, an explosion of reality that forces upon the beholder a symbolic stirring within the waters of the imagination that lead him immediately and dramatically to a vision of things Divine.

Let a man who would know this truth trace the soul of Spain as it is etched in the sombre magnificence and the irony of Velasquez. Here was a painter who painted kings and fools and peasants, but who painted the Greek gods of antiquity only to mock them. In so doing he summed up Spain's rejection of the Renaissance and her wedding to the Baroque, the art that many claim we inherited from the crusading spirit of the Company of Jesus in the first passionate moment of its existence.

Only Spain's militant Christianity makes intelligible, for example, the linking of the gay Baroque to the severe Castillian spirit. The best Baroque is most probably Italian. The best *popular* Baroque is Austrian and Bavarian where even the cemeteries are riots of dancing cherubs and rounded maidens. But the spirit of the thing was created by that final flowering of Christendom under the Hapsburgs and it found in Castille a sword.

Beyond the principle of a purest dedication to religious ends it is impossible to understand how Castille—the catalyst into which was poured all the energy of a nation born anew as a result of its final victory over the Arabs—quickened and sustained the Baroque spirit, a spirit apparently the antithesis of everything Castillian. The gray monotony of Old Castille; the stones of the Avila of Santa Teresa which legend says are the tears Christ shed over the poverty of the plains and mountains of the Land of the Castles; the austerity of the Castillian, grave even in his humor, severe even in his sins, lacking in subtlety, narrow, profoundly realistic, gross and ascetic at once, Don Quixote and Sancho Panza not mingled into a third thing but erect and separate in all their contradictions, uniform in his dances and repetitious in his songs.

The final test of the Baroque is that no artistic snob can bear it! Its final tribute is that no puritan can worship surrounded by the trappings of its spirit. I have known scores of educated Americans bent upon Europe and the Gothic or the Romanesque who are appalled at the Baroque additions to churches built and inspired in an earlier moment in time. These people fail to understand two turths essential to the human spirit: history builds upon itself and although an art form frozen into the immobility of its own moment within time may perhaps be aesthetically superior to an art that mingles with what comes after it, it is inferior humanly because man does not live in a museum but on the street and in the fields where being answers the challenge of nature itself by unfolding treasures which reveal themselves one after another in the stream of becoming and thus form what we might call the tradition of being itself. Secondly, they fail to see that the Baroque answered a challenge, which, although not new to Western civilization, was then rampant and almost victorious: the challenge of men who denied the value of creation and who were checked and thrown back, in and through the Baroque, by a blatant and flamboyant affirmation of the Goodness of God's world. The Baroque, therefore, entered into the stream of our culture and men today can be distinguished in their mutual oppositions by their own personal responses to this spirit which was a scarlet trumpet.

The Baroque is an art of rhetoric and persuasion, not an art of logic. The mind annealed in pure logic and in the frozen wasteland of a reason cut away from the things that are is irritated by the Baroque as well as by what might be called "Baroque men". This truth sweeps within itself not only the Baroque gaity and joy but also the Baroque sorrow, a sorrow so intense that it not only pierces the heart of Mary but even seems to live, if but for a moment, the agony of the Cross.

The great Holy Week processions in Spain—the most famous of which is Sevillian—win by exhortation, not be reason. I speak from experience because I am probably the only North American to be a member of one of these Lenten brotherhoods and therefore I was privileged once to march in silence with my Spanish brothers under the decent anonymity of a black hood on Friday night.

It was a very good thing to go through the darkness and struggle up hills that had known the marching feet of the Legions of Rome, crossing crabbed and frozen streets, feeling the burden of the great Images we bore and sensing in some dumb way that this act of ours was not altogether without merit. I well recall how we entered the fortress walls of the city of Avila, passed the Cathedral—itself a fortress built into the very walls a thousand years ago—and then broke upon the brilliantly lit main plaza where we promptly proceeded to frighten the hell out of five thousand French tourists. This was pure Baroque—religion monstrated rather than demonstrated, a Thing done as is life itself. It imposes and thus imprints itself upon the seer as well as upon the doer not by what it proves but by what it is.

The Baroque spirit of the late sixteenth and seventeenth centuries was essentially popular and not academic. Producing unity out of a riot of materials apparently in contradiction one to another, the Baroque was and is an art of paradox. It was almost an anticipation and a salute to the meaning of Chesterton.

The Baroque was a protest in favor of the goodness of God's creation against new theologies that were denying the decency of being and that thus permitted the world to shrivel up under the hands of men who were incapable of seeing the mark of the Lord in the things He had made. The Baroque was a revindication of Genesis which says that God looked upon all the things that He had made and saw that they were very good indeed.

ii.65

THE MAN WHO WENT
TO HIS OWN FUNERAL

In the town of Pamplona, Spain, there died on September 15, 1967, one José Antonio Tápiz Izquierdo. Tápiz can be understood only in the light of the town that gave him birth. Pamplona is the capital of the ancient Kingdom of Navarre and it is known to the world because boys run through the streets before raging bulls once a year during the celebration of the famed festival of San Fermín. But also, in that same city, just thirty-one years ago an entire people came together in the Plaza de Castillo and formed there a sea of red berets. These *Requetés* fell upon the Communist north as they spilled out of their mountain enclave, Christ the King on their lips, rosaries around their necks, Sacred Hearts on their tunics, rifles in their hands. Enormous crosses were interspersed in their ranks that made their advances over the shell pocked fields of the Ebro and before Bilbao a moving forest of faith, a cathedral in arms.

Tápiz died there in that town of Pamplona. He was a good man. A Navarro and a *Requeté*, an "Apostolic, Roman Catholic" in his own formula. Tápiz was also—and this is central to the meaning of his life—a member of the *Muthiko Alaiak* which is Basque for "Happy Lads." The *Muthiko* is a local society dedicated to Navarre, to Spain, and to Carlism, a royal house banished in the last century because of a quixotic and quite anti-liberal allegiance to local liberties and to the Church.

But why should this man, José Antonio Tápiz, dead at age thirty-seven, single, the head of a household composed of his mother and four sisters, the owner of a dry goods shop, with a life altogether undistinguished by the standards of the world, merit the honor of having his picture and his last deeds memoralized in the northern Spanish press? Why do we write of him here? Tápiz has gained fame because he embraced publicly his own death, a hideous death, with a high Catholic elegance that recalls the martyrs and remembers the saints.

209

Told that he had an incurable cancer of the throat, José Antonio—after an agonizing few weeks in which his courage was tempered in the inner crucible of his being—welcomed his death and made it a partner in the last months of his life. On March 29 he underwent an operation. Fourteen days later he came home, *sin* larynx, and that night he made the rounds of bars in Pamplona with his friends, carrying a little blackboard on which he wrote out the words he could no longer speak. Later he fell upon the *fiesta* of San Fermín with all his old vigor and boasted that he had not missed one bull fight or one wild Basque dance in the streets. Then, the hospital once again. A hole was opened in his neck and Tápiz complained of pains in his head.

On September 11, José Antonio asked for and received extreme unction. Then, still on his feet but knowing that he had left only one week of life, Tápiz stunned all Pamplona by inviting his friends to a Mass for his soul. The Church was packed for the funeral. That night he entertained his friends at an enormous feast in the headquarters of the *Muthiko Alaiak*. Surrounded by faded paintings of the old kings, by banners of the Virgin and of the Sacred Heart, the floor littered with oyster shells and other debris, the signs of good fellowship and Catholic liberty, the old walls of the *Muthiko* rang with toasts to Tápiz that lasted deep into the early morning. This young man, already dead to the world, joked away the tears of others with brandy and wine. He wrote on his little blackboard, "I am a happy man." Two days later he went to bed for good and thereafter received His God on his back. But there was no rest for the man because he had to console a parade of visitors that passed through the death room. He died on Friday, the 15th; his red beret of the *Requeté* was buried with him.

The press detailed his life as follows: he belonged to the Center of Marian Devotion, to the Society of Nocturnal Adoration, to the *Muthiko Alaiak,* and to the *Requeté*—the armed guard of the Roman Church in Spain. He was loyal to Spain, to his king and to his God. Of an almost incredible purity of heart and body, Tápiz conquered a lifelong timidity in order that he might die publicly, confessing the Faith openly by organizing and attending his own funeral and then wordlessly at a banquet with symbols scratched on a tiny blackboard, saluting old companions in arms and a world that he loved. He even remembered his friends in America and sent us two days before he died a pamphlet announcing next year's

San Fermín. The envelope was addressed in his own hand. We were his companions and we remember him here. *Adios,* José Antonio Tápiz Izquierdo, *Muthiko.*

xi.67

AS YOU WERE

As with most of my devotions I put off going to Lourdes until the summer of 1974. I spent three days in the famous shrine in the foulest of tempers because I was suffering from what Shakespeare called that worst of all diseases, "the consumption of the purse." In a word: I was next to being broke. It is intolerable to be in France and not be able to eat like a king—or a republican bourgeois. When God created the world he poured out the very quintessence of heaven on France. France is a super-endowed nation, lush and rich and incredibly well spaded by the most conscientious peasantry in the world. That peasantry is also notoriously tight. I had the most abdominable meals in the best fed nation on this earth and I remembered too late the advice of a wise friend of mine from Louisiana: take twice the cash and half the clothes. Nor could I make it up with wine because French *vin ordinaire* is comparable to vinegar. I left France a hungrier and a drier Catholic than I entered. I went back to Spain and to the *tinto* of Navarre and it was there I remembered my best story about Lourdes and here in America I decided to write it down lest it be lost forever. The tale appeals, I understand, to the spirit of the Cappadocian Fathers of the Patristic era—and at *Triumph* we attempt to appeal to every taste.

Now Navarre is Mary Country. The zeal for the Mother of God is so deep that in some villages old women pass the entire day moving their lips in silent rosary after rosary. Many of the red-bereted *requetes* in the Crusade against the Communist republic wore rosaries around their necks and these unconquerable soldiers of Christ the King, at night and on bivouac, pushing west towards Bilbao and then Santander, ended the day with the murmur of rosary mingling with the clashing of rifles being stacked and the hissing of camp fires being put out: all of this on that long and bloody road to victory.

In Pamplona I belong to a social club whose middle generation is almost totally made up of former volunteers in the Crusade of 1936-1939. In my years in Spain the *Muthiko Alaiak* occupied the second story of an old building that fronted onto the main plaza. There on any afternoon you could play *mus* (which I never did) or eat an enormous mid-afternoon snack consisting of roast suckling pig, salad, two bottles of wine, and cognac (this I often did). Or you could simply drink wine or coffee and conspire with fellow traitors against the modern world, watched by the attentive eyes of the Kings—the *true* Kings—the Carlist Kings in exile who gazed imperiously out of old paintings that covered the walls. The whole was dominated by a statue of the Sacred Heart (that statue has been machine-gunned, but that is another story). The noise was deafening.

The *Muthiko Alaiak*—this means "Happy Lad" in Basque—is prominent during the famous Fiesta of San Fermin, when its dance group is justly renowned, but the *Muthiko* is also celebrated in Navarre for its charities. Every year an orphan boy is made king for a day in the old castle in the town of Olite, medieval capital of Navarre. Lit up by torches, the castle sees the forming of the court, homage payed to a poor boy by his loyal servants, monies collected, and an education and future assured him. The *Muthiko* also organizes pilgrimages to Lourdes, just a long stone's throw across the border in France. And here too the Happy Lads of *Muthiko* are as solicitous for the well being of the poor in health as they are in Olite for boys poor in wealth. It is a very good thing indeed that at least one sick person each year get on the chartered bus that leaves Pamplona for the shrine across the mountains. After all, Lourdes is supposed to cure the sick.

But one year—this sometime after I had left Pamplona—the Lads could find no Sick Man. They hunted through the streets of Pamplona and no sick fellow emerged. His fare was payed for in advance; his food and lodging assured; but in that year there simply was no Sick Man in Pamplona, or so it seemed. This posed a grave problem indeed. It looked as though the excursion was going to be a bust: a pilgrimage to Lourdes without a sick fellow waiting on a cure is like "Hamlet" without a prince. (The Bard knew all about Navarre: he wrote that "One day Navarre will astonish the world!" Navarre did in 1936. Moscow radio today says that "The Spanish Problem" could be eliminated if this "province of drunken religious fanatics" could be eliminated.) Folk in the north of Spain tend to be exceedingly healthy, generally fortunately so, at that moment not all that fortunately so. But then the *Muthiko* did finally find its Sick Man, a middle-aged paralytic who wheeled himself about the town in a little manually propelled cart and who sold sundries to passerbys.

At first this industrious and crippled gentleman manifested no enthusiasm whatsoever about the prospect of being trundled away in a bus to Lourdes. He wasn't bothering anybody and he could not quite understand why the *Muthiko* was bothering him. No, he had not thought about the possibility of a miraculous cure—that sort of thing happened to other people and usually it happened long ago! Would he oblige the group of pilgrims? The group simply could not very well go to Lourdes without a Sick Man to take the cure. Everybody in Navarre cannot be healthy. We must give the Virgin something to do. His sense of charity thus appealed to, the Sick Man agreed to go along for the ride, albeit with some trepidation because the *Muthiko* has the reputation of landing on whatever moon it occupies and then dancing thereon, with the wine skin swinging, passed eagerly from hand to hand: "*Navarra, Navarra es* (expletive deleted) . . . *nudo—como Navarra no hay ninguna.*"(In a word this means that we in Navarre have it made and there is nothing like us anywhere else in the world: in that sentiment I concur.)

And thus to Lourdes they went over the mountains. The sing-song of the rosary prayed in unison on the bus gave way to the lilt of the *jota* and both merged into Marian hymns as the spectacular basilica signalled over the rich countryside that Pamplona was about to take over Lourdes. The cart of the Sick Man had been slung into the back of the bus and he had settled into his seat in an uneasy silence, somewhat dazed but by no means unapproving of the enthusiasm of his hosts. After all, he too was a Navarese. In Lourdes, the Happy Lads made their way rapidly to the basilica and, assembling in formation, red kerchiefs slung around necks, red berets cocked heavily over the left eye, white folk costumes glistening in starched splendor under the sunny sky, they went into their routine—Basque *jotas* that antedate the Christian era. Rapidly surrounded by the curious, the Lads became the central attraction on the ground surveying the descent to the grotto. Then someone noticed that they had forgotten the Sick Man: he was still back there in the bus. Hurrying to him and exuding apologies, a few of the *Muthiko* pilgrims lifted their guest from his seat, assembled his cart, and wheeled him towards their dancing companions. By now the main body from Pamplona was leaping and whirling about in wild dances, much to the astonishment of the assembled faithful, especially those from Omaha, Neb. Descending the decline after this celebration—accompanied by much wine (Spanish, not French) swung from Happy Lad to Happy Lad—the *Muthiko* blended into the dozens of groups bent on venerating the Mother of God. The new silence deepened and was cradled in the murmuring of *Ave Marias* by the mass of humanity that slowly moved towards its goal, the grotto: God's Mother.

Then they let the cart go! I mean the two Happy Lads detailed to wheel the Sick Man down to his cure, they just let it go—and this in a daze of piety produced by splendid wine brought across the border mingled sacramentally with the deepest of Catholic lyricism. They just let it go! And down the road went the cart, scattering the faithful from Omaha and Bangladesh right and left as pious banners and standards and crosses were rolled underfoot by the careening vehicle and occupant. Bouncing down the road with half the *Muthiko* roaring on behind on foot, the cart hit the bottom, jumped six feet in the air, turned over and spilled out the Sick Man. In the dust, his words to The Happy Lads: "I don't want to get well; I just want to be the way I was."

(P.S. When Lourdes is mentioned and pilgrimages are organized to-day in Pamplona one middle-aged paralytic, seen throughout the rest of the year wheeling his little cart in the main plaza as he goes about his business, disappears from sight. He vanishes. He surfaces again only after the buses have left town and headed north. He is—thanks to the Virgin—as he was and that is just how he now wants to be. And the moral to this tale, one known by all good Cappadocians, is the following: never give up! If you show charity to your neighbours as did The Sick Man to his, the Good Lord just might—it is an outside chance, of course; you must hedge your bets carefully in this religion racket—let you be as you were.)

xii.74

THREE DAYS WITH MINDSZENTY

His Eminence Jozsef Cardinal Mindszenty, until very recently the Prince Primate of Hungary, was called by Pius XII "The Lion of Hungary." That Lion honored the Hungarian community of Dallas-Fort Worth, Texas, with a three-day visitation, June 17 to June 19. He came unto us and he left us: a *stupor mundi*. We are humbled and even more we are astonished at what manner of man we had in our midst. In a public Mass celebrated at the Cistercian preparatory school, His Eminence said that sane and holy political existence often involves dedicating a nation to the Mother of God. We will not forget this sermon. The Cardinal is frail but when he talks he commands. He does not lean on his crozier. He holds it aloft. He spoke of Hungary, of her Catholic history and destiny, and he linked both to Hungary's pact with the Virgin Mary, all of this sealed and symbolized in the Holy Crown of St. Stephen, the Apostolic Crown.

Earlier that day the Cardinal had confirmed some sixty faithful at the chapel of the Carswell Air Force Base near Fort Worth. Trumpets greeted him as he entered the packed chapel blessing the faithful, right arm sweeping the aisle as he moved swiftly to the altar. The Bishop of Fort Worth concelebrated the Mass surrounded and assisted by Cistercian monks. The Cardinal administered the Sacrament of Confirmation and distributed Holy Communion to the faithful. That evening his public address in Hungarian was carried by Radio Free Europe. It was estimated that some eight million Hungarians, both behind the Iron Curtain and in the diaspora, would hear his words. But the Cardinal's address seemed principally aimed at those Hungarians living in exile, scattered by the tyranny of the age.

Do not forget the tongue, he said to them. Our Hungarian tongue is our history: our history is a rendezvous with God in time. Do not set parents against children through the shuddering experience of dividing the family into two languages, one spoken by the old, one by the young. And: Remember, you American Hungarians: our land is Mary's and the Holy Crown is your own—yours and every Hungarian's wheresoever he might be. More than 1,500,000 Hungarians live outside the slave state. But there is given unto all of us—Hungarians in slavery and Hungarians in liberty—a history, a language, an inheritance, and a buckler to put on—this is how we are and this is what we are.

After that stunning Mass in Hungarian, beamed across the ocean and into the lands of darkness, I saw the Cardinal call the children of Hungarian parents around him. He sat on a little stool and the youngsters swarmed over him. He asked them if they carried rosaries. He joked with them. This *alter Christus* with the small ones of the Lord dancing around him smiled and laughed, a small crimson figure in a sea of innocence. For them he laughed and smiled. But he smiled and laughed for nobody else.

A very perspicacious young correspondent for the *Dallas Morning News* noted on the front page of that paper that the reporters who had gathered for the Cardinal's televised press conference came to find in this man whatever legend it was that sounded forth from out of their own pasts. One Jewish reporter remembered how Mindszenty opened the churches and schools to the Jews during the Nazi occupation, itself a kind of prelude to his crucifixion by the Communists. To this writer and to many others then present we faced, altogether without any right to do so, the Lion of Hungary. But the Lion is in mourning.

Prince Primate: Archibishop: Cardinal—jailed by the Nazis in the early forties; released by the Allies and then jailed and sentenced by the Communists in 1948; in prison from 1948 until 1956—we pass over the torture and the trial. Then—but let the Hungarian record of that one splendid week of liberty speak for itself: Radio Free Hungary:

> At 21:05 this evening at Retsag (Nograd County) units of the Army liberated Cardinal Josef Mindszenty from his prison at Felsoptancy where he has spent the past year. His eight years of incarceration have come to an end . . . The People of Retsag were the first to greet the Primate . . . Cardinal Mindszenty said: "My sons, I shall carry on where I left off eight years ago."

Then he got into a tank surrounded by Freedom Fighters with submachine-guns and he went home to Budapest. There he gave "my pontifical blessing to the *arms of Hungary*."

When the Russian tanks came growling back into the city, and
Catholic Hungary was murdered, and the West did nothing, Jozsef
Mindszenty took refuge in the American Legation in Budapest. He
remained there until 1971, largely confined to one room. The building was
ringed by machine-guns.

His Eminence told us, dryly, that "although his welcome was running thin" at the American Legation (1956-1971: fifteen years in one
room, and this after eight years in Communist prisons, and—earlier—in
Nazi jails), he left only because he had been ordered by the Vatican to do
so. The Cardinal-Archbishop suggested that there was something faintly
amusing in a situation in which it is a crime for anybody else to leave
Hungary and a crime only for himself to stay there.

Other questions and answers. (These are taken from my notes and
are not direct quotations unless otherwise indicated.)

Question: Is the Crown of St. Stephen religious or political property?

Answer: The Apostolic Crown belongs to the Hungarian nation. It
was given to St. Stephen *for* the nation *by* the Pope. Hence the Crown
belongs to *all* Hungarians and this includes those who live outside the
boundaries of the Hungary occupied by Communism.

Question: Why did you not resign when it was evident that the Vatican
wished you to do so?

Answer: I could not resign, nor would I have resigned, because the
Hungarian Church suffers a terrible persecution. No *quid pro quo* is possible. There is an abstract constitutional right to religious liberty which is
not worth the paper it is written on. All bishops must be screened by the
government and nobody can become a bishop, can be named by Rome,
unless the Communist government finds the nomination acceptable. One-
third of all recently ordained priests cannot exercise their priesthood.
They are forced to work in factories or on farms. "The Peace Priests"
(collaborators) get the best ecclesiastical positions. They are spies and informers.

Question: Who has succeeded you now that you have been relieved of
your office by the Vatican?

Answer: I have no successor.

(The significance of this answer was missed by most of the reporters,
and understandably missed. Nobody can succeed to Cardinal Mindszenty's role as Prince-Primate because he became such under the ancient,
thousand-year Hungarian constitution which has been abrogated by the

Communist rulers. You can get another Cardinal into Hungary but you cannot get a Prince-Primate without overthrowing the Red government and restoring the ancient constitution. In the absence of a king, the Prince-Primate is the first *political* as well as religious figure in the nation. Therefore he is the guardian of the Apostolic Crown. Josef Mindszenty is not just any old garden-variety Cardinal: he was the first man in all "the Lands of the Holy Crown of St. Stephen." He *was* Hungary in legal theory; that he made this theory a reality has been the cross and glory of his life; but never did this man take onto himself something not invested in, and demanded by, his office. The Crown, in Hungarian legal theory, owns—even more, *is*—Hungary.)

Question: Why did you choose to take the road to such a long life in prison; why did you not try to come to some kind of an agreement, a detente, with the Communist regime?

Answer: (This is an exact quotation): "I did my duty. This was nothing new. One of my predecessors was killed in battle in the thirteenth century, another was killed in battle against the Turks. Five more were persecuted and jailed."

Question: "How is the Faith faring in Hungary under Communist rule?"

Answer: "Many good Catholics who live in villages cannot go to Mass because a spy is attached to each church. If you go to Mass you are likely to lose your job or find yourself persecuted and hounded. Many villagers try to go to the cities, save money for the trip, in order to attend Mass in the anonymity of urban churches. They will not be noticed there, watched by the police, or turned in by ecclesiastical spies and informers in orders. If Catholic parents insist on a religious education for their children (promised by the paper constitution), these children are likely to be failed in their courses; they will be barred from any chance for a higher education."

Hungary today daggers itself to death in despair. The country just does not seem to want to continue to exist. The incredible sacrifice of the rising of 1956-57 bled the arteries of the nation. Those who have survived see no reason to die themselves; and they seem to see no reason to give birth to a new generation. The contraception and abortion statistics are staggering. This death wish fits Russia's plans for Hungary.

But Cardinal Mindszenty is a living reminder that Hungary for a thousand years and more was the *Regnum Marianum:* Kingdom of Mary, bulwark of the West. The Cardinal insisted that he had acted, in all of his life, in the traditions of the history of his own land. (I invite the reader to wait on the publication of the monumental study on the meaning of Hungary recently written by the Dallas Cistercian Hungarian, Father Emilian Novak.) He appealed to those traditions when he first confronted the weight of Marxist arms in 1948; and he brought to bear against them the arms he then had at his disposal: processions, banners, Masses, Benedictions, songs—a Catholic people in the arms of prayer. That same people took to other arms some eight years later.

I had the signal honor during these days of having had time to speak at length with one of His Eminence's secretaries, Msgr. Tibor Meszaros. At a luncheon my wife and I were seated at a table next to the Cardinal's, our companion was his secretary. This man's contempt for detente was colossal; it was matched by his contempt for a system that aborts children. He did not seem interested in talking about the Cardinal's refusal to accept an honorary degree from the University of Santa Clara because it recently named a pro-abortion Congressman to its Board of Regents. This is the same Santa Clara that in 1956 freely offered all of its students as volunteers in the cause of Hungarian independence. I was there. From Hungarian independence to abortion apologetics is a shabby history, an almost too perfect curve of decline. Santa Clara bored Father Tibor.

The man is attuned to living primitively, close to nature and the things that are. He talked, privately, to the reporters about how you survive under the Russian boot. Tibor Meszaros lived ten years in concentration camps—"They caught me in 1948 eight months before they caught the Cardinal."

Every piece of bread, the Monsignor recalled, any small favor, is purchased at the price of a piece of your integrity. You learn how to be murdered—and of course, to accept being murdered—bit by bit, day by day, *and* you learn how to will this murder of yourself. Mass he could say possibly once every two or three months if he could steal a few grains of wheat and beat them into a host and a handful of grapes to stamp into wine. He had to hide the elements in the barracks because his person was stripped naked and searched daily. Were you tortured? Answer: Everybody is tortured in his own way, and they know all the ways that are.

I was aware, suddenly, that I was talking with a man from another world, from another order of things—that Cardinal and this priest and the

Cardinal's other secretary, a Franciscan. "Be a nothing"—words of Father Tibor to the reporters—"then you will survive and the experience is very fascinating (he repeated this several times) because everything in the world takes on a new look. You judge everything from the nothing that you are. Nobody knows who you are. You are dead to parents and friends and world. But never give an inch. To become something is to cease to be the nothing that will make you be, that will save you."

Of Cardinal Mindszenty, Father Tibor said: "He doesn't have any body at all. They broke it all up years ago and threw it away. As for his will, it nevers changes This man is a man of deep passions and those passions are always the same."

I shall remember Cardinal Mindszenty best as he spoke before the improvised altar in the Cistercian gymnasium—crozier in hand. Behind him was the old Hungarian Flag—the bars and cross mounted by the Crown of St. Stephen and its bent cross and all the bending of the world. And there was Mindszenty—erect; eighty-two years old; instructing us eagerly in the Faith and instructing millions behind the Iron Curtain who listen in danger and in hiding.

We knew—I knew—that someone from Beyond had passed our way and that something very strange had happened to us all.

vii.74

ADIOS: FRANCISCO FRANCO

The tens of thousands of mourners who stood for hours in the early Winter cold before Madrid's Royal Palace: the filing past the open coffin of the dead warrior: the sign of the Cross: the nuns and priests and soldiers and rich and poor, the veterans: the Falangist open armed and the older military salutes—Spain walked past the body of its fallen *Caudillo* and bid him good-bye. An estimated million people participated in the funeral of the General. Everyone today knows in Spain that an era has come to an end and the massive outpouring of emotion for a man who in life inspired very little emotion bespeaks Spain's fear of an uncertain and possibly sinister future. The good years are behind, at least for now. Franco was buried in the massive Valley of the Fallen just thirty odd miles out of Madrid. Carved out of the rock in a high mountain to house the bodies of thousands of soldiers who died in that distant Crusade that began on July 18th, 1936, and that ended in victory for Catholic Spain on April 1st, 1939, Francisco Franco was buried next to a man he scarcely knew in life: José Antonio Primo de Rivera, founder of the Falange, murdered in Alicante by the Communists in 1936. Franco, by one of those curious coincidences of history, died on the anniversary of José Antonio's execution in Alicante. The names of the young martyr to Spain and of the aged General are inextricably woven together in a history that is bigger than legend and more lyrical than poetry. Their bodies rest in that mountain monastery under a gigantic cross, three times the height of the Statue of Liberty, that lifts in prayer the austere Castilian hills and mountains in frozen adoration of the God to whom Spain gave its soul, one more time in her thousand-year battle for the Catholic Thing. "It is a great thing to be a Spaniard": these are words of General Franco himself, spoken not two months ago when the world once again snarled its hatred of his victory.

Adios: Francisco Franco

The Spanish Civil War—*la Cruzada*, "The Crusade"—has about it a kind of epic quality that has moved men in the 36 years since that war ended in ways which are inexplicable except in metaphysical terms. The single and lonely instance of a successful revolution against a Marxist government in the name and under the banner of Catholic civilization and of a revolution that succeeded and perdured for more than a third of a century, the Spanish adventure of those years divides men in their reactions as does nothing else. It was a cleancut war and the aging liberals of the Western world who have hated Franco with peculiar venom for having had the audacity to win confess at bottom their rejection of *any* political order that makes of the Faith its own public orthodoxy. The hypocrisy of an academic and political establishment stretching from Moscow to London that bleats over the legal execution of a handful of terrorists in the Autumn of 1975 and that refuses to even think about the 4,184 secular priests murdered by the Reds and their allies in those years of civil war; about the 2,365 religious clergy, murdered; and about the 283 nuns murdered, to say nothing of the uncounted thousands of Catholic laity butchered to death because they were existentially guilty of having gone to Mass, is simply a sign of bad will too obvious to be countered by any reaction other than contempt. Historians would like to put the Spanish Civil War in perspective, but the war itself seems to elude scholarly objectivity: it moves men in deeper regions of the soul and friend knows friend and foe from friend by just how each one does react. Nobody today ought to want to fight that bloody war over again, but the death of General Franco and the uncertainty of Spain's future demands that it be so fought, possibly in deeds, certainly in thought. The Spain of tomorrow is going to be about that war: was it fought for nothing; did a million men die in vain or must history come full circle again as though it were a cosmic wheel? The university youth of Spain today is sick of listening to stories about "The Crusade," but history will now make them tell some of those stories themselves.

Franco won and then he held the line against the whole world. He held it first against Hitler who tried to collect a debt for having aided Franco and found Franco to be deeply ungrateful when he refused to permit German troops to march through Spain in 1940: "I would as soon have three or four teeth pulled," said Hitler rather than talk it out again with Franco face to face as he did in Hendaye in October of 1940. Franco held out again against the Allies and their blockade of Spain after World

War II. A ruined nation in shambles astonished the world by simply not giving in. There were nuns—for example, in Avila—who starved to death in their convents that bleak Winter when the entire world, minus Argentina, tried to bring Spain to its knees—and Spain refused to grovel. When the cold war against Spain thawed in the United States under the administration of President Eisenhower, Franco led Spain to unprecedented levels of material prosperity. And just as European resentment of that nation is fanning itself to white heat again, prodded by Basque separatism and Communism aided by the media everywhere, Franco has now gone to "my Judge" as he wrote in a moving last testimony proclaiming from his death bed his faith in the Catholic Church.

What kind of a man was Francisco Franco? His fairly modest origins never suggested the role he was to play in history. Born on Dec. 4th, 1892, in El Ferrol in Galicia, Franco wanted to follow his father's footsteps and pursue a career in the Spanish Navy. Blocked in his ambition because of a reduction in admissions to the naval academy, Franco chose the infantry academy at Toledo. He did not know then that his army would relieve its heroic siege more than a quarter century later. At age seventeen, Franco graduated with the rank of second lieutenant. Soon thereafter, we find him in Morocco commanding an elite regiment of native cavalry. The Moroccans were always to respect him and gave him some of his finest units during the Civil War. Introverted, painstakingly honest and efficient, utterly unconcerned about money, Franco was already annealed in the enigmatic character that was to mark his entire life: a man of abstemious habits who neither drank nor smoked, a sportsman who revelled in hunting and fishing, Franco was known to be distant and aloof in his comportment with fellow officers. The man apparently never had any friends. Married to Carmen Polo, an aristocrat considerably his social superior, Franco became the youngest captain in the Spanish Army. He rose to be second in command of the crack Foreign Legion and became something of a national hero because the Legion put down the African rebellion. Brigadier general and director of the General Military Academy in Saragossa, Franco abstained from politics in the collapse of the monarchy in 1931. His wife came from a distinguished liberal monarchist family and Franco was thought to have royalist sympathies but he was absent from the plotting going on around him of generals who refused to accept the fall of the monarchy with equanimity. In October, 1934, Franco—then a major general—put down the rebellion in the mining country of Asturias. A new shift to the Left in the government saw Franco, more or less exiled, in an obscure command in the Canary Islands. Madrid thought he could do little harm there.

The rising against the Red-leaning Republic in 1936 was not initially thought out or captained by Franco. The deterioration of the Republic and the rule of the gunman in the streets, the murder of priests and nuns, the burning of churches and the rest had reached the point where the government could no longer control its own masses. The assassination of the royalist deputy in the Cortes, Calvo Sotelo, set off the rebellion but it had been planned earlier. General Sanjurjo, acting for the army, signed a pact with Fal Conde acting for the Carlist Traditionalist Communion and its regent, Prince Javier of Borbon-Parma. Both Sanjurjo and General Mola were killed early in the war. These were the two soldiers most indicated to control the nationalist rising. Although the Carlist put almost 100,000 *requetés* in the field, red-bereted volunteers wearing the Sacred Heart of Jesus on their khaki uniforms, their dream of restoring *their* traditionalist and Catholic monarchy was destined to be frustrated by a series of factors not the least of which was Franco himself. Nationalist Spain was formed out of a coalition of three forces: the army (excepting those numerous units, a large minority, that did remain loyal to the Republic); the Carlists, oldest political force in all Europe, lyrically Catholic and largely concentrated in the North; and the newly founded Falange whose leader José Antonio Primo de Rivera, as indicated, was caught by the Reds in Alicante and executed for treason: he was, of course, guilty of the charge! The Falange found its support chiefly in Old Castille and in cities such as Valladolid, Avila, and Burgos. Aping proletarian manners and Italian Fascist symbols, the Falange was a nationalist movement typical of that moment in European history. By no means a mere copy of Mussolini's Fascism, the Falange owed much to the romantic politics of its founder. The stirring hymn, "Face to the Sun," *Cara al Sol,* symbolized the Falangist rejection of the politics of the smoke - filled room and the wheeling-dealing of the discredited democratic and liberal system of the last century. Although tens of thousands of Spaniards who were neither Carlists nor Falangists fought in the war on the Catholic side, only those two movements had their own military formations, uniforms, and flags.

General Franco, who had flown from the Canary Islands to Morocco and then to the South of the Spanish mainland, was made head of the new nationalist Spain in Burgos. He pressured the reluctant Carlists into a common political party headed by the Falange: "The National Movement." An essay of this nature cannot relate once again the three years of that war, but an understanding of its structure is necessary to gauge accurately the subsequent life of Francisco Franco. The rebellion seemed to have failed in its first few days. Every city of major significance except Seville in the South remained loyal to the Republic which quickly armed the industrialized and radicalized masses even as it put down aborted nationalist risings in Madrid, Barcelona, Valencia, and elsewhere. The Basque provinces proclaimed independence and allied themselves with the central government of Madrid. But the nationalist army advanced steadily from the South. In the North, to the pleased astonishment of both Mola and Sanjurjo, the whole of Navarre, Calism's stronghold, went delirious with religious enthusiasm as it declared itself for the old Spain and against the new. Within twelve hours every republican symbol in Pamplona was gone and the colors of the old monarchy flew from every window, united with the Carlist Cross of Burgundy, the *aspas* of the Tradition. Forty thousand volunteers streamed into Pamplona from the villages on July 19th, 1936, and the war in the North took a turn unpredicted by either the army or Madrid.

Nonetheless, the Republic ought to have won. That it lost was due to a series of reasons. The Communists stupidly murdered their own allies, the Anarchists, in Barcelona. They merely surrounded them and shot them down by the thousands. In so doing, they killed the best troops that the Republic had at its disposal. The government lost whatever moderate support it once had from Christian Democrats because of its open encouragement of the persecution of the Church. The *chekas*, operating behind the lines, disgusted the population by its cruelty and brutality. Mola coined the term "fifth column" when he said that he had four with him and one in Madrid on the other side of the line. What proved to be crucial, however, was the drying up of volunteers in the Red Zone after the first flush of radical enthusiasm had withered under the Nationalist and Catholic advance from the North and the South. Nationalist provinces were fed constantly with volunteers, especially in Old Castille and Navarre. The provincial government of Navarre had to issue a decree forbidding lads under seventeen from enlisting in the *tercios* of *requetés* because somebody had to stay home and bring in the crops. Many ran away and joined the colors, lying about their ages. I know two such men who are

Capuchin priests today in Dallas. The Republic was aided by foreign volunteers in the famous International Brigades, including one from the United States, "The Abraham Lincoln Brigade." Many Communist and Socialist leaders of the post-World War II period cut their teeth in battle in those units: e.g., Tito and Nenni. Their war record was indifferent and could not match those of the Spaniards on both sides of the fence. Russia sent heavy equipment and technicians. Within six months the Madrid government ceased to be anything more than a puppet of Moscow. The Nationalists, in turn, were aided by the Condor Legion from Germany, and Spain proved to be a splendid training ground for future *Blitzkrieg* tactics. Italy sent several divisions, but the Italian troops proved to be a liability because most of them ran away under fire. Spain today is full of not particularly kind jokes about Italian valor, but the Garibaldi International Brigade on the Red side fought with excellent bravery and efficacy. Mussolini's troops, however, had little taste for a war that was not their own. They tended to get in the way of the Spaniards as they headed for the rear. The liberal myth that the war was won by foreigners for Franco is a sheer lie.

As province after province was liberated by Franco, he turned their organization over to the Falange. Himself an old-fashioned soldier with only the most conventional and distant of monarchist sentiments, Franco was never the "fascist beast" he was made out to be by the liberal rhetoric. Franco was a successful sixteenth-century politician operating in the twentieth. He used what he had at hand, and the Falnage was there, acceptable to both Italy and Germany whereas Carlism was utterly too clerical for both Fascist Italy and Nazi Germany. (Carlist families in the North were notorious for harboring Allied pilots who had parachuted to safety or drifted across the border; Carlist hatred for Nazi paganism was only matched by its hatred for Communist atheism.) The Falange, after reaching a pitch of power in Spain, declined in influence even though today it remains the one political movement which is official in the country. Some of Spain's finest men today have entered the Falange in the hope of saving their nation from a Socialist or Communist takeover.

Franco's style of governing after his victory was typical of the man. Although not given to public oratory, Franco surrounded himself with all the visual symbols of power and authority. He rarely wore mufti and he received people in his office in the Pardo uniformed and bemedalled. A diminutive man in size, he was almost dwarfed by President Eisenhower when they rode together through Madrid in an open limousine. The man kept his own council and even his most intimate political associates never knew what he was thinking about. Part of this can be put down to temperament, but part of it grew out of his enormous sense of responsibility to Spain. He loved his wife and was a good family man and he tended to let himself go only around children. This iron discipline was eroded around the edges in the last years of his life when sickness and age were wearing him out. He cried a lot, it is said, in these last two years, but he always cried about Spain and his fallen comrades in war. Franco knew how to govern. He gave full authority and responsibility to his cabinet members and then he sat back and watched. If they failed, Franco dismissed them. If they succeeded, he got the credit. A genius at playing off political forces against each other, the General encouraged an entire squad of royal princes to dream about a throne. At least one of them was on his payroll ("Carlos VIII": now dead). And all the while he kept them at a distance and thus did not offend the basically anti-monarchist Falange. Opposed by the Christian Democrats who were riding high in Europe in the Fifties, Franco domesticated his own by bringing them into the government and putting them to work. One thinks immediately of Martin Artajo and Manuel Frago Irribarne. Accused of being a creature of the new and powerful *Opus Dei,* Franco watched its influence reach a peak and then he permitted Fraga to expose an *Opus* style Teapot Dome scandal. The *Opus* lost out, but Frago had to go too. Franco remained. One joke had him dying and going to Heaven and informing the Spaniards several centuries later in a thunder clap from the sky that the Father of God had resigned. Crossed by Don Juan de Borbon, the son of Spain's last king, Alfonso XIII, Franco responded by taking over the pretender's son, educating him in things Spanish, and then handing him the throne. Thus he relegated the English liberalism of the father to exile in Estoril, Portugal, and to occasional *pronunciamientos* uttered between yachting trips. (But the father of the new king *does* remain an influence in Spain and ought to be watched.)

Franco inspired very little love in life. He may inspire more in death. But everybody in Spain respected him, including his enemies. They respected him, most probably, because they could never predict what he would do or guess what he was thinking. One wag had it that Franco's success was due to his never thinking about tomorrow but only about today: therefore, he survived into the day after tomorrow. There is some

truth in it—*but*, wait—how does this judgment jibe with the elaborate constitutional provisions he set up for his successor? It is as though Franco
wanted to govern even beyond the tomb because he trusted nobody, except—possibly—Admiral Carrero Blanco, the President of Government,
who was murdered by either Reds or separatists because his military
regularity extended to his religious piety: they blew him up with his driver
as he left Mass one morning on the precise moment when he always left
Mass every day of the week. No wonder Franco trusted nobody. His trust
was the kiss of death.

He left Spain a legacy. In a world that has known war upon war,
anarchy in the streets and instability in government, Franco bequeathed
Spain more than thirty years of peace. That nation, practically alone and
with very little American aid, achieved a prosperity nobody dreamed
would be achieved within what is a relatively poor country. Anyone who
knows Europe well has noted the burgeoning middle class in Spain; the
well-dressed people (especially the babies); the packed churches of a
believing nation; the quiet of the *siesta*; the nervous chatter and high-
spirited conversation, the good humor in bars and cafes; the plethora of
high-taxed automobiles jamming roads built for donkeys; the in-
dustriousness of a people who keep ahead of the game often by working at
two jobs at once. Spain is still outstandingly itself: a nation of proud in-
dividualists with a fiercely close-knit family structure; a people vertical in
its values and explosive in its sensibility; a race of men that copies too
much from outside its borders and thus perpetually threatens to cease to
be itself.

For the hundred off years prior to the advent of Francisco Franco's
rule, Spain averaged one new government a year. The nineteenth century
saw Spain bereft of its overseas empire in the Americas and bent on tear-
ing itself to pieces in the bloody fratricide of those who said "no" to the
French Revolution and of those who said "no" to the ancient Catholic inheritance of glory whose burden was too heavy for them to carry.

The Valley of the Fallen where Franco is now buried in that huge
monastery of granite suggests a peace come to those who have labored in
battle. The massive angels who guard the long corridor of the monastery
church carved out of the mountain rest on great swords, their eyes closed
and their heads bowed as if in sleep. Not the Resurrection but the calm of
Holy Saturday after the agony of the Cross permeates that place where
veterans of both sides repose now in peace, their war fought—and won or

lost. Franco insisted, against opposition from his own comrades, that families whose sons died fighting for the Red Republic be permitted, should they desire, to have their dead buried with their fallen Catholic foe. It was a gesture of reconciliation and it is to be hoped that all of them now rest in the Lord. But Spain's victory under Franco on this earth was by no means decisive and that victory could be frittered away tomorrow despite the almost forty years Franco had to consolidate his grip on the nation. I can see as in a nightmare the Valley of the Fallen itself dynamited into rubble by a vengeful Red Republic tomorrow. And thus an assessment of the legacy Franco left his chosen heir Don Juan Carlos de Borbon, is demanded in any eulogy to the memory of the *Caudillo*. After all, Franco warned Spain in his last message pecked out on a typewriter a few days before he went into his final coma that her enemies were alert and again at the door. Nothing is ever forgotten in Spain and no victories are decisive and no defeats are definitive.

Earlier, in the massive demonstration of support Franco received when Europe went wild with hysteria because Spain had executed five terrorists guilty of murdering three times as many policemen, Franco named Spain's enemies from the balcony of the Royal Palace in Madrid: world Masonry and world Communism. The anti-Masonic rhetoric, delivered in his feeble and high pitched voice, was drowned out by the thundering applause of hundreds of thousands of Spaniards who had rallied to their chief because they sensed themselves threatened once again from without and alone. But the rhetoric sounded curiously outdated in this age of ecumenism, and it must have struck most Spaniards that way as they later pondered the meaning of that short five-minute speech. "Masonry" for Franco and for others who had lived through the years of blockade and isolation was a kind of code word, a shorthand, for the entire liberal network of financial and political interests that make up what might be called "the Establishment" of the Western world. And that Establishment is profoundly anti-Catholic and therefore anti-Spanish. That Establishment wants the disestablishment of the Church in Spain as the publicly declared religion of the land. That Establishment today is buttressed by the support of half of the Church in Spain and of well over half of the Church outside Spain. Church and State unity is redolent of the baroque sixteenth century and the Armada and the Inquisition and the whole bag of horrors that form the Black Legend. There hangs about the head of Spain the same halo of hatred, as Chesterton put it, that hangs about the Church of God. The Establishment will not rest until Spain reintroduces the same system of parties that brought it to the brink of ruin in the nineteenth and early twentieth centuries. The Establishment simply does not know or does not care to know that every Spaniard is his own party and his own king and the kind of mechanical discipline needed to make the system work does not exist in Spain. Franco's legacy will receive little comfort and no support at all from the Western democracies, even though a Communist Spain on their Southern flank would mean the end of Europe and the total isolation of the Americas in a world turned into a Red sea. France and everything to its North and East could not survive a Communist Spain. Spanish Communists—and they are numerous and ready to move—are, after all, Spaniards: a favorite sport in Barcelona during the Civil War consisted in mounting machineguns in the portals of churches and spraying the Tabernacle of the Altar. Disinterring dead nuns and violating them publicly ran a close second. Communist or Catholic—Spain is absolutist in its convictions. If Spain turns from God, the forces of Anti-God will have gained their best ally in Europe. But these considerations do not disturb the Establishment whose unarticulated motto is "Better Red than Roman."

The Communist Party dominates the outlawed Democratic Front which headquarters out of Paris. Basque separatism is more virulent than effective politically. The movement is the result of the Madrid government's stupid policy of not recognizing ancient Basque claims to a measure of autonomy and self-government. This sentiment as incarnated in Carlism is wedded to Spanish unity. When divorced from Carlism, as it has been in large measure in recent times, the cry for Basque autonomy is converted into a cry for independence. The dream of uniting the five Spanish Basque provinces with the four that lie in France into one nation is a utopia that Communist tactics have swept into a larger strategy for the dismantling and destroying of Spain as a viable national unit. But neither the Basques nor the Communists have done well by their cause in shooting innocent policemen guarding banks or directing traffic. This kind of public offense to the Spanish Thing is what unites Spaniards who always react to the danger that they can see and never react to the danger that they simply read about.

But the majority of those Spaniards who want a measure of "liberalization" are not Communists or even Socialists. They are Christian Democrats or liberals in the classical political sense of the term and their tradition in Spain dates back to the early nineteenth century. The very word *liberal* is of Hispanic origin and was first used at the Cortes of Cadiz in the post-Napoleonic period under the reign of Ferdinand VII. In a sense Spanish liberalism forms part of the financial and commercial network that knits the Spanish aristocracy into a brotherhood all its own. These people are neither Falangists nor Carlists. They desire a ceremonial monarchy under a king who exercises some influence but little power and their political vision extends no further than 1931 when the old system collapsed and the king fled the country. For this influential class, Franco has been little more than an interlude and the horrors of the Communist Republic have been dimmed in memory thanks to the passing of time. Given that Juan Carlos's very title to the crown reaches back to the dominant liberalism of the last century, he is bound by the pressure of history to yield, if but partially and possibly reluctantly, to a class that always despised Franco even as it waxed economically on the peace he secured Spain.

King Juan Carlos finds himself in a typical double, even triple, bind: damned if he does and damned if he·doesn't. The Falangists and other right-wing elements, including the police and most of the army, want to hold the line against dismantling Franco's Spain. Their most eloquent leader today is the lay theologian, Blas Pinar. The most savagely right-wing force today is the police: too many of their own are being picked off by Communists and separatists who announced in March a policy of killing one policeman a day until the government surrendered to their demands. They are batting about 300 percent and that is good hitting in any man's league. Juan Carlos is already being pressured by the Right to resist any significant move towards change. The classical liberals of wealth, prestige, and title will expect the king to repudiate Franco and return to the old days of Alfonso XIII. They would have preferred Don Juan, but they can live with his son provided that he do their will. The powerful *Opus Dei* which cuts through all non-Communist political divisions will want some liberalization but not too much. The Church is split and polarized into Right and Left, the former being captained by the Cardinal Primate of Toledo and the latter by the Cardinal of Madrid. Premier Arias Navarro, who broke down over national television when he read Franco's *adios* to Spain, is too soft for the Right, especially the police, and he is too hard for the proponents of liberalization. At this writing he has not offered his resignation to the new king, but he is not required to do so by law. He could, of course, be fired or kept on at the sovereign's will. The post-Franco constitution is sufficiently open-ended that Juan Carlos can make of it what he wants: he can both reign and govern or he can let his ministers govern and retire discreetly into the background and assume the "English" role that the liberals have painted for him—a monarchy of plenty of pomp and circumstance but little substance. Such a monarchy cannot last for long in these declining years of the twentieth century. Much depends on the character of Juan Carlos and very little is known of his worth, except that he is a gentleman and the husband of a fiercely ambitious woman, Sophia of Greece, who inherited her passion for power from her mother. Juan Carlos has been taught some traditionalist history and doctrine by his former tutor, Fr. Federico Suarez of the *Opus Dei,* Spain's leading historian of the nineteenth century and a man whose youth was spent in the Carlist movement whose discipline he subsequently abandoned but whose ideas he has retained. In any event, Juan Carlos has been catapulted to power—or political oblivion, but nobody was ever prepared more carefully for kingship than was the prince by General Franco.

And thus Francisco Franco died at the very moment when his ancient enemies began to strike again. This man never thought of himself as a dictator. He left an elaborate constitution which gives representation in the Cortes to the heads of families and to professions and guilds. Individual members of the Cortes defied Franco from time to time on the floor before their peers and their right to do so was never denied nor were they harassed in their private lives. Franco lived by the rules he established, but his personality was such that whatever he willed became law. Those days are now dead and with them have gone the security and peace of an age.

Spain will hold the line for Christian civilization if the men in power keep their nerve. If they yield under foreign pressure, then Spain will slide inevitably to the Left and ultimately to Communism. The victory of Francisco Franco was only an interlude and a holding action in a war as ancient as history itself. And now the old warrior has been buried deep behind the main altar of the basilica of the Valley of the Fallen. A hundred thousand comrades, veterans of the war mingling with young Rightists, sang the Falangist *Cara al Sol* and cried out as one man—"Long live Franco." But he is dead, and only one lonely voice exclaimed "Long live the King" as Juan Carlos, pensive and grim of visage, watched the coffin of his mentor disappear under the mountain.

xii.75

233

PORTRAIT OF AN OUTLAW HERO

He is under a sentence of death if he enters France. He is known to the Algerians as "The Devil of the Maghreb", but he always called himself *Le Ghoul*. He was named successor of the O.A.S. by General Salan. He lost six ribs in Africa and his very existence is a miracle to medical science. Just yesterday he died to the world when he disappeared under the decency of the black habit of the Benedictines. This man is my friend, possibly the most remarkable I have known. Therefore I should like to remember him here.

André Montpeyroux, Marquis de Montpeyroux, is a legend in Africa and a police file in France. I first knew him in Madrid after he had abandoned Algeria, early in 1964. The scion of what is perhaps the most illustrious title in all France, André was then living on the edge of poverty. A tiny man, incredibly thin, some fifty years old, he gave the impression of a constantly exercised defiance to the laws of nature. He ought to have died a dozen deaths, first in World War II in France, later in prison in Germany, finally in the sands of Africa where he raised the banner of Christian civilization against a whole continent bent upon barbarism.

I would meet André from time to time in the house of a mutual friend in Madrid. He always dressed neatly and he always wore the same suit. He never took a cab. He never went to a cafe. He never spoke of himself but only of our dead world, of our civilization, of his beloved France, and of God. DeGaulle had frozen any funds which might have come from his extensive lands in France. I believe that his family estates are in Brittany, but I am not certain because I always sensed that questions about Andre's origin and history would not have been welcome. Nor did the Marquis mingle with the aristocracy of Madrid: he believes in something altogether different.

His books and pamphlets are a blend of high theology and of a lyricism recalling the France of Joan of Arc and of Bayard. There runs through them a nervous passion for adventure reflecting the spirit of this man who made Algeria remember that from out of the West there can still come men who know that the Cross is a Sword. In Algeria's agony. Montpeyroux lifted into being the *Rèsurrection-Française,* a movement which rallied to his side thousands of Christians and Moslems who followed Andre into an impossible battle. I have seen photographs of Andre de Montpeyroux covered in the white robes of the Arab, haranguing streets dominated by Moslem machineguns.

He believed in France and in the presence of Europe in Africa. But his France had nothing to do with the inheritance of the Revolution. Its roots were rather thrust deeper in the past. Andre is a French Traditionalist and Legitimist, one of the last of a band of splendidly romantic Frenchmen.

Rèsurrection-Francaise must not be confused with the O.A.S. André knew that the secret army, although riddled with decency, was also laced with former Socialists and Communists whose racism and economic interests threw them into the arms of the French Right against a common enemy. He knew that high idealism marched side by side with gross materialism in the last agonizing months of resistance.

André shot his way out of desert hideouts a dozen times. He often crossed enemy lines riddled by bullets that would have killed another man. He never seemed to die: this was the secret of his life. Therefore Andre Montpeyroux has passed into legend in Algeria as a Christian devil come out of the tombs of the past to harass the forces of Liberation and Socialist Democracy. When the moment of agony came upon French Algeria, the O.A.S. had accepted the help of *Rèsurrection-Francaise* as would any army fighting with its back to the wall accept the aid of an auxiliary ally.

Despite the charismatic fire surrounding Montpeyroux, his movement never approached the proportions of a massive reaction: its very doctrinal affirmation was perhaps too pure and too severe to achieve widespread popularity in a population not known for its Christian idealism.

With the death of his Algeria, Montpeyroux fled to Spain. I am told that André broke his self-imposed silence only once when he wept publicly upon hearing that the Cathedral of Algiers had been profaned. The story of his role in the war was broken in the European press only upon his entrance into the Benedictines.

I worked with the Marquis briefly in Madrid on a series of lectures. Working with Andre was not easy. He speaks a wretched Spanish and no English. My spoken French approaches zero. But I was astounded by the depth of erudition and at the delicacy of thought of this professional crusader. I will always remember his courtesy to men and his shy courtliness with women, the dignity of his austerity, and the depth of his charity.

The last time I saw André was in a hospital in Madrid. André had been operated on and was recovering from the removal of some mythical internal organ, shot to pieces long before by Arab bullets. I am no specialist in these things and can give no details. André never volunteered any, but the doctors in that hospital swore that he could not be alive. Although I did not know it then, André had already entered into what was soon to become his monastic destiny.

I do not think that I will see André Montpeyroux again. Religious superiors do not encourage visits to novices and I shall have left Europe long before André is ordained a priest. His family in France, across that border that he may never pass in this life, blessed his decision to disappear in the anonymity of the monastery that guards the great cross remembering the Spanish dead of the crusade against Communism. I hope that André will never read these words, which would distress him, but it is good that men everywhere within our crumbling world know of the deeds of heroes.

André Montpeyroux, Marquis de Montpeyroux, Prince of Brittany, I salute you—Knight of Christ: Shield of Christendom: Outlaw Hero.

v.65

A PARTING OF FRIENDS*

Ladies and gentlemen of the Third Summer Institute of the Society for the Christian Commonwealth. Reverendo Padre Eduardo. Don Sigirano Diaz.

Last year in this very *sala de actos* your predecessors were honored by a discourse given us by the heir to the Catholic Empire whose ancestors rest in the peace of the Lord, their remains reposing in those solemn tombs before which we have often prayed for salvation—for Spain, for America, for Holy Church, for Her triumph, and for their souls. Archduke Otto von Habsburg ended his address with the following words: "The Cross does not need Europe; Europe needs the Cross." And as my old companion in arms, Willmoore Kendall, now dead and gone to God, was wont to put it: there are two Europes, European Europe and American Europe. Both belong to the same civilization and common roots unite them, if often but obscurely, in a tree whose ample foliage has covered the world.

Today that tree is withered, its branches crippled and twisted, its leaves scattered by the winds of history. We are living out a long winter of desolation in which the absence of God has covered the world and an unholy silence—not that "sounding Silence Who is God" in the words of San Juan de la Cruz, that holy anticipation of the Word, but a silence which is an absence amidst chatter and noise—has choked the soul. Four hundred years of secularization and materialism are drawing to a close. The time has come to plant and water a new tree of civilization amidst the barbarism surrounding us.

And for that reason you came here to be with us—in Spain, in the Escorial. You came to learn how to be rebels against a society that has denied its God, that has insulted His Holy Church, that has ignored His Mother. You have succeeded to the degree that you consider yourselves to be pirates, God's buccaneers, in a society that has outlawed Him and in so doing has outlawed that band of men who raise aloft the Banner of His sacred Kingship. You truly are Knights of Banished Legitimacy. The skull-and-crossbones, flag of Catholic Spain in the so-called "War of Religion" early in the last century, is today our flag.

The Athanasian Creed tells us that the Father is Lord, the Son is Lord, and the Spirit is Lord, and that there are not three Lords but One. And the Principle of this Ineffable Fecundity which is worked in the very heart of the Tabernacle Who is God is the Father, Abba. But the Father is not King. There is no vigorous theological tradition known to me that insists on addressing Him who is the Lord Father, as King. Christ—Logos, Verbum, Glory of the Father, Light of Light—is King, as you have been taught. And He is King because He inherits—all kings inherit from their fathers—and He inherits from His Father who begets Him in all eternity. And He is King because He conquers; and title to kingship comes to all kings either through heredity or through conquest. And He conquered on the Cross through His Redemption of the human race. And He governs and His Authority is sovereign and there is no other sovereignty in Heaven or on earth.

Why have we gathered together here this summer? Some of us are here because we are bored by the vulgarity and banality of democratic liberalism, of secular humanism. Sheer good taste brought us to the Escorial. Others are here because they wish to fight for the King. Others because they wish to learn. Many—because they wish to have a good time! And this too is a very Catholic thing. God, in His inscrutable providence, saw to it, for reasons unknown to us, that we came together here—some to teach, some to study, all to pray.

We have come this afternoon to the parting of friends. Eight weeks or more we have lived together and been annealed in a common dedication to The Catholic Thing. Our very old civilization is now dead. It had some good things to offer. It was not a bad place within which to live, especially if one belonged to the upper middle classes. It was a comfortable world. God was not outraged publicly. He was simply put in a closet—respected initially as a privileged if eccentric guest; later, like some old uncle, forgotten. And the results of this absentmindedness have been the terror, the horror, of our moment in history: innocents slaughtered in the womb; the aged menaced with the smiling ministrations of a white-robed priesthood of murderers; children ripped from the bosom of the home by public officials because their parents willed that they not be corrupted by an evil system of education. None of this has been dramatic.

De Tocqueville, at the very dawn of the American republican experience, predicted a tyranny that would be suave, easy, unobtrusive, destructive in its very gentleness. That tyranny is upon us today in the United States. Speak out for the truth of God: you will be expelled from almost every Catholic university in the nation. Defend the lives of the innocent: you will be punished at the polls. Win at the polls, as in New York: your victory will be annulled by a governor's veto with the stroke of a pen. Things look very dark indeed!

And therefore I am reminded of General Foch before Paris in 1914 when the German armies were pressing in upon his serried ranks. His cable to the capital: "My right wing has collapsed; my left is chewed to nothing; my center is going down. Situation excellent. I shall attack." He attacked and he won.

I urge this afternoon, my dear friends, that you go home and attack—attack on all fronts. God is with you—more accurately, more modestly, you are with God. How can you fail? What can the ministers of this corrupt order do to you? We have a saying in Spanish: *Dentro de cien años todos calvos*—within a hundred years we are all bald anyhow!

This world can be looked at from many points of view. Astronomically we are a freakish speck of dust whirling through an awful waste of nothingness, menaced by enormous orbs of concentrated heat that threaten our very existence from eon to eon of time. Biologically, we are an improbable concentration of atoms from whence came forth consciousness, the queer ability of the world to look at itself and even become in spirit what it already was in matter. This is almost as absurd as a rock on a mountain meditating on its own weight. Einstein was right when he said that everything makes sense except that sense makes sense. Philosophically, we are a center that has no periphery, a cry for a God we neither see nor hear. Where is He anyway? Theologically, we are the lords of the cosmos, redeemed by Him Who became one with us in flesh and blood—Our Brother, Our Friend, Who is also Our God.

Now I advance to you the following proposition: this startling intervention in time, within an utterly insignificant pimple of a planet, of the Creator—of the Lord God: of the Awesome and Terrible Inner Unity Who is Trinity, of that Company Whose Face cannot be seen without incurring the pain of death by those of us on this side of the veil of existence—this intervention has made us co-creators with the Lord. The words are not mine. They are St. Paul's. If we are to create—if history will not end until all creation is brought back to the Father, through the Son, and in the Holy Ghost—then we had better get about that job of co-creation! This means, in political and social terms, that we fashion a world in which men and women can walk erect, brothers in the Lord, redeemed, and full of the joy and glory of their vocations as sons of God.

Spain did just this for centuries. Spain poured out her wealth, her genius, gave her young lads in the death of battle for generations, in the Name of Our King.

Every nation has its natural constitution: England's is, possibly, the apotheosis of the shop-keeper; France's is the apotheosis of the reason; Germany's—poor Germany—was recently the apotheosis of blood; the United States—the apotheosis of self-aggrandizement and enrichment. Spain's was always the glory of the Holy God in His Holy Church. Menendez-Pelayo caught it on the wing when he wrote: "*España, cuna de San Ignacio; martillo de los hérejes; luz de Trento; evangelizador de la mitad del mundo—esto ha sido nuestra gloria; no tenemos otra.*" "Spain, cradle of St. Ignatius; hammer of the heretics; light of Trent, evangelizer of half the world—this has been our glory; we have none other."

We have come here to the Escorial where a palace is a monastery, where a politics is a theology, where a world is a Heaven, where the very Castillian sky is a paradise, where a man is and walks—only in God. Go back to America and do the same!

You think you cannot? My guess is that none of us can. But the palm of victory, as St. Augustine teaches us, belongs to God. To us there belongs only the battle. And no other battle today is worth fighting. And a man without a battle is less than a man. He is somebody with a mortgage and a Ford.

We will make America Catholic as the *conquistadores* made half the world Catholic, and if we do not do so we will have had the satisfaction of having served the King, of having attempted to save His innocents, in sacralizing the vast expanse of our own nation, of setting down the Cross in our front-rooms and on our plains.

But now there has come, in truth, the parting of friends. In this last and solemn moment I wish you all *adios*—go with God. Forgive us, each one to the other, our faults. Remember our good humor. Walk as Catholics—heads erect. And God be with you all.

x.72

240

REPORTING

THE VISION OF CHRISTOPHER DAWSON

That a man should speculate successfully upon the origins of civil society is not remarkable; that he should prove an able philosopher is not exceptional; that he should stand among the peers of his own nation in the profession of history is a thing not altogether new; that he should command a vision profoundly Christian and altogether human—this has been done before; that he should be all these things at once and together—this is incredible.

Christopher Dawson is certainly the first scholar in the English-speaking Catholic world, perhaps in the whole world. To the Spanish intellectual, Dawson is the spirit of Catholic England; to the German, he is its mind; to the American, he may become its conscience. His subdued eloquence is just now beginning to trouble us and his very existence is a rebuke to our whole educational system.

Yet it is not upon his proposals to reform the university that I would chiefly address myself in this essay. The value of orienting the humanistic disciplines around the reality of Christian culture; Dawson's contention that history be made the hub of the wheel of education; the breadth of vision prompting him to put forth his program—these things can be understood only by discovering what history means to Dawson himself. Every book he has written is a meditation in the concrete on the life of man in time under God. To a distinguished series of studies by Mr. Dawson is now added *The Dynamics of World History*, edited by Mr. John J. Mulloy. (Republished in 1978 by Sherwood Sugden & Co., 1117 Eighth St., La Salle, Il. 61301, $7.95.) Mr. Mulloy has assembled in one book the most significant contributions of Dawson towards a sociology of history. Mr. Mulloy is to be thanked for having taken up the task. He is to be congratulated for having executed it so magnificently.

243

Addressing himself early in life to the status of "Sociology as a Science," Dawson marked out the limits of his future career. He found sociology with a vast body of material at hand and no clearly defined principles with which to organize it. In the meantime sociologists and historians faced one another with mutual distrust. What passed for history among the former was viewed with contempt by men who had given their lives to historical truth. In turn, the cheerful indifference of historians to the supposedly scientific nature of their discipline infuriated men for whom the ideal of science was sacred.

Inheriting from Comte and Saint-Simon, more directly from Frederic Le Play, the hope of building a genuinely scientific sociology; informed by a mind and a sensibility profoundly attuned to the beauty and tragedy of history; possessed of an enormous capacity for synthesis—Dawson had taken to himself the materials of both sociologist and historian. He has succeeded so well that it is often difficult to determine whether he is writing history or sociology. This irritates pedants but it bespeaks Dawson's fidelity to the real: existence, after all, is too dense and rich to be reduced to the severely defined limits professors place on their own disciplines. These limits often cloud that total commitment to being, that adherence to the real which sunders forever the whole man, Unamuno's "man of flesh and bone," from that desiccated anonymous observer whose delicate shade haunts our academies and rustles politely through the unread pages of our scholarly journals today. Existence, Gilson once wrote, "is the catalyzer of essences." The degree to which a man realizes this truth concretely measures the distance he puts between himself and the original sin of the intellectual mind: rationalism. Of rationalism there is no trace in Christopher Dawson.

Writing much later in life, and this out of the fullness of his wisdom, Dawson declares that the sense of history is born neither of scientific tools nor intellectual distinctions, but is given as a gift and a vision essentially esthetic in structure. Some men simply see the heart of a culture and some do not. We reach here, it seems to me, an absolute. The difference between seeing and not seeing can be reduced to nothing more fundamental than the opposition between sight and blindness. Thus Henry Adams, for all his Unitarianism, saw the thirteenth century; G.G. Coulton, for all his Latin, did not.

Yet vision, insists Dawson, must be pumped by the spirit, the mind, and even by the blood. He learned all about the blood from Frederic Le

Play, a sociologist who dealt in things and men, and Dawson warmed to him as to a brother. From Le Play he learned that the life of a man and of the society of which he is a part grows out of the earth itself and like a mighty tree waxes so long as it keeps its roots in the things that are. Explicitly stating his agreement with T.S. Eliot that a higher culture can be nourished only by flourishing regional cultures, Dawson insists that a "meta-culture," while transcending its origins, must always walk upon them for they are the very limbs of civilization. Amputate them and the gangrene of cosmopolitanism sets in, sapping society of its vigor and draining it of all health. This judgment lies behind the many condemnations of our rootless urban culture of today that run throughout this entire collection of essays.

Dawson finds Islam a point in question. While flourishing in faraway India and Burma under highly civilized and refined conditions, Islam never lost the blinding conception of a naked God that came once and forever to simple men annealed in the barren grandeur of the desert. And, we might add, the awful transcendence of the Almighty is softened and made human for men who live among groves and who know light airs and easy mists. For such the gods are many and the saints are friends of the Lord. What Dawson says so lucidly on the level of theory concerning what I would call the embodiment of the spirit in the womb of the world, Hilarie Belloc once said poetically in his somber meditation on "The Men of the Desert." This essay, certainly one of the half-dozen great essays in the English language, culminates in the conviction that grace incarnates itself the better in men in proportion to their natural perfection.

If both Belloc and Dawson have been accused of associating the Christian Thing too closely with culture it is because both men have seen that the God of the Catholic Faith is not the "Totally Other" of Protestant theology, but a God transcending *within* immanence, a God discovered always by men located in a world and moving within a history. To see the things of the spirit acting above and beyond history, touching men who are thereby translated out of history—to understand religion and society in this manner is not only a fall into Barthianism: it is something even worse: a failure to understand the sexual dimension of the human spirit.

While fully sensitive, as indicated, to the immanent character of religion, Dawson carefully preserves its transcendence. Here he parts company with Eliot whose *Notes Towards a Definition of Culture* tended in the direction of identifying religion and culture. A religion cannot be explained, Dawson insists, in purely sociological terms. Every attempt to do so has robbed religion of its intrinsic interest and has drained it of its crucial significance. The Church, Chesterton's "thundering chariot" swerving this way and that through all the early ages, maintained a balance between those who would have robbed Christianity of its historicity by refining the Faith into a kind of cosmogony and those who would have robbed the Faith of its transcendence by reducing the Kingdom of God to the expected reign of Christ among His saints within history. Dawson's essays on "Christianity and the Meaning of History" form the brilliant center and baroque climax of Mr. Mulloy's compilation. In a series of rapidly developed arguments, Dawson sketches "The Christian View of History," "History and the Christian Revelation," "Christianity and Contradiction in history," and "The Kingdom of God and History"; finally, he gathers the whole into one splendid vision written with remarkable economy and insight: "St. Augustine and the City of God." Here is summed up, not only the Augustinian and Catholic theology of history, but the very heart of Dawson's commitment to Christian existence.

Contrasting the Greek word with the Hebrew, Dawson sees in the former a contempt and a fear for the things that pass; an emphasis on the universal and the abstract that drained history of any substance proper to itself; a theory of cyclic return that stripped history of both its novelty and its drama. But the Hebrews knew that the unique moment in time is the crossroads at which man ever stands, pointing back to a past having meaning in its light of the present and forwards towards a future full of mystery and apocalypse. The Catholic, combining the breadth which is one with the mission of the Church with a "sense of the uniqueness and irreversibility of the historic process . . . is the heir of a universal tradition." Quoting with pride the words of Orosius, Dawson has truly made them his own: "Everywhere is my country, everywhere my law and my religion. . . . The breadth of the east, the fullness of the north, the extent of the south and the islands of the west are the wide and secure home of my citizenship, for it is as a Roman and a Christian that I address Christians and Romans."

Forever reminded by the shattering absurdity of the Incarnation that history is made, not by laws and causal sequences but by men and God, the Catholic sense of history is irrevocably opposed to the rationalist reduction of history to scientific necessity. "History is impatient of all . . .

artificial constructions. It is at once aristocratic and revolutionary." Arbitrary and unpredictable to a reason forever bent on clarity, the darkness of history is bathed in the Light of the Incarnate Word. And in this darkness lit by the lamp of faith the Catholic sees everywhere "the signs of a divine purpose and election."

That God fingered an obscure and harsh tribe, thus touching it with the mark of His Covenant; that He came into time and was born of woman; that He died on the Cross and thereby sealed the redemption of the whole human race—these follies to the Greek mind are the substance of the Catholic heart. "What has Athens to do with Jerusalem?" The taunt of Tertullian is probed with an amazing delicacy by Dawson who really understands the meaning of Donatism and the African Church. The rough comradeship of the African Church. The rough comradeship of the African Christians; their contempt of the rich and their impatience with injustice; their incomprehension before the philosophical traditions of the Hellenic world; their confident hope in an early end to worldly history; their passion to taste again the fleshly presence of Christ who would surely come soon and gather round Him His oppressed, the little ones of His Heart; the dream of Tertullian of an altogether earthly paradise here below, a paradise swept clean of Greek seduction and Imperial oppression—these are the things and this the spirit Augustine faced in Africa when touched with the dignity of the episcopacy.

All Africa seemed to be crying for martyrdom as this whole continent groaned under a cross fashioned, so men thought, not on Golgotha but on the Acropolis. Outwardly ascetic and haggard, the African spirit hungered inwardly for the luxury of a faith devoid of mind, of a God so one with man in history that He surrendered His very transcendence. This excessive contempt of the world gave birth to the irony of a Christian materialism. From the East Augustine faced a danger more insidious because more subtle: the inclination to reduce the Kingdom of God to a "supersensuous and intelligible world"; the tendency to dissolve the Faith into "a kind of Christian *Mythos*." Origen, despite his orthodox intentions—declares Dawson—produced a new and dangerous attitude towards the Church in which "the traditional conception of the Church as . . . the New Israel, and the forerunner of the Kingdom of God fell into the background as compared with a more intellectualist view of the Church as the teacher of an esoteric doctrine or *gnosis* which leads the human soul from time to eternity."

St. Augustine, while fully preserving the transcendent destiny of man, located our salvation within the City of God—a City whose source is trans-historical but whose being englobes the whole of history. Older than the world because its first citizens are the angels, "as wide as humanity, since in all successive ages Christ is the same Son of God, co-eternal with the Father, and the Unchangeable Wisdom by Whom every rational soul is made blessed," the City of God is the very spiritual unity of the whole universe.

Christ is both the Wisdom of the Father and "the fullness of time." In Him eternity and time, history and transcendence, are gathered into the bosom of the Father in whom we live and move and have our being. Sharply set off from the City of Man, the citizen of the divine city can see the Hand of God in the contradictions of history, the breath of the Spirit in each chance meeting of men in the crossroads of time. The metaphysics of time, the meaning of memory as the prism of history, the crisis of freedom, the rule of love—these Augustinian themes fill out the Catholic sense of history. It is a very good thing indeed that there be a Christopher Dawson to remind us that we are the people of history and that history is ours.

Dawson makes his own Augustine's claim that we are living now in the last age and that the end is near. With the Incarnation, the history saw its most solemn event and nothing remains, as Newman once wrote, but now "to gather in the Saints . . . the present distress . . . is ever *close* upon the next world and resolves itself into it." Yet the Catholic of the past never waited grimly for the end. He never felt constrained to husband the world against the approach of the apocalypse. This is the role of a Heidegger or of any existentialist thinker who has passed through the Calvinist rejection of being. To the Catholic people of history the world was a splendid jewel and in its goodness all were called to luxuriate. It is in the baroque civilization of the seventeenth century that Dawson finds the last great corporate expression of the Catholic salute to being. No one really understands Dawson's carefully worded strictures against modern industrial civilization who has not read his essay, "Catholicism and the Bourgeois Mind."

Ironically reminding all of us that we are bourgeois whether we know it or not, Dawson goes on to identify the bourgeois mind with the "closed" spirit, the commercial spirit that never deals in men and things and therefore never gives itself away. Following Weber and Sombart, Dawson sees the bourgeois spirit as essentially chained in the medieval world, then liberated by the Protestant insistence on faith alone and by the Protestant rejection of the sacramental character of the universe. The deadly enemy of the peasant; the aristocrat; the soldier; the priest; the mystic; the artist, the bourgeois can almost be defined by his opposition to these *existentially* Catholic types.

The baroque was thrown up in protest against the rising commercial spirit of Holland and England. Fused under the force of battle, the baroque was an artificial culture, a theatrical world affirming flamboyantly the glory and grandeur of the things God had made. It was an erotic culture that lavished itself on God and man, "an uneconomic culture which spent its capital . . . recklessly and splendidly . . . the baroque spirit lives in and for the triumphant moment of creative ecstasy. It will have all or nothing. . . . 'All for love and the world well lost,' *'Nada, nada, nada,'* "

Dawson sees the turning back of Alexander Farnese from Paris as one of the crucial moments in history. The defeat of the Spanish arms marked the victory of the closed over the open spirit, of the cautious over the ecstatic, of the prudent over the lover. Thus was the age of great love affairs brought to an end. The Praise-God Barebones won the world and the future was given over to the penny-savers. Yet the Baroque continued to fight on. A culture of the court that enshrined the *Sanctum Sanctissimum* on a high altar as befitted a Great King, it was simultaneously the spirit of the Catholic peoples of Latin and Austrian Europe. The risings in La Vendée in 1793, in Tirol in 1809, in the Basque provinces in the late nineteenth century—these, maintains Dawson, were the last sparks of the grandeur of the Counter Reformation genius.

Dawson warns us against the bourgeois spirit; perhaps it wouuld be better to call it today the post-bourgeois spirit. The "closed" heart becomes "other-directed" when it loses its nerve. We live now in an "other-directed" universe of little men. If we would preserve our own inheritance, an inheritance stretching back beyond the days of the Fathers to the time of the Prophets, we must capture again the sense of history. We must walk again with Augustine.

This brings me back to where I began. Dawson has suggested in these past few years that reform of the Catholic University to which I referred in the opening pages of this essay. He has suggested that Christian culture be made the center of all our educational endeavors. It is doubtful whether this can be done by administrative fiat. A revolution is called for, a revolution worked in the hearts of Catholic scholars everywhere in this nation. To read *The Dynamics of World History* is to be appalled all the more by the shabby efforts made today to force us to abandon our own heritage in the name of "commitment to the twentieth century," but it is also to see the possibility of the necessary revolution.

i.56

CHARLIE AND LEGITIMACY

"The visitor to Rome," commences David Daiches' elegaic prologue to the *The Last Stuart*, "is likely to find more interesting things to do than to turn up the narrow *Via dei Santi Apostoli*, where he may notice a shabby baroque building." I too have been there. The building now houses a business and language school, a *pensione*, a restaurant and barber's shop. Passing under the archway which gives upon a small courtyard, the visitor—Daiches tells us—"will hear the clatter of dishes and smell the odours of cooking from the open windows of the restaurant kitchen." To the left there is an unnoticed plaque bearing an inscription that tells the visitor that "There lived in this building Henry, Duke, later Cardinal of York, who, surviving son of James III of England, took the name of Henry IX. In him in the year 1807 the Stuart dynasty became extinct." Daiches puzzles, as did I, over the absence of the name of Prince Charles Edward Stuart who, with his younger brother Henry, was born and spent his childhood in this crumbling old edifice—and who died there. Then it was the somber *Palazzo Muti*; now it is full of the pungent spices and the noisy life of the poor that quicken Rome, always young amidst her ruins.

But what have the streets of Rome to do with the rising of the clans in the bleak wilderness of the distant Highlands of Scotland? What do the wail of the pipes at Glenfinan and Lochiel with his nine hundred and Keppoch with his five hundred and the Royal Standard unfolded by the Duke of Athole and the Young Chevalier—bent on Three Crowns or Death (these his own words)—have to do with a Franciscan convent in Rome, near by the old *Palazzo Muti*, which houses the heart of a "Queen of Great Britain"—Maria Clementina de Sobieski, mother of Charles Stuart and herself destined never to wear crown nor touch soil in the British Isles? "Queen of Great Britain"—the anomaly of these traces of Stuart Scotland in the midst of Rome is deepened by the fact that it was precisely "Great Britain" whose existence Scotland denied; the exiled Stuarts launched their thrust for independence in the name of undoing the infamous Act of Union of 1707.

The wanderings of the House of Stuart, exiled after the Protestant Settlement of 1688, have gripped the imagination of romantics for better than two hundred years—and the attraction continues even to the present, as witness the publication of this recent spate of books on "Bonnie Prince Charlie." And no wonder; no wonder Sir Walter Scott and Robert Louis Stevenson, for example, could not resist them. From Whitehall and power to exile at St. Germain and eventually to permanent banishment in Rome, the Scottish Royal House that by a freak of history inherited the crowns of England and Ireland seems, in retrospect, to have been bigger than both life and poetry. Life rarely reveals the perfect curve of decline and extinction that marked the Stuart dynasty. Nor does art permit itself the extravagance that marked this road to oblivion: artistic verisimilitude would never allow so many "Protestant Winds" to frustrate every Jacobite invasion from the continent by friendly French or Spanish fleets; it was not aesthetically credible that Seven Men should take on all the might of England—and therefore it happened: The Seven Men of Moidart, but most especially a young prince whose charm was such that he carried everything before him—for a time—simply by appealing, as he did to Lochiel, to ancestral loyalty and by stating to the clans of the far northwest: "Here I am—your Prince in the Name of Our King, my father."

Jacobitism, the Stuarts in exile, has no theory behind it. Nobody articulated any doctrine indicating why a sensible man ought to risk his all for this somewhat erratic family. Nonetheless the history of the Stuarts in their opposiiton to the rising power of the rich, concentrated in Parliament, is politically intelligible. The crown in theory stood for the poor man against the powers of this world—this was its immemorial function, its reason for existence. The destruction of royal power meant, quite simply, the turning over of England—and by extension, Scotland and Ireland—to the new capitalist class formed by the earlier Reformation. In the subsequent frustrated efforts of the Stuarts to return "to their own" the anti-capitalist—or more accurately, non-capitalist—nature of their support is evidenced by the records of the Jacobite dead: a list can be found in *The Stuart Calender, A Centenary Memorial of the Royal House of Stuart,*

London, Kegan Paul, Trench and Co., 1886—my copy belonged to the then "*Apostolici Protonotarii, Roberti Setoni*".) The names form a rosary of common men, yeomen, craftsmen, gentlemen of little wealth; very occasionally noblemen; all of them done to death by the Hanoverian government, by Whiggery.

Nonetheless Jacobitism—unlike Carlism in Spain—never unfurled its banners under the cause of the Poor of Christ, oppressed by a new order of things. The appeal of Jacobitism was deeply personal and romantic: "O Charles, Son of James, son of James, son of Charles, with you I'd gladly when the call sounds for marching." *Tearlach Mac Sheumais.*

Each of these books, written in independence of one another, is excellent in its own way. Daiches locates the entire Jacobite movement within the context of Scottish nationalism. Among the more original and brilliant insights of his study is his analysis of the clan system in the Highlands: pre-dating medieval and Frankish feudalism, clan life is not based, insists Daiches, on mutually exchanged oaths, as was the Feudal pact; clan politics is totally patriarchal, Celtic, pre-medieval. And it was this pre-medieval order that backed Prince Charles in his bid for the throne: where went the chief there went the clansmen, even to Culloden and death. Margaret Forster's *The Rash Adventurer* is the book of a woman: she both loves and hates Bonnie Charlie. He was rash but she adores him in his rashness; he deteriorated rapidly after his lost bid for the crown—and here Miss Forster shows better psychological insight and human understanding than many writers who simply damn the debauched prince into hell. Mr. John Selby's *Over The Sea to Skye* is a splendid military history of the '45. Selby is no Jacobite—or if he be one he keeps quiet about it. He even has good things to say about The Butcher of Culloden, the Duke of Cumberland, for putting some spine into an English army badly shaken by Prince Charles' victories in Scotland. And Butcher Boy *was* quite efficient: when he burned out the Highlands he neatly destroyed the clan system, that last dagger aimed at the heart of the new world.

All three new books tell a story well known, although each author tells it in a new way. Taking an army of something like 5,000 Highlanders, clansmen, from the wild north of Scotland and the distant islands to the west, interlaced with a handful of French-trained Irishmen, with practically no cavalry, the young Stuart Regent marched his army south to within striking distance of London. Rolling past hostile cities and villages, the Scots sent poor peasants and townsfolk screaming into their houses—the Whigs had told them that Scots ate babies when in the field. (These were the same Highlanders whose ladies often gave private lessons in Greek, Latin and French to small boys bent upon education.) Prince Charles marched all the way south on foot, leading his father's subjects; disdaining a mount, he was the first man on the road every morning and the last one to sleep at night. Some of the gentlemen with him murmured against his preference for the company of Highlanders: there is some truth to the contention that Charles, all of his life, wroshiped these clansmen as supermen. This was the Old Order in Arms, a pre-feudal and patriarchal society that had out-lived the Middle Ages and that even then, in the full sweep of a new capitalist world, challenged all its weight and wealth. And London was the goal.

Studied by maps—they are* available in the three books under discussion—this Jacobite push south into the heart of England looks like a delicate minuet, or the tacking of a square-rigged sailing ship off Cape Horn, trying to make it east to west against the prevailing gales. The Scottish army weaves here and then ducks there, marching always between two numerically superior English armies, either of which could have squashed the rebels. The genius behind this fabled march south was Lord George Murray—brilliant, self-assertive, righteous and altogether impossible to get along with. Lord George Murray was one of those men who is always right, even when he is wrong. But Lord George *was* wrong—once: that one time sealed the history of England and possibly of the world. Lord George forced Prince Charles to retreat from Derby.

As usual Murray had good reasons for what he did. All three authors agree with earlier authorities on this point but all three, interestingly enough, give Charles' case a fair showing. The Jacobites had looked for English support. Charles and his men had hoped for a mass rising in the north of England by Stuart sympathizers, especially in Lancashire. (Only the old King in Rome, James III, had warned his son not to count on *anything* from the English, but James was ignored by his son.) There was no rising. The English Jacobites—the Squire Western types—were splendid at drinking toasts to "The King Over the Water" but their enthusiasm waned when the wine wore off: when the Scots passed by the road, the English Jacobites remained riveted to their chairs, empty glasses in hand. The Welsh were due to come in from the west—levies up to twenty thousand! But at Derby there was no sign of a single Welshman. Everybody at the Prince's council at Derby said that London, the first megalopolis of the world, now less than 150 miles away by road, would simply swallow up the Jacobite army of 5,000 (dwindling daily) if it ever got there. What could some few thousand Celtic-speaking Scots in kilts do in the labyrinth of the streets of London? Get Lost, apparently! Murray urged a retreat and a retrenchment and was backed by the entire council minus two, one duke and the Prince himself. Charles raged in that famous and fateful meeting. His whole life hung on the decision.

"There was a considerable Jacobite party in London," Daiches reports, "led by Alderman Heathcote, who would have given their support. Furthermore, Charles' brother Henry was at last completing preparations to embark 10,000 French troops at Dunkirk and land them in the south of England." Charles knew that French support, fickle at best and always cynical, would melt away if the army retreated. The army retreated and France lost interest, exactly as Charles predicted. Charles earlier had agreed to accept the democratic principle in his councils and Lord George had seen to it that he had the votes for retreat even before Charles knew of Murray's plan. Charles lived by his agreement that day but swore then that he would never again risk his father's cause on a vote.

Charles did not march back to Scotland on foot in the midst of his men as he had done coming south. He mounted a horse and skulked behind the last serried lines of an exhausted army cheated of victory. Charles was dead right and Lord George was dead wrong—but who could have known this *then*? None of our three authors speaks of The Welsh Connection. But one day after the Jacobite army abandoned Derby a rider—it is said—on a horse almost dead from having been pushed all night, careened into Derby. He had come to tell the Prince that Wales was on the move. Finding neither Prince nor army, he went home. This gesture permitted subsequent Welshmen to boast that they had ridden out ten miles—some fifteen—on the way to England and Derby. It made for good drinking stories. This story, affirmed by earlier historians of the '45, is not touched in any of these three new books. But whether the Welsh moved or not, Charles—we now know—could have taken London. George II, that "wee German lairdie," was packed and ready to pull out by boat for Hanover. There was a run on the Bank of London that was about to ruin the Whig financial power.

But—looking at things from Derby—Lord George was right and Lord George was wrong. And Charles was right and Charles was wrong. And we leave these things to God.

Charles' heart was broken and he commenced rapidly to cease being a man.

Who was Prince Charles Edward Stuart, "The Bonnie Charlie" of Scottish song and legend? What manner of man could have turned the most progressive and advanced European country upside down with a handful of ragged clansmen for the better part of a year?

This young man who decided to win three crowns for his exiled father, the *de jure* James III and the VIII, was born and raised in the *Palazzo Muti* in Rome. But he was raised to be an Englishman. Drilled from babyhood on the conviction that he was heir to the Three Crowns, Charles lived his life under that conviction. After the failure of the '45, he disappeared for years: no one knew where he was; he lived incognito and passed into the sewers of Europe for about a decade: no one, not his father and not even the English police could find him. An indifferent Catholic, Charles refused to abandon his Faith when it could have helped him—when in Scotland and England. Later he toyed with Anglicanism for a short time; but he returned to the Faith of his youth. Truly, Charles lived only one theological proposition: sons may not be disinherited; no law passed by Parliament could unmake him, deny that he really was who he was—the son of James III and the VIII, himself the son of James II himself the son of Charles I. These adamantine truths were never questioned by Charles Stuart. He had one moment of glory—and neither Whig history nor the sanctimoniousness of moralistic prigs can deny him that moment: he landed in Scotland, Prince Regent of the Three Kingdoms with his father's writ in his coat, and he landed more alone than has any man bent upon such a vast venture anywhere or at any time in history. The Seven Men of Moidart—Charles' companions—come down to us from a very cold and rationalistic century as a kind of promise and confirmation of loyalty. Of political philosophy Charles knew nothing—and his soul was probably saved thereby. He knew all that he had to know: I am the heir to England, Scotland and Ireland. And I am that heir because God has made me the son of my father. To this heritage he gave his whole life.

These books detail Charlie's life in hiding in Scotland after Cumberland beat and destroyed the Jacobite army at Culloden. The

English were so powerful that they could take every victory Charles imposed upon them but Charles could not take, his power was too slender, the one defeat—a resounding defeat—that Butcher Boy wrought upon his cousin. At Culloden Charles should have listened to Lord George, as Murray ought to have listened to Charles at Derby: the two men never got along. The Cause was destroyed and within the day Butcher Boy put all the Highlands to fire and the sword.

Daiches and Forster detail, as have others before them, the degeneration of Charles Stuart after his one moment of glory. Both authors show considerable restraint and civility in treating of those long years of decline. What can a man do, after all, who has been trained from boyhood that he must rule—and he does not rule? Charles may have become, after his marriage to Louise of Stolberg, "a filthy clown" (Forster), but he certainly was not the brute that hostile testimony has made him out to be. That the Bonnie Charlie who chased Cope away at Prestonpans would be cuckolded in middle age by a bloody fiddler, Alfieri, is worse than tragic: this incident has about it all the savage cruelty of comedy. Charles ought to have died at Culloden as his great-grandfather ought to have died at Naseby. But God saw to it that art was frustrated.

Jacobitism died effectively with the '45 (the Elibank Plot and "The Swedish Connection" belong to the politics of desperation: I may write of them another time). But Charles Stuart lives in ballad and song and he still walks in the Highlands. This "Bonnie Who Lies Over the Ocean" is still *sung* and song is the touchstone of Christian politics. Who sings about George II?

This spate of books about Charles Edward Stuart, a man who resurrected an almost dead movement and almost brought it to success, moves us to wonder why he remains and has remained so popular through two hundred years. It is not as the old and abandoned drunk, calling for his pipes and falling into a deep stupor whenever the Highlands are mentioned to him—this in Rome in his old age—that Charles is remembered. He is remembered as the young hero of the White Cockade, who answered London's offer of 35,000 pounds on his head with 35 pounds on "The Head of the Elector of Hanover"—he wasn't worth any more! Charles is remembered in his one moment of glory with his Scottish Highlanders, with whom he found his only true home. He is remembered for leading and personifying a politics he neither created nor chose, but was born to: from birth he had been cheated of an easy crown by a father who had refused to abandon the Profession and Faith of the Holy Catholic Church; and Charles' own grandfather had simply thrown away Three Crowns because of his allegiance to that same Faith; and he knew, of course, that his great uncle—Charles II—had died in that Faith. Bonnie Charlie somehow resented all this religion: it certainly had ruined his life. But he remained a Stuart and died, as he had lived most of his life, a Catholic.

The literature of Jacobitism is extensive today; a scholar can make a career out of attempting to identify "Pickle The Spy." But a theory of the Jacobite movement is difficult to come by. Jacobitism as such had no doctrine. We can search the annals of the movement bent on restoring the House of Stuart and we can find no specific political philosophy that supported its men at arms in the four risings (counting the '89 and the '19) that marked Jacobite history. The Stuarts *had* to go—Belloc and others have demonstrated this thesis—because they were medieval anachronisms in the face of a rising capitalism. Popular monarchy simply could not continue to exist in England with the rich in the saddle. Seventeenth and eighteenth-century England was swollen with a new aristocracy of money. The Stuarts were doomed, then. But what kept men faithful to their cause, even when they were exiled? What moved the Stuart supporters—if wealthy themselves—to risk fortune and lands to restore the Old Family? What moved poor men to risk everything, family and livelihood and even life, to stitch upon their tunics the White Cockade?

Contemporary political philosophy cannot account for Jacobitism. Books and doctoral dissertations dealing with the Jacobite movement in this country have been done under the aegis of history departments. Political science cannot touch this issue because Jacobitism ultimately was a *legitimist* political movement and contemporary political theory has no criteria for dealing with legitimacy. Our typical political science professor in this area will deny any existence to legitimacy as a valid object for speculation—even as he connives to get a job for his son in the same department. Nepotism is perverted legitimacy but a recognition of legitimacy nonetheless.

Jacobitism was used by non-juring Anglicans who believed in the Divine Right of Kings. Jacobitism was an instrument for Scottish nationalism in its efforts to undo the Act of Union. Jacobitism was the only bosom into which Irish patriots could throw themselves. Jacobitism was the ally of Catholics who saw in the converted Royal House rescue from the intolerable laws against them. Some few Catholics saw something more: the conversion of England.

Charlie and Legitimacy

But Jacobitism itself was none of these things. Alfonso XIII of Spain once said that any royalist movement based exclusively on the principle of legitimacy could last only one generation. He was, of course, very wrong. The Carlist movement in Spain is about one hundred and fifty years old and the Jacobite movement lasted, as an effective political power, some eighty years. True, the Carlist movement is not exclusively legitimist: Carlism involves a doctrine. But Jacobitism had no doctrine: it only had legitimacy. But legitimacy reaches to something far deeper than doctrine: it reaches to being. A son is the son of his father and *his* father inherited before him. These truths of being are prior to every legality, prior to all doctrine: they are simply one with the agathonic structure of Existence. Fathers and mothers in their own families are legitimists: they favor their sons, push them forward, see that they inherit what they—the parents—can give them. Legitimacy is normalcy. When the political order is normal, it reflects the principle of legitimacy. When this normalcy is overwhelmingly familial, then the political order is familial: families rooted and established safely in the things which are their own throw up dynasties that represent this familial order of social existence. Christian kings are legitimate because they are heirs of Christian dynasties. In a profound sense the dynasty governs, not the man.

As Doctor Alvaro D'Ors has demonstrated in his little cameo, that work of genius—*Legitimidad familiar y formas de gobierno*—legitimacy is deeper then legality. When a society is dominated totally by families, be they rich or poor; when the family itself is considered the ultimate *political* unit of existence, says Don Alvaro, then that society quite naturally represents itself according to the way in which it is: i.e., families are governed by a family—the principle of legitimacy incarnate. However, when a society is partially familial, partially dominated by men with family *names*, and partially made up of men whose family backgrounds do not count at all, then we have an aristocratic republic: ancient republican Rome or the United States of America in the early years of its history. When, finally, we have a society made up *politically*, neither totally of families nor partly of families but rather of individuals, then—by nature—we have a democracy, in which the individual is the ultimate ontological unit of political reality.

Jacobitism must be understood as the intrusion and continued existence of an older legitimacy within a new aristocratic order of things. When the crown no longer passed naturally from father to son as does property pass from any father to his son; when the crown became dependent upon the will of an assembly, Parliament; when the crown was conferred rather than inherited, then England was torn apart. The Divine Right controversy earlier on in the history of the Stuarts was by no means the proper trench from which royalists could make a counter-attack. Roman Catholics, after all, did not believe in Divine Right: witness Robert Bellarmine against King James I; but Roman Catholics, along with Anglicans, did believe in the principle of legitimacy. Divine Right, on the other hand, was a peculiarly Lutheran doctrine. Legitimacy is not really a doctrine at all: it is simply a truth about things as they are. When a *group* of families dominates a society *as families*—and this has been so with the English aristocracy—then dynastic and popular monarchy has to be abolished. The Stuarts were between an older, non-aristocratic order and the new order dominated by familial wealth. No historian any longer ought to wonder why these Italian born and bred Stuarts turned out the entire north of Scotland in their favor: clan life is patriarchal; the defense of the clan involves the defense of the legitimate right of the king. Charlie, like Jamie the Rover, his father before him, was the incarnation of familial legitimacy. For this reason both gathered to their cause all the poetry and imagination and glamor of Scotland. Therefore all the money of London reigned against them. The Stuarts were not rejected because they were legitimate. That the Catholic Son of the Father is Himself Legitimate is a consideration into which I dare not enter, at least for this time. *Tearlach Mac Sheumais.*

vii.74

ST. THOMAS AQUINAS

This year marks the seven-hundredth anniversary of the death of St. Thomas Aquinas, the Common Doctor of The Holy Roman Catholic Church. The Dominican Saint is being honored by philosophical and theological congresses celebrated throughout the world and the significance of his thought is being commented on, respectfully if not enthusiastically, by the secular press here and abroad.

St. Thomas's life was lived in a hurry. This is the overwhelming impression I get from reading Father James Weisheipl's monumental new biography, *Friar Thomas D'Aquino*. Born at Roccasecca, Italy, in 1224, Thomas rushed to his death on March 7, 1274 in the Cistercian Abbey at Fossanova. His life was spent in a whirlwind of writing and preaching and teaching and taking up the staff or mounting the mule: what a rider and what a walker he must have been! Italy to Germany to Italy to France to Italy again and then back to France again and back to Italy and the end. His first Parisian period at the university lasted ten years and Thomas apparently did not even have enough time to learn French. Everywhere we see him writing—in a nervous and unintelligible script that always fell behind the swiftness of his mind—and dictating, often to three of four scribes at once.

Everything that he wrote was *ad hoc*. As a Master in Theology he commented on the Scriptures and on the *Sentences* of Peter Lombard as was expected of him. As a Dominican he defended the right to existence of mendicant orders against a secular clergy that challenged that right, especially in Paris. As a Catholic apologist he answered the plea to refute the errors of Islam with the magisterial *Summa Contra Gentiles*. As a professor of theology he produced a "simple" text for beginners: the *Summa Theologiae*. As an apostle of Christ who saw that the rising Averoism in the universities was corrupting the faith of students, he busied himself with the enormous task of writing a whole plethora of commentaries on the works of Aristotle. As a watchdog of orthodoxy he debated that perpetual sophomore Siger de Brabant and defended the immortality of the human soul. He answered every request made on his pen, writing on usury and the treatment of Jews and kingship. It is thought that he composed the brilliant liturgy for the Feast of Corpus Christi. He constantly preached in Latin to his own brothers in religion, to the university—wherever he might be—and often in his Italian vernacular to the laity.

This miracle of the constancy of his energy, the resolution in execution that marked his whole life—how could any one man have done all that Thomas did in so few years? He wrote forty massive treatises and dozens of smaller works. St. Thomas Aquinas literally made of his mind and his body a holocaust in the service of God and His Church. He never complained of the vast tasks put upon him. Yet his prose reads as though it were the work of an extremely calm author, untroubled by the exigencies of practical life; there is a kind of serenity of both doctrine and style that permeates everything he did. Contrasted with the burdens placed upon him and the nervousness of the comings-and-goings of a life lived always "on the move," St. Thomas defies psychological analysis. The toughness of his intellectuality—not a shade of Christian sentimentalism in Aquinas—synthesized with the charity and humility of his person would be a problem for historians today *if* he had stood still long enough for them to take a look at him.

A number of years ago the late Msgr. Gerald Phelan made the startling claim that St. Thomas is better understood in the twentieth century than he was in his own time. This claim is difficult to substantiate but it is even more difficult to refute. The vast richness of St. Thomas's teaching is simply too gargantuan to be digested by any one age or any one man. What he knit into a unity of doctrine we perforce scatter into a pedantry of specialties. Seven hundred years after his death the entire Christian philosophical tradition has not been able to catch up to him as he still hurries on donkey or foot from country to country and from pulpit to pulpit. Still today he hurries along, and he beckons the Christian intelligence into a new age.

By their fruits ye shall know them: it was the fruit of the wisdom of Brother Thomas that constrained the Church Fathers at Trent to place upon the altar, next to the Holy Scriptures, the *Summa Theologiae*. And this great tree of doctrine then brought forth the new fruit promised by Pope Leo XIII in his *Aeterni Patris* of 1876 which recommended the wisdom of Aquinas to the Catholic world. Already St. Thomas—without the cheapness of clairvoyance but with the brilliance of insight—had reconciled and transcended the genuine preoccupations of both David Hume and Emmanuel Kant. He was soon to do more. When a latter day idealism would have thrown into doubt the very being and goodness of God's world early in this century, there was Thomas to refute the insult. When a narrow fideism would have divorced faith from reason, there was the reason of Thomas in defense of the reasonableness of the Faith. When a proud rationalism would have divorced reason from faith, there was Thomas telling the world that not only can reason *not* disprove any article of the creed but that a reason divorced from the Faith falls far short of what reason can do. When a post-war Europe declared existence irrational and gave over life to the despair of nothingness, there was Thomas telling us that the Name of God is Existence—"I Am Who Am." It matters not the challenge nor the time nor place. Thomas is already there, not simply defending but attacking and advancing a doctrine that challenges us to move beyond his own conclusions, using his principles as mere launching pads. But St. Thomas is a terribly annoying teacher. We always seem to meet him once again just at the moment in which we think we have surpassed him. He walks too fast.

He said in those last months of his life when he dramatically and abruptly stopped writing—"I can do no more"—that he had seen Things making all that he had written look like straw. We have not seen those Things but we have had the grace to have known the teaching of the Common Doctor and all that we have written is to us as so much straw.

vi.74

A E I O U

Charles, the Fifth of that name as Holy Roman Emperor and the First as King of Spain, fought and won his great victory at Mühlberg, not under the colors of either Austria or Spain but under those of Burgundy: the red and gold: the Knights of the Golden Fleece.

Archduke Otto von Habsburg, the heir to the glory and burden of his name and the biographer of his illustrious ancestor, sees a profound significance in the unfurling of the Burgundian banners at Mühlberg. Burgundy was never a piece of real estate. Like the united Christendom defended by Charles on that day of victory, captured for us in Titian's famous painting, Burgundy was a state of mind.

La Cruz de Borgoña, the Cross of Burgundy, the Cross of Saint Andrew, the *Aspas* of the Spanish tradition, found its form in the Order of the Golden Fleece, the highest secular honor in the Catholic World. The shifting boundaries of Burgundy—neither French nor German but encompassing "the lands on either side of the great road that runs from the North Sea to the Mediterranean; to the east it is bordered by the high chain of the Alps which separates the Germans from the Latins, and to the west by the Massif Central"—were occupied, annexed, restored once again, but Burgundy's frontiers were quicksilver. The Knights of the Golden Fleece grew up in the new commercial and town society of the late Middle Ages which extended from Maestrick to Liege and thence to Metz, Verdun and Lyons and as far south as Avignon and Arles. Formed out of a unique and felicitous union of the older feudal order and a new and rich society reflective of the burgeoning Renaissance, Burgundy was a symbol of what all Christendom once had been: universalist in its commitment to the defense of the common Catholic culture; disdainful of the new nationalisms, yet speaking every western tongue; profoundly chivalric and religious; dreaming, in the mid-sixteenth century, of taking the Cross on Crusade to the Holy Land; the very "autumn of the Middle Ages" in the words of Johan Huizinga.

Coming upon this inheritance through the wife of the Emperor Maximilian, Mary of Burgundy, Charles of Habsburg was raised a Burgundian. This made it possible for him to be a universal Emperor and King of a Spain newly knit into unity by "The Catholic Kings," Ferdinand of Aragon and Isabel of Castille. But Charles V was born too late. This historical tragedy haunts the pages of Archduke Otto's biography. Called to defend a supra-national unity whose roots were deeply transcendental, Charles faced a world that was splitting itself into national states under the totalitarianism of monolithically imposed languages, written down and rapidly spread through the newly invented printing press—McLuhan's "Gutenberg Revolution." The difference this revolution made would later be perfectly symbolized in the persons of Charles and Martin Luther: when the German was working the definitive crystallization of High German with his translation of the Bible, the Flemish-speaking Charles was insisting upon speaking Spanish before the Pope. "Castillian is a tongue worthy of any Christian," he said, simultaneously rejecting nationalism and affirming his own acquired Spanish identity.

Facing the threat of Turks on the Mediterranean flank of Europe, Charles had the agonizing task of confronting Luther and attempting to heal the schism that was then rending to shreds the *res publica christiana*. Otto makes patently clear Charles' attempts to right what was wrong in Christendom by urging Rome to call a council. Had a council been called some ten to fifteen years earlier, the definitive schism might have been avoided. The judgment is controversial, but it is argued persuasively by the royal author.

When the Emperor faced Luther across the table at Worms in 1521, "he was not sustained by fanaticism of any kind," argues the somewhat anti-Catholic Edward Crankshaw, author of *The Habsburgs: Portrait of a Dynasty*. Willing to meet the Lutherans half-way in their demands for internal reform in the Church, Charles would not waver when the question touched the public foundations of the Faith:

> I am descended (Charles said at Worms) from a long line of Christian emperors of this noble nation, and of the Catholic kings of Spain, the archdukes of Austria and the

dukes of Burgundy. All were faithful to the death to the Church of Rome, and they defended the Catholic Church and the honour of God.

I have resolved to follow in their steps. A single monk who goes counter to all Christianity for a thousand years must be wrong. Therefore I am resolved to stake my lands, my friends, my body, my blood, my life and my soul in pledge for this cause.

The single monk was placed formally under tha ban of Empire. But the world whose lineaments were traced in those years of Reformation and Counter-Reformation owes more to him than it does to the Emperor-King.

Both Charles and the Burgundian ideal were brilliant throw-backs to the High Middle Ages. The new age of the national state, print technology, the religion of The Book, the rapid centralization of political and economic power, the drying up of regional culture, the exaltion of the Machiavellian Prince, lasted some four hundred and more years. Today the pressures of a new technology—the electric—which decentralizes even as it abolishes space as any significant "centre" from which power could emanate makes of Charles a strangely post-modern figure without the technical hardware he needed to do his work. His life of wandering from point to point within his vast possessions, his quite literal "failure" to govern from any fixed capital, were problems never solved within his lifetime. Otto von Habsburg's insistence that "the system of national states is revealed as the disastrous—perhaps even fatal—mistake that it is," seen in the light of two ruinous European civil wars and two world conflagrations that have "led the continent to the brink of complete dis-integration," imperiously forces upon us a meditation on the meaning of Charles' role within history. This meaning will alter with the changing circumstances of a new world that has rejected everything he rejected without affirming, thus far, the Faith and supra-national commonwealth built thereon that he affirmed. But new technological revolutions have the power to recreate the past even as they destroy the present. Men rebuild the past in the light of their future. Charles had no future for a long time. But his time may be very close upon us. Possibly Austria had to shrivel to the comic rump republic that it is today in order that its transcending significance take being in a new form tomorrow.

The spate of books about the Habsburgs does seem to point, if but obliquely, in this direction. Otto's book about his ancestor finds its counterpoint in Gordon Brook-Shepherd's *The Last Habsburg*, which sketches the life and moving death of Otto's father, the Emperor-King

Karl. Crankshaw's *The Habsburgs* is the kind of luxurious picture-book accompanied by text that helps show off coffee-tables and bridge gaps in the conversation of polite people. Lavishly and splendidly illustrated, Crankshaw traces the House of Habsburg from its obscure origins in Lorraine through the Burgundian inheritance of Maximilian I and "The Spanish Apotheosis: Philip II" down to what the author calls "Recovery and the long last act: Francis Joseph and Charles I."

Crankshaw's religious preferences are not revealed in the text but he is clearly incapable of understanding the Habsburgs' millenial allegiance to the Catholic Church. Because of this blindness Crankshaw cannot deal fairly with Philip II and the spirit of the Baroque Counter-Reformation. Something of the grandeur of Lepanto and the splendor of Don Jaun of Austria defending Christendom crawls around his otherwise properly secularist prose. But the man's deepest failure in insight is his incapacity to come to terms with the admittedly often misunderstood Ferdinand II. Yet despite Crankshaw's aristocratic, sectarian bias, the magic of the Crown of Charlemagne, central symbol of the West's political destiny, suffuses his pages.

The high point of the author's study is his genuine love affair with Maria Theresa. This man really adores the embattled Archduchess and "King" of Hungary. He details her homely Germanic virtues; her love for a weak and sensual but essentially decent husband; her innocent incapacity to understand the cynicism of the Prussian Frederick's surgical removal of Silesia from her inheritance; her so very womanly act of throwing herself, child in arms, on the loyalty of Hungary; her hesitation before committing her daughter Maria Antoinette to marriage with the French Bourbons. And what tragedy followed upon that act! If Franz Josef came into the possession of an empire in the nineteenth century, he could thank that ample and nubile and always pregnant woman, simple-minded in her devotion to the Catholic Thing, single-minded in her dedication to the fullness of a responsibility that half Europe would have seized from her for being a woman, and that she preserved precisely for being one.

Ideologues can never come to grips with Habsburg politics but these politics are extremely difficult to understand even in the light of conventional political philosophy. Increasingly identified with the Imperial Crown since the late Middle Ages, Habsburg never held that crown by dynastic right but by election. Destined by both ambition and circumstances, Habsburg possessed its own lands as a base in the service of a higher cause: the defense of Christian civilization against its enemies, both external and internal. In a deep sense, we can agree with Charles Maurras that the French monarchy of the Capetians was created out of the very bone of France, and that the Plantagenet dynasty of England, initially a usurper, came to be the *caput* that grew out of the *corpus politicus*. But the Habsburg dynasty was not created by a polity in order that it function as its head and representative in history. Habsburg created Austria; and Austria created Europe—the entire Baroque world that spanned half the world and that called to its mission men of every tongue and race, that gloried in the goodness of creation and that literally swam in the beauties of being that were denied by the Puritan North.

Punsters have played with Frederick III's cryptic code: AEIOU. These letters might mean: *Austriae est Imperare Orbi Universo* or *Alles Erdreich ist Oesterreich unthertham*. Charles V made the boast true. But if Austria's Empire extended to all the universe it did so, ran the ditty, because *Bella gerant fortes: tu, felix Austria, nube: nam quae Mars aliis, dat tibi regna Venus*—The strong make war; thou, happy Austria, marry: what Mars grants others, Venus give to thee.

A dynastic politics in the service of a trans-national ideal is a reality difficult to fit into conventional categories of political theory: an hereditary family in the service of a non-hereditary goal; a royal dynasty that wove a world into being; a central European house whose greatest monument is the Spanish Escorial; a paradox that is one with Europe itself. Both the ideological and the doctrinaire are bankrupt of explanations in the fact of the massive history of this House of Europe.

Today *all* politics tend to become dynastic. The withering away of ideology wrought by the new technological decentralization (earlier predicted by Otto von Habsburg in his *Social Order of Tomorrow*), the collapse of the old homogenous "citizenry" and its replacement by a swarming vortex of tribes, have shaken to the foundations the modern and individualistic impersonality of power. Power increasingly is exercised dynastically. The pitchman from nowhere with a "Cause" is by no means extinct, but today he wears the image of a nineteenth-century medicine man at the country fair. All of us in the West have been "caused" to death. But blood is thicker than water.

As the family corrodes at the base of society, it returns with a vengeance at the top thanks to the electronic glare under which we all live. Dr. Alvaro D'Ors, distinguished scholar of Roman Law at the University of Navarre in Spain, has pointed out that democracy's greatest victory consisted in banning the family from political life. Wherever the family is granted a modicum of political representation the ensuing polity is at least marginally aristocratic. Wherever the family dominates an entire society, that society is at least incipiently royalist—dynastic—given that such a community of self-governing families tends to incarnate itself in a family, a dynasty, a royal house. In a society such as our own today in which families—Rockfellers, Kennedys, etc.—govern a community whose chosen goods, whose icons, are largely non-familial, even anti-familial, possibilities for either tyrannical destruction (pleasure for them and power for us!) or a new flowering of human decency cluster together ambiguously and demand understanding in the service of survival. Unless we penetrate the nature of a familial polity we cannot comprehend our own age. Everybody today running for dog-catcher uses the royal "we" over television. Why?

Habsburg politics represented the zenith of familial politics—and also its nadir. The Imperial and Royal Family of Christendom was barred by law from returning to Austria after World War I and the ban was only lifted recently. To bring the supposed impersonality of the Law to legislate against a *family name* was an obscure attack against the very legitimacy of Being. No man can deny who he is. To require such a renunciation is to menace something more profound than all law. But if this is true, all democratic theory, founded as it is on "individuals," on non-persons without family, is beyond serious metaphysical and moral consideration.

Emperor Charles I of Austria and Apostolic King of Hungary, "the last Habsburg," was—like most men—either too late for his time or too early. But unlike most men the persecution he underwent for simply being a Habsburg approached the zone of irrational hatred. Mr. Gordon Brook-Shepherd has written an elegant and even eloquent study of this Charles who was not destined for the throne to which he suddenly became heir upon the assassination of Archduke Francis Ferdinand and his wife in Sarajevo in 1914. This was the last thorn pressed to the crown of the aged Franz Josef. Let us never forget his life of sorrow: his wife, unhappy and neurotic, murdered by an Italian anarchist; his son, a suicide with his mistress at Mayerling; his role as First German Prince, lost to the Hohenzollerns; his Italian provinces, wrenched from his sceptre; his loneliness, assuaged only by his dogged sense of duty. President Theodore Roosevelt learned from the Old Gentleman what his role in history was: "to protect

Citizen of Rome

my peoples against their governments." Another story—probably too good to be true—has a buck private in the Austrian Army complaining to Franz Josef about something or other. The Emperor's considered answer: "Don't you have any influence with a first sergeant?" The Emperor-King slept on a military cot through the last years of his life. He was a splendid man indeed! Upon the death of this First Gentleman of Europe in 1916, with Austira-Hungary locked in a losing war to the Allies and increasingly subservient to its Prussian masters to the north, Charles entered into what was to become his martyrdom.

Brook-Shepherd's study is especially significant because he draws upon the living memory of Charles' widow, the Empress-Queen Zita of the House of Bourbon-Parma. Her cooperation makes the book intensely personal, if quite naturally somewhat biased. The two evil geniuses of Charles' short reign, according to the author, were Count Ottokar Czernin, "Charles' brilliant but erratic and disloyal Foreign Minister," who undermined the emperor's attempts to seek peace with the Allies through the intervention of the brother of the Empress, Prince Sixto; and Nicholas von Horthy, who rode to power in Budapest in 1921 pretending to be Charles' man and who then twice banned his own sovereign's return to the throne. This vulgarian even demanded the Order of the Golden Fleece from his master. But the Golden Fleece is only for Catholics; Horthy was a Calvinist. Little else need be said about him.

Charles, from very early in his short life, had fixed upon a free and equal federation of nations as the political solution to the problems of his multiracial Empire. But the tide of nationalism—financed from London and backed by the silliness of Wilson that eventually created such monsters as Czechoslovakia and Yugoslavia—was too strong for the young Emperor. Forced into a Swiss exile after the war, thwarted by the fat and comfortable Horthy in his efforts to return to Hungary as its rightful King, Crowned and Apostolic, Charles and his wife were exiled by the Allies to Madeira.

The foul climate and inadequate medical treatment brought the exiled monarch to a premature death. His health, already sapped by years of fighting at the front, by sleepless nights spent at the impossible task of waging war, preparing for peace, and governing the ungovernable, snapped. Charles of Austria was no more. Democratic Europe and America turned him into a statistic.

Brook-Shepherd is an Englishman; he is not at home with the Baroque. Yet he does justice to this essentially simple and very noble heir to a

270

glory that was for him a burden and a cross. Very early in his book the author comments, rapidly and with typically English reticence, on the heightened *goodness*—he pardons us the word and so do I—of the subject of his study. What others took for weakness and vacillation in the Emperor-King Charles emerges as an almost overly sensitive respect for the other man; an unusual patience and willingness to hear everyone on every subject; an heroic willingness to fight the enemy on the front and to refuse to find any enemy behind it; a tenderness toward the poor of his ravished Empire and a kind of pathos before children; an unexpected purity for a man in his position; an innocence almost too Catholic to believe. His character is very difficult to describe historically. The young man wanted to be known as "The Emperor of Peace"—this, when the guns were thundering on the Western Front. He may well be known one day by a loftier title.

In 1949, twenty-seven years after his death, a "Process for the Beatification of the Servant of God, Charles of the House of Habsburg," was introduced at the Vatican. Charles was utterly too much a Habsburg ever to have posed like a saint, but he may very well be one. In accord with canon law, his tomb was opened recently at Madeira, in the presence of Vatican officials. His son was there, too, the first layman in the Catholic World, according to Pius XII. It was there, in Madeira—in a stinking hell-hole of a house—that this ruined and broken man called his young son to his bedside so that he might know, and this in his agony, how "a Catholic and an Emperor dies." Yet it is typical of the dying Charles that he afterwards regretted having to face his son with his own agony. This man was too kind for our world. It is perhaps strangely fitting that his delirious prayers in that hell-hole to which he was consigned to die by Democracy were in both German and Latin, the language of his family and the language of the Church to which Habsburg had ever given its word.

Too early? Too late? Both of them were both: The great Charles V who dies at the monastery at Yuste found his biographer in the son of that latter day Charles who was offered up as a last sacrifice on a remote island to a very bitter and very evil old world, which killed him in exile, which was fought by the earlier Charles, and which today—thank God—is itself dead and unmourned.

vii.72

REJECTING

HARVEY COX'S
SECULAR CITY: CITY OF NIGHT

The apostles of secularization have found in Dr. Harvey Cox an eloquent spokesman, certainly the most celebrated of our time. *The Secular
City* has swept the American scene in recent months with such force that
Cox has come to symbolize the radical dissent that today marks the New
Protestantism. The book has already gone through five editions; it has
also formally reached the academy—at Southern Methodist University,
for instance, it is used as a theological text. In Catholic circles, *Commonweal*, faithful to its reputation for piety where things heterodox are concerned, devoted the better half of two issues to an analysis of Cox's thesis.
Another Catholic journal, *Ave Maria*, speculated that *The Secular City* may
prove to be the major theological work of the decade. Even were the book
to lack any intrinsic value, its very popularity would be symptomatic of a
national mood and hence would merit attention as a sign of something
deeper than itself.

The book does possess a certain power. It forces from the reader a
total response, an unqualified yea or nay to secularization. The secularized West—desacralized, disenchanted, deconsecrated, urbanized,
anonymous, purged of objective meaning, disembowled of decency efficient, slick—emerges so starkly that the serious reader is compelled to
ask himself a truly sundering question. Granted that the Secular City does
not yet fully exist, granted that Dr. Cox's dream is only now tracing its
lineaments upon the ruins of what was once Christendom—would I serve
the completed City loyally or would I live within its technologized walls a
secret traitor?

The publicity given Cox's book would lead the uninformed reader to
believe that its author was the first scholar to have dedicated himself
seriously to the subject of secularization. But students of history have
known for some time that the desacralizing of Christian civilization began

at the very moment Christendom reached its zenith in the thirteenth century, as George de Lagarde demonstrated in his *La naissance de L'esprit laique*.

Secularization as an ideal, if not as an actuality, is at least as old as Marsilius of Padua's *Defensor Pacis*, published in 1324. Anti-clericalism, egalitarianism, popular sovereignty, the separation of church and state, a secularized political order—all these beads on Dr. Cox's modernist rosary are as old as Marsilius. From that moment forward, Western man, tired perhaps of the burdens of transcendence, began not only to distinguish but to separate secular things from the spiritual order, and from that order's representative in time, the Catholic Church.

Historians also know, however, that these tendencies have never "won out"—that compromise has marked the Western experience in its dealings with secularization. From the fourteenth century until now, Western man has lived in a civilization that has increasingly secularized its political and social institutions, but that has never become secularized in the absolute sense. Despite the occasional activity of fervid enthusiasts for total secularization, the West has hitherto tended to blend the profane and the sacral in such fashion that historians and philosophers have been perfectly justified in using the term "Christian civilization" to describe the occidental experience and to distinguish it from other civilizations.

Partial secularizations, effected under the pressure of the French Revolution, have hitherto invited partial reactions in the West—reactions commendable to many for their balance and moderation. The American experience is an instance, possibly the most instructive in history. The Declaration of Independence is an essentially Christian document. While the Declaration's rhetoric is typical of the Enlightenment, its authors took great pains to root their cause in God, and to commend the country to Providence. On the other hand the Philadelphia Convention established no state church. The American commonwealth was thus understood by its founders to be Christian, and the American government to be secular. The compromise represented a balance between a society still heavily sacral in its convictions, yet permeated by the secular spirit.

In another context, the Catholic theologians of nineteenth-century Europe developed an elaborate doctrine that sharply distinguished between "thesis" and "hypothesis" in the matter of church-state relations. Where a people had retained its Catholic faith integrally and organically (the thesis), its institutional representation in the political order was recommended as being both normal and proper. But where a high degree of religious pluralism had taken root due to the collapse of the Counter-Reformation (the hypothesis), governments were commended to neutrality in religious affairs. Britain provided still another case. Religious tests designed to penalize Dissenters and Catholics were abolished in the nineteenth century, although the Church of England retained its established status. The change indicated an awareness that the United Kingdom had ceased to be integrally one with the Protestant Settlement of 1688, but that conditions still sufficiently reflected the sense of the Settlement to merit retention of the Anglican Establishment. Compromises of this kind have been a mark of the West until very recently, and even modern Western thought on the subject has been shaped accordingly.

For instance, Will Herberg and others have advanced the thesis that Christians and Jews have stamped this country with a tripartite pluralism. The Protestant-Catholic-Jewish relationship, the argument runs, has set in motion a perpetual conversation that produces a "consensus" on the ultimate meaning of our common American orthodoxy. A related position has been developed by those Catholics, both American and European, who constitute what might be called today "the moderate left." Such Catholics have tended to support Jacques Maritain's contention that a new lay Christian society is emerging in the West, a society whose spiritual roots reach deeply into the hearts of men without, however, touching their freedom to dissent, their religious liberty. The Christian-democratic order of the future, they maintain, will be based on an essentially Christian ethos, but will not institutionalize its religious convictions.

Yet these views, which only yesterday seemed so advanced, today wear the look of very old age in the light of the teaching of Dr. Cox. From the Andover Newton Theological School comes the news that the moderates who have heretofore commanded our attention *cannot* have it half way. This distinguished priest of the New Protestantism anounces (with echoes already discernible from the "New Catholicism") that the god of secularism does not permit a tempered devotion. Those who would still strike a balance, who are reluctant to go the full distance, will be thrust aside by that lord of all gnostics—History: which is the ally of the Secular City.

According to Cox and his friends, the West, to say nothing of the rest of the world, will never again support a civilization whose ground is essentially religious and whose culture bears the lineaments of a common faith. America's future will not be formed, even in myth, by a Herbergian Protestant-Catholic-Jewish trialogue. The future of all humanity, on the contrary, will be defined by a radical deconsecration of the temporal—by *pure* secularization. Tomorrow will not bring forth a world existentially Christian but essentially laicist or secular in its structure, as the Maritainians teach. The Secular City, mothered by historical necessity, will be thoroughly purged of every trace of the religious in its public life. The man of the future will not even experience a spiritual void, as does the existentialist today, for the ultimate meaning of our civilization will not have been given by God, or even by Christians annealed by the Word of God. Meaning will have been formulated by men resolutely dedicated to secular goals.

As might be expected, the classical and medieval inheritance of philosophy is part of the tradition that History will sweep away in the name of the Secular City. Natural law's last vestiges will disappear. No longer will statesmen be permitted even an implicit appeal to an objective moral order as a sanction for the programs they advance or defend. Their preferences will be formed pragmatically, and judged exclusively in the light of their utility in solving concrete secular "problems." And the attempt to solve these problems must never, under any circumstances, involve religious charisma, or even the more modest, Aristotelian concept of the common good. So not only must the body politic's religious backbone be cut away; but the traditional philosophical head of the *respublica* must also go to the block to meet the axe of the secularist executioner.

"Value systems" will be based upon a "new social consensus," having more to do with the United Nations' Declaration of Human Rights than the "American founding documents." Why the preference for the UN formula? Because the Secular City will reject all "affirmations concerning the inalienable right by which men are 'endowed by their Creator'."

In a word, the Christian faith, or what is left of it, will be so thoroughly "interiorized" by the configurations of the Secular City that it will never again act as a positive force in history. The City's soldiers may be sent to die in distant lands, but they will neither be buttressed in battle nor comforted in death by any presumed affinities their cause might bear with the will of Him whom earlier generations were free to call the God of Justice.

Having glimpsed, thus beiefly, the kind of City Dr. Cox thinks we will soon be living in, let us look more closely at the philosophical and historical analysis that underlies these conclusions.

Not surprisingly, Cox's ethical relativism is based on an epistemological skepticism concerning the capability of the instruments of knowledge to deliver the goods they promise—that is, the Truth. Our author comes out strongly, very early in his book against *any* corporate adherence to *any* ethical system understood as an absolute. According to Cox, "the Copernican Revolution" has so "relativized" moral affirmations that we must admit that all codes of conduct are dependent on the historical conditions that gave them birth. They lack any ultimate grip on reality, and will therefore be discarded tomorrow in favor of more enlightened, if equally provisional, ethical systems. Thus Cox's distaste for the idea of natural law, and for the Greek philosophical tradition which helped give that idea to Christendom.

Curiously enough, Cox does hold that a plurality of ethical systems is a *good* thing for civilization, even though his own moral nihilism would logically preclude saying anything whatever about good and evil. He defends the *non sequitur* by arguing that inasmuch as his own "values and standpoints are relative," they have no right to exclude other values which are equally relative! After all, no one's values are "directed" towards any "reality." Philosophical common sense, however, reveals the foolishness of this position: if my "values" were recognizably unrelated to reality, *a fortiori* they could hardly be embraced as *my* values. If there is, in fact, no goal towards which purposive action can be directed, how can I act at all? A conviction that every gesture of decency (or depravity) is directed towards Nothing would simply paralyze action in most persons and probably produce insanity in the more intelligent. Cox hastens to deny that his position leads to "individual or group solipsism," but the principle of contradiction forces us to just that conclusion.

A genuine "ethical pluralism," I am saying, must involve a common agreement about at least a minimum of ethical standards. And to be objective, these standards must, in turn, be rooted in some *tertium quid* recognized by all parties. If this minimum is not insisted upon. Hitlerian racism or Congolese cannibalism have just as much right to enter the conversation as do the moral sensibilities of Dr. Harvey Cox. And, to do him justice, Dr. Cox does have strong moral sensibilities, as witness his condemnation of the *Playboy* sexual code.

Cox's moral relativism, of course, is one with Mill's radical skepticism. Far from guaranteeing the liberal toleration that both Cox and

Mill want for all opinions in the market place of the spirit, the teaching of both men is vulnerable to Bertrand de Juvenal's point that if no one opinion has any intrinsic value its suppression by public power is no crime. On his own showing, Cox comes off no better than *Playboy* or the Congolese cannibal.

At bottom, however, Dr. Cox is not honest in posing as a moral relativist. Moral relativism is really a cloak used to hide *his* absolute: the Secular City. This book abounds in moral judgments urging us to do all manner of things from smashing the "last remnants of Christendom" to seriously opposing "the romantic restoration of the sprites of the forest." Cox, like all pitchmen of the human spirit, is grimly realistic in his own moralism. Were he a true moral relativist, he would shrug his shoulders and permit us poor believers to enjoy the remnants of Christendom while he basks in the secularist centers of the West. Moral relativism, honorably entertained, can surely make no choice between these alternatives. But Cox will not permit any opposition to the building of his beloved Secular City.

Behind Cox's myth of historical necessity glints the bayonet's steel: whether we like it or not, we are all going to have to live in the Secular City. Like all men, Cox lives by orthodoxy, although his orthodoxy is someone else's heresy.

Ethical nihilism usually masks a philosophy of history to which the ethical order is transferred by sleight of hand. There are no absolutes rooted in a supposedly fixed human nature, the nihilists maintain; but there *is* an absolute in that stream of becoming in which the supposed constancy of human nature is washed away. It is called History.

Modern political philosophy, thanks largely to Eric Voegelin's *The New Science of Politics*, furnishes the theoretical instruments we need to understand Cox's philosophy of history. As already suggested, Cox is a gnostic. This conclusion escapes us at first because *The Secular City* argues that Christianity *de*divinized the world of Nature, thereby distinguishing the secular from the sacred; yet gnoticism, as Voegelin shows, consists essentially in a *re*investing of time with attributes belonging properly to a transcendent God. But despite his representation of the world as non-divine, Cox succeeds in smuggling the Absolute back into history when he makes the construction of the Secular City the imperative basis of time itself. All history moves inevitably towards secularization. It follows that secularization, as understood by Cox, takes on the absoluteness that truly characterizes only God Himself.

Cox's gnosticism is insidious, precisely because it presents itself as anti-gnosticism—as a call to chase the gods from the world. But once the gods are banished, man is left confronting a naked, empty world that beckons dumbly, yet irresistibly, forcing from him a promise to spend his whole being in its service. Cox's "secular order" is so radically worldly, so utterly cut off from God, that it looms before the mind and will as the sole field of activity for the spirit and hand of man.

Once comprehended, Cox's gnosticism is so conventional that it could be used as a text-book case to illustrate the Voegelinian thesis. According to Voegelin, gnosticism invariably divides history into three moments, each succeeding one of which allegedly involves a civilizational "advance" over the previous moment. So does Harvey Cox. According to the Voegelinian analysis these advances are always interpreted in the light of some "law" thought to be intrinsic to time itself. Thus also with Cox. According to Voegelin, gnostic movements always find some scripture to announce their message. So too does Dr. Cox, with his special reading of the Old and New Testaments. Every gnostic movement looks to prophetic leaders who will point the way to the secular paradise. So again does Dr. Harvey Cox: the prophetic leader of the Secular City is Cox's Jesus, whose message has found a peculiar resonance in our time in the persons of John F. Kennedy and Albert Camus!

Cox's "history" may be traced as follows: Historical progress must be understood as an advance from the tribe, into the town, towards the city. Born into the tribe, men were linked together by a "common mythological past," as well as by the chemistry of consanguinity. Assured of a well-defined place within his community, tribal man so wove religion into the business of life that not only the great events of birth and death and marraige and war, but every gesture of day-to-day living, was saturated with a preternatural significance that gave direction to human existence. But thanks to human inventiveness the tribal vision was destined to disappear. "The appearance of currency and the development of the alphabet," Cox says, "supply two essential ingredients in the shattering step from tribe to town." Diversification of function, introduced by the beginnings of commerce and spurred on by the rationalization of work through technology, tended to break up "the familial patterns" thitherto "directed by tradition."

The growth of town culture coincided with the sanctification of work, and reached its apotheosis in what Weber called the Protestant Ethic.

(Cox is far more severe with the Protestant Ethic than with the Catholic and Latin genuis for leisure.) The highly individualistic effort demanded by the transition from tribe to town was made possible by an asceticism which bent the back of man to the service of both market and machine. For these two masters were first seen as symbols of rectitude and sanctification, although they later became purely secular tools stripped of all religious significance. Cox's "town culture" thus functions as the antithesis that has steered the march of man from the thesis of the tribe to the synthesis of "technopolis."

Contemporary man, fashioned anew by the demands of technopolis, lives in an order of things that necessarily annihilates his sense of place. Radical social mobility has been made a feature of this order not only by the rapidity of modern transportation, but also by the magic of electricity, which makes space coterminal with consciousness. (Cox could have buttressed his argument by invoking Marshall McLuhan's *Understanding Media*.) Moreover, the pressures of mathematized technology have so atomized the new order that every dimension of human existence is regarded as an enemy of every other: work is separated from play and play from ritual, the economic from the familial, and the familial from the political. They have banished all sense of living in an enchanted world.

A progressively atomized existence is simply the price men must pay for the, building of the Secular City, whose inner genius can be defined—we may gloss the text—in terms of a demiurgical iconoclasm. This iconoclasm cannot tolerate formally distinct essences annealed into unity through the catalyst of existence. As Cox sees it, whatever unity in life man may have created out of the darkness must now be fragmented into that "differentiation of function" that technology is bound to impose. The small farm must go, and with it all sense of communion with nature. The remnants of craftsmanship must disappear. Family economics must be suppressed. Interpersonal relationships must not disturb the smooth functioning of the "technopolitan" machinery. The anonymity of the city becomes, not a moment of personal repose from a too public world, but an ideal to be cultivated. Wives are even admonished not to be interested in the work of their husbands. Work is one thing, marriage another; and the two must never meet, under pain of treason to the City. Everything shall be itself *and nothing else*.

That "and nothing else" is the key to the thinking of Dr. Cox and his followers. That key is important, moreover, for the mind that produced the thesis of *The Secular City* is really far more interesting than the thesis itself.

As a venture in scholarship, the book is strictly derivative. As we have already noted, what Cox says about secularization was said years ago in Lagarde's monumental five-volume work. What Cox says about the inner dynamism of technology was sketched out more than two decades ago by Friedrich George Junger. Cox's sociology is David Riesman plus gnosticism. His theory of historical progress is simply a poor man's rationalism, a kind of Americanized Marx, already unmasked by the scholarship of Lowith and Voegelin, among others. When sound, Cox is banal; when weak, he is a pure journalist. It is Cox's mind that is fascinating. It reveals the symptoms of what Plato would have called a pathology of the human spirit. Harvey Cox is sick with Manicheanism.

I do not use the term Manichean as an epithet, but rather with the full force and sense of its traditional meaning. The Manichean spirit—a many-headed serpent—has always been marked anaolgically, throughout its myriad manifestations, by an excessive dualism: a conscious effort not only to seek distinctions within being, but to force these distinctions into separations and the separations into divorces.

Spirit and matter, heaven and earth, body and soul, God and the world, church and state, are not only distinguished formally—as they are in Christian orthodoxy—but are forced into dramatic opposition by Manicheanism. As a result, Manichean psychology is always characterized by what could be called an itch for "reductionism," in which all differences harden into hostilities. Just as Descartes reduced all ideas to their clearest and simplest components by purging them of extraneous elements, so too the Manichean spirit is bent upon atomizing the complexity of existence, urging the Many to declare war on one another in the name of the One. Manicheanism converts the true universality of being into a kind of cosmic solipsism in which every category of the real is liberated from its communion with the whole, in order that it may pursue its own lonely destiny.

It seems to me that the secularizing spirit, so handsomely articulated by Dr. Cox, is guilty of just this kind of reductionism. First the City of Man and everything found in it is divorced from the City of God. Religion is then interiorized, forbidden expression in the public forum, and the forum is forbidden any traffic with the temple. The fragmenting of life gathers momentum due to the secularists' monopoly of demiurgical science. The secularists are eventually able to dissect man into *homo ludens, homo amans, homo economicus, homo politicus, homo artisticus*, etc., severing nerve after nerve of the human spirit until man finally collapses into the many, having lost the unity with which he emerged into being from the hand of God.

Cox's Manicheanism tips its hand in his constantly reiterated insistence on the "liberation" supposedly achieved by secularization; the Secular City liberates not only the secular from the religious but everything from everything else. This desire for liberation is one with the Manichean fastidiousness for the absolutely pure, for purity understood as purgation.

For Cox, politics is not pure until purged of every element of the sacred. He is so much the snob that he would even deny England's Majesty the pomp of coronation because this ceremony, no matter how empty it may seem in our day, at least suggests the dependence of the temporal on the spiritual, of the world on its Creator. Indeed, the dedivinized world speaks with such authority that Cox is constrained to warn us away from any *future* commitment to the Christian mystical tradition. Such a commitment would turn tomorrow's man toward the delights of communion with an Unseen God. Thus his duty to secular and worldly ends would not be fulfilled. But the Catholic tradition says that Martha, "careful and troubled about many things" (Luke, X, 41) can be seen to be Martha only when contrasted to Mary. If we remove Mary and "the better part" which she chose, then Martha becomes an "absolute" absorbing the whole of life.

For Cox, nature is not pure until all the leprechauns (the example is his own) are banished from the forests. Economic activity is not pure until it is so removed from familial affairs that not even a tiny remnant of men may work where they live. Work itself is not pure until divorced, not only from the Catholic sacral order and the leisure with which it is humanized in the Latin world, and from the Protestant Ethic of Anglo-Saxon culture, but even from any relation to income. Production is one thing and consumption something else, and never the twain shall meet! Sex is impure until totally stripped of every vestige of romance and chivalry. No tipping of hats to ladies in this Secular City, as that suggests the cult of the Virgin, a horror equal to the *Playboy* morality. This passion for "purity" in every order of life is a kind of heroic imperative that requires the Secular City to separate and divide everything that man has hitherto tried to knit into unity.

The metaphysician can read here a rationalist fascination with pure essences that bespeaks a sensibility ill at ease with the complexity of existence. The political philosopher can detect a kind of fanaticism that insists on violating the given in the name of a new procustean bed. The moralist will read an impatience with men as they are. But the theologian will nail the thing to the wall when he condemns it as a hatred of creation, a Manichean disease—a heresy.

It is ironic that this prophet of secularization and celebrant of the world actually loathes the richness and the superabundance of creation.

That men sign their work with the seal of their commitment to the transcendent is so innate to the human personality that the instinct is rooted out only by violence. That men have suffused the world with their awareness of the divine in song and sculpture and music is so at one with human nature that any other order of things seems monstrous. That all art worth the name is ultimately religious, and all politics capable of moving the heart profoundly sacred, is less the deduction of a philosopher than the observation of a sensibility uncorrupted by rationalism. That the sacred and profane, the economic and playful, the familial and the public, be woven into an historic unity, *that man sacramentalize the whole of being*—this is what Catholic Christendom has always meant by the sacral order.

The sacral order is simply the vitality of a world that is always *more than itself*—always so supremely vital it spills over into prayer, exceeds the possibilities of its own nature, is always more than it might have been.

But Harvey Cox is the enemy of the sacraments. This is his gravest heresy. He tells us that Christianity did precisely what it did *not* do—desacralize the world. The issue demands clarification.

Antiquity identified divinity with nature, but for antiquity nature was not, nor ever could have been, a sacrament. Sacraments partake of the meaning of signs, and signs point to something beyond themselves. Beyond nature, as understood by the classical world, there was nothing at all. There were no signs pointing out towards an unexperienced transcendence until the emergence of the Christian sacramental order, which abolished the conflict between transcendence and immanence.

The Church as the dispenser of the seven sacraments became the instrument of God's working in and through the world, but God does so through *His* power and not the world's. In one supreme, ineffable thing, the Eucharist, the world *is* God, but only through His own divine priesthood and not through anything divine that creation possesses of itself.

It is against the rock of the Sacrament of the Altar that the secularizers, both within and without the Church, are bent upon doing battle. It is as if the tides of history were sweeping in upon us once again today, and we were breasting the full flood of the sixteenth century's negations. Then the faithful found in the Sacrifice the strength needed to stand fast against heretics who preached a return to an earlier and simpler Christianity.

The doctrine of transubstantiation was then, and remains now, a gauntlet thrown in the face of men dedicated to the violent separation of the sacral from the temporal order. For those who accept the formula of Trent—the Real Presence and everything It implies—Cox and his fellow apostles of secularization are not only the enemies of civilization but the enemies of the sacramental God in whose name Christendom was born and has been sustained through centuries of combat.

Cox's secularized world is such a wasteland that he can even speak of a salutary "atheism" introduced into history by what he calls "the Gospel." But our God is so intimate that He can be found by simply walking across the street to the nearest Catholic church.

If both the Sacrament of the Altar and that common sacramental, Christendom, whose "preservation is the standing grace of this world," in Hilaire Belloc's phrase, simultaneously arouse the fury of latter day Manicheanism, it is because both are united in a mystery too profound for full human comprehension. The medieval town had at its center the cathedral, and the center of the cathedral was the tabernacle. Cox and his allies, as Cox admits repeatedly, are the sworn enemies of the God in the tabernacle. That they are also enemies of the civilization built around Him is nothing but a corollary.

Cox's hostility to the idea of sacramentalizing the world constitutes his second heresy. From his point of view, all things temporal must be separated from the religious in order that they may come into their own pure fullness unhindered by the sacral. He has not mastered the Thomistic teaching that establishes an analogical relation between the being or existence of the world and the Being of God. It is this likeness that makes all things "vestiges" (in the language of St. Bonaventure) of the divine. They speak to man of their Creator. This insight has made possible the Catholic tradition of natural theology, a tradition that finds its character in St. Paul's insistence that "the invisible things of God, from the creation of the world, are clearly seen, being understood by the things that are made, His eternal power and Divinity" (Romans, I, 20). And if St. Paul could add that the Romans were "inexcusable" for not having known the existence of the One True God from meditating on the things that He has created, so we may say the same of the secularizers who refuse to find the least trace of the Creator in the world surrounding them.

Because in the secularist dispensation things do not reveal themselves as coming forth from God, they cannot be viewed as signs pointing back to Him as the source of their being. They cannot become sacramentals. Only a world which is *not* God but gestures back to Him can be divinized. This too is the teaching of St. Paul. It would seem evident by the principle of contradiction that we can divinize, sacralize, only that which is *not* divine in itself. And when Christian man divinizes the world, through the Grace of God, the world remains both what it was before he acted and it *becomes something more than it was.* In this fashion grace perfects what is already present in nature, teaches St. Thomas Aquinas. The sacramental makes of the world a new sign of the Lord and hence a recipient of what Christ wrought within time. This is why we burn palms blessed on Palm Sunday after they have served their purpose. They are too sacred to be left to a chance profanation. This is why we Catholics bless our fishing fleets. This is why we annointed our kings in medieval times. This is why the Irish today begin their constitution with the Sign of the Cross, sealing that document with the solemnity of the Name of the Trinity.

Possibly most crucial to Cox's thought is his understanding of God. Actually he offers us two gods with very little in common. His first is deistic and European. His second is despostic and Oriental.

The first Coxian god creates an unfinished universe and by calling upon man to name the beasts and the other things that are, commands him to complete the task. There is little here to surprise the orthodox except Cox's insistence that there is some kind of contradiction between the traditional concept of Divine Providence and human freedom. According to Cox, man's freedom is less an effect of divine freedom than an addition to it.

Cox's first god is reminiscent of those old-fashioned fathers who educated their children only up to a certain point, then threw them out into the harsh world with the admonition to "go it alone."

My own belief is that Cox's theoretical objections to reconciling divine and human freedom were raised and settled some fifteen hundred years ago by Boethius, who pointed out that any attempt to project the temporal concepts of "before" and "after" into eternity not only destroyed the meaning of the Divine Eternity but rendered impossible the fact of human liberty. In any event, Cox's deistic god is a cosmic spectator who surrenders the fashioning of the world into the hands of man. This god intervenes, however, from time to time and in a most surprising and despotic fashion, thus revealing the Oriental facet of his dual personality.

(Before proceeding with this divine schizophrenic we should note that his creator, Dr. Harvey Cox, has no patience with contemporary semanticists who try to conjure away the question of whether God "exists," on the grounds that the meaning of "existence" is purely verbal. He is equally harsh with those theologians who try to build a doctrine around "no-god-at-all." *The Secular City* was published before the god-is-dead people gained notoriety, but one can surmise that Cox stands somewhere to the right of the pallbearers. He insists that there is an enormous difference between the Hidden God of Scripture who "refuses to bark at man's whistle" and the "no-god" of contemporary atheism. Moreover, Cox confesses his debt to Bonhoeffer when he tries to articulate a "non-religious" god approachable not as a "Thou" but as the "You" who is the unseen "partner" in the building of the Secular City. But despite this emphasis Cox's Hidden God remains "The Totally Other" of the Lutheran tradition, not the Catholic God who cannot be spoken of in such terms [themselves formally "immanent"] as "the Same" or "the Other.")

Harvey Cox, the iconoclast, has shaped his "second" god according to his own image. Being an iconoclast, he has turned God into one.

This Coxian god is a wild and savage Force bent upon destorying all of the icons and statuary thrown up beside the road by Western man on his pilgrimage through time. Cox commends what he calls "the biblical God" because this god makes his presence known in history by smashing the "idols" of men and by humbling the "spirit of pride." This god is truly a tribal god—a god of the desert, a whirlwind out of the clouds, a god so remote that we must address him not as "Thou" but as "You," as the "You" out there in the darkness, the unknown and unapproachable partner in civilization's destruction.

Like all Iconoclasts and Manicheans, the god of Harvey Cox has come riding out of the wastes of the East, determined on the destruction of Christendom's glories.

But this god is not our God, the Triune God of Nicea.

Our only response to Harvey Cox's god must be resistance, with the hope that he will be driven back into the desert.

Nor is the Jesus of Dr. Cox our Christ. Nor is our Church the great "cultural exorcist" destroying every trace of beauty sketched in the darkness by civilized man. Our Church is not the advance guard of a new barbarism.

Our Church is the claim to infallibility, the triumphant and flamboyant "Thou art Peter," made not in the desert but daily in the streets of Rome, the Eternal City, capital of Christendom, and center of Creation. These things must be said so that men may know even in this age that "we have not loosely through silence," as Hooker wrote, "permitted things to pass away as in a dream."

1966

LESLIE DEWART:
HELLENE OR HERETIC?

A man who attacks the hellenic heritage of Christianity and then proceeds to use Aristotelian logic with rigor and even delicacy is resourceful. Leslie Dewart, in *The Future of Belief*, has stacked the cards in his favor. His thesis: Catholic Christianity must consciously expunge the Greek mind that it assimilated in the first flush of the Patristic Age. His advantage: any opponent who uses that same philosophical inheritance in order to oppose the arguments advanced can be dismissed as having failed to get the point of the book.

The St. Michael's College (Toronto) professor hammers that point home early in the game: "today's everyday experience requires not merely the *demythologization of Scripture* but the more comprehensive *dehellenization of dogma*, and specifically that of the Christian doctrine of God."[1] He reminds us of the point time and again and occasionally pleads for it rhetorically: "Is there any intrinsic need, due to fidelty to the Christian faith, to believe that the basic metaphysical notions of the Greek philosophical tradition are true?" Dewart grants that hellenization accounted for the brilliant early development of dogma; yet dogma petrified after the Council of Chalcedon, and Christianity has had to make do through some fifteen hundred years with an "underdeveloped" and impoverished doctrinal expression of faith.

We shall examine this thesis in due course, but a logically prior matter deserves notice at the outset. *Dewart's entire argument rests on presuppositions that cannot be demonstrated metaphysically, but that can only be advanced rhetorically—by appealing to experience.* These presuppositions are: Catholic dogma, as enshrined in the historic creeds, cuts no ice with modern man

---

1.* The emphases in quotations, are, throughout, Dewart's.

and is, in fact, unintelligible to him; the modern consciousness is superior to all that went before and marks a coming of age by a civilization that has taken too long to get out of its swaddling clothes. From these two premises Dewart draws the obvious conclusion: the Catholic Church must jettison its doctrines, burdened as they are by an unsophisticated metaphysics, and adjust itself to a secular world which is more adult than the Church. He carefully warns against interpreting this conclusion merely as a call to a deeper penetration into the content of doctrine already formulated by the Church; he insists that any fresh restatement in contemporary symbols of the truths of the Faith would drain his proposed reform of meaning and interest. Dewart wants new truths and new doctrines, and he wants them at the expense of the old ones.

Now these presuppositions are, obviously, open to challenge. Those of us who have dealt extensively with converts, men and women drawn to the Church out of the very vortex of contemporary industrial civilization, know that the typical approach to the Faith involves a *rejection*, even a contempt of the "contemporary consciousness"—that it is often united with an almost savage cleaving, not only to the most venerable traditions of the Church, but even to the peculiarities of that Mediterranean mind Dewart busies himself disparaging.

Dewart can also be challenged for everywhere taking for granted the intellectual and moral superiority of contemporary man over his ancestors without offering one line of evidence. Since his whole case, not for doctrinal *aggiornamento*, which he rejects, but for doctrinal revolution, depends on the supposed superiority of modernity over the past, the witness of those who experience the world quite differently in their daily lives surely ought to be taken into account. It seems strange that a man so fond of Gabriel Marcel has failed to follow his example of never building a philosophical position upon arguments not buttressed by a delicate phenomenology. Not one paragraph in the book, otherwise marked by careful and measured reasoning, is given over to demonstrating, by example or insight, that contemporary man is so mature that he merits from the Church a job of aesthetic surgery upon the very body of her teaching, in order that she might become attractive enough to merit the attention of the truly splendid age in which we live.

In other matters Dewart is quite respectful of "conservatives," crediting them with a practical wisdom not often acknowledged by "liberal" innovators. Therefore his awareness that they are not "the stupid party" ought to have moved him, not through courtesy but through curiosity, to have investigated *their* contention that the only decent reaction to the contemporary experience of the secularized West is that of the young man in Anthony Burgess's novel, *Tremor of Intent*, who "went. . . into a corner," heaved his shoulders, and "tried to throw up the modern world." If those whom Dewart regards as the party of tradition agree with Mr. Michael Lawrence "that the modern world needs to be vomited out of history," it follows that the professor ought to have paused long enough to consider their evaluation of the supposed maturity and superiority of modernity before launching into a program of doctrinal reform whose end is adjustment to this very contemporary consciousness.

In a word, conversation with Dewart cannot center on the way in which he experiences the modern world. On this level we can simply exchange testimonies and let the chips fall where they may. There is a sundering abyss separating those who agree with Eliseo Vivas that it is a mark of decency to be ashamed to have been born in the twentieth century and the Dewarts who hold that our moment in time reflects not a decline, but an advance in consciousness and spirituality. But while a man's evaluation of the secularized West neither supports nor detracts from Dewart's philosophy and theology, from a dialectical point of view, the evaluation is crucial existentially. It is crucial because a sick world—and we radical Christians think that the world is very sick indeed—calls for surgery upon it and not upon the Church it has rejected.

The point is that the *politics* underlying *The Future of Belief* rests upon assumptions that Dewart neither questions nor demonstrates. Most reactions to his book, moreover, will be formed in terms of this politics and not in terms of the philosophy supporting it. Only a fraction of the multitudes being urged today by awed reviewers (Catholics foremost among them) to rush to the nearest bookstore for that blue jacket promising "theism in a world come of age" possess the philosophical training and learning necessary to follow his thesis intelligently.

And yet that thesis is not without interest to philosophy.

I propose in the space available here to do three things with it—(1) summarize the thesis briefly in a way that will familiarize the lay reader with the kind of thing that is recommended in many quarters today as "Catholic" philosophy; (2) suggest a critique of the thesis that evaluates its claims to philosophical novelty, but that presupposes a professional's familiarity and competence to deal with the metaphysical details of

Dewart's argument; (3) explain in less technical terms the spectacular failure of the thesis—its failure to grasp the truly radical implications of orthodox Christian metaphysics—and the disastrous consequences to the Faith of seeking radical solutions *outside* of orthodoxy. In warning the layman of the difficulties of Part 2, I mean only to say that the argument there can be bypassed, that it is not essential to an understanding of why Leslie Dewart is either a very backward Catholic philosopher, or is not a Catholic at all.

I

Dewart's central argument is that we must work out a new formulation of our understanding of the nature of truth—one that conforms to modern man's experience of the world. And once we have done that, he concludes, it is clear that we will have to discard traditional dogmas, reinforced by Scholastic philosophy, asserting the Existent, Personal and Trinitarian God of Catholic orthodoxy. The Scholastic synthesis holds, to put the matter briefly, that truth is the conformity of the human intellect to *being*—a relation that is established in the intellectual act of *judgement*. This view, as Dewart is aware, precludes the possibility that "old" truths about revelation may fall into obsolescence and give away to "new" ones. Thus, in order to propound a revolutionary theology, he must first propound a new theory of truth.

Now this task, in turn, requires a new theory of knowledge. According to the Scholastics, knowledge is the intentional act through which a human subject unites himself to an object—an act through which the intellect unites itself to being. Truth, therefore, is found in the knowing human subject's awareness of his relation to the object in question, to being—an awareness that, since it results from an intentional act, takes the form of a "judgment." Dewart will have none of this because none of it jibes with modern man's more refined understanding of the elements of knowledge. According to Dewart, we can now understand that knowledge is a process through which an initially undifferentiated experience is penetrated and illuminated by the human consciousness. A man's consciousness, moreover, takes the form of *concepts* which are culturally and historically structured. They are so structured because "consciousness is not an essentially original and private event afterwards communicated (through signs) to other human beings"; rather it is a public event from the beginning. For Dewart, the "concept" (or knowledge) is itself "*the cultural form* of human experience."

Having rejected the Scholastic theory of knowledge, and therefore of truth, Dewart is able to advance his own view of truth—namely, that it is located formally within "concepts." Any "concept is true *to the degree* that by its elevation of experience to consciousness it permits the truth of human experience to come into being." Thus he has apparently discovered a "truth" beyond "the truth."

This discovery does not, however, enhance the stature of God. The reduction of all knowledge to concepts has quite the contrary effect.

For Dewart, the Christ of the creeds and the God of Christianity becomes a "presence"—and *merely* "a presence"—perceived in conceptual consciousness in precisely the way in which everything else is perceived by man. The "experience" of God is, to be sure, somewhat different from other experiences. "God is, among other ways in which we can conceptualize the matter, that which we experience as the open background of consciousness and being." God, Himself, however, has no being. Therefore, we cannot say that He *is*. We can no longer believe that God *exists*. There is a sense, according to Dewart, in which God is a "reality"; but the sense is so ephemeral that we are advised not to try to give Him a name. In the future, Catholics as well as other "believers" might better worship Him in silence.

II

Dewart's theory of truth is unacceptable to any Thomist. The Thomist holds that truth is never found in concepts at all—and this because of his anti-Platonic conviction that truth is not a meaning or an intelligibility but an existential relation between meanings and things. St. Thomas's teaching that truth is rooted in the very *exercise* of existence caused him to locate the mind's possession of truth in an act—the act that affirms or denies being. Concepts, in Thomistic epistemology, are existentially neutral in the sense that they can by purged of an explicit reference to singular existents in the course of scientific or any other kind of inquiry. Indeed, if the conceptual order did embrace existence, there would be no such thing as an unanswered question.

In propounding his view that truth is found formally within concepts rather than within judgment, Dewart attacks Scholasticism for failing to give an account of error or falsity. A more sophisticated understanding of intentionality would have taught him that false judgments *intend* (in the technical sense) the term of the relation of knowledge *merely as a term*. What exists as an object of knowledge in such cases exists merely and solely as an object and not as a subject of existence. Although the judgment remains relational, in other words, the relation has not been referred to extramental reality. I recommend to Professor Dewart Francis Parker's essay in *The Return to Reason*, "Realistic Epistemology." (Dewart's rejection of the doctrine of intentionality as outmoded is curious; for after falling into disuse for centuries, the doctrine has been revived precisely in the modern age to which Dewart is so anxious to adjust. I think of the reappearance of the doctrine in Husserl's phenomenology, which is traceable to his contracts with Brentano and to the subsequent expansion of an understanding of man as intentionality—some of it illicit in my view—in the existentialism of Heidegger and Sartre.)

Thomistic epistemology, then, reflects a metaphysics of being that insists upon an essence-existence polarity—essence being captured noetically in the conceptual order and the existent being affirmed in judgment. This psychosomatic act implies the marriage of soul and body: although man affirms being through his intellect, he encounters the material world through sensation. Dewart takes issue with this metaphysics on the grounds that the real distinction between essence and being in creatures renders "the *intellect* incompetent for knowing the actual existence of *any* essence, be it created or uncreated." But this is an odd case for the prosecution to lay before the jury because the defendant in question, St. Thomas, has already built *his* whole case around a confession of the very point. Thomistic realism, that is to say, is radically pessimistic about the intelligence being able to know anything at all in isolation from sensation. That the intellect cannot "know" created or uncreated existence (*esse*) is, according to Thomists, both a matter of human experience and a consequence of the abstractive nature of intellection.

But it is also a consequence of something far deeper: the structure of being itself. Dewart seems to be aware of this; he strikes at the Thomistic metaphysics of being with such vigor—apparently because he knows that unless he can discredit it, he cannot reduce truth to the conceptual order and, without doing *that*, he cannot call for a theological revolution. It is instructive to watch our author come to grips with St. Thomas on the meaning of being: Dewart seems sure that he knows what Aquinas was up to.

(He even pauses to act as a moderator between Gilson and Maritain on their reading of the Common Doctor, opting for Maritain.) But that he actually knows a little less than he supposes is clear from the following crucial mistake. Dewart understands Thomas to have based his "real" distinction between existence and essence on the grounds that *"a reflective analysis of our knowledge reveals* . . . in created being a real distinction between" them.

St. Thomas inherited this teaching from Avicenna, and repeated it often; but he was fully aware that it was convincing only in the framework of a metaphysics that conceives of existence as an Aristotelian "accident" added to an already constituted essence. Now since the human mind is, in fact, forced to "conceive" the situation in this way, the argument of Avicenna is useful as an introduction into the deeper meaning of being. St. Thomas's use of Avicenna, however, is little more than a ceremonial bow in the direction of a worthy pioneer. The true distance between Avicenna and Aquinas can be measured only by understanding that for St. Thomas existence is the very act of being, without which there simply are no essences at all—not even in thought. The Thomistic distinction between existence and essence (or better, their "non-identity") is not established by a "reflexive analysis of our knowledge," but through a process of reasoning that distinguishes that-in-the-real through which things *are* from that-in-the-real through which they are *what* they are. If "being X" belonged to the very structure of being, then it would follow that "being" always implies "X." But fidelity to the Many precludes our absorbing them into a monism of being, understood as an undifferentiated ontological block. The Thomistic essence, then, emerges ultimately as "the so much and no more" (Gilson) of an act of existing. Essence is an inner limit posited in being by the existential activity that it structures and determines.

In short, the tail Professor Dewart is wagging is not the Dumb Ox's at all, but Avicenna's. Which is really not surprising because, as Gilson never tires of repeating, Thomas's revolution in metaphysics was so profound and radical that not even his immediate disciples such as Giles of Rome knew what he was up to.

That the Christian revolution in philosophy has not been grasped by our latter-day revolutionary in dogma, Dr. Dewart, is further evident from the line: "truth cannot remain *the same.* It would make as little sense to say that existence remains *the same.*" It is true that existence never "remains the same"—but not for those reasons that forbid a parallel conclusion about truth. Created existence (what I like to call radical extramentality) is neither "the same" *nor* "the other." Both of those concepts are reducible to the quasi-transcendental—what St. Thomas called *aliquid*, and both enjoy only logical existence. When projected out into the real, they are tricks we play on ourselves.

And these tricks lead to bad theology. Dewart's repeated contention, following Luther and Barth, that "God is the Totally Other"—the absolutely Transcendent—reveals a failure to break through to the ultimate frontiers of the real: God is neither "same" nor "other" any more than the created act of existence is reducible to this logical geometry. A wholly "transcendent god" must be defined in terms of the immanence denied him; but that god is obviously not the Catholic God.

Here may be the place to drop some hints (without attempting to elaborate them) as to the direction that a deeper probing of Thomas's teaching on the meaning of existence might take in our day. Before philosophers join Dewart in doing away with "existence" in the name of "facticity" and "presence," they might consider the following propositions:

—Created existence (*esse*) neither is nor is not. (The tradition affirms this by insisting that existence is "non-subsistent" in the creature, but the tradition here truly is burdened by the hellenic mind.)

—Created existence is neither affirmable nor deniable.

—Created existence is neither "the same" nor "the other."

—Created existence is non-identity. Existential Identity is God Himself and the creature encounters its identity in His Being. Ultimately I am not God because I am not my being (*esse*) and because my being (*esse*) is not.

—Created existence is non-contradiction understood as radical extramentality and not as a principle governing the intelligence: i.e., the principle itself of non-contradiction "out there" in the real (the spatial metaphor seems inevitable) *is* the act of existence.

—Created existence is non-cessation which must not be confused with either "the dynamic" or the "static."

—Created existence is not tautological—it cannot be repeated. How could that which neither is nor is not, but without which nothing is at all, be repeated?

—Created existence is neither past, present, nor future; it escapes all three ecstasies of time.

—Created existence is not a "now" or an "already" because it is not a "presence" (*pace* Dewart) at all.

—Created existence is the act of synthesizing the analytic order. By contrast, created essence—through *esse*—is the dynamics of the analytic order. Essence is causality, Aristotle's four causes.

—It follows that created existence is a "plus" or an *excessus* as St. Thomas teaches (but without exploiting the insight) in *In Divinis Nominibus*. Existence escapes every analytical operation and all concepts. The activity of existence is the "beyond" that is lost the moment we reduce the complexity of the real to its constitutent parts. Existence is what is left behind when the lover ticks off the excellences of his beloved to a friend or to himself; it is that without which she would not be at all.

—Created existence is not a "presence" (sorry about that, Professor Dewart) because it is never given to us in this life. It is interesting that Dewart, having tried to destroy the "correspondence theory of truth" early in his book, eventually returns to a measure of Thomistic good sense by affirming that "the existence of *things* is self-evident." In this case "existence" presumably determines the mind irrespective of "cultural concepts." But this is a shallow Thomism. For it is precisely not "the existence" of things that is self-evident; rather it is "the things" that are evident (although not *self*-evident). Were their existence evident, they would not be.

III

The trouble with Dewart is that he is not radical enough. Having failed to understand how far St. Thomas progressed from Avicenna—and thus that the job of dehellenizing Christian thought was done centuries ago—Dewart has failed utterly to grasp the stupendous implication of Thomas's insights into the structure of being. Some of these implications, indeed, seem to have been hidden from Thomas himself. But they may now serve as a framework for—more, as an urgent invitation to—truly radical explorations into a theology of the future.

Thomas understood that the logical distinction between essence and existence in God, which so fascinates Dewart, is not central to the metaphysics of existence. As he put it in *De Potentia Dei,* the real problem lies elsewhere: "God does not enter the essence of created things, but (nonetheless) their *esse* cannot be understood unless seen as deduced from the divine *Esse.*" This meant that Nature, stripped of its pagan and Greek divinity by Christianity, could now be penetrated without any reference whatever to God. But note that this charter of independence from any metaphysical or theological totalitarianism, granted to science by the Catholic Church with her customary graciousness, is linked paradoxically with an absolute impossibility even to think of existence unless "it" be thought of as "in God." Once the human spirit has cracked the limits of nature and encounters the astounding miracle of being, either God must be affirmed or the spirit must fall into the anguish of existentialist Nothingness. Being elicits our allegiance to God, or being slips away in Heideggerian *Angst.* In no sense do we require—nor is the metaphysician granted—the "presence" of God. God is affirmed to be *without* appearing, and thus without filling the night of the intellect with the Light which is Himself. This misery of metaphysics, in the felicitous phrase of Maritain, might very well be the philosopher's paraphrase of St. John of the Cross (who, however, was dealing with far graver matter): *"y en el monte, nada."* The metaphysician has not found God, and He has not emerged before the philosophical reason either as an object or as a presence. But the philosopher now knows in the darkness of his reason that unless He be, nothing is.

Here is where Dewart misses an opportunity. By insisting that God is merely a "presence," he not only flattens the Christian experience of God, but misses his best chance to build a true theology for the future around the only metaphysical reality that *is* the Future: Christ.

We can approach the issue by meditating on Aristotle's clue to what might be the deepest dilemma in purely human or political life. In the *Rhetoric* the Stagirite suggests that the wise and good man—the statesman annealed in philosophical truth—can never propose the *being* of moral excellence (*arete*) to the populace because the populace, not possessing this virtue, will never understand the philosopher. The philosopher must be content with suggesting what goodness will *do* for the community rather than what it *is*. Behind Aristotle's pessimism lies a truly deep understanding of the nature of the political act. Belonging as it must to the future (there are no political acts with consequences in the past), the political, or human, act is addressed to what is not. The future has not yet been determined, and hence cannot be said to exist. This is true of every future except the only Future that is: Christ, "The Fullness of Time."

In the words of St. John the Evangelist: "We are now the sons of God; and it hath not yet appeared what we shall be. We know that, when He shall appear, we shall be like Him because we shall see Him as He is." Our very personalities are *not* discovered through conceptual consciousness and are *not* "emergent" in experience as Dewart imagines, but will be revealed to us only when we confront our future who is the Incarnate God. Dewart holds forth the prospect for man's future of a "beyond personality"; but this "beyond" truly *is* the Person in whom I find my own identity, who in truth *is* that Identity. In his fondness for Teilhard de Chardin's evolutionary Omega Point (our author has the good sense to caution against some of the French Jesuit's philosophical weaknesses), Dewart misses the utter radicalness of Christianity's teaching on the future. Anybody who builds a theology around an emergence from the past, no matter how "cosmic" it might be, anyone who seeks Christ *there,* is simply backing out of the present into the future with his gaze transfixed on the past. This is certainly not a theology for tomorrow, whatever else it might be.

Dewart and those who think as he does would *determine* our encounter with Christ by adjusting the Church, His Mystical Body, to a secular eschatology masking itself as maturity, and to an already dead secular way of life. This is sheer reaction; it fails utterly to grasp the *absolute* liberty that the radical Christian senses. The secularized world has already come into being. Thus it is a past to me as I stand at the crossroads of time. It cannot determine my future, and I owe it not the slightest allegiance. It rejects both the liberty of man and his being in the Person of Christ, his only tomorrow. The world to which Dewart would adjust God can be wiped away with all the astonishing absoluteness with which sin is annihilated in the confessional. A theology of the future transcends this world or it is nothing.

The openness, the fullness, the "futureness" of God also escapes Dewart in his discussion of the Trinity, which, he fears, the modern Christian will have to do without. "Christian theism might in the future not conceive God as a person—or indeed as a Trinity of persons." Dewart is dissatisfied with the orthodox understanding of the divine "processions" in terms of a triune personhood. The Christian tradition is alleged tò have treated God as an Aristotelian first cause to which it later attached, as a kind of afterthought, three. persons. By building these metaphysical "blocks," theologians tricked believers into an implicit tritheism. However, as I have written elsewhere: "Every community of nature grows itself out of the ecstasy of personality . . . God, for the patristic mind . . . is a personal and *hence* self-giving Act: this Act, an infinite ecstasy and fecundity, is expressed within Himself in the Trinity and beyond in the act of creation. The priority of personality over nature caused the Greek Fathers to approach the mystery of the Holy Trinity from a point of view which differs from that of the Latins. Whereas the Latins began with Unity of the Divine Nature and attempted to understand the Three Persons in the light of that unity, the Greeks began with the three persons and saw the Unity of Nature in the light of the Trinity of Persons. Their eminently personalistic theology was made possible by a theology of the real that saw the ultimate meaning of being in *agape*, in ecstasy as rooted precisely in God as personal, as superabundant."*

The Trinitarian structure of being, adumbrated in this life in the family, where the very existence of the child grows out of a "we," implies an understanding of personality which is one with *agape*, with what St. John Damascene called "superabundance." This law of unity in variety and variety in unity is regarded by Donoso Cortes as the fundamental law of being. Chesterton did not hesitate to call God a "holy company," and we do well to remember his terrible line: "We Trinitarians have known that it is not good for God to be alone."

Not surprisingly, Dewart's perverse view of the future also moves him to relieve God of authority—concretely, His superiority over men. For the notion of "superiority" belongs to those wicked "hierarchical relations" from which modern man has been emancipated. Modern man, then, is not only clearly superior to all of the men who went before him; he can now look even his Creator straight in the eye. And so God slinks down the road of the "future" and slips out of history; it would be pleasing to know that God were not personal and so could be spared this impudence.

What, in fine, are we to make of a talented Catholic scholar who finishes off an attack on traditional Catholic philosophy by stripping God (all the while piously insisting on the tentativeness of such conclusions) of His authority, His personality, His Trinity, His very being—much as a bemused child finishes undressing a doll by twisting off its head? First, suspect the protestations of tentativeness: the sincere man who is merely

---

* *The Metaphysics of Love*, 1962.

tempted by heresies is not likely to write a book aimed at the bestseller lists explaining their plausibility. Second, give the man the benefit of the doubt; give him a chance to explain how the "reality" of God in which he professes belief can be reconciled to reducing God to "experience," to an "open background of consciousness and being." It would seem that only two gambits are open: either "reality," as attributed to God, means the experience of God and nothing else; or "reality" somehow stands behind being as an ultimate ontological principle. If Dewart goes with the first possibility, then he is formally an atheist in the sense the Catholic Church understands the term; moreover, he has not escaped the charge of modernism, his protestations to the contrary notwithstanding. If he goes with the second, he has fallen back into the very hellenism he would discard. The idea that "reality" is a radical background to "being" is precisely the teaching of Avicenna, who distorted his own intuitions, having at hand nothing more than the old bottle of Greek essentialism into which to pour the wine of a creationist doctrine of being. That Dewart rejects the term "essence" matters not at all. Once "the real" is allowed to be more profound than being, the intelligence is beset with the contradiction of an ontological zone—call it "open background," "presence," whatever—that somehow is before it is. The only escape from the contradiction is semantic.

But there remains the fact of the book, and of its enthusiastic reception in Catholic circles. As I put down *The Future of Belief* I wondered how young untrained Catholics might react to the book and to its reception. I was gripped by an icy vision of a future "human church," bare, stripped of homage and of all comeliness, bereft of hierarchy and order, its temples emptied of beauty and swept clean of grandeur. In my vision the faith had gone out of the Church, and God had altogether departed. This church blindly worshipped a blind idol called Man. But then I shook off my vision as a bad dream unworthy of the hope that fires men who look to a Future called Christ.

1969

REDEEMING

WHY I AM A CATHOLIC

God is trundled through the streets of England once again. The Mystery Plays of York are revived. In medieval times, God was seated high upon the top level of a triple stage; an old gentleman with a great beard carried about on a cart by the guildsmen of the city. Below Him Christ was lying in a manger, was dying on the Cross, and was rising from the tomb, and on the lowest stage—at the very bottom—"Sathanus the fiend" was roasting in hell.

This drama in York symbolises the Faith I have known in the Catholic Church. To domesticate the drama of creation and redemption, and thereby to throw into awesome relief the tragedy of the fall of man and the evil that thus entered into the universe, is to fix as by a sign those truths of the Faith that have gripped me most powerfully all my life. For me, creation has always been unique, local, and therefore domestic. All those philosophies beyond the Church that have exalted the cosmos at the expense of the shrine seem not only lacking in truth, but failing in poetry and dignity. So too, our Redemption is wrought not through some system of ethical abstractions, but through a Divine Person. This answers a deep-rooted need of mine: loyalty. Outside the Catholic Church, where is there any suitable object of absolute loyalty? Could I be loyal to a man who lived long ago and preached a noble doctrine on the shores of the Sea of Galilee? For those of us who were born into the Church, this is not enough: we have the living Christ.

In the old days, the men of York dressed Christ as one of their own in the rough doublets of the country yeomanry. In the chivalric Book of Hours, Our Lady appeared as a young woman of the court. In so doing, the men of the Middle Ages proved themselves profoundly historical and profoundly Catholic. It is said everywhere that medieval man had a low sense of history; the judgement is Hegelian or Marxist, or both: in any case false. To be so full of the past that it is clothed in the garb of the present is not to miss history; it is rather to thrust history forward into the very courtyard of the present. But this truth merely prefigures the essence of history which is Christ present forever in His Mystical Body.

Finally, to place Satan just a few feet under Our Lord on the same cart as it is pulled down the narrow streets for all to gaze upon in wonder, is not only to remind man that he is involved in a "terrible aboriginal calamity", but also to teach him that what looks like a meaningless and absurd universe is not. Although things *are* what they seem to be, sin can make what is *not*, look as though it *were*. Appearances to the contrary, sin and evil are not the texture of the world, and therefore we must harden ourselves in hope.

The Catholic Church explains herself. She is an absolute, relative to nothing but God. Even more, since the Church bears God within her bosom in the Sacrament of the Altar, by participation the Church Supports the whole of His Creation. Thus she harbours the beauty of this world, and in blessing all things as she does wherever her life is lived in its fullness, she sends them forth, enjoining them to be themselves and to lead the life prefigured for them in the Wisdom of God.

A born Catholic, aware that he is a member of a "chosen race, a royal priesthood, a holy nation, a special people", and asked why he finds himself within the Church, can only answer that he really does not know. God gives him the Faith, but why God gives it is among the inscrutable things. God desires his salvation, but why God does is hidden in the Divine Will, and although he can know sometimes what the Will of God is, he cannot know why He wills as He does. Still, as God creates each man separately and endows him with an existence that is his own and incommunicable, so too does the Church come to each man as to an individual person, filling needs that are his own, and giving vision to those private intimations of the truth he may have traced in the darkness of his reason. The man born into the Church, baptised into its membership as an infant, discovers frequently enough that some of the Catholic truths have always informed and given depth and substance to needs and judgements he is prone to think peculiarly his own. Or he may find he has not really understood some doctrine of the Faith until its cogency struck home only after much living in the world finally forced him to judge things and men to be as they actually are.

I see the things that are and need not be. I believe that what once was, must in some sense, now be. Nothing is really lost; history is contemporary with the present. Through all the years the Church has fulfilled this early vision, and has confirmed this persistent belief: the mystery of being and the majesty of Christendom transfigured in the twin doctrines of the Creation and the Mystical Body. But there is a third Catholic doctrine that never meant much to me as a boy: the doctrine of sin and evil. As a child, I thought myself incorruptible, both morally and physically. Sin had only the vague outline of a reality within my mind. Now I know its monstrous tragedy. Evil thus seen has not dimmed my first wonder at the mystery of things; my early belief that the entire course of history is united in sharing the gift of existence is still intact; I still hold that being calls forth from man the pledge of loyalty both to the gift and to the Giver. This grasp of evil and imperfection locks with my affirmations on creation and history, and the three of them provide an approach to my own personal understanding of the Faith. Of course, no Catholic grounds his Faith on his own speculations. The Church is an absolute, and is measured only by God.

To look at the universe and fail to see it as created by God is to judge it a world completely absurd. This is the only sane judgement that can be made by a man who will not affirm God. Facing reality today, those thinking men who are not of the Catholic Church (and who are not influenced by her) usually react in one of two ways. Some accept an absurd world and try to live with it as best they can; these are the sceptics who have always known it was either Rome or disillusion, and who, like Santayana, have not been afraid of disillusion. Others are sceptical of God, but not of man; the civilised integrity of thorough-going scepticism is too exacting for them; they cannot bear to live without meaning; they place their faith in human perfectibility, and then they go on to introduce their own kind of order into the universe; they attempt to dissolve the absurdities in existence; they tidy up the mess. These last are the "secular humanists". They are numbered by the millions in the Western World today. This is their century, and they know it.

I have a great sympathy for the first kind of man—the absolute sceptic—because he neither denies the mystery of things, nor does he wound an already bleeding universe. He does not add to the absurdities. For the second kind of man—the secular humanist—I confess no sympathy at all. To pretend to a sympathy I do not feel in order to gain an apolgetic foothold in the secularist camp would be to fall into a great lie. This kind of person irritates, and the irritation is rendered the more difficult to bear because the men in question wish to dissolve the absurdities inherent in existing reality, and they succeed only in adding to them.

It is time I defined my terms: by absurdity I do not mean tragedy in the strict sense of the term. The ancients knew well enough that tragedy is invested with a high nobility; there is a sombre meaning, a black intelligibility, running through all genuine tragedy, filling it with the dignity of drama. We can follow the tragic hero to his destruction, and although we suffer with him, our reason is satisfied; we know why he came to his end. This is not the case with absurdity. The absurd is the meaningless. Not only does this kind of evil wound, but it bewilders. We see no reason for it; it is a vacant stare upon the broken countenance of human existence. Absurdities are everywhere. Each man can make his own list. This is mine: the cynicism of the rich, the cheapness of love, the loss of innocence in children, the blindness of the learned, the scattering of the family, the suffering of the sick, the death of infants and the carrying of coffins. Surveying this desolation of withered expectations—steadily, without panic—the sceptic must, and does, estimate the world senseless, a place empty, and altogether without hope. "Depart from hope all ye who enter here": thus Dante, inscribing the portals of hell; thus the sceptic, pronouncing judgement on this world. "If Christ be not risen, our Faith is in vain." Without Him risen, and without God creating, the world is as the sceptic declares it to be. The sceptic is in the Pauline tradition. He reminds us that we are ransomed men; men rescued from his own vision of existence. He is part of the furniture of the Faith.

But the sceptical breed is vanishing in our day. It is being replaced rapidly by men of the other sort: the "secular humanists", those men who, refusing to recognise sin and evil as part and parcel of the universe in its present fallen state, refusing to see the world as fundamentally absurd from every canon of "secular" reason, ignore or sentimentalise evils that are absolutely unredeemable, and view all the others as "problems" to be dissolved by themsleves through techniques developed in their own wills. This philosophy parades under many names, but perhaps the "secular humanist" label is the most accurate of all: "humanist" because man is made the measure of all things, and "secular" because salvation is thought to be within the reach of the powers of nature as mastered by scientific and social action.

Like Milton's Adam and Eve, the secular humanists go forth into life with "the world all before them", reaching for "the happy end". And this is the irony of their programme: they heal no wounds; they dissolve no absurdities; they rather add to them. The secularists think they can eliminate human suffering, and for every cripple they send forth whole in body, they admit to their temples a man sick in mind. For every border raid they put down, they loose upon humanity a war more hideous than the last. They extend the franchise, and they cheapen the citizenry. They broaden the base of education, and they lessen the product. They suppress superstition, and raise up a mob of cynics. Wisdom is nothing to them, and the Christian tradition—full as it is of chivalry and romance— is utterly beyond the pale of their narrow and mechanical comprehension. They pull down the moral law in the name of freedom, and set up a hundred prohibitions in its place. They preach life, and establish by law murder clinics for the unborn in Sweden. Addicted as they are to measuring and counting, they would quantify all existence, level away every distinction, destroy the memory of the past, and finally stifle the movement of the human heart to rise above the level of the collectivity.

Secular humanism is man's conferring divinity on himself, and is thus not only a violation of the First Commandment, but is also the crowning absurdity within the whole history of the human race, for what could be more ridiculous than man worshipping himself? Absurd, for when man begins to admire himself in a mirror his pride makes him less attractive than before. Meaningless, because the vaunted earthly paradise is not at hand, because suffering is still with us, because the universe still groans under evil, because men are not better than they were, because men are worse than they were.

I admire the realism of the pure sceptic in confronting the fact of human absurdity. I deplore the refusal of the secular humanist to look existence in the face; he is a latter-day Pollyana, blithely dancing through a graveyard, gathering roses while he sings songs of the happy time.

To refuse to look at evil is to fall into secular humanism. To look once at evil is to see it as the sceptic sees it. To look twice is to see it as the Catholic sees it: as a wound, a laceration cutting away the edges of being, but leaving intact the central mystery—the truth that men and things are, and are good. Reality is not what it ought to be; all things falter, and nothing falters more than man. Unless he take to worshipping himself, any man who thinks at all must be outraged at his own paltriness; he becomes aware that the actuality is but a mask, hiding the face that should be his own. This is a discovery of lost perfection, for I could not be horrified unless there was a memory inscribed in my nature of what I was intended to be. When I survey the wreckage of the human soul, I hear music curling round the ruined city of man; I hear trumpets sounding through the recesses of the human heart, proclaiming dignity, a lost paradise, and the promise of an eternal fatherland.

The irony of human reality and human possibility, the disproportion between what we are and what we can be, is an evident fact of experience. Seen together they trace a cosmic tragedy. Tragedy, once again, is full of meaning, and the Church alone possesses that meaning. Lying at the origin of all literature is the story of a Golden Age, and lying in the centre of every human soul is the hope. But only the Church guarantees the story, and only she fulfils the hope, bringing, as she does, grace through Christ, reconciling all fallen things to God. Without the Faith, we could be doomed to discover the possibility of perfection and beatitude, without discovering any means for their fulfilment. But "what we cannot do by ourselves, we can do through our friends", says St. Thomas Aquinas. The Church offers the friendship of God through Christ our Brother in the flesh, and this friendship is not only the hope of the world to come, but is also the only hope for mankind within history. This last truth I do not take on the teaching authority of the Church; I take it on my own experience and on whatever judgement I may possess concerning the history of Western civilisation.

St. Paul tells us that Faith is of things unseen, but I do not need Faith to know that I am not what I ought to be, that I am involved in sin along with the whole of mankind. I do not need Faith to teach me that wherever the Catholic Church is accepted in the fullness of her teaching, there will I find men fully human and themselves. To contrast the secularised world with the remnants of Catholic Christendom, is to come to know all the more, if not the final meaning of grace, then certainly it effects in history. "Faith is of things unseen": true enough, but "by their fruits ye shall know them". These fruits cause me to rejoice in the patrimony that is mine. They root me all the more firmly to this holy company, the Catholic Church.

What kind of man does the Church make? I do not mean what kind of man does the Church shelter; she shelters all men, and it is one of her glories that those rejected by the world can find friendship and hope only within her walls. But the full Catholic, the man made by the Church through and through—the fruit of the Faith—what is he like? He is the man who, finding himself in a finite universe, looks within his soul and discovers, not only a nature limited in its very substance, but a nature wounded by that "terrible aboriginal calamity". The first of his virtues is humility: the realist acceptance of finite perfection. The second of his virtues is loyalty: a firm cleaving to the reserves of reality at hand for the creation of a decent personal life, and a just social order. The Roman Catholic conserves whatever God has given him, whatever his ancestors have bequeathed him. A profound reverence for creation informs his mind, stamps itself on all his art, is translated into the way he wrestles with nature in the struggle for survival, colours his relationship with society and with the state, steadies him in success, and anneals him in adversity. He knows the meaning of contingency, and he treads gently upon being, lest he shatter that most absolute of Gifts. He does not tinker with existence. He rather celebrates reality. The vine and the cup are not foreign to him: he knows the meaning of sacrifice: he knows mystery.

I wish to be united with such men; not simply with those who are walking around the crust of the globe at this moment, but with all of them—those dead, those living, and those still to come. This attitude toward history is neither Greek nor modern, but Roman.

To the Greeks, history was nothing but time, and human salvation was achieved only by a flight into the abstract order. For the Greek metaphysical mind the only things worth saving from history were ideals. But the salvation of ideals does not, in the words of Newman, "warm the desolation of my heart". Nor does a handful of ideals satisfy a man burying his dead. As for the modern conception of history, it has even less depth than the Greek. It is untouched by imagination, and is altogether pedestrian. Nothing so refreshes the man of today as to be told he has met the challenge of history by moving with the times. Mobilism has become, not only a sign of intelligence, but a mark of virtue, and an evidence of high moral probity. But there is no poetry in all this; nor is there courage; this is a trick relieving men of the duty of fighting the times when they are bad, and although the times are always more or less bad, today they are worse than ever before. The Roman view of history was something completely different. It was rooted in the fundamental human need for familial and corporate continuity. It was full of piety. Man was not looked upon as an isolated atom, drifting amorphously in the fluidity of time. Men

311

counted for more than "the flies of a summer morning". The famous *pietas* united all men in one society.

To the old Roman at his best (and at his worst) the family is knit together by blood and a common land turned over by hands that have received their patrimony from a line of ancestors stretching back to the youth of the race. The dusk falls on the back of each man as he retreats down the road of time, but as he has received from the past, so has he given to the future, and as they lived in him, so shall he live in them. And this is promised him by the household gods, and even when he no longer believes in his gods he still keeps them, for they are the badge of his service and the pledge of his immortality.

But what was symbol to the pagan, is reality for the Catholic. The Mystical Body of Christ unites all ages into one company, and I can talk to Augustine, not as to a memory, but as to a man. The Incarnation did not destroy time, but raised it to an altogether new dimension. When St. Paul speaks of the "life of Christ" he usually does not mean the thirty-three years Our Lord spent on earth. He means, as Mgr. Knox has said, an "energy" poured out on the world, filling all times, and transcending each one of them, uniting together the whole course of mankind, making the Franks before Tours the companions of the heroes of the Alcazar. The Catholic holds his youth against an ageing universe; he begins his eternity while still a wayfarer within a world that passes.

The Catholic sees reality at the centre, and the centre is Christ, and as Christ is He through whom all things are created, the Catholic sees creation. Very early in life I was filled with the mystery of being. When quite young I got down to the meaning of contingency, without knowing the name. Although I am not what I ought to be, I exist, and I do not have to exist at all. I find myself in a world that reflects my own fragile hold on being. To say that the universe of things need not exist does not mean that the universe need not have ever existed. *It is to say that here and now it need not be.* There is nothing in it, absolutely nothing, calling forth its existence. The head demands the arm, and the arm demands the hand, but neither of them demands being. Chesterton's line about the "impossible things that are" sums up this absolute mystery lying at the centre of reality. Things are impossible in themselves, and at first sight it seems far more reasonable that there should be nothing, rather than something. Yet nothing is not; things are, and all of them keep on doing something so utterly mysterious that it dizzies the intelligence, and rocks the imagination. Defying abstract formulation, even the poet falters when he attempts to express it. That which things keep on doing, is—being. As a dancer does an act of dancing, so do all things do an act of being, and why they should so act, no man knows. St. Thomas expresses this, of course, in terms of participation. Each thing that is, shares in an existence not its own by right.

To pierce thus into reality, to go below the surface swarming as it is with sin and disease and evil is to affirm this world to be as it is: not an accumulation of sense phenomena, not my "representation" as Schopenhauer declared, not a series of "problems" to be explored by secular humanists, not a vast cosmos of raw materials to be exploited by a machine—but as the heritage of existence: a barony held in fief for the Lord.

For we men are, in truth, vassals, and the claim we have on existence is borrowed, and thus we own allegiance to the God who gives us being, and even to the being He gives us, since the being is God's being, although not the Being of God. Fealty, piety, loyalty, the swearing of allegiance, the pledging of swords, and the bending of the knee—these are the realities that are always playing out their chivalric drama in the back of my consciousness, and neither doctrine nor polity that fails to place them to the forefront can ever receive from me more than passing curiosity, or half-hearted attention. The Church has come to me all these years preaching her awesome doctrine of the "I Am Who Am" and of His terrible Love, and of His betrayal and death on a Cross of Wood, and of His Kingship over all men in His Body the Church. This is my vision of existence. This answers.

1954

THE SOVEREIGNTY
OF CHRIST OR CHAOS

We celebrate here in this special edition of *The Wanderer* one hundred years of life in the service of the Church and of Western civilization. The century which spans the years from 1867 to 1967 has been marked by the victory of Liberal secularism in the Western world. The same years saw the disappearance of the Austro-Hungarian Empire, the last great Catholic Power in the world; they noted the liquidation of the Papal States and the reduction of the worldly role of the Roman Pontiff to the Vatican; they marked two ghastly World Wars and the rise of Communism and its subsequent enslavement of half the world; and today they close upon what must certainly be the deepest crisis through which civilization has passed since the fall of the Roman Empire—even more, a crisis itself deeper because today the Church itself is wracked from within by a spirit of rebellion and doubt that reflects the final desacralizing of that society which was once Christendom. We have won victories in these past hundred years, but they have been isolated, sporadic, and extraordinary. They have bent against the grain of the times. It would be illusory here to count those victories or to glory in them because they have not turned the tide.

Looking ahead to the next hundred years, those of us who are faithful to the full inheritance of the Catholic Thing, those of us who do not glory in our own petty consciences but who make of our intelligence and of our will a holocaust before the See of Peter, must not only map a strategy for our counterattack, but we must locate that strategy within a sweeping vision of the meaning of the crisis within which our world anguishes at this moment of time. Our strategy must fit an accurate reading of the times. If we read our times of troubles in provincial terms, we cannot prepare ourselves for what might very well be a splendid opportunity to strike a

314

startlingly brilliant blow for the Faith. To see the crisis in the economic terms of a battle between socialism and capitalism, and socialism gradually winning the day, is to see the business provincially: Socialism is an enemy, but it is not the enemy. To see the crisis in terms peculiar to the American political experience, as though the battle enjoined were one between the forces of freedom and its enemies, would be equally provincial: freedom can never be an absolute goal for a Catholic who must see it as an instrument, albeit a peculiarly noble instrument, in the service of salvation, in the service of love. To see the crisis in the light of the destruction of local liberties and the growth of the mass state would be to see a significant truth, but to reduce the crisis to those terms would be, once again, provincial.

I suggest to the readers of *The Wanderer* that at its deepest level the Western world today is in the very last death rattle of a crisis in Authority. Given, however, that Authority is ultimately God's Authority, this crisis is simultaneously a crisis of Faith.

Western man, very early in the game, distinguished carefully between Authority and Public Power or Government. Authority was the Truth incarnated by a community and Power was that same community organized politically for historical action. Both Power and Authority grew out of one given society, but they articulated themselves into two distinct dimensions of the social order. The Romans grasped this truth in the seedtime of the Republic when the judges, later the senate, were the repositories of all Authority and when the magistrates, headed by the consuls, and the machinery of government managed by them, were the repositories of Power. To Power was given the role of asking questions of Authority in order that Power might act justly and wisely. To Authority there was given the role of answering those questions put to it. The distinction was blurred in the late Empire due to the centralization of power in the hands of the emperors, but even then the Roman Order maintained the fiction of a distinction: the imperial title had to be ratified by the senate.

In Greece the Power-Authority tension was heightened and symbolized by the death of Socrates at the hands of the Assembly. Plato lamented in his *Republic* that the Authority of Philosophy did not possess the Sword of Power. It was his firm conviction that unless Wisdom could wed itself to the force inherent in Power human societies would be perpetually doomed to live in corruption and evil. Aristotle suggested a tactic that involved the education of statesmen by philosophers in order that government, Public Power, might thus be imbued with the Authority of Wisdom. In any event, Greece as well as Rome understood that Authority is one thing and Power something else, although Greece, unlike Rome, did not have the practical genius needed to institutionalize Authority and thus make it a working partner in the business of governing men.

Both Greece and Rome sensed that Authority was personal, reposing in the hands of judges and senators in Rome, and in those of the philosophers in Greece. Authority was the prerequisite of the wise. But these men possessed Authority by what they knew and by virtue of the moral excellence achieved within them. Authority did not accrue to them because of who they were.

The Incarnation of the Son of God changed all this. Christ—The Way, the Truth, and the Life—not only has Authority, but He IS Authority. He alone commands simply by being. In that Christ is the Perfect Wisdom of the Father, in Whom all things are created, it follows that all Authority is His and all Power—called upon to heed the voice of Authority—is His.

Here we discover the theological roots of the doctrine that proclaims the Kingship of Christ. In Christ the tension between Power and Authority, experienced in the political community, dissolves because—being God—His Authority is His Power in the deepest metaphysical sense of the term.

This doctrine articulated by the Fathers of the Church, and most especially by St. Isidore of Seville, bloomed in the High Middle Ages and was reflected in the enormous transformation undergone by society in the centuries following upon the fall of the Empire and the hammering into unity of Catholic Christendom. The destruction of the highly centralized Roman Order and the growth of the new medieval kingdom gave birth to new relations between Power and Authority. Given that Europe, a dust of Germanic tribes emerging from barbarism thanks to being put to school by the Church, had to rebuild itself from the very foundations, those centuries were marked by the growth of a cluster of institutions, self-governing and administering, autonomous, almost anarchically free. Guilds, townships with charters, provincial parliaments (beginning in the Basque country in the North of Spain, spreading then rapidly into France and England), and universities and schools burgeoned into being and soon structured society around the reality and the theory of a series of authorities in the political community that both checked the political power of the king when it tended towards tyranny and that advised and voted subsidies to it in moments of extraordinary stress and danger to the entire body politic. If all Power resided in the government of the medieval king—and it did—, then all Authority—multiple and hierarchically structured—belonged to society itself. Crowning this thicket of authorities that ran from guild regulations concerning its own affairs to feudal relationships between lords and vassals was the Authority of the Church concentrated in a unique fashion in the magisterium of the Roman Pontiff, God's Authority on earth, given the Keys to bind and to loose. Political power was checked from below by the Authority of customary law which could not be violated with impunity and from above by Rome's Authority to pronounce definitively matters pertaining to ultimate moral acts and to sound doctrine. Very often kings consulted Popes on the morality of this or that military adventure, and the rightness or wrongness of many a royal alliance or proposed annulment of a marriage was debated openly in the universities. It is absurd to speak of the "Power of the Church" in the Middle Ages. The Popes had about as much power as does an aged father laying down the law to his robust son, which is to say that papal authority was what authority always is and must be: moral. The Authority of the Papacy stood so high that it did not need any power to buttress it in its role as arbiter of Christendom. The Popes first acquired a modest power in the Renaissance when they determined to become Italian princes, but by then, ironically enough, their authority was already in full decline.

This network of autonomous authorities—running from trade unionship through the thicket of feudal relations governing a predominantly agrarian society, reposing within the jealousy independent universities and spread through society politically in customary laws which were intensely local and hence personal, crowned by the Church and her magisterium—was the social and existential incarnation of the theology of the Kingship of Christ. Ultimately all kings are royal through Him. Ultimately all Authority, even that of a master craftsman in all that pertains to his trade, comes from Him in Whom "we live and move and have our being." This is the meaning of the Royal Sovereignty of Jesus Christ.

We can approach the issue speculatively if we attend to a distinction emphasized by my old master in political philosophy, Yves Simon. Whereas Law is always impersonal and universal, Authority is ultimately personal and concrete. A father cannot "pass laws" for his family because he is not charged with the care of an entire political community, but the "rules" he lays down in his household bind because he has authority over his children and his wife. The very natural law itself, impersonal and hence lacking in concrete effectiveness in classical antiquity, took on the personal Authority of its Author, God, within the Christian Order in Europe. To break the natural law for a Christian was not simply to break a law: it was to break a Heart, Christ's. Standing thus as Center and King of creation, Sovereignty was His and His alone.

The distance between medieval Christendom and modernity can be measured by the birth of a new political phenomenon, the State. The State was brought into being by the absolutizing tendencies of the French monarchy in the Renaissance and it was articulated in theory by the apologist of that same monarchy—Jean Bodin. Expressing the matter as trenchantly as possible, Bodin identified the Power of the Prince with an Authority which was Absolute and which resided in himself. He thus rendered the Prince a Sovereign in the full ontological, and not merely in the ceremonial, sense of the term. Instead of governing according to customary law and in harmony with the spiritual Authority of the Church, the new Prince governed according to a Sovereignty which was his own, a Power united to an Authority which was unbounded and un-limited. The font of law as well as of Authority, the Prince of the Renaissance and of the early centuries of the modern epoch might or might not, at his pleasure, recognize the Authority of God's Church. He might or might not make himself the servant of the Lord. The decision was ultimately his because *he* was sovereign and not God. Politically the crea-tion of the absolute and sovereign State entailed the gradual destruction of local liberties, the withering away of the force of customary law, the crea-tion of a system of public schools, the centralization of both Power and Authority, the reduction of the Church, first to a fifth spoke in the wheel of royal absolutism, and later to a private superstition persecuted and tolerated by starts and fits by the Revolutionary State, itself the repository of the earlier absolutism. Liberalism simply substituted the Authority of the Assembly (symbol of that myth, "The People") for that of the King. Under the banner of a fake "Liberty, Equality, and Fraternity," one-fourth of all Spain's land went under the auction block in the last century and thus both the Church and the townships lost their old economic in-dependence without which nothing can be done in this world. Under that same banner the economic liberalism of a new capitalism destroyed the free peasantry, dealt craftsmanship its death blow, and enthroned economic liberty in the center of society upon the ruins of the older Catholic order. The crowning of the supremacy of economics coincided with the enthroning of a whore as the Goddess of Reason in the Cathedral of Notre Dame. Under that same banner the religious orders, most especially the Jesuits, were persecuted throughout all Catholic civilization. Under that banner, Man became Sovereign, even though he paid for his new divinity by losing those liberties and concrete rights that had been his own under the dispensation of Catholic civility.

By an historical irony the English colonies in North America preserved better the medieval inheritance than did most of the older European provinces of Christendom. They escaped the Renaissance and therefore they both gained and lost. The neither knew the grace of its statuary and the splendor of its poetry, nor did they experience the last Catholic synthesis in the West which was the Baroque civilization of the Habsburgs. But they did carry into the new world a number of institutions which were typically medieval. The sheriff and the posse of our Western mythology are simply medieval institutions with six-shooters rather than long bows. (how many know that the posse of a John Wayne movie is the *posse comitium* of the Catholic tradition of law?) More significantly, the tradition of local liberties and self-government, of "States' Rights," and an independent judiciary were all heritages of a world that was already dying in Europe when Columbus set his caravals westward in search of the Indies. Wounded by the crippling influences of a Puritan soul, damaged by the influences of the rationalist Enlightenment, the American experience in government did at least escape both the absolutism of the French monarchy and the deeper absolutism of the French Revolution. The State was never Sovereign here—not until recently.

But the history of the West has been governed by a curious law rooted in the geographical movement from East to West. Everything that is typically our own in Christian civilization has come out of the East as did our God Himself. But everything then has moved West. This has been true of both the grace of God and of every heresy that swept out of the Eastern deserts to fall upon, and thus damage the soul of Christendom. Thus it was that the unity of Catholic Europe, itself a medieval ideal, when abondoned by the rest of Europe, was taken up in the first decades of the modern era by Spain, the most western province in European Christendom. Thus it was that Charles the First of Spain and the the Fifth of the Holy Roman Empire, born a Fleming and buried a Spaniard, placed—in his own words—all his kingdoms, his wealth, and his friends at the service of the Holy Roman Catholic Church, at the precise moment in time when the Lutheran heresy threatened all the North; and when France and England were busy themselves with bloating the power of their kings in the name of a royal nationalism (in the case of France) and in the name of a royal narcissism (in the case of England). Thus it happened that the remnants of medieval liberty, scattered upon the Eastern seaboard of this American continent by men who in many ways were throwbacks to an earlier time, grew into that mighty thing, the American Republic, itself a strange and not altogether unlovely mingling of a Catholic body politic which housed a Puritanical soul. But secular Liberalism as well, itself born in Europe from out of the absolutizing pretensions of the modern State, has also travelled East to West.

It has now arrived here in our own United States. We are witnessing today in our land events which reached their apotheosis in Europe decades ago. Swamped as we are by the consequences of Rationalism and Liberalism, our government is converting itself into a European-style State—font of justice and law, dispenser of ideology, dictator of education, a vortex of power into which the best brains and most ambitious spirits in the nation are swept inexorably. Just as the Revolution insisted upon a secularized France in the first flush of the Jacobin victory in Paris, so too today the drummer boys of the future march us towards a total secularization and desacralization of the social and political orders. We once recognized a public orthodoxy of morals and liberties whose roots were deep in the tradition of the natural law and in the Christian inheritance. That is today dead. The government, from the riders that it puts to South American aid in favor of birth control, to its public pretensions of agnosticism in things absolute, proclaims that it has shed itself of any Authority deeper than itself. Judicial decisions against prayers in public schools, the blackmail which is one with the threat of withholding Federal funds to education unless the subjects taught comply with the secularist democratic ethos, simply reiterate again here in this land what happened long ago on the European continent. A new time-serving clergy, hat in hand, eager to please the powers of this world in all things and bent upon the secularization of the Catholic patrimony of universities and schools, recalls those French Bishops and priests who swore allegiance to the Revolutionary State in the first flush of national reconciliation which followed upon the Terror. King Louis XVI of France, when he was trundled to the guillotine by the Jacobin secularists, longed to make his confession before he faced the knife, but he disdained the services of the government's priest because this man had taken the oath to a godless State. How many Catholic educators today have secretly sworn allegiance to the secularist world that both surrounds and feeds them? And it would be illusory to expect that our youth can resist as did Louis XVI: after all, they have not been trained in his high code of honor. This last is the effect of much living in a Catholic civilization.

Men speak today of an attack upon States' rights. But that attack was already launched and won in France by the late eighteenth century when the secular-liberal-democrats abolished the provincial parliaments and with them every vestige of local liberty in France. In the nineteenth century three bloody civil wars were fought in Spain—Carlist Wars—over that very issue of States' rights and the partisans of local liberties (they were also those of the Church) were beaten by mercenary armies paid by English and French liberal capitalism. States' rights, after all, are a medieval and Catholic relic utterly foreign to the dynamism of the modern State.

We are, therefore, playing out in this nation—very late in the day—consequences of the identification of Authority and Power that were played out to their grim end in the late eighteenth and nineteenth centuries in Europe. The game was decided in favor of the Revolution. American scientific and technical mastery often create the illusion of utter modernity. Americans are usually pleased to fool themselves (it is an innocent illusion) about having shaken off the European past in the name of a new world, etc. But the truth, by an irony which is really sardonic, is almost exactly the reverse. This country has been the last stand of medievalism in things political. (I abstract here from the moral and theological, and restrict myself to the purely political.) What we are witnessing in our land today is the liquidation of the vestiges of the medieval order, of that very order which Lord Acton insisted created every typical instrument of liberty and human dignity known to the West.

But history never simply repeats itself. The march of ideas and of passions from out of our geographical East into our West always carries with it the weight of its own past. Thus it was that the Spanish-Austrian Empire of the Habsburgs in the sixteenth and seventeenth centuries did not simply repeat the medieval experience: it created something new out of a baroque wilderness of materials that were not present in the High

Middle Ages. Thus it is also true that the secularization of American society today is not simply repeating the European past. Secularization here, carrying behind it the weight of the entire European experience, is far more profound than anything hitherto known in the Catholic world which, after all, did divide into a secularist bloc and an intransigent Catholic bloc, thus giving birth to Two Frances, Two Spains, Two Italys, and so on. And our American secularization is bending back upon its European origins. In so doing, it is deepening a movement towards total secularization which today is truly worldwide, which has even invaded the Communist orbit and which produced the reaction of the Red Guards in China who rightly feared that the true Marxist gospel was being contaminated through Russia by western ideas.

This last points up in a dramatic fashion the deepest meaning of this moment in history. The secular liberal West is now entering into its own agony. I insist that the modern State, buttressed by the secularist philosophy, is on the point of dying after having run its course—its three-score and ten—through four hundred years of historical experience. Secularism is failing today precisely because it has succeeded. It always did play the stock market of the human spirit and it always played it short. Secular Liberalism's goals were low, so low that they have been accomplished in the industrialized nations of the West. Secular Liberalism seized the modern absolute and sovereign State. What did it promise? A high standard of living; a maximum of comfort; an easing of the pains of illness and the prolongation of life; earthly salvation through education for the masses; the destruction of hierarchy in the name of the myth of human equality; the standardizing of culture; the reducing of religion to the realm of private superstition and the banishing of its fake authority from the marketplace; the easing of the harshness of traditional morality and its substitution by a vague "humanitarianism"; technical efficiency; the literal worship of science, jammed down the throats of the nations by the bayonet when necessary. These premises were to be made good by the modern State that concentrated within itself all power—the State that was the ultimate source of all Authority, even in matters moral. (Permit me to cite here but one instance, if dramatic, of the State's absorption of Authority unto itself. When it was determined that this nation was to put a man on the moon, neither philosopher nor theologian was consulted. The taxpayers were simply dragooned into supplying the millions, possibly in time billions, needed to set an astronaut on the moon—and this altogether without any military justification, either defensive or offensive, being given the nation. We were told we were going to do this because the State so willed it out of the progressivist and gnostic dream illusions entertained by those who exercise power within the land.) I suggest to the reader that the Liberal program has been carried out. It has been a stunning success. Pockets of poverty do exist here and there in the United States, and in Germany and Great Britian. But these pockets are ·simply challenges to a technocratic order that already possesses the instruments needed to eliminate them in time. Nothing fails like success. Secularist-Liberalism has achieved its goals. It has no place to go. It cannot lift the human heart to the distant hills. It cannot move men to actions which are spiritual in their source. Secular Liberalism tries to fill up the vacuum by sending off its youth to distant lands in order that they might clean up the garbage with greater dispatch. But a civilization whose only goal consists in cleaning up somebody else's garbage has lost what T.S. Eliot called an "objective correlative" for its energies. The secularist West has no destiny. It aimed low: it won: it is finished in history.

As we insisted in *Triumph*, the Black Revolution in our nation was a vivid proof of the bankruptcy of secular Liberalism. The Black Brother was not satisfied with the mammon offered him by the Sovereign Liberal State. He does not know what he wants but he senses in the roots of his being that his deep cry for justice and dignity, born out of centuries of Protestant Calvinist oppression, will not be satisfied by an integrated neighborhood, a color television set, and a new Buick. He too lacks an "objective correlative" for his revolution, but he does have one for his rage: Secularist, White, American society, Calvinist in its reflexes, Rationalist in its mind, and hedonist in its intentions. But the Black Revolution is not the deepest sign of the collapse of the Liberal order. The widespread use of drugs by our youth, the hippie revolution, the truly abnormally selfconscious separation by youth from any tradition at all, well expressed by the phrase: "Don't trust anybody over thirty," the open defiance of government by those who glory in civil disobedience, the spread of crime for crime's sake, indicates that Authority, once shifted from God to the State, has now shifted—following the dialectic of the Protestant Principle—from the State to something called "the individual conscience." While not precisely rejecting the materialist panaceas of secularism, while still largely symbolizing their rejection in terms of Liberal myths, whole segments of the population have abdicated from

Society. The collapse of respect for Authority within the Church is, of course, the effect of the spiritual exhaustion of millions of Catholics who are shellshocked from being in the trenches for so long a time. This is true as I have suggested elsewhere, but this collapse is also the effect of a general disenchantment with Authority in all its public forms. Society—liberal society, the West as we know it—is simply breaking up. This is truly unpleasant because Liberal Western society is comfortable, reasonably civilized, safe from public violence, and its permits people even to be Christians if they so desire. But the whole business is collapsing today. Ask anybody who lives in Washington!

A moral vacuum is being created in a land that has ever prided itself on living by law but that today lives thanks to the bayonet between it and violence. Given that all nature abhors a vacuum, this vacuum will be filled. I suggest that there are two candidates for the job: a crusading and charismatic Communism of the Castro or the Red Guard type or a new and radical "instauration" of a Catholic society structured around the Sovereignty of Christ the King. I think that the odds are in favor of the former, but as a radically traditionalist Catholic my prayers are on the latter.

In the light of the above I make the following suggestion to the readers of *The Wanderer*. We owe not the slightest allegiance to the Western secularist and Liberal order. It destroyed the Catholic order and it did so by murdering our ancestors in nation after nation in Europe and South America. Let secular democracy stew in its own juices as it is stewing today. Meantime, let us keep our powder dry until the right moment, God willing, emerges on the horizon of history and calls for us to act in the name of Christ the King. Let us not waste our time and energy by shoring up the modern State. Let us rather do everything in our power to see that it collapses. (I use the term "State" here as formally defined in opposition to "Government" within this essay.) Let us also avoid, in thought and in rhetoric, any suggestion that we defend the nineteenth-century order in things political and economic: in both dimensions they were enemies of the Church and therefore they are our enemies. We are enemies of all kinds of Liberalism, economic as well as political.

Although this essay has not been addressed formally to the crisis within which the Church finds itself today, we can affirm confidently that the Church will emerge from this ghastly historical moment, leaner, stripped of the weak and with the fat burned away. This may not happen in the lifetime of those who read these words, but it will certainly happen within the next hundred years. In the meantime, let us be traitors to the Secular City and thus taste the sweetness that is one with all treason, both good and evil. Let us be the last rebels in our salute to but one Sovereign, One Lord, Christ, King. Let us, therefore, ignore, fight, shirk, undermine, every authority that supplants or ignores His. In existential terms this means that we must cleave to the Authority of Rome which is that of Christ's, against clerics and prelates if necessary.

We shall, therefore, build up a Power for Peter's Authority, capable of acting in every dimension of life and even unto death by arms should it be necessary. This will cast us out of polite society and into a wilderness where we will be buttressed by neither institutions nor by that weight of prejudice with which every society maintains itself in being. We are losing our universities today—Webster, Notre Dame, St. Louis, San Francisco. Let them go. Men cannot swing swords in a sea of marshmallows. We are losing our clergy by the thousands. Let them go. May God have mercy on their souls, but we don't want them administering to ours. Our liturgy is in ruins. We will cling to the essential Thing: the Real Presence on the Altar, Christ, King, Eucharistic Lord. And in so turning our backs on respectability, we will be feared as we hover in the wilderness awaiting our moment in time, feared as was the Red Guard in China. And Peter, at first fearful of us, will come in time to call upon us, his own soldiers, the Power for his Authority, the Sword of God. We will then fill up the vacuum and sweep away the debris and thus create a new Catholic Order out of the chaos. (This will be easy to do because the enemy lacks guts.) And if all of this does not come to pass, if we are never so feared, if we hestitate because of worldly respect, if we disguise our cowardice under the rubrics of a false prudence, if we wait for a new Athanasius instead of forming ourselves into his spirit, then we will have let pass this our last chance in history. I fear to think of what barbarism would then fall upon the world.

1967

CHRISTMAS IN CHRISTENDOM

Let us now go even unto Bethlehem, and see this thing which is come to pass, which the Lord hath made known unto us. And they came with haste, and found Mary, and Joseph, and the babe lying in a manger.

A note of haste sounds clearly in the staggering text of St. Luke: the shepherds run to the new-born God as would an army of men, upon the breaking out of peace after a long war, run to their hearths and to their own.

The early Church was in a hurry to celebrate Christmas. Pagan antiquity had become bankrupt spiritually and intellectually by the time that God deigned to become Man. Philosophy had failed. The handful of sages who had made Greek *episteme* their own and who actualized the lofty moral precepts of Stoicism lived out their lives in a quiet desperation, convinced that human existence is little more than the lot of a condemned prisoner who waits in his cell upon the call of the executioner. A cold wind full of despair whistles through Marcus Aurelius' contention that "it is possible to be a good man, even in a palace." The final irony of classical antiquity consisted in its having wrought civilization out of barbarism as it chiseled palaces out of stone quarries: it had to suffer stoically, as does a man a burden or a secret tragedy, the very glory that it created.

So it was a very tired and sad world that hurried to the Good News of Bethlehem: "For unto you is born this day in the city of David a Saviour, which is Christ the Lord."

Observers from another world would presume that the doctrines of the Incarnation and the Ressurrection, and their promise of a final victory over the tomb, would have fixed the eyes of the men of this time upon a distant but guaranteed salvation—and blinded them, consequently, to the world. And this did happen, of course: the flight of the monks to the Egyptian desert, the severe and often savage asceticism of the early Fathers, the joy of the martyrs as they elbowed aside their fellow Christians in the colosseum and then embraced the lions in the service of a final crown—all bespoke a contempt for this world by men whose faith was so palpable that things visible were but a pale screen between them and an Eternity they already experienced in the flesh.

But Christianity—formed as is its Cross of a cluster of tensions that are never resolved—while permitting and even encouraging this flight from the world, simultaneously exalted Creation as the work of God, and therefore judged it to be very good indeed, as did the Father when He rested on the seventh day. Although the "*world*" might be very evil (the terminology is Pauline), "*Creation*" was sacred. And it was Christmas that made possible—better yet, that concentrated within itself—this distinction. For if the Son of God, the Eternal Glory and the Wisdom of the Father, He in Whom all things are made, was born of a Virgin, and thus entered time as a Perfect Man, then there was a double reason for saluting existence. Not only are all things made in His Image, but He entered time and as a man became one with these things of the world as He mixed Divinity with the clay of the earth. In those first moments of His birth as a Child thrashing about in swaddling clothes, He sanctified not only the straw upon which He lay and the clothes of His mother as he groped for her milk, but He hallowed all reality unto the most distant star.

Christmas, in the early centuries of the Church thus focusing attention on Christ's humanity, lifted the sadness that had settled over the world due to the failure of classical paganism. Before the Child at Bethlehem no real Christian could doubt that the Nicene formula, "true God and true Man," knits together our most daring theological convictions as Catholic adults with that moment of blinding innocence and joy which is the Christmas of a child in Christendom.

The Church was in a hurry about Christmas in those early centuries; but many churchmen were not. There was a quite natural hesitation about assigning a specific date to the birth of Christ for fear that it would be confused with the innumerable "birthdays of the gods." The first evidence of the feasting of Christmas comes from Egypt around the year 200, where the sacred date was thought to have been May 20 in the twenty-eighth year of the reign of the Emperor Augustus. But the sermons of St. John Chrysostom in Antioch show that by the fourth century, the

December date was firmly fixed. The famed Golden Tongue publicly urged the Faithful to unite with their brothers in the West in the celebration of Our Lord's birthday on December 25. There had been a reaction by the Christians in that city back to certain Jewish rites and feasts; but from Thrace to Cadiz, argued Chrysostom, the churches have united around December 25 as the birthday of Christ. This very spontaneity, he went on, was a sign of the genuineness of the day. His vigor won over the doubting brothers of Antioch. And December 25 it was to be: Christ was born on that day liturgically and the subject was then closed forever. But the Church came to this decision, rather boldly, less for reasons of historical accuracy than out of a desire to replace popular pagan feasts.

There is strong evidence that the solar feast of *Natalia Invicti*, in honor of the Unconquered Sun and observed on December 25 throughout the Mediterranean world, is responsible for our Christian date. A solar cult of the Mithraic religion competed with Christianity for dominance within the Empire. Set up to climax the older Saturnalia which lasted from December 17 to December 24, the feast of the Sun climaxed a period of merrymaking when all classes of society mingled together in a carnival spirit of gift exchanging, the carrying of torches, and the wearing of colorful and outlandish costumes. In grafting the spirit of that pagan celebration onto Christmas, the early Fathers transmuted heathen revelry into Christian joy.

Far from the warm Mediterranean, beyond the frontiers of the Empire, the Germanic tribes in the vast forests that covered half of Europe would break the monotony of a bitter winter by observing the solstice. This festival centered around the old barbaric worship of "the mother tree," which grew in the center of every settlement and was thought to be the source of all life, its roots reaching down to the springs of being. When baptized by missionaries, the Teutons retained their feast, but transmuted its nature into the custom that survives today in the Germanic Yule log and tree. This tradition, linked with the Latin fig tree (descendant of the tree under which Romulus and Remus had been suckled by the she-wolf), came in time to be associated with the burning bush of Exodus, where God told Moses His Name; and all of them together mingled with the Tree of Life in the Garden of Eden; and the combined symbolism looked forward to the Tree of the Cross. Thus the entire weight of the tradition of the Christmas Tree, *Weinachtsbaum*, reminds us that with the birth of Our Lord all Creation was born again.

By the twelfth century Christmas was celebrated in every nation in Europe, reflecting warmth and humanity and the good will of man to man. But the thirteenth century deepened profoundly these emotions in a new celebration of Creation that not only emphasized the humanity of Christ and the cult of the Virgin, but that gloried in His helplessness as a baby, and His poverty, born as He was in a cave. It was at this time that Christmas became the feast of the poor and the outcasts, of defiance against the cold blasts of winter. Thus did the pain of God's poor—humbled and in misery—defy the mystery and cruelty of the powers of this world. But this defiance was never bitter. Rather it was filled with good cheer, comforted by the knowledge of the conditions surrounding the birth of Christ. The English Christmas of Dickens, of Tiny Tim, rescued in the end by a Scrooge converted by the Spirit of Christmas Future, extends backwards in a straight line to the High Middle Ages.

We owe to those centuries our first Christmas carols, and also Saint Nicholas, whose feast falls on December 6. This bishop whose bones lie in peace in the Antalya Museum in Turkey was renowned in his time for his charity toward the poor and for his love of children; but he came into his own only many many centuries later. St. Nicholas—Father Christmas in England, *Papa Noël* in France, *Pelznickel* in Germany, *Sinter Klaus* in Holland, our Santa Claus—was most loved by children, for whom he occupied the position held in the earlier tradition by the Christ Child: bearer of gifts, "Christ bundles" full of good things to eat and wear. As Daniel Foley says in his splendid little book, *The Christmas Tree*, "the gifts were given on the basis of good behaviour. Thus, children at an early age were introduced to the basic tenets of theology."

Gift-giving was the prerogative of Saint Nicholas and of the child Jesus in the north of Europe; but the children of Spain have always had to wait for the Three Kings to come at Epiphany. Heralded by fireworks and by the illumination of the walls of the town, Gaspar, Melchior, and Baltasar have ridden out of the centuries into the plazas of every city and village of the Hispanic world. Surrounded by servants groaning under enormous casks and trunks filled with presents, the Kings of the Orient still scatter largesse in the streets, often to the booming of cannons from the town walls, climaxing the Twelve Days—Christmas to Epiphany—formally sanctified by the Second Council of Tours in 566.

The three Masses said on the day of *Christ's Mass* date from 1110. St. Thomas Aquinas defended the liturgical custom of saying such a plethora of Masses on Christmas—at midnight, at dawn, and *in die*—by alluding to the triple "birth" of Christ: in Eternity, in Time and in the Souls of the Faithful. It was at the third Christmas Mass, in the year 800 of our Lord, that Leo III crowned Charlemagne Holy Roman Emperor and thus knit altogether into one the history of the West.

Christmas thus became the central festival within Christendom. Easter advanced what were possibly better abstract and liturgical grounds for preeminence within the Christian Year, but the popular conscience seized upon Christmas as its own proper day, knowing intuitively that the sense of the Incarnation circles around and is one with Christmas. And the Church, always wise, judged the dissertations of the theologians in the light of the truth of our popular Christmas. That defiance of the poor against the bleakness of a life grim and harsh, a defiance bent upon a happiness that would not be gainsaid, found in the Mother and Child a reality deeper than all symbols, because it united into one things never mixed otherwise—fecundity embraced innocence and thus banished the price that each must pay for being at all. This was the popular Catholicism that stormed heaven with the spires of the Gothic, the same faith that sought the wisdom of children before the manger. "Little children will enter the gates of heaven, and unless you become as one. . . "

The Puritan heresies smashed this Christmas of ours. Although Lutheranism had done little to alter the old feast, the French, Dutch and English Puritans, burnt from within by the bitterness of their hatred for Creation, confused by what they viewed as the Roman myth of the Virgin, forbade the celebration of Christ's Mass and of His Day. An Act of Parliament in 1644 declared Christmas a *fast* day, of all things. Shops were forced to remain open, plum puddings and mince pies were condemned as heathen and popish (which, of course, they are). Even before Oliver Cromwell legislated Christmas out of England, the deed was done in the American Colonies. Cotton Mather denounced Christmas in sermon after sermon, and the General Court of Massachusetts levied its stamp of disapproval of the popish holiday by enacting, democratically, a statute "for preventing disorders" (i.e., fun) on that day. The peculiar fanaticism of these our ancestors makes interesting reading:

> For preventing disorders arising in several places within the jurisdiction by reason of some still observing such festivities as were superstitiously kept in other communities, to the great dishonor of God and offense to others; therefore that whosoever shall be

found observing any such day as Christmas or the like, either by forbearing of labor,
feasting or any other way upon any such account aforesaid, every such person so offen-
ding shall pay for every offense five shillings as a fine to the county.

Five shillings from the poor of the colonies! This was the gigantic
fraud out of which grew our modern world, a world dour and grim, devoid
of an older code of honor that it repudiated along with Rome. In this con-
certed attack upon the hallowed traditions of Christmas past, launched in
the name of Bible Worship and Money, Puritan capitalism fingered the
central issue with all the nervous brilliance of the mind of its founder,
Calvin: if Creation is evil (and John Calvin and John Knox and Cotton
Mather would have it so); if God is an awful Transcendence, a Totally
Other, removed as is innocence from the taint of sin, the world; if this popish plot, the world, is concentrated in a unique fashion within the body of
Woman (Did not sin come into the world through a woman? They looked
into their Book and found the answer.); if this evil spills out in the bodies
of small children, full of evil and marked with the sign of predestination; if
the vast bulk of humanity, unwashed and filthy with sin is condemned
from all eternity by our God who told us all this out of His Book; and if
but a handful are elected to be lifted out of the caldron and signed with
salvation (a visible effect of which is cleanliness and earthly wealth, for
does not the Book write of filling the barns of the just?)—then it follows:
first, that the Incarnation—God's coming into the world—was totally
superfluous and in fact an utter waste of time; second, that children are
nothing other than potential adults, fields for education by the Elect with
their Book, in themselves depraved little devils rotted by original sin and
without any claim to special wisdom into the true meaning of the real;
third, that the Romish cult of the Virgin simply perpetuates and deepens
through the feast of Christmas a silly love affair with Creation which
covers over the sin of the Woman, all women, and the depravity of the
Child, all children. If all of this be true (and John Calvin and the Holy
Writ would have it so) then carols as well as the Masses, the tree along
with the manger, the Mother along with the Child must go. If the world is
utterly hideous, then man must build another one. When the technocratic
secularists today, in the name of the "modern world," strike at Christmas
and attempt to prohibit its public celebration, they can take comfort in being in a tradition that goes back to the fining of poor men five shillings
because they danced on Christmas Eve. Secularism and all the mythology

331

about the "absolute separation of church and state" is simply a Puritanism debased, its original corruption compounded.

But in this ghastly simulacrum of civilization that we call the twentieth century, where all honor is forgotten, there are still children in the high plains of Castille who are romping now through cobbled streets covered in snow, the night bitter and cold under a sky swept clean of clouds. And they are singing, these children: "*Ande. ande, ande, la Mari morena; ande, ande, ande, qu's la Nochebuena.*" Dark Mary, Our Lovely, please hurry and give birth to Your Son, because tonight is the Good Night. Like the first shepherds, in haste, they flee from a tired and sick world in order that they might find Emmanuel, our Great God. Stumbling and falling along the roadside, fleeing the banalities of a world without Him, they bear Her along and buoy Her up. Tonight they will fling themselves before His manger and sate themselves, gluttons for God, in adoration. Come, Dark Mary, deliver us tonight Christ, Our God, Our Lord, Our King.

xii.67

REJOICING

THE MIRACLE OF WINE

Mr. Alec Waugh's *In Praise of Wine* (Sloane, $6.00) is a book that every hack who scribbles notes upon other men's books ought to read. It will teach him the meaning of civility and it might teach him how to write. At its best it will tell him all about wine, about the grape grown, trodden, bottled, aged, corked, decanted, and drunk.

Like a good Englishman, the author disdains any pretensions to a superior knowledge of wine, but the man commissioned by the House of Gilbey to write its history is certainly among the leading amateurs in the Western world, and those who read him will go away instructed, enlightened, and in need of wine. Waugh's prose breeds a passion for a big wine, for a Burgundy, and he quotes with relish from Hilaire Belloc's address to a Saintsbury Club dinner: "And when I depart from this earth to appear before my beloved Lord to account for my sins, which have been scarlet, I shall say to Him: 'I cannot remember the name of the village; I do not even recollect the name of the girl, but the wine, my God! was Chambertin!' "

Waugh has spent a lifetime in pursuit of the grape. In so doing he has fulfilled and completed an apostolic injunction, for if a little wine is good for thy stomach's sake, a noble comentator upon the text has added that much wine is good for thy soul's. Waugh has made the pilgrimage to the Bordeaux country, to the Douro in Portugal where they still tramp the grape barefoot; he knows the island of Madeira; the Champagne; and he left Jerez de la Frontera in better shape than I did.

This is a splendid book whose spine is stamped all over and up and down with grapes but whose cover looks more like a Pink Lady than Tavel Rose. There are those who will never forgive Waugh for having included that potato-bred potation, that poteen universal, that goes by the name of whiskey. But there is an irritating urbanity to this book that proves even to the satisfaction of those of us who belong to the Vinous Order of the Strict Observance that Scotch was brewed before the Reformation and that thus permits us to go on doing with an easier conscience what we have been doing all along: *i.e.*, drinking, if never paying for, Scotch. Waugh has the Exchequer Rolls for 1494 to prove it to us: "Friar John Cor is issued bolls of malt wherewith to make *aqua vitae.*"

In Praise of Wine ought to be read by all writers who drink wine. If they drink this book over wine they will think long on the kind of book that *they* would have written about wine. This will make them happy and pleased with themselves. It will also heighten the excellence of Mr. Waugh's achievement: he, at least, is interested in wine for itself, in this divine essence which once made a great medievalist of our time doubt, if but for an instant, that existence is superior to essence.

But had *I* written about wine I would have written a very bad polemical tract for the better beating upon the head of all my enemies. I would have proved the superiority of Merrie England to its Whiggish aftermath by pointing to the gin-sodden figures of Hogarth, and I would have praised the yeomanry of a more decent past, a yeomanry that ate and drank its own. I would ponder long over the observation of that friend of Erik von Kuehnelt-Leddihn who maintains that the martini is a left-wing drink and, being of a fanatical and reactionary cast of mind, I would measure every polity by the excellence of the wine it grew and by the quantity of the wine it drank, for most assuredly the consumption of much wine is among the few infallible signs of liberty. When Mendès-France raised aloft the standard of milk against wine some years ago in France, I—without ever having heard of him before—deduced even to his last speech his shoddy and canting career.

But Mr. Waugh does not relieve the feelings of his civilized readers (uncivilized ones this book will never have) by political tub-thumping. He sticks to the point: Wine. One suspects that he is possibly a bit too civilized. Although he excoriates and destroys once and for all that most obnoxious of beings, the wine snob, Mr. Waugh is certainly not a wine and cheese man. I would hesitate to cross swords with him on most of the business pertaining to wine, but I would maintain that crumbling cheddar, a slice of apple, and port make a meal all by themselves. I also question why his brief appendix devoted to California wines omits Wente Brothers Pinot Noir, a wine certainly superior to that found anywhere else in the United States.

The Miracle of Wine

In Praise of Wine makes me want to know Mr. Waugh in the flesh, a bottle of wine on the table between us. I could tell him about Pisco sour which I learned to like in a four-masted barque off the coast of Peru some years ago, a divine liquid hoarded by a captain with bad kidneys who already had reason enough to suspect the vinous propensities of his American supercargo. And I could ask him why his splendid wine map fails to sketch in Navarre and the Tyrol where they bring forth red wines as clear as the mountain air and the freedom that is bred only in those final conclaves of Western liberty and heroism: there I have drunk to king and emperor more than once with wines that tasted as distant bells sound in early morning when placed high in the hills and apart from all things modern and vulgar. But more than anything else, I should like to ask Mr. Waugh why he ruined his final line, writing "the miracle that is *in* wine." Is not wine itself *the* miracle? Excepting Bread alone, only Wine is God.

19.i.59

By the author of
"Escape from Scepticism: Liberal Education as if Truth Mattered"—

JOY WITHOUT A CAUSE:
Selected Essays of Christopher Derrick

1940 and the 'Ballad of the White Horse'
A World of Profit and Delight
The Rules of the Game
Pavane for a Dead Liturgy
In Defence of Stagnation
In Defence of Triumphalism
Population or People?
It's All Done by Mirrors
Quare Fremuerunt Gentes?
Do People Matter?
The Pageant of Our Redemption
Something Beautiful for God

Liberation and the Gospel
To Feed the Hungry
Assumption Day in Catholic Poland
The Facts of Life
Liturgy and the Consumer
The Word 'Catholic'
Resurrection, Ecumenism, and Witness
The Scandal of Particularity
Confitebor Tibi in Guitarra?
A Solid Chunk of Wood
Why Bother About Religion?

254 pages

"Mr. Derrick is a bold man who writes charmingly."
—*Russell Kirk* in *National Review*

$4.95 including postage and handling

Sherwood Sugden & Company, Publishers
1117 Eighth Street,
La Salle, Illinois 61301

ESCAPE FROM SCEPTICISM:
Liberal Education as if Truth Mattered

CHRISTOPHER DERRICK

"I found *Escape from Scepticism* a perceptive, witty and engaging account of the present troubled condition of liberal education. Derrick's book offers a disturbing indictment of today's colleges and universities, the fancied dwelling-places of wisdom, for their failure to provide young people with any reasoned defense against the prevalent scepticism of the age or any encouragement to stand against it."

—Nathan M. Pusey, President Emeritus, Harvard University

"It may seem absurdly pretentious to compare this book with Newman's *Idea of a University*, but the comparison is apt . . . . Derrick has wit and a brilliant aphoristic style. Every sentence is packed with thought. His little book could well serve as a manual . . . for the reform of Catholic higher education today."

—Paul H. Hallett in the **National Catholic Register**

"*Escape from Scepticism* has my vote for Book of the Year!"

—Ron Kennedy in the New Zealand **Tablet**

"This is a short book. But it is brilliant and easy to read. If you know any parents of high school or college students, recommend this book to them. If you are such a parent, read it prayerfully. And act upon it."

—Professor Charles E. Rice in **Faith and Reason**

" . . . the author demonstrates a remarkable capacity to present his strongly held views in the most uncompromising fashion, while sparing his reader the tone of arrogance or pontification. The book is simply brilliantly written, in an easy style, reminiscent of that of his famous Oxford tutor [C.S. Lewis]."

—Robert Emmet Moffit in **New Guard**

"The occasion for *Escape from Scepticism* was a visit to Thomas Aquinas College. The school is significant because it was the first tangible indication of a Catholic educational reformation. It was followed in close succession by Magdalen, Newman, and Christendom Colleges, all dedicated to a fully Catholic education. "It works," says Derrick of the kind of education offered by these schools, and so does his book: It works, and it makes sense."

—Karl Keating in **The University Bookman**

$2.95 including postage and handling.

Sherwood Sugden & Company
PUBLISHERS

1117 Eighth Street, La Salle, Illinois 61301

BEYOND DETENTE:
TOWARD AN AMERICAN FOREIGN POLICY

Paul Eidelberg

" . . . *far and away the best, and most constructive, critique of Détente I have read . . . .*"

—The Hon. Clare Boothe Luce

" . . . *refreshing and engaging, precisely because the author attempts to supplement the straightforward approach to foreign diplomacy with a consideration of those moral and philosophical principles on which a sound and practicable foreign policy must rest.*"

—A. James McAdams
in *Modern Age*

". . . *Eidelberg's book . . . goes beyond an academic discussion of foreign policy and international relations to discuss* politics *in foreign affairs. For most academic specialists, foreign policy is something which takes place "out there" as governments maneuver on the global game board. This view, while adequate for some purposes, ultimately fails as a guide to action. Foreign policy is what we do, and what we do determines who we are. More than the nation's power is at stake in contemporary international politics; its essence is at hazard.*"

—Thomas F. Payne,
Southwest Missouri State College

"*In dissecting with surgical precision the nature of our current foreign policy and the reasons for its development, Dr. Eidelberg spells out with frightening clarity just how dangerously bad it really is, and how essential it is that it be changed before it is too late. . . . Cautionary note: One does not curl up with this book; one wrestles with it. It makes great demands on the reader—but it repays him many times over. In this reviewer's opinion, it is a virtuoso performance.*"

—Vice Admiral Ruthven E. Libby, USN (Ret.)
in *Strategic Review,*
United States Strategic Institute

$12.95 including postage and handling.

Sherwood Sugden & Company
PUBLISHERS

1117 Eighth Street, La Salle, Illinois 61301

DYNAMICS OF WORLD HISTORY

by

CHRISTOPHER DAWSON

Edited by John J. Mulloy

"Christopher Dawson is perhaps the most thoughtful, stimulating, and suggestive historian of the Catholic faith who in this century has devoted himself to the general history of civilization. He is more down to earth and convincing than Spengler or Toynbee. . . . This is a book which no thoughtful historian can safely ignore, and it is as timely as it is illuminating."

—Harry Elmer Barnes, *The American Historical Review*

"*Dynamics of World History* is a splendid synthesis of Christopher Dawson's historical thought. It is a book that should be read and reread not only by all students and professors of history but also by all others who wish to obtain a deeper understanding of civilization, its dynamics, and its meaning."

—*Martin R. P. McGuire*

"For breadth of knowledge and lucidity of style he has few rivals . . . . He knows what his European and American colleagues are doing and his judgments on their work are exceptionally fair. . . . it is safe to say that this selection of his best writing will also be read with interest outside academic circles.

—Geoffrey Bruun in *The New York Times Book Review*

"It is difficult to think of any living writer who has made so laborious and scrupulous an attempt as Dawson to understand the widest variety of social phenomena without denaturing them in terms of something other than they are. His extraordinary range of learning is seen in two essays here on St. Augustine and Gibbon, which in their percipience and richness of reference are, I think, the best studies of their subjects in English."

—Martin Wight in *The Observer* (London)

$7.95 including postage and handling. **489 pages** +xx

Sherwood Sugden & Company
PUBLISHERS
1117 Eighth Street, La Salle, Illinois 61301

A BETTER GUIDE THAN REASON:
STUDIES IN THE AMERICAN REVOLUTION
by
M.E. BRADFORD
with an Introduction by
Jeffrey Hart

"The publication of Professor Bradford's essays in a single volume represents something of a milestone in contemporary conservative thought." — **Samuel T. Francis** in *The University Bookman*

"Bradford's angle of vision is unique and so challenging that it will doubtless stir controversy even among conservatives . . . . But whatever the reader's conclusions . . . he can hardly fail to be impressed by this subtly crafted and trenchantly argued volume."
—M. Stanton Evans in *National Review*

" . . . Many would agree with Bradford that the American Revolution was a conservative event, but no other writer has matched his portrayal of why and how that was so. . . . For Bradford, in a stunning feat of intellectual courage and originality, has done nothing less than to provide us with the necessary means to rediscover our founding, the original basis of our commonwealth." **—Clyde Wilson**

" . . . . in this enterprise Bradford brings to bear a unique combination of skills and perspectives, principally those of the political theorist, literary critic, textual analyst, and historian. What emerges are provocative and challenging propositions.
—George W. Carey in *National Review*

" . . . these are exciting essays to read. Bradford provides a necessary warning that once a nation tries through positive law to establish social equality, it has embarked on a never-ending course of unfulfilled promises and unreasonable expectations destructive of community and at odds with the nature of republicanism."
—William C. Dennis in *Modern Age*

"Bradford is surely a consummate stylist; the prose within this beautifully produced book fairly sparkles; is graceful, yet muscular. The scholarship . . . is impeccable."
—D. R. Bustion in *The Dallas Morning News*

Cloth: $12.95; paper: $4.95. (Prices include postage & handling.)